Suffer the Little Children

THE INSIDE STORY
OF IRELAND'S INDUSTRIAL SCHOOLS

In 1999, **Mary Raftery** wrote, produced and directed the internationally acclaimed three-part documentary series *States of Fear*. Winner of an Irish Film and Television Academy Award, *States of Fear* also received a Special Jury Gold Award at the WorldFest in Houston, Texas; a Silver Screen Award at the US International Film and Video Festival in Chicago and a World Medal at the New York Festivals. In addition, it was judged as one of Europe's top ten documentaries for 1999 by the Prix Europa in Berlin.

A Senior Producer/Director with national broadcaster RTE and a former Woman Journalist of the Year, Mary Raftery currently lives and works in Dublin.

Dr Eoin O'Sullivan is a lecturer in Social Policy at Trinity College Dublin. He is the foremost expert in Ireland in the area of industrial schools, and was the consultant to the RTE documentary series *States of Fear*. He lives and works in Dublin.

Suffer the Little Children

THE INSIDE STORY
OF IRELAND'S INDUSTRIAL SCHOOLS

Mary Raftery
Eoin O'Sullivan

Continuum • New York

2001

THE CONTINUUM INTERNATIONAL PUBLISHING GROUP INC
370 LEXINGTON AVENUE, NEW YORK, NY 10017

First published by New Island Books, Dublin, Ireland
Copyright © 1999 Mary Raftery and Eoin O'Sullivan
This edition published by arrangement with New Island Books.

Library of Congress Cataloging-in-Publication Data
Raftery, Mary.
   Suffer the little children: the inside story of Ireland's industrial
schools / Mary Raftery & Eoin O'Sullivan.
   p. cm.
 Includes bibliographical references and index.
 ISBN 0-8264-1337-4
 1. Reformatories--Ireland--History.   2. Trade
schools--Ireland--History.   3. Problem children--Institutional
care--Ireland--History.   4. Problem youth--Institutional
care--Ireland--History.   I. O'Sullivan, Eoin. II. Title.
 HV9148.A5 R33 2001
 365'.42'09417--dc21
                         2001017195

*Grateful acknowledgement is made to all those who gave permission to use
material contained within the book. The publishers have made every
reasonable effort to contact the copyright holders of material produced
therein. If any involuntary infringement of copyright has occurred, sincere
apologies are offered and the owners of such copyright are requested to
contact the publishers.*

Cover design: Slick Fish Design
Cover illustration: Katy Simpson
Typesetting: New Island Books
Printed by The Bath Press, Bath

Contents

ACKNOWLEDGEMENTS

The authors would like to acknowledge the great assistance they received from the following: David Gordon, Tom Boland, Peter McDonagh and Margaret McCarthy from the Department of Education in Dublin, who greatly facilitated our access to the Department's industrial schools files; Tony D'Alton, Carmel Egan and Eddie Harte from the Department of Education in Athlone, whose enormous help was most appreciated, especially given the now greatly increased workload of the Special Schools Section of the Department.

To many others, we would like to express our gratitude for their generous help and support: RTE, Catriona Crowe (National Archives); Augusta McCabe (Department of Health); Tom O'Donnell (Limerick Local Radio); Sue Nunn (Kilkenny Local Radio); Tom Lynch (Boys Town, USA); Sheila Ahern; Kevin Cummins; Siobhan McHugh; Alan Gill; Bernard O'Connell; Christine Buckley; Bernadette Fahy; Paddy Doyle; Anne Daly; Margaret Kennedy; Fintan O'Toole; Colm Toibin; Dermot Bolger; Mavis Arnold; Mary O'Doherty; Tommy Morris; May and the late Kevin O'Sullivan; Tony McCashin; Caroline Skehill; Noreen Kearney; Helen Buckley; Robbie Gilligan; Paula Mayock; Barry Cullen; Mary Ellen Ring; Jarleth McKee; the Staff at the Anna Liffey Bar, New Haven; Rachel Moss; Ciara and Niall McSweeny; Colm and Grainne O'Suilleabhain; Lisa Berlinger.

Austin Clarke's poems are reproduced with the kind permission of Dardis Clarke, 21 Pleasants St, Dublin 8.

Finally, a word of gratitude to Joe Joyce, whose sharply observed comments were very much appreciated, and to Edwin and Ciara at New Island Books for their endless patience and great support.

All of the above, of course, bear no responsibility for any of the views expressed in this book, which are those of the authors alone.

A SIMPLE TALE

A casual labourer, Pat Rourke,
Who hurried from bricking across the water
With wife and babes, could find no work here.
All slept in a coal-hole, heard
(When light, that dwindled through the grating,
Was Wicklowing from strand to hill)
The gulls, loop-lining near Dublin Bay,
Squabble for offal, rub of cur
Or cat around a dustbin, till
A-bang in breadshop, dairy. Brought
To Court, the little screaming boy
And girl were quickly, for the public good,
Committed to Industrial School.
The cost — three pounds a week for each:
Both safely held beyond the reach
Of mother, father. We destroy
Families, bereave the unemployed.
Pity and love are beyond our buoys.

Austin Clarke, 1963

Introduction*

On the 11th of May 1999, the Irish Government called a press conference to issue an apology, on behalf of the State, to the tens of thousands of children who grew up in Ireland's extraordinary network of what were called 'industrial schools'.

This historic and unprecedented event coincided with the broadcast on Irish national television of the final part of *States of Fear*, a series of three documentaries exposing the astounding levels of both physical and sexual abuse suffered by many of these children while in the care of the Catholic religious orders who ran these institutions.

States of Fear† had provoked an enormous response from the Irish public. Outrage at the crimes committed against these children was expressed continuously for the three weeks of the series, across acres of newsprint and hours of radio broadcasts all over the country. The Government apology was perceived as a direct response to this furore, as was its promise to establish a Commission on Child Abuse to inquire into the issues raised.

Minute examination of official State records, together with extensive testimony from those who grew up in industrial schools, combine to make this the first full account of the vast and largely hidden system used to lock up so many thousands of Irish children. Their vivid human stories convey both the extraordinary levels of cruelty and suffering experienced by them as children, and their tremendous courage and resilience in surviving the often savage way in which they were abused.

---

* This new introduction updates some of the material in the text.

† Dr Eoin O'Sullivan, co-author of this book, was a Consultant to *States of Fear* (RTE Television, broadcast on 27th April, 4th May and 11th May, 1999). Mary Raftery, his co-author, wrote, produced and directed *States of Fear*.

Now, almost two years since the historic apology by the Irish Government, several parallel processes are in train. The Irish police investigations continue with regard to several of the schools. Most of these cases had begun before the broadcast of *States of Fear*, but so far none have come to trial. A total of nine Christian Brothers are facing multiple charges of child sexual abuse with regard to the industrial schools in Salthill, Galway and Tralee, County Kerry. Allegations of abuse in St Joseph's Industrial School in Letterfrack, County Galway continue to be investigated.

The largest police operation in this area concerns Artane Industrial School in Dublin — in fact, it now constitutes one of the most extensive child sexual abuse investigations to have been conducted anywhere in the world. However, to date only one Christian Brother has been charged — he faces multiple counts of sexual assault. Completed files on approximately twenty others have been sent to the Director of Public Prosecutions, and most have now been awaiting a decision on whether to proceed to charges for over a year.

The slow pace of bringing cases to court has been a source of considerable frustration to many of the survivors of abuse of the Artane institution. Over 500 formal statements of complaint have so far been lodged with the Gardaí, with new allegations continuing to be made on a regular basis. Up to 150 Christian Brothers have been implicated, a number of whom have left the order, some have died, and the remainder continue as serving Brothers.

About half of the Artane allegations concern physical abuse only, with the remainder comprising both physical and sexual abuse. The Gardaí conducted full investigations into the complaints of physical abuse and sent a number of files to the Director of Public Prosecutions. However, the DPP decided that no charges would be brought as a result of these. It is understood that the lapse of time, over 30 years in all cases, was the primary reason for not charging any of the Artane Christian Brothers against whom allegations of physical abuse had been made.

It is interesting in this regard to note a recent case in Scotland, where a nun was convicted on charges of child

4

cruelty relating to her work in two residential children's homes from the 1960s to the 1980s. These were run by the Poor Sisters of Nazareth, who had an extensive network of such institutions throughout Britain and Northern Ireland. Maria Docherty, also known as Sr Alphonso, had faced four counts of repeatedly abusing, humiliating and cruelly treating young girls. Since her conviction, 50 nuns have been named in over 400 compensation claims from former child residents of Nazareth homes in Scotland.

Descriptions of conditions within the Scottish institutions are very similar to survivors' accounts of Irish industrial schools. And yet in all such Irish cases so far, the authorities of the State have declined to use the sanction of the courts against the perpetrators of almost identical physical abuse of children.

During the past year, many of the survivors of Irish industrial schools have strongly objected to the way in which such firm distinctions have been made between sexual abuse on the one hand, and on the other, the physical violence to which they were subjected as children. They argue that for the perpetrators there was a strong element of sexual gratification involved in the kinds of extreme beatings which they meted out to their small victims. However, it appears that Irish law as it stands does not share this view, and that the only recourse now open to those who were physically abused is to testify before the Commission on Child Abuse.

This Commission, chaired by High Court judge Mary Laffoy, has had a bumpy ride since its inception. It has now begun hearings before its Confidential Committee, in which survivors are provided with a sympathetic forum in which to tell of their experiences, and where no cross-examination is permitted.

The Commission's Investigation Committee, which will fully test and rule on cases of child abuse (physical, sexual, emotional and neglect) within all institutions, including ordinary schools, has yet to begin hearings. It has been delayed by issues relating to compensation for survivors of this abuse. However, in October 2000, almost 18 months since its initial apology, the Irish Government finally announced its intention to establish a separate Compensation Tribunal. Although there are as yet no details as to what form this will take, the religious orders implicated in the abuse of children at their institutions have agreed in principle to make some financial contribution towards compensation.

It is interesting to look at the extensive international experience in this regard, as institutional child abuse at the hands of Catholic religious orders is by no means an exclusively Irish phenomenon. The past decade has seen the uncovering of widespread abuse of children from the 1920s to the 1980s at residential homes run by Catholic religious orders in Australia, most notably by the two Irish orders of the Christian Brothers and the Sisters of Mercy. The Government of Queensland, where several of these institutions were located, has contributed $1 million to a Trust Fund to provide assistance to those whose lives were destroyed by this abuse. So far, however, no financial contribution has been forthcoming from the relevant religious orders.

It has been left to survivors to pursue the religious orders through the courts, as indeed is happening in Ireland and in Canada. To date, the Sisters of Mercy have paid an undisclosed sum in an out-of-court settlement to sixty former residents of their Neerkol orphanage, ending what had become one of the largest litigation cases in Queensland's history.

The Christian Brothers agreed to pay $3.5 million to over 260 former residents of their orphanages and schools in Western Australia. Widespread sexual abuse of children by members of the order had been uncovered at its Western Australian institutions, covering a period dating back to the 1930s.

However, it is in Canada that the most detailed and comprehensive attempt has been made to identify means of redress for those who have had their childhood stolen by abuse in institutions. Prominent among the Catholic religious orders implicated in child abuse in Canada are once again the Christian Brothers and the Sisters of Mercy, with the addition of the Oblates of Mary Immaculate who ran the notorious Daingean Reformatory School in Ireland.

In March 2000, the Law Commission of Canada published its Final Report on Responding to Child Abuse in Canadian Institutions. It is undoubtedly the most thorough study of this tragic phenomenon, and should provide a blueprint for the Laffoy Commission in Ireland.

The Canadian Law Commission conducted a series of studies to identify the "needs" of those abused as children within Canadian institutions. Different groups of victims across Canada were asked what they wanted, what they had received and how they would improve the situation for other victims. Their responses had several points in common, even as the groups varied. Their reasons for pursuing their claims included: establishing a historical record; acknowledgement; genuine apology; accountability; access to therapy or counselling; access to education or training; financial compensation and prevention.

In its final report, the Law Commission makes over 50 specific recommendations on both how to deal with the victims of past abuse and how to prevent future institutional child abuse. The report concludes that it is the survivors of such abuse who can best articulate how they have been harmed, that the focus of all interventions should be to right the wrongs done to them, and crucially that this process should cause them no further harm. How to achieve this key objective resulted in a report of over 450 pages.

The Commission notes that the goals of achieving accountability, apology and reconciliation are often in conflict with the objective of providing financial compensation in existing processes such as public inquiries, criminal trials, criminal injuries compensation schemes and civil trials.

Interestingly, in the light of concerns in Ireland about the role of elements of the legal profession in representing clients of institutional abuse, the Canadian Commission recommends that law societies should review their Codes of Professional Conduct to ensure that appropriate rules are in place to safeguard against the exploitation of survivors of institutional child abuse, especially with respect to recruitment of clients and fee arrangements.

The Canadian Law Commission concludes that what matters most is the attitude of those in authority in terms of dealing with this issue. New initiatives will mean little to survivors of institutional abuse if those in positions of power are not fully committed to redressing the harm done. Similarly, irrespective of what a survivor seeks, authorities must respond with full honesty. No information should be strategically withheld, and no procedural tactics should be deployed simply to gain an advantage.

In practice, however, achieving these principles has proved difficult. For example, since the publication of the Law Commission of Canada final report, it has emerged that the Christian Brothers seriously misled a Canadian court in an attempt to protect millions of dollars worth of their assets from creditors, according to court documents filed in Ontario.

In a strategy centrally devised by senior Christian Brothers in their Rome headquarters, the order put its Canadian assets into liquidation in 1996 when it was facing large civil claims for compensation from 126 alleged victims of child abuse at the order's Mount Cashel orphanage in Newfoundland.

At the time, a high-ranking Canadian Christian Brother had sworn in an affidavit that the liquidation would ensure that a "maximum amount" of assets would be "employed compensating all of the claimants in a fair and expedited manner". The court was informed that the total value of the assets of the order was approximately $4.2 million.

However, it has now emerged that the Christian Brothers in Canada had internally calculated that they had in fact had, "in conservative terms, well over $100 million in assets". The plan was to minimise any possible payments to victims of institutional abuse, leading the court-appointed liquidator of the Christian Brothers of Ireland in Canada (their official title) to raise "questions about the bona fides of the decision by the Christian Brothers to wind up Christian Brothers of Ireland in Canada for the purposes of maximizing compensation to the victims of abuse, and demonstrates possible ... breaches of an undertaking to this court."

The Canadian experience may give some inkling of what lies ahead for the Laffoy Commission, the Compensation Tribunal, and the various civil actions in Ireland. So far, the Irish Commission has held three public sessions, mainly to explain how it intends to function. During the summer of 2000, it heard formal submissions from many of the survivors' support groups and from the religious orders responsible for the industrial schools system in Ireland.

In spite of their public apologies to the children abused in their care, the submissions from the religious orders displayed scant evidence of contrition – in fact, they manifested in some cases a degree of hostility towards several aspects of the Commission's operation.

The Christian Brothers, for instance, objected to the Commission's decision to use the word "survivor" to designate those who grew up in industrial schools. Former residents had welcomed this – they had previously been generally referred to as victims, a term which they felt humiliated them. However, the Christian Brothers indicated that the use of the term "survivor" implied that some had not survived, an inference which they considered "distressing".

A number of the religious orders considered that the process was unfair to them, that it was "pro-accuser and anti the accused". Justice Laffoy firmly rejected any imputation of unfairness concerning the Commission. Ominously, however, some of the orders indicated that they reserved their right to mount a legal challenge to the entire process. The Commission is acutely aware that every aspect of its operation is likely to face a series of court challenges from the legal teams representing the religious congregations involved.

Meanwhile, the Catholic Church in Ireland maintains its policy of secrecy with regard to publicly releasing its records on children's institutions. Diocesan archives in this area remain closed, and despite repeated requests for access to their archives, the religious orders concerned remain equally secretive.

It is easy in this fraught legal landscape to forget that what is at the heart of this issue and this book is the wilful and systematic ruination of thousands of lives, children subjected to appalling and horrific treatment from their earliest years.

Their stories, together with the exclusive access given to the authors to official State records, provide a searing insight into a tragedy whose scale Ireland is only beginning to understand. In most cases, those whose experiences are recorded here decided to be identified by their first names only. Some asked for their names to be completely changed in order to protect their privacy. Those individuals identified by their full names had specifically asked that this should be so.

Without exception, they all spoke eloquently about the importance to them of recording publicly the terrible events of their childhood, no matter how painful they were to recall, so that children in the future would never have to suffer as they did, either from direct abuse or from the decades of disbelief, denial and indifference which they as adults had faced at the hands of Irish society. Their motivation in this regard is identical to that found by the various commissions of inquiry into institutional child abuse elsewhere in the world – across three continents, survivors of these horrors share the hope that they may contribute to improving the lives of the next generation of children in care.

Mary Raftery
Eoin O'Sullivan
January 2001.

One

The Myths

It would be difficult to find an area of Ireland's recent past that has been more bedevilled with myth than the country's enormous system of industrial schools. Irish society continued until very recently to have little idea as to the real nature of its child-detention system. Even people who themselves went through that system shared many of the misconceptions surrounding the area — several of which had in fact been perpetuated by the religious orders who ran the schools.

The first and most pervasive myth was that the children within the system were objects of charity, cared for by the religious of Ireland when no one else would do so. The children themselves were repeatedly told by their religious keepers that were it not for the charity of the Catholic Church, they would have been left on the side of the road, abandoned and starving. In the absence of anyone to contradict this, the children themselves accepted it, as did the general population.

However, it was a fallacy. The system was entirely the responsibility of the State, established by law, funded and regulated by the Department of Education. The State paid a grant to the religious orders for each and every child committed by the courts to be detained within the system. While the level of this funding was not by any means overly generous, comparison with wage levels of the time clearly shows that it should have been enough to feed and clothe the children adequately. However, both the personal testimonies in this book and the Department of Education's own files illustrate the extent of severe material deprivation suffered by the children in these schools.

The charity myth was undoubtedly most useful. It served to explain away the often thin and ragged appearance of many of the children in industrial schools. While usually kept apart from the general community, the children were nonetheless highly visible within their localities — in towns the length and breadth of the country they were to be seen walking in file every Sunday along the roads. Many who remember this spectacle often describe it as a sad and pathetic sight. However, the general view remained that the religious, especially the nuns, were doing their best under difficult circumstances.

The second important myth is that these institutions were 'orphanages', and that the children behind their walls were orphans. The use of the word orphanages was highly inaccurate — under law, the vast bulk of children's institutions were specifically defined as industrial schools, established and funded for the industrial training of the children within them. Most of the children within the system had either one or both parents still living, and so could not in any sense be described as orphans.

The 'orphanage' myth reinforced the perception by society of the supposedly charitable nature of these institutions. The description of the children as 'orphans' was far more likely to elicit sympathy for both them and their religious carers. It also undoubtedly assisted with fundraising and a range of other activities.

The reality — namely that thousands of children were detained in a State-funded system essentially because their parents were poor — would not have produced the same levels of either sympathy or charity from the wider community. Had there been a proper understanding of the true nature of the system, it is likely that it would not have survived for so long. Public concern would most probably have been voiced at a much earlier stage (as in Britain) about the inappropriate nature of such institutions for child care. In Ireland, the State's policy of removing children from their families and funding religious orders to care for them remained unchanged until 1970. The 'orphan' myth essentially meant that the obviously preferable option of giving that same funding to families to allow them to keep their children at home was never publicly debated.

This misconception was so pervasive that even many of those who grew up within the system were not aware that they had actually been in an industrial school. This deeply-rooted misunderstanding of the system was publicly repeated as recently as 1996, in the seminal television documentary *Dear Daughter*, which dealt with the appalling abuse suffered by Christine Buckley in what was known (and referred to by the documentary) as Goldenbridge 'orphanage'. In fact, this was St Vincent's Industrial School, Goldenbridge, and had never been an orphanage. It was funded, inspected and regulated as an industrial school by the State.

It is important to note that there were indeed several real orphanages in Ireland. A small number were Church of Ireland institutions, but most were run by Catholic religious orders. The majority charged fees, and were usually described as catering for the children of the middle-classes who had fallen on hard times. They served a very specific purpose in maintaining a rigid class divide between children from different backgrounds — a strategy which was clearly and publicly stated by the Catholic Church in its various Handbooks for Catholic Social Workers during the 1940s and 1950s.

Another myth relating to the system was that it mainly dealt with the children of unmarried mothers. While it is true that there were a number of such children within industrial schools, they always made up only a relatively small proportion of the general child population detained.

One of the more damaging misconceptions concerns the industrial schools for boys over the age of ten. The religious orders running these schools were far less likely to refer to them as orphanages. In fact, there was an erroneous view among the general public that these institutions were reformatories for children who had been found guilty of criminal offences.

Once again, this was largely untrue — only a relatively small number of the children in these schools had any criminal convictions. The vast majority detained in senior boys' industrial schools such as Upton, Glin, Artane, or Clonmel were there because of the poverty of their parents. This association between the boys' institutions and criminality was to dog the footsteps of many of those who grew up there.

Allied to this specific misconception was the general view that the system was mainly for boys. In fact, the opposite was the case — girls significantly outnumbered boys for most of the hundred years of the existence of the industrial schools in Ireland. This was so marked during the 1930s and 1940s that it was the cause of considerable concern to the Department of Education.

Yet another myth, which continues to this day, is that no one really knew about the nature of these institutions and the suffering of children within them. While it is true that the public at large were probably unaware of the enormous scale of the system for detaining children within the Irish State, it is nonetheless evident that there was a clear popular knowledge of the existence of a punitive and incarceral system for children.

In every part of the country, people remember how as children they were threatened with specific industrial schools. The threat was made in the knowledge that these were highly unpleasant places to be. While it is probably true to say that the general population did not know the true horror or extent of the abuse and maltreatment, it is clear that people knew that children could be and often were locked up and punished.

In recent years, a number of arguments have been made to mitigate the stories of horrific abuse which have emerged from the industrial schools. Primary among these is the contention that it is unfair to judge what happened in the past by the standards of today — that in the Ireland of the 1950s children everywhere were badly treated, and that this was the accepted norm. Consequently, the argument goes, it is unfair to single out the religious orders in the industrial schools for blame. This is an important argument, and bears close examination.

Any detailed analysis of the system reveals a far more complex picture than this argument supposes. There had, for instance, been a number of statements from leading Christian Brothers, including their own founder, Edmund Ignatius Rice, that corporal punishment of boys was wrong and should be discontinued. These had often been repeated internally through the decades. The fact that this particular congregation chose to ignore these views does not mean that they were in ignorance of an alternative and more enlightened way of relating to the children in their care.

From within the Department of Education, there was also some dawning understanding of the needs of children caught within the industrial schools system. In 1943, the Medical Inspector of Industrial and Reformatory Schools, Dr Anna McCabe, attended a conference in England on child psychology. She strongly recommended the establishment of child guidance clinics to assist these most vulnerable of children. Her recommendations were ignored, once again not out of ignorance of the value of such an approach, but rather out of a choice made that such clinics would cost too much.

Fr Edward Flanagan, the Irish priest who founded the famous Boys Town in the United States, also published long articles in the Irish papers in the mid-1940s, condemning the highly abusive and punitive culture within Irish industrial schools. He recommended a more child-centred approach, based on communication and understanding rather than physical violence. He was very clear in his condemnation of the regime used in the country's industrial schools. He also was ignored.

It can be argued from these and many other similar examples that there was, certainly from the 1940s onwards, an awareness of the complexities of dealing with children in need of care. This awareness was clearly not acted on. The norm remained one of frightening levels of physical violence within industrial schools, combined with complete emotional deprivation of the children. To say that no one knew any better at that time is to ignore the important attempts which were made to reform the system.

The reality is that the Catholic Church and the State in partnership made certain choices, not so much out of ignorance but more for reasons of financial expediency. The institutional model for the processing of children into adulthood by religious orders was undoubtedly the cheapest option available. From the State's perspective, any of the more enlightened approaches that they were aware of would not only have cost more, but would also have been strenuously resisted by the Catholic Church as an erosion of its power.

Two other interesting lines of argument have emerged to mitigate the accounts of child abuse within the industrial schools. The first is the "bad apple" theory. This holds that in every group of people there will always be one or two who behave reprehensibly, and that this should in no way detract from the good works undertaken by the others. Furthermore, that in this regard, the Catholic Church is no different than any other area of life.

Were this true, it would indeed be a valid point. However, the scale of the abuse of children within the industrial schools system was so vast as to pose the most fundamental questions about the nature of religious orders in this country. The testimony in later chapters of this book gives a clear sense of the overwhelming extent of that abuse — children were savagely beaten and treated with extraordinary levels of cruelty by their religious carers in almost every single one of the fifty-two industrial and reformatory schools which existed in Ireland for most of the twentieth century. Very large numbers of the boys in particular were sexually abused and raped by male members of religious orders into whose care they were entrusted.

It is undoubtedly the case that by no means all nuns or Brothers within institutions were cruel to the child detainees. However, it is equally clear that those who did not either beat or abuse children did not stand in the way of the often sadistic excesses of their fellow religious. This is a point repeatedly made by the survivors of this abuse. It is a crucial area which the religious orders themselves have so far failed to address publicly. This specific issue provoked much comment in the wake of the *States of Fear* series, but no explanations or reasons for it have so far been advanced by the religious congregations involved.

The final line of argument to excuse the behaviour of the religious orders in the industrial schools is that the system was never really an Irish one — that it was imposed on Ireland by the British Government, and that this country merely inherited its flaws. Chapters Three and Four deal in considerable detail with the origins of the system, and how it changed and adapted to post-independence Ireland. Suffice it to say that the system became very much one of an Irish creation in the 1920s, at a time when Britain itself was beginning to see the dangers involved in institutionalising large numbers of children. The British Government had decided even at that early stage that such a system caused more harm than good to its small inmates, and had begun the process of reform. The newly independent Ireland took the opposite course. It decided for reasons which had very little to do with child welfare to consolidate even further the institutional system.

The legacy of the industrial schools continues to pervade many aspects of Irish life. The revelations in recent years of such severe child abuse within the system have shocked the nation. It is probable that such revelations will continue as the Government Commission to Inquire into Childhood Abuse, headed by High Court judge Mary Laffoy, begins its hearings of testimony from the survivors of the schools.

There are also many hundreds of cases for civil damages waiting to be heard before the courts. So far, they are being vigorously contested by both the religious orders involved and by the State. While this is of course their entitlement, it does appear to somewhat mitigate the effect of the various apologies issued to victims by these agencies.

Perhaps most seriously, the Gardai are now in the process of investigating hundreds of allegations of sexual abuse and rape against members of several of the congregations who ran the industrial schools — to date, allegations of this nature have been made against up to 150 Brothers. Eleven have been charged so far and are awaiting trial.

As the enormity of the crimes committed against so many tens of thousands of vulnerable children begins to dawn on the general population, the question most frequently asked is how could it have happened. The following chapters provide some clues as to the ways in which industrial schools became such living hells for their child victims.

Two

The System

To understand fully the operation of reformatory and industrial schools in Ireland, these institutions must be viewed as part of the larger system for the control of children and, to a lesser degree, women, in this country. It was a vast structure, with its origins in the second half of the nineteenth century. Several Catholic religious orders established a large number of institutions with the specific aim to "save the souls" primarily of women and children. While these were to provide a crucial element in maintaining social control of the population, they were also to constitute the frontline in the intense sectarian warfare between the Catholic and Protestant Churches in Ireland. They included State-funded reformatory and industrial schools, private orphanages, county homes (the replacements for the old workhouses), Magdalen laundries, and Mother and Baby homes.

All of these institutions were linked together in two key ways. Firstly, many of the religious congregations who managed the reformatory and industrial schools also operated Magdalen laundries. Several orders of nuns had constructed large complexes, containing an industrial school, a reformatory and a Magdalen laundry all together on the same site. Secondly, these institutions helped sustain each other — girls from the reformatory and industrial schools often ended up working their entire lives in the Magdalen laundries. Many of the children of unmarried mothers, born in the county homes and Mother and Baby homes, were placed in the industrial schools. In some cases the mothers themselves ended up in the Magdalen laundries.

This massive interlocking system was carefully and painstakingly built up by the Catholic religious orders over a number of decades. It was to result in huge numbers of children, and to a lesser degree their mothers, being incarcerated for transgressing the narrow moral code of the time. The majority of these institutions were run by female religious congregations, and it is ironic that those they most harshly punished were women. Interestingly, women placed in such institutions, particularly in the Magdalen laundries, were always referred to as girls, regardless of their age.

A number of both statutory and voluntary bodies continuously argued for the development of non-institutional systems to deal with destitute children. However, such was the domination of Catholic congregations in this area that no alternative care system was allowed to develop. The religious congregations were suspicious of all non-institutional means of providing services. This largely reflected their own institutional structures, but also their inability to assert total control over anything outside of their own institutions. One clear example of this was the demand from the Catholic hierarchy that children no longer be removed from industrial schools to be fostered with local families.[1]

From the perspective of the twenty-first century, it is difficult to comprehend the extent of the system developed by the congregations of the Catholic Church. Yet there can be little doubt that few families in this country were not touched by it. How many families had a daughter or other relation placed in a Mother and Baby home to avoid the disgrace of lone parenthood? How many families have suffered the guilt of wondering what happened to these children?

The sheer scale of the system has in part resulted in the strange public silence on these institutions for most of this century. While there were some courageous expressions of concern and dissent, the general absence of questioning was profound. Yet the majority of these institutions were not hidden away in remote areas. They were situated in prominent locations in towns and cities all over Ireland (see Appendix 1).

The Children

There were four distinct groupings of children within the 'care' system. The largest of these were in the industrial schools, committed by the courts because the State had decided that their parents were either unsuitable or unable to look after them. The second group were those children convicted of criminal offences, usually minor acts of delinquency, who were sentenced by the courts to a period in reformatory school. The third grouping were those children in so-called orphanages, which were mainly fee-paying institutions for the middle classes. Finally there were the children under the care of the local authorities, who were either destitute or had been born to unmarried mothers. Some few of these were "boarded-out" or fostered, but most ended up detained within industrial schools.

Industrial Schools

A total of over 105,000 children were committed to industrial schools by the courts between 1868 and 1969. At its peak at the turn of the century, this system contained a massive seventy-one schools in Ireland, detaining up to 8,000 children at any one time. For most of the first half of the twentieth century, there were fifty-two such institutions in operation. Up until the 1950s, they contained over 6,000 children at any one time.

From the mid-1950s, the numbers of children detained declined, largely because of a growing reluctance by the courts to commit them to industrial schools. By 1969, only thirty-one industrial schools remained, incarcerating just under 2,000 children.

From 1917, after the last Protestant industrial school closed, Catholic religious congregations managed all of the schools, bar two. The exceptions were the Baltimore Fishing School and the school in Killybegs, both of which were managed by parish priests in the area. The Sisters of Mercy were the single biggest provider of industrial schools. Their institutions alone detained a staggering total of over 40,000 children.

The role of the courts was central to the way in which the system operated. It was they who committed the children, passed the information on to the Department of Education and relevant local authority, who then between them funded each child by way of a capitation grant which was paid to the religious order running the particular industrial school in which that child was detained. It was this court procedure, with the children usually having to appear before a judge, which created such a strong association in the public mind between criminality and the industrial schools.

The actual court hearing was normally quite perfunctory. Barristers or solicitors were generally not involved. When the child appeared before the judge, he or she was usually not spoken to. Evidence would be heard from whoever had made the application for the child to be committed to industrial school. In many cases, this was the local inspector from the National Society for the Prevention of Cruelty to Children, to become the Irish Society or ISPCC in the early 1950s.

These inspectors were known colloquially as "the cruelty men". If relatives wished to have a child committed to industrial school, very often the local inspector would be called upon to organise it. He would also have been alerted by Gardai or a local parish priest that they were aware of particular children in need of care. Occasionally a Garda or priest might also give evidence in court as to the reasons why a child should be committed. The children themselves had no representation in court, and were not consulted either before, during, or after the event. They had literally no one to speak up for them.

The legal mechanism used was the Children Act, 1908. It had essentially incorporated, modified and repealed much of the existing legislation in relation to children under its broad remit, thus becoming the first legislation to deal with children in a comprehensive manner. In recognition of its scope and progressiveness, it became known as the Children's Charter. This Act (and its various amendments) was to form the legislative basis for child welfare services in Ireland for much of the twentieth century.

Until the 1950s, the Department of Education published in its annual reports a detailed breakdown of the numbers of children detained under each category specified in the 1908 Act. These included "found begging", "found destitute" and "found wandering without any home or settled place or abode, or proper guardianship, or visible means of subsistence". From the

1950s, these categories were collapsed into three broad headings: "lack of proper guardianship", "non-attendance at school" and "indictable offences".

Approximately eighty per cent of all children committed, and over ninety per cent of the girls, came under the category "lack of proper guardianship". In practice, this was a catch-all heading, which included children of unmarried mothers not eligible for adoption, children who had lost one or both parents, those whose parents were incapacitated through illness, or whose families were unable to look after them due to poverty. Homeless children came within this category, as did those whose families had been broken up because of desertion or the imprisonment of one parent. However, in all these cases, the language and procedure of the courts was to place the onus of guilt on the child. And the State, rather than attempting to address the poverty that existed in these families, chose instead to fund religious orders to effectively incarcerate these children.

About ten per cent of the total were committed for non-attendance at school. However, it is important to remember that these children had committed no offence. Rather it was the parents of the child who were guilty of a breach of the law. But in all cases, it was their children who paid the price, ending up detained in industrial schools for periods as long as eight years.

The numbers committed to these schools for criminal offences were equally small — less than one per cent of all girls and eleven per cent of boys. All of these were either under the age of twelve or else it was their first offence. These children were not criminals in any modern sense of the term. In most cases they had committed minor acts of larceny or delinquency. However, no account was taken of their circumstances, and they were made serve out long sentences in industrial schools. From the mid-1950s, St Joseph's Industrial School in Letterfrack, Co Galway was used almost exclusively for young boys convicted of these minor offences and for those who were not attending school. However, Letterfrack was unique in this respect and was utterly untypical of the remainder of the industrial schools.

Of interest is the relatively small number of children committed who were literally 'orphans', despite the popular connotations of such institutions as 'orphanages'. The Committee of Inquiry into Widows' and Orphans' Pensions suggested that there were only 350 orphans in industrial schools in 1933, representing 5.3 per cent of the overall population within the schools in that year.[2]

The total number of girls in the industrial schools at the end of each year between 1869 and 1969 was always in excess of boys. This was largely due to the fact that girls were usually committed at an earlier age than boys, thus spending longer periods of time in industrial schools. Just over nineteen per cent of girls admitted to industrial schools between 1870 and 1944 were aged under six compared to just over ten per cent of boys. There was a marked tendency in this context to commit girls for reasons of "protection".

'Poor Law' Children — "The Forgotten Ones"

Another group of children placed in the Industrial schools were those who came through the local authority system. These had been born mainly in the county homes, the old workhouses. Most of them were either the children of lone mothers or of those who were unwilling or unable to use the courts system. Their background was invariably one of severe poverty, and did not differ significantly from the circumstances of the children who had been committed through the courts.

There were approximately 25,000 of these local authority or 'Poor Law' children sent to industrial schools, giving a grand total of over 130,000 who spent their childhoods in these institutions. While the local authorities had a statutory obligation to find foster homes for these children, in practice many of them chose the institutional option. This became especially pronounced from the 1950s — the religious orders had mounted a successful campaign to secure more of these 'Poor Law' children to fill the vacancies caused by a decline in children coming through the courts system at that time.

As fostering fell into disuse, it became clear that the local authority children were among the most seriously neglected within the system. While the Department of Education had specific responsibilities to inspect the children committed by the courts, the 'Poor Law' children had no agency which had responsibility for their welfare. This led one of the inspectors within the Department of Health, who had long championed the cause of these children, to name them "the forgotten ones".[3]

Orphanages: A Class Apart

In addition to the industrial schools, and often confused with them, a number of private orphanages existed. These were generally outside of the State system, and most were clearly defined as being for children of "good character from respectable families". There was thus a clear class distinction between orphanages and industrial schools, reflected in the fact that many orphanages were in fact fee-paying institutions.

Many of the children within them were not orphans in the strict sense of the word. Most had either one or both parents alive, or some other relative prepared to pay their fees at the orphanage. Because these institutions were not regulated in any way, there is very little information on them. In many cases, it appears that the fees were usually higher than the amounts paid by the State for the upkeep of children in the industrial schools. There are equally no figures available to show how many children were in these orphanages. In 1970, it was estimated that there were 1,700 boys and girls in a total of forty-two orphanages in the country[4] — it is likely that there were at least twice that number of children there during the middle decades of the century.

The picture is highly confusing as many of the industrial schools for junior boys and for girls were widely and inaccurately called orphanages. However, the class distinctions were a defining aspect of the differences between these two types of institutions for children. It is interesting in this regard to look at some of the ways in which the orphanages described themselves. For example, the Dominican Orphanage of our Lady of Sion in Dublin's Eccles Street stated that it was for "the orphan daughters of parents of the professional and mercantile class who have seen better days".[5]

Many orphanages were run by the same orders who also managed industrial schools. In this way, they made clear distinctions between the children of the poor in their industrial schools, and those of the middle classes who were directed towards their orphanages. The Sisters of Mercy, for instance, described their orphanage in Cork as being "for girls of the upper class [to] be comfortably maintained and receive a superior education".[6] In addition, this same order ran a total of three industrial schools in Co Cork, all for the children of the poor.

The Presentation Sisters, who ran two industrial schools in Tipperary, also had the George's Hill orphanage in Dublin. For girls to be received there they had to have "respectable parents who have met with reverses of fortune". It promised to educate them fully for such positions as governesses, school teachers, shop assistants and even nuns.[7] The best a girl from an industrial school could hope for was usually a job as a domestic servant.

The only notable exception to this pattern appears to have been St Brigid's Orphanage in Dublin. This was described as not being for "the orphan child of rich Catholic parents", but rather for orphaned and destitute children "upon whom the double calamity of physical and spiritual destitution has fallen".[8] Indeed, several orphanages saw it as their specific mission to rescue children whose Catholic faith was perceived to be in danger. The Sacred Heart Home in Drumcondra, for instance, was "to provide a home for girls rescued from the dangers of proselytism".[9] It is interesting to note that even into the 1950s and 1960s, the sectarian battles which had raged throughout the nineteenth century remained alive. The religious orders continued to perceive a serious threat from the various Protestant denominations — the prospect that they would steal away Catholic children and forcibly change their religion remained very real in the minds of these Catholic congregations.

There were a number of specifically Protestant orphanages, catering for several hundred children up to the 1970s. They were generally run by secular Boards of Governors, but with a clear Protestant ethos. The largest of these were the Bird's Nest Homes, the Cottage Home and Miss Carr's Home.

A microcosm of the precise and minute class distinctions in Ireland for much of the twentieth century can be seen through the Christian Brothers' institutions for children. They ran most of the industrial schools for boys over the age of ten in the country. They also had two other institutions for a different class of boy. St Vincent's Orphanage in Glasnevin catered for "boys of middle-class families who are orphans through the death of one or both parents".[10] It was funded by the Society of St Vincent de Paul.

Their second institution was for even better-off boys, those from the upper middle classes. The O'Brien Institute in Dublin's Marino was funded through a legacy left by two sisters of that name specifically to be used "for the education of the sons of gentlemen of reduced circumstances". Places were strictly limited, and each application was vetted personally by the Archbishop of Dublin. The Christian Brothers thus catered for three distinct social classes of children — upper middle class, middle class, and working and lower class — each in their own clearly defined and separate type of institution. This use of child care by the religious orders to methodically entrench and perpetuate a rigid class system in Ireland remains one of the most hidden aspects of these structures.

Given the generally better-off backgrounds of many of the children in orphanages as compared to industrial schools, one might expect that they received kinder treatment at the hands of their carers. In some cases, they were indeed better off. Some of the women who grew up in St Joseph's Orphanage on Tivoli Road in Dun Laoghaire have happy memories of their childhood. This institution was run by the Daughters of the Heart of Mary, who had no involvement with industrial schools. However, in a number of the orphanages run by orders such as the Sisters of Mercy, the Sisters of Charity and the Christian Brothers, who also ran industrial schools, the descriptions are of somewhat harsher and more brutal regimes. But even here, none of the children faced quite the same level of deprivation or abuse as experienced by those detained within the industrial school system.

Reformatory Schools

Reformatory schools, although closely associated in the public mind with industrial schools, were legislatively quite separate institutions. They were exclusively for children convicted of criminal offences. However, in most cases their crimes were so minor that these children could not by any stretch of the imagination be described as criminals.

The boys' reformatories were run by the Oblates of Mary Immaculate. They were St Kevin's in Glencree, Co Wicklow, and St Conleth's in Daingean, Co Offaly. In 1940, Glencree closed and the boys were all transferred to Daingean.

The main girls' reformatory school was St Joseph's in Limerick, run by the Good Shepherd nuns, who also had a large industrial school on the same complex. In 1944, St Anne's Reformatory School in Dublin's Kilmacud was established by the Sisters of Our Lady of Charity of Refuge.

Between 1858 and 1969, a total of 15,899 children were committed to these reformatory schools. There were always vastly more boys in this system, 13,428 in total, compared to only 2,471 girls. Between the 1930s and the 1960s, the courts sentenced an average of 150 children a year to periods of several years in reformatory schools.

In the context of current sentences handed down by the courts to adult offenders, it is interesting to examine the approach in this regard to children in the early part of the century. For instance, a twelve-year-old boy from Green Street in Dublin was sentenced to five years in the Glencree Reformatory in 1908 — he had been found guilty of vagrancy, and was described as uncontrolled and as someone who sold papers in the street. Another case was that of a thirteen-year-old from Dublin, "a regular street arab" whose father drank a little and whose mother was "good, but a Protestant" — in 1915, he got five years in Glencree for stealing two suits of clothes. In 1928, a twelve-year-old from Cork was committed to the Daingean Reformatory for a period of four years and four months. His offence was to have stolen a quantity of apples and pears valued at thirty shillings.

The establishment of St Anne's Reformatory School in 1944 is of particular interest. It was set up to "receive girls under seventeen who either (1) are convicted of legal sexual offences or (2) are placed in dangerous surroundings and have marked tendencies towards sexual immorality".[11] Its establishment derived from the desire of the Good Shepherd Sisters to expand their reformatory work to Dublin. They were particularly keen on the detention of girls deemed to be "sexually aware". Up to the 1940s, they had generally moved these girls directly into one of their Magdalen laundries — they ran a total of four of these around the country, in New Ross, Waterford, Cork and Limerick.

However, the Good Shepherd nuns cut down on this practice in the early 1940s in an attempt to force the Department of Education to fund a new reformatory school for them in Dublin. The Archbishop of Dublin, John Charles McQuaid, also took an interest in this area, but decided that the Sisters of Our Lady of Charity of Refuge were more suitable to run such a reformatory. His wishes in the matter were granted by the Department of Education. St Anne's detained only about twenty girls at any one time, and was the only school to be funded on the basis of an overall grant rather than a capitation fee per child.

Mary Norris's Story, St Joseph's Industrial School, Killarney (Sisters of Mercy), 1944-1948

"I don't remember kissing my mother goodbye. We must have done, but I think there was too much fright. She was screaming, and with the little one feeding on her breast. We were all screaming. They took us out and up to the village, where there was a court. We were like sheep going to a fair, to a slaughter. We all stood there in front of this judge, and he put us away."

Mary Norris was born in 1932 near Sneem in Co Kerry. She was the eldest of the eight children of Daniel and Brigid Cronin, who had a small farm. Her father died of cancer when Mary was twelve years old and her youngest sister only six months.

"Some time after Daddy died, my mother started seeing a local man and he was visiting the house on a regular basis. I think maybe on some occasions he stayed the night. It didn't interfere with me or my siblings. We saw nothing that we shouldn't see. He used to bring us a few sweets, and we saw our mother a bit happy.

I was getting ready for school one morning, and down our narrow boreen I saw this car. It couldn't get up to our house, but a Guard and another man asked was my mother inside. I later discovered that this man was what we called the Cruelty Man, the local inspector for cruelty to children.

Now the man that my mother was seeing was in the house, he'd stayed that night, and I would assume that the house was watched. That's my reading of it — that they wanted to catch him in the house. And they said, 'We're taking the children'.

When they marched us up the village, we could see all the people looking at us. I was doing my best to comfort my brothers and sisters, who were all crying. After the court, the Guards gave us some dinner. Then they took us by car in the dark to Killarney, along the mountain road.

We came to a place above Blackwater, and I asked to go to the toilet. They let me out, and I thought, I'm running away, because I knew that I could get home from there. And then I thought, I'll never see my sisters and brothers again. So I got back in the car.

The first thing when we arrived at the orphanage in Killarney, we were stuck into a bath of disinfected water. We went into this bath thing — no kiss, no cuddle, no 'you'll be all right', and they gave us these old dresses, like a mohair sort of a dress and knickers.

Then we went down and got supper: bread and dripping, cold cocoa. And I thought, in the name of God, what are they bringing us here for, we had better at home. It mightn't have been much, but it was nicer. For the first few days, I couldn't stop crying, crying, crying. I suppose it was the shock of it all.

My brothers were taken to the boys' section, because they were too young to go to the Christian Brothers. They were kept apart from us, we hardly ever saw them. And my younger sisters and myself were in three different dormitories. I mean, as a big family we'd be used to sleeping together and being close. It was like the minute you got in — cut, that's it. You're a family no more.

I now know why all this happened to us — the local parish priest was behind it. He considered my mother a bad woman, not fit to be allowed keep her children. They didn't lock us up because we had no shoes or because we were neglected. We were not neglected, our mother was doing her best for us. We were taken in because they decided that our little souls were in danger. Not our bodies, just our souls. They didn't care about our bodies. Just so long as the little souls were safe.

I straight away took a dislike to this particular nun, and she took a dislike to me. I want to name her, I'm not going to protect her — Sister Laurence she was, and she's dead now. A few days after we arrived, she sent for me and she said, 'Your mother could have kept you, you know, but she's a bad woman, an evil woman, no good, and I hope you don't turn out like her.' And all I could say was, 'Yes Sister, yes Sister, yes Sister.'

And then the beatings started — awful beatings. I used to wet the bed, and I'd get beaten for it. Sister Laurence would make me go down the back stairs carrying my mattress on my head. I'd have to carry it all the way across the yard to the drying room. All the other kids would be lined up, chanting 'Mary Cronin wet the bed, Mary Cronin wet the bed". And I mean I was going on thirteen then. And the bed wetting had only started up since I came to Killarney.

When we'd be having our bath on Fridays, Sister Laurence used to come down and I would have to stand there, dripping wet, no clothes on. She had a belt around her, which was part of her regalia, I think, that she took with her vows, part of her poverty chastity and obedience. But she used it as a weapon.

Can you imagine when your skin is wet and somebody is hitting you with leather? She was a big strong woman, and she'd be there hitting me with all her force. And without no word of a lie, she would be frothing at the mouth. It was only years later that I thought she got some pleasure out of that, other than hitting me. And I mean I got very badly beaten, but mainly only by her.

We used to have a nickname for this nun. We called her the devil. And one day, didn't she hear me muttering it. 'What did you say, Cronin?' she roared at me. 'Nothing, Sister,' I said.

'Do you realise', she said, 'that you are speaking to the bride of Christ?'

Now, the other girls used to listen to me, because I'd been on the outside and knew things. I'd seen bulls and cows and calves and the rest of it, and I knew what was what. And coming in at twelve, they hadn't broken me.

So, my head sideways, I said: 'Ah, Jesus, he must have been hard up.' And didn't she hear me again. Well, I got a walloping. But I couldn't stop it — it just came out of me. Of course the others were delighted, because they couldn't say anything like that. They wouldn't dare laugh in front of her, but they laughed about it afterwards.

She would hit you on the body, always on places where the marks wouldn't be seen. And it was usually in front of everyone. And in front of another nun, a lay nun who used to say to me, 'Listen, Mary child, cry because if you cry she'll stop.' But I couldn't cry. I wouldn't give her the satisfaction of crying, because I felt if I cried she'd won.

That Christmas, I was still wetting the bed. There were a few what we called matrons in the orphanage, they were ordinary lay people. One of these matrons got married down the town of Killarney, and her husband was Santa Claus that year. A lovely man. And when it was my turn to get a present, he said to me, 'Are you Mary Cronin? I can't give you anything, I'm afraid. I've been told you wet the bed.' This was all out loud. And he passed my by. He didn't want to, but the nun was there beside him.

Christmas wasn't too bad, though. The food was a little bit nicer. We might get a sausage or something. The games were taken down, the ludo and stuff. And the only time I ever got an egg was Easter Sunday, just an ordinary boiled egg.

The rest of the time, the food there was atrocious. In the morning you got a bit of bread and margarine and cocoa. At dinner-time you got stale bread, and they would get the blood from the butcher's shop and it would be poured over this bread, and the bread put in the oven. And then at three o'clock, you got porridge, and it was like something that they would give to the pigs. It wasn't really porridge at all. I remember the hunger, going to bed really hungry.

And the nuns, of course, they had wonderful food. God forgive me, they were like pigs. I mean, they were living off the fat of the land. There would have been about sixty of them in Killarney at the time, between the schools and the orphanage.

There was a lovely woman — her name was Agnes — who worked in the nuns' kitchen. And there were a number of lay sisters, of course. And the food, oh, you'd smell the onions and the steak and the beautiful bread and butter pudding and rice, tapioca. We used be over washing up in the scullery, and Agnes would give us what would be left. We'd eat a bit, and then take the rest out to our friends in the yard.

Most of the lay sisters were very nice. They did a lot of work around the place, in the kitchen and that. They wouldn't be allowed to eat with the other nuns, they'd have to eat afterwards. I think maybe they identified with us. They were kept down as well.

From time to time, the inspector would come. It was a woman, I can see her, with her grey suit on her. She'd taste a bit of the food. 'Oh, lovely', she'd say. It was pandy — mashed potato with butter. 'Oh, that's lovely, do you like your food?' 'Yes Ma'am', we'd all chorus. You couldn't say but what we got yesterday was shite. And what we'll get tomorrow will be shite. Because the nun was standing there with her.

As well as that, the nuns would always know when the inspector was coming. Another orphanage in Cork or wherever would say she's on her way. They knew.

And then the preparations would start. We'd have new clothing. We were all polished up, and we'd get a ball to play with. We'd be so happy. The toys would be brought down. There'd be little toys put on beds and things like that. We used to have tin mugs — ponnies, we called them — and tin plates and spoons. No such thing as a knife and fork. And when the inspector would come, all that would disappear, and nice things were put out instead. I mean, if only she had opened the cupboards, she'd have seen what was in there.

She never really asked us any questions, she never talked to us on our own, and I blame her for that. I don't blame the nuns for that. Because if she'd wanted to talk to us, they couldn't have stopped her. You know, I've always felt and I will always feel that I and many others who went through this will blame the nuns, and justifiably so. But there was another organisation that had control, and that was the State, the Government. They were responsible, they had overall control. But they didn't come and check out properly who these nuns were, and what they were doing to us. They were lacking, they let us down.

You know, it's not just the physical beatings that they gave you, the emotional things are just as bad. There's one thing that I'll carry with me to my grave. A lot of the children in the orphanage came in from the county home in Killarney, the workhouse, and it was run by the nuns as well. Until the day I die I'll remember the way some of the nuns treated the children from the county home in comparison to the other children.

And I was doing the same. 'You're only a county home baby, you've got no mother or father', I used to say to them. The hurt I must have inflicted on them. It's no consolation to me for anybody to say, 'but Mary you didn't know any better, you treated them as you saw the nuns treating them'. That's no consolation — I was the one who hurt them, and I have to carry that with me.

I never minded having to do work around the place, cleaning and laundry and so on. It was never too bad. One of my jobs at one stage was to mind the smaller ones, and some of them you loved. One little one, Kathleen, who was running around the yard one day, and she kept falling. So one of the nuns, Sr Amanda, she's the nice lay sister, she said to me, 'Mary child, go down and bring her up, she's sick.'

Kathleen had a very good mother who used to visit her every Sunday. I think she was a farmer's daughter who got into trouble and had a baby. She was a lovely, lovely person and she adored her daughter. And it turned out that little Kathleen had meningitis, and she died in the fever hospital in Killarney.

After the funeral, her mother came back with one of the women that worked in the convent and she was in the kitchen, crying. I was down at the other end of the room, putting dripping on the bread for the supper, and this brute Sister Laurence came in.

'What are you crying for?' she said in a rough way to the child's mother. 'You do know that this is the punishment now for your sin.' Wasn't that a great consolation to a mother who was after losing her child? I had a big knife in my hand for the bread. I don't know how I didn't just go up and stick the knife in that nun. That's never left me either.

My own mother, she didn't really visit. She might have come once. She married the man who had been visiting her and had two more children, but he was a tyrant. She was kept locked in, she had a dreadful life with him.

She got away from him eventually and went to England. I mean, the resilience of the woman! She got a job in England, and she had a bit of a drink problem. But for the last eight years of her life, I looked after her. She only died in 1989, surrounded by her family who all loved her.

She found it very hard to talk about what had happened when we were all taken away from her. I think the local priest had drilled into her that she sacrificed her children for a man. And she had that guilt now. Sometimes, in my moments of maybe depression, I would say nasty things to her, I'm afraid. But everything was all forgiven before she died

And my brothers. What happened to them was very sad. For a while, they used to come to school in our place, and so we'd still see each other. And then one day they didn't come up. I asked where they were and was told they'd gone to the Christian Brothers in Tralee. Just like that. No goodbye or anything.

So far as I know they were not well treated in the Tralee place. From what one of them said later, I think they might have been sexually abused. They both became alcoholics. One was burned in a fire in the south of England in 1969. The other was murdered in North London in 1978.

One of them had been boarded out from the Tralee school to a local farmer. One of my sisters was boarded out to the same farmer when she was about ten. She told me years later that she was sexually abused by that farmer. She said there was no penetration, there was just feeling. But why did the nuns send that girl out to a farmer when my mother wasn't asked permission? Were they able to just send children out without asking anybody?

My two younger sisters have much better memories of Killarney. They were tiny when they went in, and they were quite happy there. I would have been gone at this stage, and Sister Laurence had moved on to be Reverend Mother of the

entire convent, so they had no contact with her. And some of
the younger nuns who came in were very nice. So the whole
place improved. I'm really happy that my sisters have good
memories.

I quite liked school — the nun who taught us was nice.
You'd get smacked in school alright, but it never worried
me. It would be maybe on the hands, and you usually knew
what it was for. Not at all like the beatings in the orphanage.

And I was bright. It has always been a bone of contention
with me that I was well able for it, but all they taught me
was to be a servant. Just to be a skivvy. The nuns ran a
secondary school as part of the convent, but it wasn't for the
likes of us. And I always felt that the better nuns were put
teaching the town children. The doctors' daughters and so
forth.

Now, when I was sixteen, I decided I'd be a nun. I
decided then I would make them like me. All I ever heard
was 'your mother's a tramp, you'll turn out just like your
mother, no good.' And I thought, 'Oh, God, maybe that nun
is right. Maybe she knows something that I don't know.
Maybe my mother is a tramp.' And even though I didn't
want to believe her, it set up this doubt about my mother.

They said they were looking for nuns to go to Australia
to help the aborigines. I didn't know what an aborigine was,
but I said 'I'll go!' Another girl put up her hand as well, but
she wasn't picked. We all knew it was because she was born
out of wedlock.

So off I went to be a nun. They took me down the town to
get the hair permed, to make me nice for going away to
college to be a nun. And they made me a dressing gown,
and took me in to eat with the matron so I would be able to
use a knife and fork and a serviette. And off I went to St
Matthew's College in Trim.

But I hated it and I didn't last long. I went to the head
nun, and told her I wanted to leave. 'I'll get the priest for
you,' she said. The priest arrived and said, 'My child, when
you're near to God the divil wants you.' But I told him that
the divil had nothing at all to do with it, I just didn't want to
be a nun.

So they got in touch with the Sister Laurence in Killarney, and she said 'I knew it'. I don't really know what I was thinking of at all. I suppose I wanted to make them like me, that maybe for once they would touch me. And they did. But you know, it wasn't enough.

So after that, they got me a job working for a family in Tralee. I got 2/6 (just over 12p) a week for milking the cows, cooking, washing and cleaning every day. I was allowed out one night a week to the pictures. I lived for the pictures, Betty Grable and all. That and buying magazines about Princess Elizabeth and Princess Margaret. I had no interest in boys at all.

They used to change the picture twice a week. One particular week, I asked the woman of the house could I go out a second night, and she said no, that I'd been to the pictures already this week. I was desperate to go. I'd been working like a slave that day to make up the work. She still said no. But I said, 'I'm going.' And I went.

I came back that night straight after the pictures. The woman was sitting in the study with cups of tea ready, she was falling all over me. God, I thought, maybe I'd get out two nights a week. Next day, up comes the same man who four years previously had taken me to the orphanage. The Cruelty Man.

'Get your stuff together, you've been a very bold girl, I'm taking you back, the nuns want you back in Killarney,' he said. So he took me back, and the nuns locked me in a room there.

The next day, I was taken down to a doctor, and he examined me, gave me an internal examination. And I remember him saying to the matron who had brought me down, 'What in the name of God is wrong with them up there, this girl is intact.' But I had no idea what intact meant. The next day I was sent to the Good Shepherd convent. I wasn't even allowed to say goodbye to my sisters, to anybody.

The Good Shepherds was what they used to threaten us with if we were bold. It was a Magdalen laundry in Cork. I was sent there to work, to slave in that laundry. The nuns in

Killarney had no right to do this — I had turned sixteen and was out from their power. But I didn't know that at the time. I thought I had to do what I was told, as always. The way I see it now is that it was one load of nuns giving servants, skivvies, to another lot of nuns to run their laundry, their workroom.

The first thing I was asked when I arrived at the Good Shepherd was my name. I said Mary Cronin. 'We'll have to give you another name,' the nun said. I objected, but she said I'd be called Maire from then on, and that I wasn't to tell anyone why I was there. 'Well, I don't know why I'm here,' I said. 'All I did was go to the pictures. I've done nothing wrong.'

When I went in there my dignity, who I was, my name, everything was taken. I was a nonentity, nothing, nobody. I had a white collar, starched, and a white little cap — the cap represented penitents. I sat there for days, crying. Then I was put working in the laundry. And one day in the laundry I was talking to this woman, we were whispering. You couldn't talk to anybody, if you did you were moved. You had to pray, out loud, all the time, to stop you talking to anyone. But she asked where I was from, and I said from Sneem. 'Oh,' she said, 'so am I.'

And I remembered straight away my dad telling my mum about this poor girl who'd had a baby, and this must be her. Then I realised, Jesus, most of them had babies and that's why they're here.

The younger ones were from orphanages like Killarney. The youngest I remember was fourteen, she was from Cork. They hadn't had babies at all. Most of them were there like me, as a punishment for disobeying an order. There were two girls from my own orphanage. One was sent because she wet the bed.

When she arrived, and I said, 'Helen, why are you here?'. She said, no, I had to call her Regina. They had changed her name to Regina. She was just barely sixteen. They had told her they were locking her away for wetting the bed.

The work was very hard. It was a commercial laundry, a huge place, with about a hundred women and girls working there. The stuff would come in from all the hospitals, the hotels. You started at about eight o'clock in the morning. I was in the washing room, and you'd get all the sheets from the hospitals with all the blood on them. No such thing as rubber gloves or anything.

They used to bring in bags from a bacon factory on a Friday, and they'd be full of white maggots, with the heat, you know. It was a big industry, and the nuns were making a fortune. And I spent two years there, and didn't get so much as a penny for all that work.

How I got out was that I had aunts in America, my father's sisters, who'd been writing to the nuns in Killarney wondering where I was, because they hadn't heard from me for so long. So I was sent back to Killarney, and they got me another job, this time skivvying in another Mercy convent in Limerick. Eventually, I saved up enough money, and went to England.

At first I had a great time. Got a good job and just enjoyed myself. But I made a bad marriage, and ended up with depression, going to psychiatrists and that. You see, I'd never dealt with what had happened to me with the nuns. Just put it on hold. But I met my present husband in 1967, and that made a big difference. We've been very happy.

I thought that nothing would turn me around from the hatred that I had inside me for the nuns. The counselling I got helped, but I really did it myself. Because not all Mercy nuns are bad. There were many good nuns. At the end of the day, I'm glad that I don't end up hating them, because if I hated them I think they'd have won.

But I'd also say to people: hold on to your anger. You've got every right to be angry. You can put anger to good use, and I hope that I've put mine to very good use. But let go of any bitterness. Bitterness is like a cancer that eats you. It's no use.

The apology the Mercy order has given meant nothing at all to me. It was a punitive apology. I mean, they said they were sorry 'if' anyone was damaged or had suffered. What do they mean 'if'? It means that they don't really believe that they have done any wrong. They're in denial about it. If they had made a proper and full apology, I believe that a lot of people wouldn't be taking litigation, and they could get on with their lives. People are going to court because of that 'if'.

I know some people still feel shame of having grown up in an orphanage. But I don't. I feel that it's other people, the people on the outside, who should feel ashamed. I think that the shame lies at the door of the Catholic Church, because they instructed the people, and the people allowed all of this misery to happen.

And of course the damage wasn't just to the children themselves. It doesn't stop with them. Because I often wonder what kind of mothers and wives they made. I know I wasn't the best myself.

I knew a girl in London who grew up in the Mercy orphanage in Clifden. I went up to see her one day, and her baby was about three months old, and mother of Jesus, she was walloping him. And I asked her what in the name of God she was doing. 'Well, that's the way we used to make them stop crying in the orphanage,' she said. It was really sad to see it.

When you sum it all up, the thing that I missed most was love. No love. I don't think the nuns knew the meaning of it. The only love they knew was the love of Jesus Christ. And how can women — and some of them had to be intelligent, they were teachers — how could they comprehend it in their minds that you loved Jesus, but you can't love little children. Jesus said suffer the little children, he didn't say beat the fecking hell out of them."

Mary Norris now lives in Co Kerry with her husband. Her only child, a daughter, is a nurse in England. A few years ago, Mary started a campaign for the erection of a headstone to mark the final resting place of the Magdalen women who died in the Good Shepherd convent in Cork over the decades. In stark contrast to the carefully maintained graveyard of the Good Shepherd nuns themselves, the laundry women were laid to rest in an unmarked plot. Mary is determined that, at least in death, these women will finally be given due recognition.

Don Baker, St Conleth's Reformatory School, Daingean (Oblates of Mary Immaculate), 1963–1965

"My first memory of arriving in Daingean was one of terror and shock. I was twelve years old, and I was brought into this small dark office. The priest had a pencil which he pointed at my penis and the first words he said were 'Do you play with that?' I was absolutely shocked. I couldn't believe that someone could ask me such a question."

Don Baker was born in Whitehall on Dublin's northside in 1950. He was very ill as a young child with tuberculosis, and was hospitalised for long periods. His parents broke up, and Don ran away from home on a number of occasions. He was convicted in the courts for minor offences, and sentenced to two years in Daingean.

"This same priest then gave me a big lecture on the rules of the place. I was completely intimidated by him. I was brought off and had to undress and give over my clothes. He gave me these things too wear instead — the jacket was about three sizes to big for me and it was like something out of the last century. The pants were the same, they were huge, and I had to wear rubber boots like wellingtons.

Then he led me out to the yard. I thought I looked bad until I saw all the other boys. They looked ten times worse — they'd had to wear these clothes for years, they were the only ones you got in your time there. When I saw them all in the yard, it was like something out of *Oliver*. I was in total shock all that first day.

My home background wasn't great. My dad was an alcoholic and there was nothing but trouble at home. I think they loved me in their own way and they tried to do their best for me. Every time I ran off I really just wanted them to come after me, to show they really cared about me. I did silly things like break into the local shop and turn on all the taps. I stole chocolate, and I'd climb into people's back gardens and steal their apples. I suppose I was a troublesome child, but it was all silly stuff. Thank God I was never violent, I never harmed anyone.

41

When I was caught, the courts ordered me to go to a psychologist. She asked me all these ridiculous questions. For instance, she showed me a picture of a cowboy with a bow and arrow, and an Indian with a gun, and she asked me what was wrong with this picture. It was really silly, and you know they never once questioned why is this kid like this, what is going on at home. I think my parents should have been sitting there instead of me. But that wasn't the way at that time. They labelled me a nut and I actually believed them. I thought I really was a headcase, and that's why I was being sent to Daingean.

It's amazing how quickly you can adjust to a place like that. After the first shock, I just fell in line and tried to survive. The routine was that you were woken at six each morning. Then you'd wash, just your face and hands — we never had any hot water, and in the two years I was there I never had a shower. It's funny, but I never felt dirty, even though we must have been filthy.

Mass was at half-six, and it was compulsory. That changed about a year after I arrived, and you didn't have to go. But everyone went. You felt the Brothers would get you if you didn't. After Mass, we go out into the yard and hang about until nine, when we'd get breakfast, or what they called breakfast — a quarter loaf of bread with a lump of margarine jammed in the middle of it. A tin plate and tin mug, with one of the boys going round each table with a big bucket of tea, scooping out a mug-full for each child. Then back out into the yard for about another hour, until you were called for work detail.

The food was unbelievable. There were eight boys to a table and for lunch there'd be a big plate of potatoes in the middle. But they had maggots in them, so you'd be peeling around, trying to find a bit you could eat. In the evening, it was the same as breakfast, the lump of bread and marge and the bucket of tea. I remember I was so shocked by this at first that I didn't eat a single thing for days. But then I just got used to it.

I was put to work sweeping and cleaning the chapel in the grounds. Because of what happened to me there I turned

42

into a complete nervous wreck. I know it's hard to believe, at the age of thirteen. But I had nervous twitches all the time, my eye kept twitching. I couldn't stand anything at the back of my neck. I kept fixing my shirt down the back of my pants all the time. I remember one evening saying the rosary and I had a major panic attack. I was frightened, so frightened. I went green and I was literally shaking all over. It was horrific — I was heading for a nervous breakdown at the age of 13.

What was happening to me was that this Brother was terrorising me every day in the church, where I worked at the cleaning. It was my job as well to ring the Angelus at twelve o'clock. Bits of straw used to fall down on my head when I pulled on the rope, I'd always be picking them out of my hair.

I was very isolated, there was usually no one else around the chapel. This particular Brother would come down and he'd start to question me in a sexual way. He'd ask me do I get an erection. He didn't use those words — he'd say 'Did you go hard today' and things like that. And you have to remember that I was just twelve or thirteen, and he was towering over me. He was a great big man, well over six foot, with his crucifix stuck in the big band they wore around their habits.

This went on day after day, and he'd be asking me did any of the other boys go hard, and did I ever see them doing anything. I would be terrified of him arriving. Every time the door would open, my heart would jump, my whole body would just go tense. The only way I could cope with this interrogation day after day was to pretend I didn't know what he was talking about. I'd just tell him I didn't have a clue what he meant. I believe to this day that that's what saved me.

Finally, after almost a year of this, it came to a crunch one day. He came in and he stood over me and took a small letter out of his pocket. He said that he'd been told that I had kissed a boy, and of course I hadn't. He hit me on the side of the face with his leather, and he said 'Tell me the truth'. I said that I was telling the truth, and he hit me on the other side of my face. Every time I said it, he hit me again. Both my cheeks were roaring red at this stage. And then it was really strange. He said 'I believe you', and then he said 'Give me a hug'. He lifted me up, hugging me, and I remember trying to keep away, even if it was only half-an-inch. Then he put me down, walked out, and not another word was said.

Shortly after that he called me down from the dormitory at night and he flogged me. They'd beat us on the stairs below the dormitories, and the sound of the strap hitting you would echo all over the place. I was stripped naked, and had to lie spread-eagled on the stairs. One Brother stood on my hands to keep me there, and another held my legs. Then the Brother who had made my life such a hell in the church flogged me with the leather. I always felt that this was his way to get me — if he couldn't get me sexually, then he could do it by beating me.

After that, I was put out working on the bog. The work was hard, but for me it was a great relief. I was with the other boys, and this particular Brother didn't come after me again.

I told my friend Skinner about the Brother in the church. Skinner was bigger than me, and he immediately told me that only that morning another Brother had asked him to masturbate him and that he had threatened the Brother he'd kill him if he ever tried anything like that again. So I began to think maybe I wasn't the only one it was happening to.

There was another incident that happened to me as well. This particular Brother took me to Tullamore with him one day to collect some doors. On the way back in the truck, he started putting his hand on my leg, and saying sexual things to me. I got so frightened that I made for the door. I actually opened it when the truck was going at maybe fifty miles an hour. He had to reach over and grab me to stop me falling out. When we got back, he asked me not to say anything about what had happened. He said he was sorry, that he had only been joking. I knew he wasn't joking, but I didn't say anything about it.

There was one time we were all marched into the church during the afternoon, which was very unusual. The head priest went up to the pulpit, and we were all looking at each other, wondering what all this was about. This priest, I remember it well, he took off his glasses and put his purple gown on the ledge of the pulpit and began screaming at the top of his lungs 'Wanking, wanking ....' He was literally frothing at the mouth. We were all in total shock.

It sounds funny now, but it wasn't a bit funny at the time. He started to tell us this story about a boy who masturbated so much that he became ill and had to be confined to bed. His mother got the priest around, and they knelt by the bed every day saying the rosary. And he told us that they had to strap the boy's arms to the bed with belts. This went on for days, he said, but one morning the mother asked the priest if he'd like a cup of tea. So they went downstairs to the kitchen. When they went back up a half an hour later, the boy had got a hand loose and was dead in the bed.

We believed every single word of that story. When we were filing out of the church, we were all looking at each other saying never again, you know. I can laugh about it now as an adult, but I don't know what was going on in the heads of those priests and Brothers. They seemed to be obsessed with sex and masturbation. The mind boggles when I think back on that particular time.

There was no attempt ever made at rehabilitation, or even education for us. For your first week there, you went to school. I think it was a kind of assessment. But that was it. I was there a year when they introduced a woodwork class, but only about five per cent of the boys were picked to go on it. I was one of them. But for everyone else, there was nothing. I don't remember ever seeing any inspectors either. No one ever came in to talk to us, to ask us anything about how we were getting on.

About halfway through my time there, a new priest took over. He improved things a bit. He got rid of the bucket for the tea, and we used to have a big teapot. We got bread that was actually sliced, and they started giving us butter as well.

They had their own dairy there, and that's where the butter came from.

I remember one morning we got an egg and two sausages. It was incredible. We thought it was Christmas, that we'd got our dates mixed up. It's funny the things that get to you. I'm here crying because we were so pathetically grateful just to get an egg to eat.

The Brother who worked in the refectory, he was a really good guy. He loved football and handball. He'd take us out to play games, and we'd have a bit of a laugh. You felt safe with him, you felt you could be a child. Because for most of my time there, I felt like an adult. We always saw it as a prison, never school. I used to call it 'Little Auschwitz'. I know that's going too far, but for years it's the way I felt about the place.

You were supposed to be tough and take your punishment. You couldn't say you missed your mother or your father. The truth was I missed them both terribly. My mother used to come and visit me, but you didn't want to worry her by telling her what the place was really like.

I remember some time back going in to one of the schools for boys in trouble to play a concert for them. And I looked at all those young lads, all acting the way I used to, all trying to be tough. I remember saying to them 'Is there anyone here who misses their mother?' No hands went up. So I told them about my time in Daingean, and how I felt about it. I sort of poured my heart out to them, and how it had affected my whole life. And at the end of it, when I asked them again about their mothers — they all raised their hands. It's hard to put words on it, but that really moved me."

Don Baker is now an acclaimed singer, composer and actor. He has spent years in therapy and counselling, trying to come to terms with the experiences of his childhood. He is a strong advocate of the value of counselling for those who have experienced similar abuse.

"I'm not interested in blaming people for what happened to me. But I do think that the people responsible, the people who ran those places, should admit to it. Because we all blamed ourselves for what happened, we all believed it was our own fault. I call it toxic shame, the shame of believing that you were to blame for what they did to you. And it's very hard to find your way back from that, to really knowing that it wasn't your fault at all.

In my case, it has had a very bad effect on my life. I'm much better now, but for years it contaminated any relationships I had with other people. I failed miserably at them, I just couldn't trust anyone.

You see, the only way we could survive Daingean was to bury it, to deny that it had happened. But the problem is that it doesn't go away, it just goes on festering deep inside you, ruining everything you touch. There was a time I drank a lot, just to feel half normal, but then that caught up with me too. It wasn't easy for me to realise that it was all connected back to my childhood and Daingean, but I really don't resent them or hate them anymore. I can forgive them now, and I can learn from it. But that wasn't always the case.

I remember being on stage one night, years ago, singing and playing the harmonica. When I was finished the concert, Christy Moore was there, and he came up to me and asked what I was so angry at. And do you know, I looked at him as though he had two heads. I wasn't even aware that I was angry. That'll show you just how deeply I had been denying everything that had happened to me."

Anne's Story, St Joseph's Orphanage, Mountjoy Street, Dublin (Irish Sisters of Charity), 1954–1963

"We used to have a little concert every Sunday evening, just among ourselves and the nuns. Each of us would do our party piece. The nuns always seemed to love the sad songs. Things like 'Two Little Orphans' and 'A Mother's Love Is A Blessing' were their favorites. One girl had a lovely voice and she normally sang 'I'll Take You Home Again, Kathleen'. But this one time, she had learnt the words of the Elvis Presley song 'Return To Sender', and she sang it for us on the Sunday. Well, she got battered around the place by the nuns. How dare she sing a song by a vulgar person like that! They really gave her an awful hammering."

St Joseph's, Mountjoy Street, was an orphanage, not an industrial school. Run by the Irish Sisters of Charity, it was fee-paying and is described in the Catholic Social Workers Handbook of 1947 as being for "children whose parents occupied a good position in the world". During the 1950s, it catered for just over forty children.

Anne was born in 1949, and was an only child. Her father had tuberculosis, and was not working. Her mother supported the family with her earnings as a shop assistant in Eason's bookshop. The family lived in Blessington St, only around the corner from St Joseph's.

When she was five years old, a little case was packed for her and she was moved full-time into the orphanage. She knows that her parents paid a substantial fee for her to be cared for in St Joseph's, but she was never able to find out why they put her in there in the first place. Her mother would never discuss it with her in later years.

"We were never allowed mix with the outside girls that would be in the same class as us at school. The nuns told us that we were superior to them, and should not be talking to them. I don't know why they said this, because it wasn't true. We were all just the same. But you'd be punished if they caught you talking.

48

Nobody told me anything when I went in there first. I thought that it was just for a few days, and then I'd be back home again. But after a while I realised I'd be there for good.

Mammy used to visit me once a week on visiting day, and bring me in a big bag of sweets. But as soon as she was gone, the bag would be whipped out of my hands, and I'd never see it again. Sometimes it was the nuns who took it, other times it was the lay staff. I remember once in my innocence I asked a nun could I have something out of Mammy's bag, and I was told I was a greedy little bitch, and that there were plenty of children worse off than me.

The food was good, though. We always got meat for our dinner, and potatoes and vegetables. We had dessert as well. Every Sunday morning we'd get a fry, with just black and white pudding. Some of our mothers would leave eggs in for us, and your name would be written on the egg, and you'd get that boiled for breakfast as well.

Everybody ate their dinner without question. But I wasn't long in the place and there was a piece of parsnip in my dinner, and it was dirty. I politely put it to one side of my plate, and ate everything else. The nun came down and told me to eat the parsnip. I said no. So she force fed it to me, and I got sick. Then she force fed that to me as well. And she started to beat me with her belt.

But that wasn't all. She went over and got the ladle out of the soup pot and put it on my hand. It was burning hot, and I still have the mark of that burn to this day. There was a day-girl who lived in Fontenoy St close by, and she went around to tell my daddy what had happened.

He arrived along alright, but the nuns managed to calm him down. They said 'Sure, she's grand now, aren't you' to me. And I was afraid to say anything, in case they'd do something worse to me. I never really told my parents about what went on there. I never felt that they could have done anything about it anyway.

Girls who wet the bed used to have their faces rubbed in it. I didn't wet the bed, but I did wet my knickers, from nervousness I think. They used to rub the knickers all over my face, and then I'd have to wash them out. This was from when I was five, and lasted for about two years — getting my face rubbed in urine-soaked knickers every day.

Even though our parents paid fees, we still did all the work around the orphanage — all the cleaning, the washing, the laundry and some of the cooking. I got abscesses on my knees from washing floors, I still have the marks on me. But abscesses or not, you still had to clean the floors.

I broke my leg when I was about 7. I just fell. Two girls carried me up to the dormitory and I was warned by the nun not to wet the bed. I was awake all night with the pain and the fear of wetting the bed. They didn't send me to hospital until the next day.

I really enjoyed being in hospital. I was there for two weeks and there was great freedom. And then they sent me out to a convalescent home in Mount Merrion as well. So I really had a great time.

I never remember any inspectors or anyone like that coming in. The nuns told us never to tell anyone 'what goes on inside these doors'. So it was very strange — on the one hand they made us believe we were superior, and on the other they were beating us and telling us we were no good. I think they were confused, and they certainly confused us.

When you were beaten, you got it all over your body. I remember a little three-year-old getting lashed on the legs because she wouldn't eat her dinner. She had five or six older sisters in the place, and they couldn't do anything to protect her. We were all helpless.

I remember a big fuss in the dormitory one night. I was still very young, and the nuns had done a raid on our lockers. Two of the girls had got packets of sanitary towels from their mothers, and the nuns found them. Sanitary towels were forbidden in the orphanage.

The nuns held them up to us all, and most of us were far too young to even know what they were. And then they started preaching about scandalising — 'he who scandalises one of my little ones' and so on. We hadn't a clue what was going on, but I'll never forget the sermon about scandalising.

A nun did actually tell us about periods, so it didn't come as a total shock to me when I had my first one. What they gave you, though, was one hand-made pad of some kind of material. It was a desperate thing, about an inch thick and awfully uncomfortable. You only got one and it had to last you. You washed it out yourself.

When the nun was explaining all this to us, she made us kneel down and say the Hail Mary, and she stopped us when we got to 'the fruit of thy womb Jesus'. And she explained to us what a womb was. And then she told us that a seed comes out of men, and that it can be an evil seed. We were no wiser, really, afterwards than we had been before her little talk.

I always liked school, and my mother was paying to have me go to the convent secondary school. But by the time I was nearly fifteen, I had had enough of it. I ran home to my parents' house, and said I was never going back. My mother wanted to send me back, but I got a job in a local shop, and that seemed to settle it that I could stay at home.

I genuinely believe that my parents thought they were doing the right thing in sending me there. They thought I'd get a good education and they thought I was happy there. And there was the social thing as well. I remember a neighbour saying to me once 'You're a poshy, you are', just because I was in that orphanage."

Anne worked at several jobs until she was nineteen. She then married, and has three children. She still lives in Dublin, and has been waiting for years for the chance to tell the real story of what happened to her in Mountjoy Street.

"I made a disastrous marriage. I was so frightened that my children might be taken into care that I let my husband away with murder. And I loved my children dearly, but I couldn't give them a hug when they were growing up. I didn't know how to. I can do it now, but they're all grown up.

I think it's amazing to see all the stuff about abuse in orphanages coming out now. Because I was stupid enough to believe that it was only us in Mountjoy Street who had a bad time. I even believed that when I left, no one else was being badly treated. And now it seems it was the same in loads of places. But at least we're facing it now, rather than hiding it. We hid it for years because no one would believe us, but that's over now, thank God."

Three

Saving Little Souls

The first reformatory in Ireland was established on the 21st of December 1858 in Drumcondra, Co Dublin. This was the High Park Reformatory School, established for the reception of Roman Catholic girls under the recently passed Act to promote and regulate such schools for juvenile offenders in Ireland. A number of months later, the St Kevin's Reformatory School in Glencree, Co Wicklow was similarly established for the reception of Roman Catholic boys.

Ten years later, on the 25th February 1869, the first industrial school in Ireland was established in Sandymount in Dublin, known as St Mary's Lakelands, for the reception of Roman Catholic girls. Over a year later, the famous Artane Industrial School was established, the first such institution for boys.

The running costs of these institutions were financed by the State, who also had a responsibility to inspect their operations. By the time the system was effectively abolished in the early 1970s, nearly 150,000 children had passed through these schools. Artane Industrial School alone, the largest industrial school ever built, incarcerated just over 15,000 boys during its existence. Visited by the Prince of Wales and Prime Minister Gladstone[1], Artane was the pride of the British empire and was held up as a model of child care all over the world. However, reformatory and industrial schools were not the first institutions to be developed to care for destitute and delinquent children, and in many cases were significant improvements on what had existed before their establishment.

Orphans and Foundlings: Patriots and Priests

The foundling hospitals were the first State-funded institutions specifically established for looking after destitute, orphaned and abandoned children. The best known was the Dublin Foundling Hospital: its revolving cradle on the wall remains strong in the Dublin folk memory. This was a shelf with a basket attached. Once the baby was placed in the basket, a bell was rung, and from the inside a porter turned a wheel attached to the shelf which brought the child into the hospital. It was an anonymous means of disposing of unwanted children.

Founded in 1703, the Foundling Hospital was originally the Dublin Workhouse, with only a small section for children. It had been provided more out of a desire to relieve the gentry of the nuisance of beggars, particularly children, rather than for any philanthropic purposes.[2] It was a time of great hardship and destitution and large numbers of children, abandoned by families who couldn't afford to keep them, wandered the streets living rough. Twenty years later, the child population of the workhouse had grown enormously, and it had become the Dublin Foundling Hospital.

This children's institution was described by the Royal Commission on the Poor Laws of 1909 as "the most gigantic baby-farming, nursing, boarding-out and apprenticing institutions that these countries have ever seen". Its closure in 1831 was preceded by an investigation by the House of Commons, which had found that of the 12,768 children admitted between 1790 and 1796, 9,786 had died and 2,847 were unaccounted for. For most of the eighteenth century, a staggering average of nine out of every ten children admitted to the Foundling Hospital died within a matter of months. There was also evidence of continuous embezzlement by the staff and of the severe maltreatment of children.

Interestingly, the well-known Irish patriot Henry Grattan blocked attempts in the late eighteenth century to reform this hellish institution. Grattan in the House of Commons argued against lessening the control of Dublin Corporation over the hospital, saying that allegations of abuse were "a most gross, scandalous, and unfounded libel upon the good name of the country".[3]

In reaction to the savage conditions in the foundling hospitals and the fact that children in them were brought up as Protestants, a range of 'orphanages' were established for the maintenance and protection of Catholic children of the poorer classes. The first such orphanage for Catholic children appears to have been the Patrician Orphan Society established in Dublin in 1750.[4] According to Thomas Osler, an early chronicler of Catholic orphanages in Ireland, this was established in reaction to the

> ... appalling state of the Foundling Hospital [which] disgusted one decent minded unmarried mother who left her child at the door of 'Adam and Eve' chapel, off Cook Street. Some of the traders of the district combined to look after the foundling's welfare. The news spread abroad that Catholic foundlings were being taken charge of in Cook Street, and the deposited increased in numbers. The Charitable Catholics realising the advantage to the Church of the possession of the Catholic babes, began to deposit pennies for the foundlings in the poor box of 'Adam and Eve' chapel. The pennies became so numerous that the Franciscan fathers formed a society for the protection of the foundlings, and called it the Patrician Orphan Society. It had for its motto: 'Lend an Ear of Pity to the melancholy Tale of the Poor, and Pay with Cheerfulness the debt of Charity.[5]

The number of orphan societies grew during the latter half of the eighteenth and early nineteenth centuries, particularly in Dublin after the cholera epidemic of 1831-2. The majority were parish-based and often had the express aim of rescuing children from proselytising agencies. Most of these 'orphanages' were non-institutional in orientation, rather they boarded-out orphan children. For example, the Franciscan Orphan Society stressed that

> ... each child, when admitted on this institution, shall be immediately or as soon as possible, consigned

to the care of a woman residing in the country, who shall produce a Certificate signed by the Minister or Priest of the Parish where she resides, as to her bearing a good character, and that her circumstances are fully competent to do justice to the child entrusted to her.[6]

The small number of orphanages operated by the religious congregations, however, tended to use an institutional form of care for the children under their supervision. One key exception to this rule was St Brigid's Orphanage, established in 1857 by Margaret Aylward, who eventually founded the Sisters of the Holy Faith. St Brigid's, which operated a policy of fostering, continued to operate until the early 1970s.

Takeover

From the 1820s, there was a substantial growth in both male and female religious orders, particularly indigenous congregations established to educate and care specifically for the children of the poor. Many of the parish or lay body orphanages were absorbed by these congregations or simply ceased to operate.

From the 1850s, three female religious orders in particular — the Sisters of Mercy, the Irish Sisters of Charity and the Daughters of Charity were to the forefront in establishing new orphanages or colonising existing orphanages and adapting them to fit their model of intervention with children of the poorer classes.

All of this was happening against a background of considerable Catholic Church reorganisation and expansion in Ireland and of fierce competition between rival Churches for souls and for power and influence. The new Archbishop of Armagh, Paul Cullen, appointed in 1849, was a central force in moulding the Catholic Church into a highly disciplined organisation in the latter half of the nineteenth century. It was keen to exert centralised control over a wide range of philanthropic activities, principally in order to combat the proselytising efforts of many of the Protestant Churches. These sectarian battles provided the background and remained an important influence on the thinking and practices of the

Catholic Church in the fields of education, health and child welfare well into the twentieth century.

Examples of the consolidation included the take-over by the Sisters of Charity in 1866 of St Joseph's Orphanage in Mountjoy Street, Dublin which had been founded by "two humble tradesmen in 1770"[7]: the amalgamation of the Franciscan Orphan Society with the Society of St Vincent de Paul Orphanage in Glasnevin in 1859, which in turn was to be managed by the Irish Christian Brothers in 1863[8]: and the take-over by the Sisters of Mercy in Cork city of an orphanage for "children of gentle birth who were left destitute" in 1877.[9] More significantly, the boarding-out system operated by many of these orphanages was in most cases dispensed with and the institutionalisation of children became the norm.

The Catholic Church's preference for the institutional model of care in Ireland dates from this period. While it was certainly an efficient means of maintaining the maximum control over the recipients of this care, it also had other significant advantages for those running it. Financially, it was cheaper to gather large numbers of the "deserving poor" under the one roof, with considerable economies of scale becoming possible in the case of large institutions. This was a phenomenon which was not unique to Ireland, as Mary J Oates has shown in her study of the Catholic philanthropic tradition in the United States.[10] It is also a model that several Irish religious orders exported around the world with great enthusiasm. But there is no doubt that children in need of care were significantly disadvantaged by this approach. All attempts to provide them with a normal family life effectively ended with the rise of these institutions.

Thus, by the mid-1850s, the majority of the parish-based orphanages, which had followed the boarding-out or 'outdoor orphanage' method of rescuing orphan and deserted children had been largely phased out. Virtually all orphanages were now operated by religious congregations,[11] primarily nuns, and used an institutional model of child welfare.

Those orphanages that continued to operate into the twentieth century received no money from the State and depended on funding from the relations of the children placed in the orphanages and on charity sermons.

In contrast to the institutional provision of child welfare services by Catholic bodies, orphan societies operated either by the Church of Ireland or the Presbyterian Church in Ireland generally continued to use a fostering system. The Presbyterian Orphan Society established in 1866, provided for

> ... the maintenance and education of Children on the roll of the Society by continuing them under the care of their mothers or other suitable relatives, of by placing them with families in connection with the Presbyterian Church, residing within a convenient distance of a place of worship belonging to the said Church, and of a suitable school.[12]

Similarly, both the Protestant Orphan Refuge Society and the Protestant Orphan Society placed children in respectable families in the countryside rather than in institutional care.[13] While Protestant societies did manage several institutional structures for orphan children, and certainly in Dublin, according to Rosa M Barrett, a keen supporter of non-institutional services for children,

> ... the Roman Catholic ones are generally larger, far too large often, for individual care, and the love these poor children so supremely need cannot be given where the numbers congregated together are very large. Moreover, to work large institutions much machinery is necessary; consequently when the inmates go out in the world they are at a loss how to do even ordinary housework, washing, &c, without the machinery to which they have been accustomed. The object of institution life should be to train the inmates that they may become good citizens and made fit for ordinary everyday life as speedily as possible, rather than the development of the military or drill system which is almost unavoidable in large institutions.[14]

The Poor Law: Workhouses and Boarding-Out

Throughout this time, there were also substantial numbers of children in workhouses. These had been established on a large scale with the introduction of the Poor Law to Ireland in 1838 and were filled to capacity with orphan and destitute children in the aftermath of the Great Famine in the late 1840s. By the 1860s, there was a recognition that these institutions were not appropriate places for the care of children. There were growing concerns about the religious and moral hazards of rearing children in workhouses. There was also a belief that special institutions were required for children exposed to criminal influences.[15]

In 1862, an amendment to the Poor Law Act allowed Poor Law Commissioners to board-out children under the age of five from the workhouses and for them to be placed with foster parents. Although the scheme was restrictive initially, and subject to a degree of abuse, subsequent amending legislation and greater scrutiny of prospective foster parents did put in place a viable alternative to the workhouse for destitute children.

From the 1870s onwards, the numbers of children in workhouses declined sharply, due to the boarding-out policy, and, of course, to the establishment of the industrial schools system. However, there were still over 800 children in county homes (the old workhouses) in 1950, but by 1966 there were only fifty-three children resident within this system.[16]

'Baby Farming'

There were also concerns expressed about the system of private fosterage or 'baby farming' for children. These resulted in the passing of the Infant Life Protection Act 1872 which allowed the officers of local government to inspect homes that were fostering or 'nursing' more than one child. Children in private fosterage, or 'Nurse Children', were placed in foster homes by their own relatives — often unmarried mothers — or by philanthropic societies or other persons who paid for them. They were not supported out of the poor rate or any public fund. In March 1902, The Lord Commissioners of His Majesty's Treasury sanctioned the employment of a lady as an inspector, and the appointment of a second lady inspector in November

1902. The duties of these inspectors were principally concerned with the boarding-out and hiring out of pauper children; but they also reported upon the administration of the Infant Life Protection Act, 1897. Shortly after their appointment, they were in a position to claim that: "A good deal of care is now generally exercised in the selection of applicants for nurse children."[17]

Despite the introduction of these non-institutional schemes to deal with deprived children in need of care, some were of the view that from 1869 the new industrial schools were the most appropriate way to cater for these children. The Rev Curry writing in the *Irish Ecclesiastical Record* argued that:

> There is a better way to provide for such children than sending them to the poorhouse, or by 'farming' them out, and that is by having them committed to industrial schools. Under the care of religious — generally of holy nuns — who feel a Christian love for them, and who minister in a Christian spirit to all their corporal, mental, and religious requirements.[18]

Reformatory Schools

The establishment of industrial and reformatory schools in Ireland was strongly influenced by similar developments in England and Scotland. Industrial schools were pioneered in Scotland through the efforts of a Sheriff William Watson who initiated day industrial schools for vagrant children in Aberdeen in 1841, a model that was quickly adopted in other Scottish towns and cities. These schools were non-institutional in character and even after the passing of the Industrial Schools Act 1854, the Scottish system contained a high number of day industrial schools.

Initially this Act applied solely to Scotland, and was only extended to England and Wales in 1857. Reformatory schools were legislated for in England, Scotland and Wales following the passing of the Youthful Offenders Act 1854.

In 1856, a "Bill for the Better Care and Reformation of Juvenile Offenders in Ireland" was introduced to the House of Commons, but was defeated through the efforts of the Irish Catholic members of the House. They argued that it did not sufficiently protect juvenile offenders from the activities of Protestant proselytising societies. The MPs insisted that young offenders could only be sent to reformatory schools managed by those of their own religion.

As a consequence, on the 2nd of August 1858, a "Bill to Promote and Regulate Reformatory Schools for Juvenile Offenders in Ireland" was passed which satisfied Catholic opinion with "the aim of the reformatory ... to train, not to punish".[19] At the time reformatory schools were a considerable improvement for children convicted of criminal offences, when young offenders were placed in ordinary prisons with adult criminals. As a result of the establishment of reformatories, the number of children aged under sixteen in prisons declined rapidly.

The first boy was admitted to the Glencree Reformatory on the 14th of April, 1859.[20] By 1870 there were ten reformatory schools certified throughout the country, five for girls and five for boys. The number of children committed to the reformatory schools rose from 140 in 1859 to 740 ten years later. However, in the hundred years between 1870 and 1970, only one new reformatory was certified, and the number of reformatory schools declined. Many handed in their certificates and reclassified themselves as industrial schools when this system was introduced in 1868.

The sectarian rivalries, which the legislators had been anxious to avoid in drafting the Act, were initially evident. Apparently, magistrates were not exercising sufficient care in ascertaining the religion of the children committed. The secretary of the Protestant Reformatory in Dublin complained in a letter to the Inspector of Reformatory Schools in Ireland that some of the prison officials were attempting to prejudice young Protestant inmates in favour of the Catholic Reformatory School in Glencree. In a case highlighted, "a turnkey named Carty... told the boy that the Glencree Reformatory would be much better for him."[21]

However, the *Londonderry Journal*, a critic of the reformatory schools legislation, posed the question, with scathing irony, as to how any boy could bear *not* to go to Glencree with:

> ... prime feeding three times a week, the band of delicious Irish music, making the rocks and valleys ring with planxties, jigs 'Garryowen in Glory', 'Patrick's Day in the Morning' and 'Morgan Rattler', while the footballs, excursion parties and the free run of the mountain added positive enchantment to the other delights of St Kevin's Paradise. Poor starving urchins must be either incorrigibly virtuous, too inhumanly careless about life and its enjoyments, if they can resist the temptation of doing the very moderate amount of crime that is necessary to qualify then for admission into the bowers of Reformatory happiness, with a snug life — provision at the end of roastbeef and school merriment![22]

Management of the reformatory at Glencree was allocated to the Oblate Fathers who had experience operating similar institutions in England.[23] The Oblate Fathers were also to manage probably the best known reformatory in Ireland, St Conleth's Reformatory School in Daingean Co Offaly, which was opened on December 22nd, 1870.

The primary purpose of reformatory school training, according to the Glencree manager, Fr Louis Foley, OMI, was:

> ... to correct the evil habits acquired and supply the defects in the upbringing of the boys committed. Its work is to make up for the want of the influences of school- and home-life and to train a boy, if possible, to be able to earn his living. The boy, then, should leave the institution with, at least, an elementary education, trained to habits of regularity and work, and determined to keep straight.[24]

Industrial Schools

Along with the desire to provide more suitable places of detention for young offenders, there was a growing awareness of the need to provide residential care for the young homeless and destitute children of Ireland. After much debate the industrial school system was applied to Ireland in 1868, based on the models already in operation in England and Scotland. According to the advocates of the schools, their objective was:

> ... to dry up the principal source of the criminal class by training the neglected children wandering about the streets of our large towns. The children must live somewhere. There are four courses with regard to them we may adopt. 1. Leaving them alone to grow up thieves and robbers. 2. Prosecuting and imprisoning them, which usually has the effect of quickening their progress in wickedness. 3. Putting them into reformatories, a course far better than the preceding, but still a costly one, and which cannot usually be adopted until the children have commenced their depredations. 4. Taking them in their early childhood, training them to industry and good conduct, and so preventing the necessity of pursuing either of the latter courses. The latter proceeding is by far the cheapest and best in every point of view, since it saves the expense of prosecuting and imprisoning the children; and what is more important, by preventing them from becoming criminals, protects the community from the losses and evils they would inflict upon it.[25]

The institutional structures for children that had been pioneered in Britain were eagerly developed in Ireland. What is striking is the similarity in outlook in this area between Victorian Britain and the Irish Catholic Church, which enthusiastically embraced the new incarceration system for children. In the eyes of the Catholic Church and Victorian reformers, working-class children were seen to exhibit characteristics that were at variance with the ideal nature of the child. The role that they ascribed to children was one of purity and innocence. They wished to reform those whom they viewed as miniature adults, in order that they become children once again. A leading advocate of the schools, Matthew Davenport Hill, expressed the view that:

> The latter [the delinquent] is a little stunted man already — he knows much and a great deal too much

of what is called life — he can take care of his own immediate interests. He is self-reliant, he has so long directed or mis-directed his own actions and has so little trust in those about him, that he submits to no control and asks for no protection. He has consequently much to unlearn — he has to be turned into a child again.[26]

It is abundantly clear that the Irish reformatory and industrial schools were designed for the children of the poor, who were perceived as a threat to the social order. It was these children who were inevitably targeted for incarceration, in particular young girls. As PJ Murray, the first Inspector of Reformatory Schools in Ireland argued in 1865:

In a thousand ways the vices of the poor affect the richer classes. The children of our neglected homes spread the contagion of their vices abroad. The little arab of the streets becomes a tempter in his turn. The outcast girl who is cast upon the pave by the intemperance or neglect of her parents, becomes the seducer of our youth. Look where we will, we find that every sin of neglect brings back a punishment from divine ordination there is no escape.[27]

A key concern for advocates of the industrial schools system was that religious segregation be maintained. The Right Reverend Patrick Francis Moran, Bishop of Ossory, gave evidence to the Commission of Inquiry into the Reformatory and Industrial System of Ireland in 1884. He stressed that it was not for criminal offences that children were to be committed to the industrial schools. These institutions he said were for those

... children who would otherwise be exposed to great danger of contracting habits of idleness, and habits of vice, but in the industrial schools they are preserved from these dangers, and are trained to habits of cleanliness and industry, and they grow up in a healthy moral and religious atmosphere.[28]

The System Grows

To establish an industrial school, certification had to be obtained from the office of the Inspector of Reformatory and Industrial Schools. The Inspector visited the premises to be used and sent a report about its suitability to the Chief Secretary's office. If successful, it would then be certified for the reception of the categories of children outlined in the Act. The Inspector determined the number of children that each school could receive.

Only the children within the limits set by the Inspector were entitled to State funding. Unlike in Britain, State funding was not made available in Ireland for the building of industrial schools. This was largely because of Protestant fears that such funding would allow for the expansion of the activities of the Catholic Church in Ireland. Instead funding was available to the schools for each child committed to them. This was known as the capitation system.

Many existing Catholic orphanages applied to be certified as industrial schools. For example, on 29th September 1842, the Sisters of Mercy in Wexford had accepted management of an orphanage which had been founded by the Redmond and Talbot families of the town in 1829. It was certified as St Michael's Industrial School for 106 places in 1869.[29] Not all existing orphanages were certified, however. The Sisters of Mercy orphanages in Castletownbere, Navan, Kells and Kilrush were refused certificates for industrial schools. Their orphanage in Ennis, completed in 1875 for the reception of 100 children, was granted an industrial school certificate in 1880, but only for forty children.

However, the number of industrial schools nonetheless grew rapidly, and extensions to their certificates were frequently requested, a process which continued into the twentieth century. In some cases these extensions were granted, but by 1880, attempts were being made by the Office of the Chief Secretary to curtail the growth in numbers committed to industrial schools. The State was becoming alarmed at the almost uncontrollable expansion of the system.

In 1898, a circular urged magistrates to make orders of committal to industrial schools only when the children came within the strict scope of the Industrial School Acts. Reaction to this circular from the managers of industrial schools, the Irish County Councils' General Council and various philanthropic bodies was uniformly critical. They argued that this policy would cause "grave injury to the industrial school system". In a pamphlet published by the Irish County Councils' General Council, letters from the managers of the majority of industrial schools on their experience of the implementation of the circular were reproduced. The manager of the largest industrial school in Ireland, and indeed in Britain, the Artane Industrial School, Brother TJ Butler argued that:

> A circular of one kind or other may have been called for, perhaps, to check some abuses in the committal of children to Industrial Schools. It is not, however, the correction of an abuse that is aimed at in the circular of October, 1898, but a total change in the administration of the system in this country, and the introduction of the English system instead.

He went on to highlight his perception of the substantial differences between industrial schools in Ireland and industrial schools in England:

> The English Industrial Schools are Semi-Reformatories filled with juvenile criminals taken largely from the large manufacturing towns, and sent to those schools for some misdemeanour or breaches of the law. This is not so with our Irish Industrial schools. They are not to be found in any considerable numbers in this country .... Here in Ireland, we have, comparatively, very little juvenile crime, but we have much poverty and destitution, hence we require few reformatories but many Industrial Schools, for the very poverty of our orphans and guardianless children would soon lead them into evil ways, unless rescued in time under the Industrial Schools' Act, and this is what our Industrial Schools are accomplishing in Ireland.[30]

The relationship between the British State and the managers of the Irish reformatory and industrial schools during the nineteenth century was often highly combative — a sharp contrast to the general way in which the newly independent Irish Government dealt with the system in the twentieth century. From the extraordinarily detailed annual reports of the last century and the voluminous correspondence that has survived in both the National Archives and the Department of Education, a clear picture of the State's energy and concerns emerges.

These substantial records from the nineteenth century stand in sharp contrast to the relative paucity of information that exists within the files on the operation of the schools for most of the twentieth century. These early Inspectors, Patrick Joseph Murray (1860-68), Sir John Lentaigne (1869-1886), George Plunkett O'Farrell (1887-89), Rowland Blennerhasset (1890-96) and John Fagan (1897-1910) were consistently critical of both the relentless expansion of the system and the conditions that existed in a number of the schools. Their annual reports and correspondence to the Chief Secretary's Office show a growing unease at the worsening conditions in the schools. Most importantly, they showed a determination to castigate the religious managers of the schools for failing to attain the high standards the inspectors set them.

Rowland Blennerhasset, for example, had a habit of examining the physical condition of both the children and the buildings with a magnifying glass, in order to ensure he would miss nothing of importance. This was a cause of acute annoyance to those in charge of the schools.

John Fagan in particular condemned many of the schools for the insufficient diet provided to the children, their lack of cleanliness and the inadequacy of the after-care provided, particularly for girls. In his first annual report in 1897, he launched a blistering attack on many of the aspects of the management of the industrial schools. He argued that girls under the care of Catholic religious congregations were "brought up in an atmosphere of religion, carefully guarded from the slightest breath of worldly wickedness; their moral values are developed to a high degree of sensitiveness; and their knowledge of, and relationship with, life outside the convent walls is of the slenderest kind". As a result many of the girls ended up as "simple, pious fools".

He found in most of the schools that the children "were well fed, well clad, bright, intelligent, and happy". However, in a number of schools the children were "untidy, careless and not clean" and a minority of schools, the children were "dull, spiritless, ill-fed, ill-clad, subject to chilblains, stunted in growth of body and mind".[31]

In his second annual report in 1898, he wrote of the deception orchestrated by the managers of many schools for the benefit of visitors. These, he noted, were "impressed by nicely laid out grounds, well-kept halls and corridors, by the shining faces of the lads over clean holiday collars, and by the orderly appearance of the beds in the dormitories under snow-white coverlets".

However, there was another side to the schools. This was a side that the inspectors appointed by the Department of Education from the 1920s onwards appeared not to notice, of if they did, did not act on. This side was, according to John Fagan, the "neglected untidy state of the living rooms and other apartments, the dirty neck under the clean collar, and often a condition of things under the white-coverlets that is better imagined than described".[32]

Although John Fagan and his predecessors were fully aware of the window displays that the managers produced for the benefit of the public, their successors appeared to have been largely taken in by it.

Four

Independence for Whom?
(1921-1939)

When Ireland achieved Independence from Britain in 1921, it made little difference to the 7,000 children who were detained in Irish industrial and reformatory schools. Under the new Irish authorities, the system remained totally intact, a simple continuation of what had gone before.

This is in sharp contrast to what was happening in Britain at the time. As the British system for locking up children was being reformed and phased out, Ireland was in fact going in the opposite direction. The numbers of Irish children deprived of their liberty under the newly independent State actually showed an increase.

This was in spite of the fact that the Department of Education, which assumed responsibility for the system, stated during the 1920s that the British legislation governing the area was unsuitable to Irish conditions. This legislation was the Children Act 1908, which still remains in force on our statute books to this day.

Although there was some minor amending legislation during the 1920s, and a major inquiry into the system of industrial schools in the 1930s, none of these resulted in any significant alteration of a system that was to prove remarkably resilient for the greater part of this century.

By 1924, there were more children in industrial schools in the twenty-six counties of Ireland in total than were in all of the industrial schools in England, Scotland, Wales and Northern Ireland put together. This was noted by the Irish Department of Education which suggested that the reason was "the fact that

Industrial Schools are utilised to a much greater extent for destitute poor children in Saorstat Eireann than in England and Wales".[1] Despite the recognition of the very high numbers of children in Irish industrial schools, no attempt seems to have been made to examine the reasons why, and more significantly, no attempt was made to take on board the enormous changes that were occurring in the UK.

The complacency of the Department of Education with regard to the schools in the Free State was not mirrored either north of the Border or in Britain. A major debate had begun there as to the unsuitability of large institutions to the welfare of children in care. Numbers of children committed to industrial schools in Britain went into sharp decline, and the system was eventually abolished in 1933, with the creation of new "Approved Schools", modelled on different, more child-centred lines.

As part of this radical re-think in Britain, the management and funding of their schools underwent substantial change over this period, and the autonomy of the voluntary bodies who by and large managed the schools came under increasing strain.[2]

The basis for these changes in the UK can be traced to a number of inter-related developments. The report of the Departmental Committee on Reformatory and Industrial Schools in 1913 highlighted the fact that although the Home Office was providing the funding for the schools, it had little control over their management or admissions policy. This Committee was established following allegations of deaths of children and practices of excessive cruelty at the Akbar Nautical Training School, which was a certified reformatory school. The establishment of a Children's Branch within the Home Office shortly after the publication of the 1913 report was to exert considerable central control over the schools in Britain, but had little influence in Ireland.

The antipathy of the Children's Branch to the system of reformatory and industrial schools can be gauged from their first report where it was argued that:

> ... comparing the schools today with what they were ten years ago, the greatest change perhaps lies in the decrease of 'institutionalism' to use an ugly

word for an ugly thing. The result has been mainly secured by two methods — by giving greater attention to the child as an individual and by bringing him into closer contact with the outside world. It is a tendency of all institutions to treat the individuals comprising it in the mass and to rob them of responsibility.[3]

A key element in the British Home Office's strategy for controlling the management and admission policies of the schools was the abolition of the per capita system of funding the homes — it was replaced with an annual budget from 1919, to be met by local authorities and central government. This allowed the Home Office greater control over the management of the schools and removed the incentive for schools to hold on to pupils in order to avail of the per capita grant.[4] The capitation system of funding the reformatory and industrial schools in Ireland was only abolished in 1984, sixty-five years after it had been removed in Britain. Its retention by the Irish Government was a major contributory factor to the massive number of children contained in the schools in this country (see Chapter Five).

Another development in Britain not mirrored in Ireland was the vigorous application of the Probation of Offenders Act 1907.[5] The use of this Act had provided an alternative to detention in industrial or reformatory schools in the UK, but it was not applied with even remotely the same enthusiasm by the Irish courts.

Thus, the key factors responsible for the reduction of children in reformatory and industrial schools in Britain — the abolition of the capitation system of funding, the development of a comprehensive probation service, voluntary agencies campaigning for change and strong central government control over the management and policies of the reformatory and industrial schools — were all notably absent in Ireland.

In Northern Ireland, reform of the system took somewhat longer than in the rest of the United Kingdom. There were sixty-eight children detained within the reformatory schools in the North, and 690 in the industrial schools at the time of partition, but already these numbers were in decline. By 1936, there were only 278 children in industrial schools in Northern Ireland. However, the system was effectively not dismantled until 1950, some fifteen years after similar developments in the rest of the UK.

Thus, in the other jurisdictions in the 1920s which developed reformatory and industrial schools at roughly the same period as Ireland the foundations were laid for the abolition of the system. The number of children placed in such schools dropped rapidly and new administrative structures were put in place to deal with them. Perhaps most importantly, there was a growing antipathy to the institutionalisation of children, and it was the State that took the leading role in bringing about the demise of the schools. The considerable activity in these jurisdictions stands in sharp contrast to the stagnation evident in Ireland. It was not until 1934 that a committee of inquiry was to report on the operation of the schools in this country. This was the Cussen Report, chaired by Justice GP Cussen.

Locking up the Daughters

A unique feature of the Irish system was the extraordinarily high numbers of girls in the Irish industrial schools system. This is most marked when seen in comparison to the numbers in the United Kingdom. Taking 1933 as an example, the figures show 1,123 girls within the system in all of Britain, as compared with a staggering 3,628 in Ireland.

Part of the explanation for this lies in the nature of Irish society in the decades after independence. A strict Catholic orthodoxy prevailed and nowhere can this be seen more clearly than in the treatment meted out to unmarried mothers and their children.

How to deal with single mothers and their children was hotly debated during the 1920s in Ireland. A lengthy discussion took place as to the most appropriate mechanism to meet the needs of 'fallen girls' and their children in the pages of the *Irish Ecclesiastical Record*. Joseph A Glynn, a prominent member of both the Society of St Vincent de Paul and the Catholic Protection and Rescue Society, proposed that a large hostel/factory, capable of looking after upwards of 500 girls, be established in Dublin. This institution would be under the control of the bishops, but should be managed by a lay committee "owing to the difficulties of getting girls to enter a home controlled by nuns".[6]

The Rev MH McInerney argued against this proposal, suggesting instead the necessity for a large number of small rescue homes scattered throughout the county. He wrote that the Sisters of the Sacred Heart of Jesus and Mary had agreed to establish a rescue home in Cork with the consent of the bishop, noting that "the county which had the glory of giving birth to Mary Aikenhead and Nano Nagle, will have the honour of leading the vanguard in the forward movement for the crushing of souperism".[7] In a further contribution, an anonymous writer describing himself as 'Sagart' argued against the establishment of such homes as:

> ... the prominent existence of Rescue Homes, suggesting as they would, a certain indulgent attitude towards moral lapses, would be calculated to lower the high ideals of our people, and is therefore, to be avoided, except in the very last extreme.

He advocated instead, the continuation of the system of individual treatment provided by a range of Catholic societies, saying that:

> ... its avoidance of scandal, its adaptability to various needs, and its enlisting of the force of personal sympathy, seems to be the right method of dealing with this complicated and delicate problem. There seems also, under God, every reason to trust that, if the system were developed prudently, it would be able to catch in its net practically all the girls who now flee to Proselytising Homes, to unsafe Maternity Homes, to far-off Unions, or to England.[8]

Crucial in this debate was the segregation between what were to be described as 'first offenders' and 'recidivists'. This would also have a major impact on the fates of their children. The language of criminality was deliberately invoked, highlighting the perception of such women as 'criminal'. Such a distinction between women who give birth outside of marriage for the first time ('first offenders') and those who gave birth a second time ('recidivists') was originally recommended by the Poor Law Commission of 1906, but not acted upon until the early 1920s. The basis for this distinction was that 'first offenders' were capable of reformation and their children in theory only slightly tainted, compared to those women who were supposedly incapable of being rescued and therefore needed to be confined for their own salvation.

Such "fallen" women were perceived as doubly dangerous. There was a strongly held view that not only was the unmarried mother a threat to the social order, but her child could be infected with the deviant genes and perpetuate the threat to order. It was because of these fears and the perceived failure of the workhouses to sufficiently imbue such women with so-called responsibility, that separate institutions for 'first-time offenders' developed. With the establishment of these new charitable institutions, the workhouses retained only those women deemed beyond saving.

Children of 'first offenders' were generally quickly separated from their mothers. For a period of a year they were carefully vetted for abnormalities, and if showing no signs of such, they were informally adopted. Through this process, children could be "normalised" and the demand from middle-class couples for children was satisfied. If, however, the adoptive family were dissatisfied with the child, he or she could be returned to the Mother and Baby home.

Children of 'second offenders' on the other hand, remained subject to Poor Law regulation and were either transferred to industrial schools or fostered.

In 1922 the Sacred Heart Home in Bessboro, Co Cork, managed by the Sisters of the Sacred Heart of Jesus and Mary was opened "for young mothers who have fallen for the first time and who are likely to be influenced towards a useful and respectable life".[9] These women also generally came from families who could afford to pay a fee to the home for this service. Similar homes were established by the same Order in Roscrea in 1930 and Castlepollard in 1935. The Daughters of Charity of St Vincent de Paul opened an institution on the

Navan Road in 1918 and the Sisters of the Good Shepherd opened a home in Dunboyne, Co Meath in 1955. Within these, according to an internal Department of Health memo "every facility is given for the girls to enter the homes with the minimum of publicity. The area covered by the homes is sufficiently large to give a girl every chance of keeping her secret".[10] The mothers of the children in the 'first offender' homes were generally held there for up to two years, because as the Matron of Bessboro argued in 1931 "a number of the girls are very weak-willed and have to be maintained in the Home for a long period to safeguard them against a second lapse".[11]

The numbers of women within these institutions averaged approximately 1,300 during the 1930s and 1940s, but appears to have decreased from the early 1950s, largely due to the emigration of unmarried mothers to Britain.

The number of single mothers going to England became a particular concern to the authorities in the Catholic Church. The Archbishop of Dublin requested that the sister in charge of St Patrick's Guild, an quasi-adoption agency run by the Irish Sisters of Charity, prepare a memo for him on this subject. The Department of Health was contacted on the issue and Miss Litster, the Inspector of Boarded-out Children, prepared a draft memo. This memo graphically describes the stigma attached to lone motherhood during the first decades of Independence. She sent the memo to the Secretary of the Department of Health, who deleted a number of its sections. This deleted text, marked in italics, provides a unique insight into the conditions for lone mothers in Ireland, insights that the Secretary of the Department obviously believed the Archbishop would not appreciate reading!

> The Irish unmarried mother in Great Britain who has gone there to avoid local knowledge of her condition is reluctant to return to Ireland. *(What have we to offer her here in comparison with the concealment, comfort and facility for adoption offered in Great Britain).* In this country she can obtain shelter during her waiting time, good food and care, skilled attention during confinement, care, attention and kindness to her baby. In the English home whether voluntary or

under PAAs [Public Assistance Authorities] she will have all of this, possibly less kindness, probably greater comfort both of mind and body. *We offer her just as much secrecy and possibility of concealment as may be hoped for in a large maternity home where she fears from day to day to find a neighbour of her own. In the English home she will be free from this fear.* We ask her to remain for one to two years after confinement. In the English home she will be kept from three to six months. If she wishes to have her baby adopted she will generally have to arrange this through a society and may have to find an adoption fee of from £60 to £100. In England, she will have no difficulty in securing adoption without any cost to herself, but there is no guarantee that this adoption will be into a Catholic home. *If she wishes to keep her baby, and rear it herself, the hand of Society is against her here. In England, she will be able to find employment in which she will be allowed to keep the child with her. This is no doubt mainly due to the scarcity of domestic workers. But - workers are scarce here too, and how many employers in Eire will take baby as well as mother?*

Miss Litster went on to describe the consequences for the children of the lack of facilities for lone mothers in Ireland (all of this section was omitted by the Secretary in his report to the Archbishop):

About a fortnight ago, three infants were found abandoned in or near Dublin. One was a baby of about three weeks old, expensively clothed and beautifully cared for. It had been left concealed by a bed of nettles in a field near Dundrum and was dead when found. One was abandoned in a telephone booth. It was alive. One, newly born, was found pushed up a chimney in the mother's home. It was dead. It may be argued that to provide a home to which babies may be admitted without their mothers is to encourage sexual immorality. I doubt if considerations of this kind enter into sexual immorality at all. The fact remains that not to have such a home is to encourage

> *murder. These three hapless babies are not the only infant martyrs of convenience, respectability and fear. The Church is perhaps waiting for the State to do something. The State is perhaps hoping that the Church will do something. The Irish Catholic woman displays less initiative in such matters than her English counterpart. Welfare societies or groups of women with a social conscience will start a small voluntary home for mother and child in England, equip and maintain it themselves. Here we wait for Church or State to move.*[12]

The stigma attached to lone mothers was in part responsible for a significant and continuous supply of children to the industrial schools. The introduction of legalised adoption from the early 1950s did not significantly effect this pattern, as it was largely the children of 'first offenders' who were legally adopted, and such children had tended to be informally adopted in any case. More significantly, it provides a salutary reminder of the treatment and perception of single mothers and their children by the Catholic Church and by Irish society as a whole. It was against this social background that in 1934 the Cussen Committee was appointed to examine the operation of the institutions which incarcerated a wide variety of children, including of course those who were labelled 'illegitimate'. While the Committee had been appointed by the Government, it was treading in an area which the Catholic Church viewed as its own untouchable bailiwick.

The Cussen Report

The Cussen Report is of considerable importance — it was the first investigation into the operation of the schools since the foundation of the State, over a decade earlier. The basis for the inquiry was that many changes had occurred in Great Britain and that "at present the Free State is behind most European Countries in its arrangements for dealing with this important social question". And that "before introducing reforms the Minister for Education wishes to have the whole position enquired into and reported on."[13]

The Commission's report became commonly known as the Cussen Report, after its chairman, GP Cussen, a senior judge.

He appears to have been an interesting appointment, as an internal Department of Education memo observed that during his term as judge between 1930 and 1937, he was "reluctant to send persons to certified schools".

The only significant intervention of the Department into the operation of reformatory and industrial schools during the period prior to the establishment of the Cussen Committee was the introduction of amending legislation to the Children Act 1908 to make it possible to have destitute children committed to an industrial school without the existing requirement of being convicted of an 'offence'. The necessary legislation was enacted as the Children Act 1929.

The Cussen Report found fifty-two industrial schools and two reformatories in operation throughout the country, all but two under the management of Roman Catholic religious congregations. (These two were run directly by parish priests.) The Report had a number of reservations about the operation of the industrial schools, mainly concerning the nature of the education and training obtained, the large numbers of disabled children to be found in the schools, the lack of support from local authorities and the stigma attached to the schools. However, the Committee was otherwise satisfied with the system, reporting that it "affords the most suitable method of dealing with these children and that schools should remain under the management of the religious orders who have undertaken the work."[14]

Interestingly, the report also observed that the last industrial school under Protestant management closed in 1917, but argued that "it may be conveniently stated at this stage that we did not receive any evidence which would point to the necessity for the establishment of such a school. Where Protestant children have committed offences it is usually possible to make arrangements privately for their detention in various institutions, the expenses being borne by the relatives of the children or by their parish."[15]

It is a most remarkable feature of the surviving archives within the Department of Education that there is virtually no reference whatsoever to the Cussen Report. All material related to it seems to have disappeared without trace. This is in fact a general feature of the archives for the period from Independence until the late 1930s — almost all the documents relating to industrial schools for these years have vanished. The files for the individual schools during the twentieth century all uniformly begin with an entry in 1939 by the newly appointed Medical Inspector. This was Dr Anna McCabe, the creation of whose post was one of the recommendations of the Cussen Report.

What emerges from these internal files as soon they begin in 1939 is a very different picture to that described by the Cussen Report a bare three years previously. Dr McCabe, writing about her initial impressions of the system in 1939, said that she was "appalled" at the conditions of the schools and their children. This raises a serious question over the generally positive conclusions of the Cussen Report, as it is highly unlikely that the conditions so graphically described by Dr McCabe could have arisen in such a short time. Her reports on the schools were to highlight the consequences of State apathy in the key decades after independence.

Margaret's Story, St Joseph's Industrial School, Clifden (Sisters of Mercy), 1927–1939

"Some girls used to wet their knickers, probably out of fright. And God help them, they had to go up in front of the whole school and lift up their dresses to let the head nun feel their knickers. And then she'd beat them. I didn't wet myself, but there was one day I was covered in sweat for some reason. She lifted up my skirt and felt the sweat on my knickers and from then on I had to join the queue to have her feel my knickers. I can't tell you how humiliating that was."

Margaret is now seventy-six years old. She lives in Wales and is a mother and a grandmother. When she was three-and-a-half years old, her parents had herself and her older twin sisters committed to St Joseph's. They kept the boys at home — it was just the girls they put away.

"At that time I suppose the way they looked at it was that boys could help out around the farm, but girls were useless. But they did wrong, very very wrong. Because my aunt who lived close by and was just as poor, she had eleven children and wouldn't part with any of them. My parents just got rid of us.

The convent in Clifden was run by the Sisters of Mercy. It was a beautiful building. Bright red bedspreads on the beds, lovely clean sheets. If people went in to visit they would have thought it was the most beautiful place they had ever seen. But it was a horrible place.

Straight away the head nun couldn't stand the sight of me. I had a beautiful head of black curls, and it was like a red rag to a bull to her. She hated any girl who might be pretty, and she beat us all the more for it. All the years there, she told me I was the ugliest thing she ever saw, and that I was vain. I didn't even know what vain meant.

I dreaded the bath day, because when my hair was washed it turned into a mass of lovely shiny curls. And she'd beat me even more. I spent hours trying to pull my hair to make it straight. I'm trying not to cry talking about this, but it's no good. I'll cry till the day I die about that place.

All my life I believed that I was ugly. Until I was in my fifties, I couldn't look in a mirror I hated myself so much. I know now that I really was pretty as a girl, but I wish I'd known it earlier. It might have given me a bit of self esteem.

From when we were four and five we had to work on the farm. During the summer, they took our shoes off us and we went barefoot. They had two men, farm workers, who cut the hay with a scythe, and we had to go in the fields, walking on the stubble in our bare feet, to turn the hay with our hands. And our feet used to get cut to ribbons.

When we got back to the convent, the floor would be covered in blood from our feet. The nun would pick out some of us to beat, saying it was our fault. She always seemed to pick me.

We'd work on the bog as well, standing the turf in what they called stooks, six or seven pieces standing up to let the air through them. Then we'd put it into canvas bags and carry them down the hill. It was heavy work, especially for little ones. I remember the thirst — our throats would be so dry, and they gave us nothing to drink.

But we'd take chances when the nuns weren't looking, and one of us would nip across to a bog hole and take a drink of the bog water. You wouldn't care whether it was clean or dirty — it would take the thirst away. There were nuns sitting there watching us to make sure we did the work. They used to have lemonade and sandwiches and cake. We got nothing.

I remember the hunger. We were always starved. When we were out for walks, we'd eat weeds, we'd call them cuckoos, I don't know why. We'd fight over these weeds, we were so hungry. We also pulled up bulbs from the ground to eat, we used to call them nuts.

When we worked in the nuns' gardens, we'd eat the tops off all the flowers. They had an orchard and we'd steal apples. They always made us sick — I think they were probably crab apples — and then we'd be beaten for being sick.

The slightest thing, and you'd be beaten. They used a piece of wood, like a part of an orange box. We always had splinters of wood in us, cuts all over us. They beat us on the arms, the legs, on the neck. I don't know how we didn't die. Our hands were all ripped to pieces.

One of the nuns used to get two girls to hold us down, she'd pull our knickers down and she beat us. And you wouldn't be able to sit down afterwards, you'd be wriggling about, and they'd beat us for that. God, were they monsters, were they human at all? That nun would have been ideal for the concentration camps. She used to love punishment.

Thank the Lord we were never sexually abused. But those nuns couldn't do what they did and still believe in God. How could they live with themselves after putting the little girls through all that?

I used to hate polishing floors. One child would put the wax on to a section of the floor, and about three of us behind her had a canvas bag for polishing. There'd be a nun behind us, saying 'up, down, up, down' and we'd polish away until it was like glass. And then we'd move on to the next section and so on until the floors were done.

It was hard work, but I didn't mind it — what was worse was the fear of not knowing when you'd get a crack across the legs or the back from the nun behind.

My father came to see us once. I was about five. I remember my two older sisters standing beside him, and he took me up on his knee and I nearly died of fright. I didn't know what he was. I just wanted him to put me down. My sister, Annie, told me that he said to them 'Aren't you lucky to be in a place like this. You're the luckiest girls alive.'

My mother came once as well. She brought my younger brother with her — he was a year-and-a-half. I never saw her again. They wrote some letters to us, and used to send us a box of nuts about once a year. We'd be allowed a few of the nuts, and the nuns would keep the rest for themselves. Whenever I wrote back, the nun would dictate the letter to me.

I was devastated when my sisters left. They were twins, six years older than me and they had looked out for me so well. When they left I was nine, and I screamed the place down. I realised I was completely on my own, I had no one left who cared about me. I must have gone hysterical, I remember being in bed for a while. I'll never forget the agony of them leaving me.

We used to have a bath once a month. There were three baths, and two girls in each bath. We'd queue up naked. We were petrified of taking our clothes off and queuing up, we were so shy. I remember when I started growing hair on my body I thought I was turning into a monkey. So I used to be in bed at night trying to pull out each hair one by one, but of course they were just growing all the more. No one ever talked about anything like that, so I didn't have a clue. We all tried to hide it, never spoke to each other about it. None of us understood what was happening to us.

The worst time of the lot was when we started our periods. Oh my God! I was just over fourteen. It was Christmas Eve that year.

They never gave us any pads. I used to see blood on older children's legs, but I never knew what it was. I used to wonder why the nuns were beating them when they had blood on their legs — surely they should bandage them if they were bleeding. I used to feel so sorry for these girls getting beaten because of the blood on their clothes.

And then it was my turn. When it started, I was petrified. The first time I thought I was bleeding to death. I think I was quite happy to die. But I remember going into the broom cupboard and kneeling down and praying to God just to let me live until Christmas Day. Because for the first time I had got a big part in the plays that they put on at Christmas. I just wanted to be in that play, and then I could die in peace.

One girl did die, I don't know what the cause was. She was about nine or ten. She was laid out in her coffin wearing her First Communion dress. And we all had to kneel around the coffin and say a prayer. I prayed and prayed that I could die and be able to wear a dress like that. We were so innocent.

There were two other nuns who were nearly as bad as the head nun. One of them was sick once, and a girl would have to stay up with her every night. When it was my turn, I remember sitting there — I was about nine or ten — praying to God that she would die. She used to beat hell out of us. She only lived a short while after that, and we were so happy the day she'd died.

We used to have a medical inspection once a year. A doctor came in and would just glance at us, all lined up in front of him. That was it. And whenever anyone came to visit, they'd take us out of our old clothes, which were made out of some kind of sacking. We'd change into lovely dresses which would be taken off us the minute the visitors left. They were such hypocrites, those nuns."

Margaret left Clifden at sixteen and worked as a domestic servant for a few years with several different families. All of them treated her badly, and she emigrated to Wales in 1943 at the age of twenty-one.

She eventually married in Wales, but her husband became an alcoholic and was violent to her. She has one son, and he and her three grandsons are the delight of her life. She has never been able to tell her son about her childhood at the industrial school in Clifden. However, she recorded her experiences onto tape for him to listen to after her death. These memories are taken from that tape.

"All my life I had terrible nightmares. I'd wake up screaming in the night. Three years ago, my doctor told me to go to a psychiatrist. When I went to her she said that the reason for the nightmares and the waking up screaming was the convent. She told me to think always that they were only dreams, and that no one could do anything bad to me anymore. I think it has helped me. I still sometimes get bad dreams, but I don't wake up screaming any more.

Even last night, for instance, I had a dream that the head nun in Clifden was standing beside my bed. I don't know if I was frightened or not, because I woke up so fast. I'm on valium now, and I think it's doing me some good. God willing, it will at least keep the nightmares away."

Marion's Story, St Joseph's Industrial School, Summerhill, Athlone (Sisters of Mercy), 1937–1954

"I remember a girl who had to get her appendix out. When she came back from the hospital she was supposed to rest. But the nuns made her get up to do work. This was before antibiotics or anything to keep infection away. A few days after they forced her to get up, she died. She was a lovely girl, and she was only fifteen years old."

Marion was put into St Joseph's Summerhill, just outside Athlone Town, in 1937 when she was still only a baby. To this day, she still doesn't know why she was taken away from her family. Her parents were married, and the family was poor. But both her mother and her father were still alive when she was committed to the industrial school.

"I remember lots of children dying. The nuns had their own graveyard, but the children were put somewhere else. There wasn't even a flower or a cross to mark where they were buried. I never remember any funerals or Masses said for them. They weren't really recognised, you know.

There was a lot of sickness. The nuns used to keep us clean alright, but we all had chilblains from the cold — I remember the blankets used to stick to my feet in the mornings. I was in a lot of pain.

I had a lot of abscesses as well. I couldn't walk at one stage. I kept passing out, particularly at Mass in the mornings. When I was about nine, I was very sick — I had a big lump under my arm, and they had to put poultices on it. They wouldn't call a doctor, because they'd have had to pay for that. I was just locked in the dormitory all day, and they'd bring me some food.

The dormitories were always locked anyway, even at night with us in there. They gave us a bucket to use as a toilet and then locked the doors.

It was lack of nourishment, vitamins, that used to make us sick. I suppose the nuns didn't have the money to buy us food. We were hungry all the time. I remember when the outdoor girls from the area used to come into school, they'd sometimes throw away bits of their lunch, bits of bread, for the birds to eat. I'd chase away the birds and run to grab the scraps.

We'd get scraps from the nuns' table as well. I used to be sent up to the convent to help with the washing up, and I'd get bits of food out of the refuse bucket. We ate grass, I remember that very clearly. And we'd rob turnips — the nuns had a farm there. I don't know who got the stuff from the farm, maybe it was the nuns. It certainly wasn't the children.

I remember one summer we were out for our walk on a Sunday and we rushed ahead of the nuns to get at the blackberries on the hedges. We were climbing up and ripping the berries off and eating them. The nuns made us turn back and we were put to bed without our dinner.

But there was one lovely nun. She worked in the nuns' kitchen, she had nothing to do with us. But whenever she'd see one of the children passing, she'd always give us a slice of bread and jam. I think she knew we were starving. She was very kind, she loved the children. Sister Joseph was her name, I'll never forget her.

Whenever the inspector came, the nuns would take out the lovely plates and cups. They were beautiful. Normally we drank out of tin mugs, some of them rusty. They put new bedspreads in the dormitories, and we got different food.

We spent a lot of our time working. We worked in the laundry, at cleaning, and we used to have to stuff mattresses with a kind of fibre. I don't know what it was, but we had to tease it out, then pack the mattresses with it, and sow them up. The dust was terrible — we'd be coughing and choking all the time. They were slave drivers, it was slave work.

And then there were the beatings as well. I was beaten across the legs with a cane for years for wetting the bed. We'd all queue up in the dining room, and the nun would beat us. We were black and blue. I remember shaking with fright, waiting for my turn.

You were beaten for other things as well, and often for nothing at all. There was one time I was cleaning the dormitories — you had to move all the beds, about fifty in each room, and they were very heavy. I made a mark on the floor moving one of them, and this staff member, a lay person, hit me on the head with a brush. She knocked me unconscious. I was about eight or nine at the time.

When I went to school the next morning, the teacher sent me up to the nun in charge, and she asked me what had happened to me. I was white in the face and my hair was stuck to my head with dried blood. My eyes were turning up in my head. I remember being very frightened.

It was after that that my epilepsy started. And I used to get terrible headaches. But nothing was done about them.

There were a few lay staff there. They were like us, I suppose, they had been in the orphanage themselves. I don't think they got paid or anything. But they used to beat us as well.

I remember three lovely girls, sisters, who came from Dublin. They all had gorgeous long blond ringlets in their hair. One of them ran away shortly after arriving. She was found on the railway line, trying to get back home to Dublin. When they brought her back, they cut her lovely hair, shaved her head to the skin.

The people in Athlone were good to us. They'd give us a day out at Christmas, they came in their cars to collect us. A big party was organised, we went to the cinema, and then the Army band used to give a concert for us. It was marvellous.

Santa would come as well, and we'd get presents of toys and books. But as soon as we were back in St Joseph's, the presents were taken off us. We never saw them again. I don't know what happened to them — they were sold, I suppose. I don't think the people in Athlone ever knew that we weren't allowed to keep their presents. They thought they were doing a good deed, helping the children at Christmas. And they were — it wasn't their fault.

They used to feel sorry for us, I think. We'd go into the town every June, to walk in the procession, and we'd have to wear shoes. But we had no socks, and the shoes didn't fit us. So our feet used to be bleeding. I remember people looking at us, saying 'Look at those poor children, and their little feet'. But we just had to put up with it."

Marion left St Joseph's Summerhill in 1954 when she was sixteen. The nuns got her a job as a domestic servant with a well-off family. She worked in a succession of jobs for families, most of whom treated her badly. She worked at one stage in the laundry attached to a work house in the West of Ireland. The institution was run by nuns, and Marion received only her board and lodging as payment.

However, she did manage to scrape together enough money for her fare to England, and in 1960 she emigrated. She worked in factories and hospitals all over England. Marion has now returned, and lives in Ireland.

"I'd love to have been a nurse, and some of the girls did go on to train as nurses in England. But without the education, there wasn't much I could do. And there was the epilepsy. I never got any medication for that until I went to England.

I was always told I wasn't good for anything except housework. As soon as you left the orphanage, they didn't care about you any more. I worked for families in Castlerea and all around there. They never paid me. You'd be on your feet, working all day long. You were never allowed to have your meals with the family. They looked down on us really. They didn't even recognise you were a human being.

The whole thing had a very bad effect on me. I had a nervous breakdown and was in and out of psychiatric care for years. I still have nightmares. But what happened to us children wasn't talked about then. It was all bottled up, people didn't like to hear it. They'd just say that everyone was poor back then, and that it's time to forget about it.

But I think everyone has a right to speak their minds, and we have a right to know about our backgrounds. There's still things I don't know about my family and why they put me into St Joseph's, but I'm trying to find out. Maybe with things becoming more open now, someone will tell me eventually."

Five

An Act of Charity?

As various scandals have erupted in the Irish Catholic Church during the 1990s, particularly in the areas of education and social services, a strong line of defence has been propagated by various spokespersons for the Catholic Church. They argue that if were not for the dedicated work of the religious in Ireland during the nineteenth and much of the twentieth century, few educational and social welfare services would have been provided. They contend that that such services were provided from the financial resources of the Church itself, with the Irish State playing only a marginal and miserly role.

This interpretation of Irish history has been accepted by many — often expressed that 'if it were not for the Christian Brothers or Sisters of Mercy, no one would have received an education in this country'. Put simply, the primary argument is that the Church provided charitable services to Irish society when the State was unwilling to do so. In the specific context of industrial schools, it is interesting to note the all-pervasive use of the term 'orphanages' to describe what was in fact a State-funded system in which orphans made up only a minority of the children. This of course gives credence to the general impression of charitable effort.

This argument is essentially based on a highly simplistic interpretation of Irish history, and it contains a seductive mixture of fact and fiction. It is a fact that many of the educational and welfare services provided by the Catholic Church — and indeed the other Churches — were pioneered in the early to mid-nineteenth century, and initially provided from their own resources. This was particularly the case in Ireland, where unlike in Great Britain, no grant was available for the construction of industrial schools. However, as Maria Luddy in her comprehensive history of philanthropy in nineteenth-century Ireland argues, the primary concern of these Church bodies was "moral and spiritual neglect and abuse".[1]

The sectarian battles of nineteenth-century Ireland exerted an enormous influence on the development of these services. There are constant references at the time to the proselytizing activities of rival churches, and accusations that each was stealing children from the streets in order to change their religion.

It was the Catholic Church which emerged triumphant in Ireland from these battles. Its domination of the social welfare services essentially amounted to the exertion of universal control over the lives of Irish women and children in particular. The introduction in 1868 of State funding for children committed to industrial schools was to provide a substantial financial incentive to the Catholic Church to continue to maintain that control.

With the advent of independence, Catholic Church control over educational and welfare services in Ireland became unchallenged. However, contrary to the view now expressed by the Church, and generally uncritically accepted to date, the vast majority of Church-operated services were in fact substantially funded by the Irish State. Nowhere was this more true than in the reformatory and industrial schools.

The Catholic Church's first public use of inadequate funding to excuse the inadequacies in its industrial schools dates from 1971. The Kennedy Report, published the previous year, was highly critical of the operation of the schools. The religious orders immediately responded by attributing all of the defects of the system to poor State funding.

The Bishops' Conference on Social Welfare organised a major conference on child care in Killarney in March 1971. The Kennedy Report was vehemently attacked. A senior member of the Good Shepherd order of nuns, responsible for the management of four industrial schools and one girls' reformatory, stated that "there is not one word of appreciation or even commendation of the work done by voluntary bodies. We are told in the report if it were not for the dedicated work of many of our religious bodies the position would be a great deal worse than it is now! Talk about damning by faint praise. The one stark and most obvious fact in the situation is nowhere stated. Just how could any body, voluntary or statutory, be expected to provide a skilled and humane service on the pittance granted by the State?"[2]

More recently, in the conditional apology given by the Sisters of Mercy to those who suffered abuse in their industrial schools, they stressed that their orphanages were "under-funded, under-staffed and under-resourced …. In these circumstances many sisters gave years of dedicated service. Notwithstanding these facts, clearly mistakes were made."[3]

This line of defence has also been used by the Catholic Church in other countries where abuse has been perpetrated against children in institutional care. Australian Christian Brother Barry Coldrey argues in his book *The Scheme*, commissioned by the Order to investigate its history in child care in Australia, that "childcare ranked low on the political agenda until the 1960s. Decision makers might sentimentalise 'orphans' on an occasion and patronise 'the wonderful people' who cared for the children, but were unwilling to divert scarce resources to their support."[4]

Although this issue has been a constant theme, privately and publicly, for the past fifty years, no conclusive evidence has yet been presented by the religious to demonstrate the inadequacy of the State grant for children in industrial and reformatory schools. No set of financial accounts by any congregation involved in managing the schools has been made public that could show that they were under-funded. In fact, it is clear from Department of Education files that it believed several of the schools to be actually making a profit.

More importantly, it has never been explained how the level of State funding, regardless of its inadequacy or otherwise, could have resulted in regimes of such horrendous abuse and degradation of vulnerable children.

It is important to point out that neither the *States of Fear* documentaries nor this book ever accepted that the State funding of industrial and reformatory schools was overly generous. It is clear that the State could and should have given considerably more money in order to have had an even barely adequate child care system. It is, however, highly arguable whether this money should have been given for this purpose to the religious orders running the system, who have now been shown to have had such an abysmal record of caring for these children.

Without doubt, the most telling incident in all of this was the effective refusal by the religious orders of additional State funding for the industrial schools in 1951. They stubbornly refused to provide financial accounts to show how they were spending the money they already received, and so the State was not prepared to increase that funding in any substantial way. It is absolutely clear from the events of 1951 that the religious orders' determination to avoid what they saw as State interference overbore any concerns which they may have had for the welfare of the children in their care.

Origins of Funding

When the reformatory and industrial schools system was established in Ireland in the second half of the nineteenth century, the basic capitation rate per child per week was set at six shillings for reformatory schools and five shillings for industrial schools.

The reasons for the use of a capitation grant per child, as opposed to a block grant per school, are interesting. The British Government was unwilling to provide funding directly to particular religious denominations, being most concerned to allay any accusations of sectarianism. This was a very real fear, given the context of the virulent battle between Protestant and Catholic power groupings for control of social services at the time. So instead, the relatively uncontentious formula of giving the funding directly to each child was adopted.

A direct effect of this was to create an enormous incentive to maximise the number of children committed to these institutions, and so increase the funding from the State. It was this single factor which was responsible for the fact that Ireland had such vast numbers of children detained in these schools. Unlike in Britain, the capitation basis for the funding of industrial schools was never changed, and so the numbers of

Irish children detained remained very substantial until well into the middle of the twentieth century.

When the first industrial schools opened in Ireland in 1869, there were 183 children committed to them. A mere five years later, that figure had risen to over 3,000. This initial rapid growth in children detained was viewed with alarm by the British authorities. They moved to place limits on the size of the schools and the numbers of children to whom the capitation fee would apply.

Firstly, the Treasury would not pay a capitation fee for children under the age of six in industrial schools. This made sound sense — the schools were for the industrial training of children, and those under six could hardly be expected to benefit much from industrial training.

Secondly, a rather complex system was established which resulted in each school receiving a separate certification for numbers of children for whom the Treasury would pay and a separate accommodation limit. Thus, for example, an industrial school could be certified for the reception of 100 children, but have a certified accommodation limit of 120. Although the school could take in up to 120 children, the Treasury would only pay a capitation fee for 100.

The intention behind this administrative order was that industrial schools should be reserved for certain categories of children as prescribed under legislation, rather than as the kind of catch-all institutions envisaged by the religious congregations operating them.

However, those children placed in an industrial school under the age of six or in excess of the certified number generally received a capitation fee from the local authority from where the child originated. The reasons why religious congregations, nuns in particular, accepted children under the age of six was partly out of charity, but more importantly out of what they perceived as the necessity to "protect their faith". They were also keen to ensure that a reserve of children existed who could be put on the State grant as soon as a vacancy in the certified numbers occurred. This was consistently stated in their campaign to have the certification system abolished in the 1930s.

The determination of the religious to maintain the catch-all character of the schools was in order to ensure that as many destitute children as possible would end up in the religious-controlled reformatory and industrial schools, as opposed to under the Poor Law and in the non-denominational workhouses.

In 1908, the new Children Act was passed, which placed a duty on local authorities to provide a contribution to the schools for the maintenance of children placed in them by the courts. This power had been discretionary until the passing of the Act. As a consequence of this, the financial position of the schools improved considerably.

In 1919, the direct State grant for children in industrial schools was increased to 7 shillings and 6 pence per child per week. In addition to this State grant, the local authority contributions netted on average a further 5 shillings a week. Children under six at this stage received only the 5 shillings grant from the relevant local authority.

The Cussen Report, which reviewed the operation of the schools between 1934 and 1936, noted that it was exceedingly difficult to arrive at an exact figure that would adequately reflect the cost of providing appropriate care for children. It showed that costs between the schools varied considerably. The Cussen Committee attributed this variation to the ability of large numbers of schools to provide food, clothing etc. from the labour of the children on the extensive farms that many schools owned, and from the workshops that they operated.

Overall, the Cussen Report concluded that children under the age of six in the schools should be funded by a central government grant of 5 shillings a week, in addition to the local authority grant which they received anyway. From 1939, a total grant of ten shillings a week was given in respect of each child under six (as opposed to twelve shillings and six pence for those over-six).

The Cussen Report also recommended that the system of certified numbers and accommodation limits should be revised. It further argued that teachers in the schools should be paid directly by the Department of Education and not from the fees received by those schools. In 1945, the Department of Education agreed to fund the entire salary of teachers within the schools. It was hoped that this would "go far towards making teaching posts in these schools as attractive to fully qualified teachers as posts in ordinary national schools, so that a rise in the standard of literary education may confidently be expected to follow".[5] However, the experience of those who grew up in the schools during the following decades shows that this was to be a forlorn hope.

'Parsimony'

The recommendations of the Cussen Committee regarding the funding of the schools were enacted in the Children Act, 1941. But despite the increase in funding, serious problems began to emerge in the schools. In 1945, the Secretary of the Department of Education wrote to the Department of Finance regarding the "grave situation which has arisen regarding feeding and clothing of children detained in industrial schools".[6]

This memorandum identified children in several industrial schools as being severely malnourished, in some cases under half their desired weight (see Chapter Six). The reasons for this were stated to be "parsimony" and ignorance on the part of the Sisters of Mercy running the particular schools, combined with the increased cost of living. Compared to the horrors being uncovered by the Department of Education's own inspectors, the language used in this memorandum was most restrained. Internal departmental reports were making reference to the "criminal negligence" of at least one particular nun running an industrial school for small boys.

However, to deal with the cost of living factor, the grants were increased and those payable in respect of children under six were immediately raised to bring them into line with the other children. The grant for each child was now fifteen shillings a week. The certification limits were also removed, allowing the schools to take in even more children and thus increase their income.

However, in sanctioning these substantial increases in funding, the Department of Finance issued a grave warning. It expected that the additional money "will be devoted to the welfare of the children committed to industrial schools, and…to emphasise the duty which devolves upon your Department [of Education] to ensure that the physical well-being of these children is not neglected by the conductors of the schools to whose care they are committed."[7] This stricture was in turn passed on to the religious managers of the schools.

The Government also introduced a scheme of building grants for the schools at this time. They had justifiably argued that they received no funding at all for buildings, and in 1946 this was remedied. However, it was to be short-lived. In order to receive the grant, it appeared that the Office of Public Works had to be satisfied with the quality of work to be carried out. The religious orders were unwilling to be subject to this condition, and so would not co-operate with this funding scheme. It was discontinued two years later.

To deal with the ignorance of some of the nuns running the schools, the Department of Education proposed in the mid-1940s to set up and fund a special summer course for nuns to instruct them in the proper feeding of the children. However, the funding for this was rather callously vetoed by the Department of Finance.[8] A suggestion to the religious orders that they themselves should set up such a course was firmly rejected.

As for the "parsimony" explanation for the starvation of children in industrial schools, the Department of Education also insisted on the removal of two of the worst offenders — the Resident Managers of Lenaboy Industrial School, Galway, and of St Michael's Cappoquin in Waterford (see Chapter Six). Both were Sisters of Mercy, and neither went quietly. In the case of Cappoquin, the Department in desperation was preparing to appeal for help to the local bishop.

The Department of Finance was not to forget the meanness of some of those religious who ran the schools. All increases in funding throughout the 1940s and 1950s were accompanied by a sharp reminder from Finance that this money was to be spent directly on the children. It is also clear from a reading of the Department of Education's files that there continued to exist over the decades a suspicion that in varying cases, not all of the funding paid to the industrial and reformatory schools was being spent on the children.

Meagre Accounts

This suspicion was evidently a major consideration in the continuous efforts made during the 1940s by the State to insist that industrial schools furnish proper financial accounts. But it was an uphill struggle. Only a handful of schools responded to the Department's repeated requests, and the accounts submitted were skimpy and uninformative.

However, even at that, one of the few sets of accounts provided, from St Joseph's Industrial School in Letterfrack, showed that the school actually made a substantial profit of £1,200 in the early 1950s. (It then made a loss during the late 1950s, when its numbers declined). Letterfrack had a large farm, on which the children provided free labour. While their accounts were too vague to be able to see exactly how the school had made its profit, there can be no doubt that the children's labour contributed in no small part.

It is interesting to note in this regard a letter in 1951 in which Noel Browne, the then Minister for Health, made representations for an increase in funding specifically for the Letterfrack school. The Christian Brothers running this school had claimed to Browne that they were in a serious financial state. However, their accounts as lodged with the Department of Education tell quite a different story. This was clearly a case of the religious orders shooting themselves in the foot, and is a possible explanation as to why they even today refuse to release any of their financial records dealing with the schools.

To get some idea as to the real levels of funding, it is interesting to convert the value of the grants into today's money. This shows that when a school like Artane was at its height during the 1940s and 1950s, with its full complement of 800 boys, it was receiving from the Government the equivalent today of about £1 million pounds a year. In addition to this, several of the Christian Brothers at the school were paid full salaries as national school teachers from 1945. Artane itself was an enormous operation, with its numerous trades workshops selling their produce on the open market, together with its fully operational 290-acre farm, worked mainly by the boys. They kept a large menagerie of farm animals, and even bred horses for sale. However, the Christian Brothers argued vehemently that none of this income was relevant, and should not be considered in the context of setting the levels of State funding. Needless to say, they never provided the Department of Education with any information as to the extent of their profits from the farm or workshops.

The determined refusal by the religious orders to supply proper accounts came to a head in 1951, and was to have lasting consequences in terms of the State's relationship with them. The religious managers had organised themselves some years previously into the Association of Resident Managers of Reformatory and Industrial Schools. During the late 1940s, this organisation mounted a sustained campaign for increased funding. It was regarded with some scepticism by Government.

An internal memorandum within the Department of Education concluded in 1946 that "no good case exists for an increase in the capitation grants payable to Industrial schools based on the financial statements submitted by these schools. The information given in their statements is rather meagre, and it is not easy to determine what is included under certain headings." It was concluded that the matter would be considered in the following year if the cost of living continued to rise.[9]

In 1947, the Department once again requested proper financial accounts from the schools. But despite their refusal to provide these, and after some haggling over the amount with the Department of Finance, a very substantial increase in the grant of four shillings a week per child was given. This was only one shilling less than the amount which the Resident Managers had themselves stated was necessary to run the schools. The capitation grant now stood at nineteen shillings a week for each child.[10]

In June 1950 a letter was sent to the Department of Education by the Resident Managers Association requesting a further increase in the capitation fee. A meeting was organised between the Minister, General Richard Mulcahy, and representatives from the Association in July to discuss the issue. Following this meeting, a further memo was sent to the Department of Finance requesting that the capitation grant be increased to thirty shillings a week for industrial schools and thirty-four shillings for reformatory schools.[11]

The rationale for this proposed increase was that the religious managers claimed that average weekly losses to the schools amounted to three shillings per child. There was also need for improved accommodation in schools, for a more varied diet, better clothing, facilities for more effective training and for brightening the children's school life. However, the response from the Department of Finance stated that "The Minister considers that in the present conditions he could not feel justified in approving increases in excess of 5 shillings per head."[12]

The Department of Education disagreed and asked that Finance reconsider the proposal for an increase of eleven shillings.[13] The Department of Finance on the 2nd of February, 1951 stated that they were not in a position to increase the grant by anything further than five shillings as the matter had been decided by a cabinet sub-committee.

It is clear from this exchange, and several others, between the two Government departments that several Ministers for Education were generally much more willing to accede to the demands of the religious managers running the industrial schools. Even in the absence of proper accounts from the managers, they usually appeared prepared to give them the benefit of the doubt, in spite of their various expressions of scepticism through the decades.

The 'Thin End of the Wedge'

In order to break the logjam with the Department of Finance over funding in 1951, Education Minister Richard Mulcahy obtained authorisation to establish an inter-departmental sub-committee to conduct an inquiry into industrial and reformatory schools. The terms of reference for the Committee were "to inquire into the conditions and circumstances of the industrial and reformatory schools under the control of the Department of Education and to make recommendations as to how they might be most efficiently and most economically organised and conducted."[14]

However, to the surprise of the Minister, the Association of Reformatory and Industrial School Managers reacted negatively to the proposed inquiry. They stated in March 1951 that they "consider the terms of reference somewhat vague and fear that the recommendations of the committee of inquiry may raise issues affecting the relations which have hitherto existed between the Department and the schools".[15] They looked for more details as to the nature of the proposed inquiry, which were provided to them.

On the 6 April, 1951, the secretary of the Association, Brother Hurley, wrote to the Minister stating that "resulting from a lengthy discussion on the proposal, I have been directed by the Association to inform you that the members are strongly of the opinion that no useful purpose would be served by the holding of such an inquiry".[16]

In response, Mulcahy held a meeting on the 23rd of April 1951 with Fr Reidy and Br Hurley, president and secretary of the Managers Association. The detailed minutes of this meeting indicate that Br Hurley gave several reasons for the Association's rejection of the proposed inquiry:

> (1) that it was felt that the inquiry reflected on the management of the schools and that the Association took particular objection to the Departments of Finance and of Social Welfare being associated with the inquiry when the Department of Education was already fully aware of the circumstances of the schools;
>
> (2) It appeared to the Association that the inquiry would be the thin end of the wedge in an attempt by the State to impose its control on the detailed management of the schools. The Managers were very satisfied with the present system of inspection and believed that the present system of management was ideal.
>
> (3) They were particularly suspicious of the Department of Social Welfare appearing to interfere in the conduct of the schools and they also objected to the Department of Finance insisting on the inquiry.

The Minister in reply informed them:

(1) that the State had no intention whatever of using this inquiry to obtain a further footing in the schools. His policy was that the State should assist the schools and once it is satisfied that the work is being done efficiently by the management to interfere with them as little as possible.

(2) the Managers were mistaken in the view that the enquiry had been insisted upon by the Department of Finance. As a matter of fact, he himself had insisted on the inquiry and only with the greatest of reluctance did the Department of Finance agree to it. What had happened was that the schools were being given only half the increase they had asked for and he was not prepared to leave the matter there. One of his objects in this was to bring the officials of the Department of Finance face to face with the realities in the schools. It had been suggested that the Department of Social Welfare should also be associated with the inquiry and he had welcomed this as he regarded that Department as a potential help in his struggle for an increase of grants.

Fr Reidy and Br Hurley responded that this threw a very different light on the proposal and in these circumstances they, personally, were quite willing for the proposed inquiry to proceed. It would be necessary, however, for them to hold a meeting of the managers. Fr Reidy then asked what would be the nature of the proposed inquiry and the Minister said that it would cover the physical and general welfare of the pupils, their training and aftercare subsequent to discharge and above all their food, clothing and housing: "It might be that the Department of Finance representatives would desire that the schools' accounts should be available in a uniform form. The Minister thought for his part that it would scarcely be necessary to visit all the schools, that visits to ten or so typical schools would be sufficient. However, that was a matter for the committee."[17]

The religious orders, however, were having none of it. On the 6th of May 1951, the religious managers passed the following resolution: "That the Association is unalterably opposed to the holding of an inquiry into the schools under the terms of reference laid down." As a result, the Minister decided that no useful purpose would be served by proceeding any further with the proposal to set up his inter-departmental committee.[18]

This row was to leave a lasting impression on the Government. No further attempts were made by the Departments of either Education or Finance to hold the religious orders to account for their spending of taxpayers' money for another twenty years. That, of course, was the Kennedy Committee, which resulted in the gradual dismantling of the entire system.

Despite the failure of the Minister's attempts to hold an inquiry in 1951, the schools nonetheless got their way, and a further increase in the capitation fee was granted in early 1952. The grant in respect of each child now stood at thirty shillings a week, almost exactly the figure sought by the religious orders. This represented an increase of over one hundred per cent in funding over a ten year period, when the cost of living rose by only fifty per cent. However, as the wide range of testimony in this book from the former inmates of the system so clearly indicates, the children remained hungry, miserable and bereft of even the most basic comforts of living.

In granting the large 1952 increase, the Department of Finance once again expressed concern about how this money was being spent and the lack of accountability by the religious managers. They argued that "in arriving at a decision to approve a substantial increase in the capitation grants payable in respect of children detained in reformatory and industrial schools, the Minister was impressed by the necessity for improving the quality and variety of the diet in these institutions, and he assumes that your Department will take all possible steps to ensure that the authorised increases are … utilised for that purpose."[19]

This communication continues in an interesting vein, displaying a certain lack of confidence in the Department of Education's ability to carry out its duties with regard to the schools. It stated that:

> ... it was represented by an official of your Department that regular visits by the Inspectors of Reformatory and Industrial Schools are a sufficient means of determining whether the increased grants will so be used. The Minister would prefer a more objective test and he feels that only the production of properly audited accounts by the school managers will demonstrate unambiguously what portion of the grant is actually spent on food. I am accordingly to reiterate the Minister's [for Finance] views that schools should be encouraged to keep properly authenticated records of their income and expenditure.[20]

Throughout the history of industrial schools in Ireland, no such records were ever submitted to Government departments.

Cows Better Fed Than Boys

Even the Department of Education, with its willingness to placate the religious orders, could not ignore the lamentable conditions in St Conleth's Reformatory in Daingean, Co Offaly. Run by the Oblates of Mary Immaculate, it catered for boys between the ages of twelve and sixteen.

The archives of the Department of Education contain an extraordinary report from the Secretary, following his visit to Daingean in 1955. He was clearly shocked by what he saw, and his report to the Minister is remarkable for the sense of anger it displays directed at the Oblates. He dismisses outright their excuses that the miserable condition of the boys and the institution are due to poor funding.

He described the living conditions for the boys as being Dickensian, and compared them to the excellent facilities provided for the farm animals kept by the school:

> In contrast to the conditions for the boys, the conditions of the milking herd were excellent ... beautifully clean and the cattle well cared for ... the attention paid to the cattle was in marked contrast to the care for the feeding of the boys ... I am of the

> opinion that very handsome profits are made on the
> farm, but I can see no evidence of any of the profits
> being ploughed back for the benefit of the boys or for
> the improvement of the building.[21]

The farm at Daingean comprised 220 acres of "very good" land, and was reputed to be most efficiently run. The resident manager during the mid-1950s was a Fr Reidy, who was a leading light in the Irish Farmers' Association. Indeed, so busy was he with these extra curricular activities, that he was unable to be present in the school during the Secretary's visit. He had left word that he had had to attend an IFA meeting in Dublin.

The Secretary was clearly (and somewhat justifiably) miffed at this. He remarked in his report to the Minister that "the Department finds it difficult to see how this school is run at a loss as Fr Reidy has claimed, the more especially since Fr Reidy prides himself on being a scientific farmer who plays a very active part on local and national farmers committees." He went even further, saying that "I doubt very much if there is any real attempt made to reform any of those boys, as one ordinarily understands the term. I doubt also if the tradition and general attitude of the Fathers in charge of these boys are the right ones for the purposes of the school."[22]

The Secretary also informed the Minister that Dr McCabe, the Medical Inspector of Reformatory and Industrial Schools,

> ... has been pressing for years on the authorities of
> the [Daingean] school certain improvements in the
> interests of the boys, both spiritually and materially.
> Some of these have been carried out, though with
> considerable reluctance. The almost invariable
> answer given to her when she suggests improve-
> ments is that there is no money available for such.[23]

However, in the by now standard pattern of inaction within the Department, awareness of problems did not mean that anything was done about them. With regard to Daingean, no action was taken, and it continued detaining hundreds of boys in miserable conditions for a further sixteen years.

Increase in Touting

Interestingly, no attempt appears to have been made by either the resident managers or by the Department of Education to reform the system of capitation grants. This system of funding the schools had been abolished in Britain in 1919 and replaced with an annual budget, which was met jointly by local authorities and central government. It had three great advantages over the capitation grant system. Firstly, it allowed the Home Office increased control over the management of the schools; secondly it removed the incentive for schools to hold on to pupils in order to maximise their income; and thirdly, it had led to rapid increases in the funding for child care in Britain, which was roughly three times higher than in Ireland.

In this context, it is interesting to note the deluge of correspondence in the Department of Education archive during the 1950s from religious orders begging to be sent more children. The numbers committed by the courts had begun to decline, and the religious were most concerned at the impact of this on the income of the schools.

One of the reasons for this, they claimed, was the use of the Probation Act by District Justices. The religious argued that far too many children were getting probation rather than being committed to industrial schools. They even complained about the influence being exerted by the Society for St Vincent de Paul in attempting to keep children out of detention and with their families. This view was especially strongly expressed by the Oblates in Daingean, and was described by Department of Education officials as "a strange attitude".[24]

Even when the children were committed to industrial or reformatory schools, the religious orders bemoaned the fact that the duration of their detention periods was becoming shorter. This, the managers argued, resulted in the schools becoming uneconomical.

In response the Department of Education caustically commented "that it would be well to bear in mind that the schools exist for the children and not vice-versa". The managers, it said, should not overlook the fact "that children should not be committed to schools or unduly detained therein merely to make certified schools economic."[25]

There was a history to the Department's suspicion of the motives of the religious orders in their drive to have children committed to industrial schools. During the 1940s, the Department became concerned at the large number of girls placed in the schools. It baldly attributed this to:

> ... the fact that the Managers have an organised system of 'touting' for children. They have social workers who act as a sort of agent and get children committed to the schools. We have no means of preventing this practice but I suggest that we consult the Department of Local Government with a view to getting the assistance of the local County Managers to ensure that children are not committed without sufficient reason and to obtain periodical reports on the parents' means when children are committed on the grounds of poverty.[26]

There is only one reference in the Department of Education's files to a possible alternative method of distributing funding to deal with children in need of care. This came from an Assistant Secretary in the Department in 1945. In it, he showed a rare understanding from the Government's point of view of the problems associated with the capitation funding and what this meant to the lives of children within the system.

In his memo, the Assistant Secretary referred to the problems in having children released from industrial schools:

> The committal to an industrial school (or any other institution) of children whose parents are of good character and are willing but unable to support them is wrong on moral and on social grounds. It is also a rather extravagant arrangement, since it costs fifteen shillings a week from public funds for each child. We have tried to have some of these children released when their parents' means improved, but our experience has shown that it is very difficult to get this done.[27]

The memo argued that at least one-third of the children detained in industrial schools at the time fell within this category — roughly 2,000 boys and girls. The Assistant Secretary then went on to suggest the desirability of a fundamental change in the Department's arrangements — namely to examine the feasibility of providing grants to the parents to enable them to keep their children at home, and the family unit intact. This, he says, would be "more satisfactory and economical".

This is such a blindingly obvious and desirable alternative to industrial schools that it is remarkable that it had not been mooted before this. What is more shocking, however, is that the proposal died a death there and then. It was not examined in any detail, and was never suggested again within the Department. One can only speculate on the reasons, but primary among them is likely to have been the Department's anxiety about opposition from the Catholic Church. Strange as it may seem, the undoubted reality was that to remove a substantial source of funding from the religious orders and give it instead to parents to look after their children would almost certainly have been vehemently opposed by the Church.

To offset the declining numbers of children committed during the 1950s, the religious orders began to cast about for other groups of children who could be detained in the schools, thus gaining them valuable revenue. They set their sights on the group of children who were the responsibility of the local authorities. Many of these had been born out of wedlock or were otherwise destitute. It was Department of Health policy to have these children raised in foster families (or boarded out, in the expression of the time). The local authority bore the entire cost of this scheme, which was a much more modern and progressive approach to child care.

However, during the 1950s, the religious orders pointed out in correspondence to the local authorities an ingenious way for them to cut their costs in this area. If instead of fostering, they were to place the children in industrial schools, the local authorities' costs of maintaining those children would be halved. The other half would automatically be paid by the Department of Health.

This strategy for cost cutting appealed so much to the local authorities that fostering declined dramatically in the 1950s, and the children ended up detained in industrial schools. The religious orders were equally delighted — it ensured for them a steady supply of children from local authorities at a time when the courts were showing a reluctance to commit children to the schools. The only losers were the children, who would probably have been better off in a family setting than in an institution, even though the fostering system was itself lax and poorly inspected.

Accountability and Control

The evidence presented in this chapter demonstrates that funding of the reformatory and industrial school system is infinitely more complex than the views presented by the Catholic Church in recent years. There is little doubt that the funding of the schools was not generous. However, it has always been the contention of the Catholic Church that one must view these institutions in the context of the times. This is an interesting and revealing exercise, though possibly not exactly what the Church had in mind.

It is appropriate to compare the capitation grant to two different sets of wages at the time — manual labourers and farm labourers. These are chosen for the reason that the fathers of a substantial number of the children in industrial schools would have worked in these areas. They are also the jobs which would have been secured by the vast majority of boys leaving industrial schools at sixteen years.

In the mid-1940s, when the capitation grant for industrial schools children was fifteen shillings a week (rising to nineteen shillings in 1947), the minimum wage for a farm labourer was £2 a week. Any benefits in kind which he received were deducted on a set basis from this £2. The testimony of Terry (see page 110) is interesting in this regard. His father was a farm labourer, feeding his family of six children on his meagre wages during the 1940s. But Terry describes the food he received at home being far superior to anything he was fed in St Joseph's Industrial School, Clonmel.

The other comparison of interest is to the wages of an unskilled building labourer. This shows that during the 1940s and 1950s, the industrial schools capitation grant was equivalent to just under one third of this wage. Once again, it must be remembered that the grant was payable in respect of *each* child in a school. Building labourers by contrast would have to feed and clothe their often very large families on a wage only three times greater than the capitation fee. What these comparisons do show is that it should have been possible to feed and clothe children in industrial schools adequately on the basis of the State grant.

In this context there is strong evidence that the Government was not convinced that the State funding was always spent on the unfortunate children, who were the victims in some cases of no less than "criminal neglect" at the hands of the religious orders. This suspicion was heightened by the fact that various Government Departments found it virtually impossible to obtain accurate sets of accounts from the managers of schools.

The capitation system of payment, which neither the managers nor the State ever appeared to have opposed, resulted in the managers "touting" for children in order to ensure the economic viability of the schools. Yet, nowhere is there a sense that the religious orders in any way questioned the system of institutional care for children. Rather, their stated aim to provide the children with a sound moral and religious training for life led them to battle to maintain a system over which they exerted almost complete control. Their success can be measured by the fact that in 1969, the capitation grant payable per week per child stood at £8, which was precisely the figure they had campaigned for.

The greatest insight into the motivation of the religious orders undoubtedly lies in the events of 1951, and their refusal of additional funding in return for greater accountability and transparency in the way they managed their schools. It is clear that they deemed religious control of the schools to be more important than additional money for the children in their care. As a consequence, it is reasonable to argue that their constant pleas of poverty to excuse the often appalling conditions in their industrial schools can be treated with a degree of cynicism.

Terry's Story, St Joseph's Industrial School, Ferryhouse, Clonmel (Rosminians), 1952–1959

"My first impressions of Ferryhouse was seeing millions of boys in the yard, all with tight haircuts. They looked hunched, bent over. I realised later that this was because of the boils they all had on their necks."

Terry's mother died in childbirth when he was eight. His father was a farm labourer, and with the help of the children's grandmother, he managed to keep his family together for almost a year. But then it was decided that four of the six children would have to go into care. Terry was then nine, and himself and his five-year-old brother ended up in Ferryhouse.

"The first thing that happened was we were given numbers. I was seventy-seven, my brother was seventy-six. They called you by your name as well, but your number was what you went by.

I was lucky, I didn't wet the bed. But my little brother, who was only five, did — he'd come up to me in the morning and tell me, and my heart would bleed for him because I knew he'd be beaten. Then some mornings, he come up and tell me that he hadn't wet it, and oh sunshine, we'd be so happy.

Sometimes he'd soil himself as well — he was only a little fellow, not much more than a baby. The Brothers would make me clean him up. I didn't mind at all, especially if it saved him a beating.

But one time, one of the Brothers handed me his strap — a big, black, heavy thing — and told me to beat my brother with it. This was the only way to make him stop soiling himself, he said. So I gave my brother just a little tip with the strap. The Brother took it off me, and said: 'I'll show you how to do it', and gave the little fellow a wallop. I refused to take the strap again after that, and the Brother got in a rage and gave him an awful hiding.

There were quite a few little lads there, four and five year olds. The youngest was three. Any of them that wet the bed were beaten. In all about fifty boys wet the bed, big lads as well. A Brother used to go round the dormitory with a list. He'd shout 'Sailors, turn over', and anyone who wet the bed had to lie on their tummies and they'd be beaten with the strap.

It was terrible to have to witness that, with boys crying and shouting. But some fellows would just sit on their beds calmly reading comics through it. I don't know how they did that. It used to really upset me. It was the things I saw happen to others that had a worse effect on me than anything they did to me directly.

After a while they gave up beating the bed wetters in the dormitories. They'd have to line up outside the office to be punished. It was terrible to see them coming out afterwards, crying and in pain.

There was one fellow with a big caliper on his left leg, and they used to beat him every day. I remember another lad being taken into the office with a sheet wrapped around his head and face. One boy came out once with his shorts down around his ankles and he couldn't pull them up because of the pain in his hands. It was really awful.

When I was working in the boot shop at one stage, a boy was called out and told to go to the office. When he came back, he was pale and shaking. He said that while they were flogging him, he was being held down and had his face pressed hard against the cassock of one of the Brothers. He said that he hadn't been able to breathe. He was in a terrible state. He felt that they had nearly killed him.

The worst thing that happened to me personally was a beating I got for having sores all over my head and body. The nurse brought me up to the Brother and said 'Look at the state of him'. The Brother told me to kneel down, and gave me a terrible hiding. It went on and on, and I shouted at him: 'Do you want to kill me?' And he started beating me all over again. But I wasn't beaten very often, and I don't hold any grudges.

I was very keen on boxing and on hurling and football. They'd help you if you were any good at sports. Even some of the brutal Brothers would spend time with the boys at sports. I had a great time with the boxing. I went to championships all over the country and won various trophies. So it wasn't all bad."

Terry also has fond memories of some of the lay teachers. While the boys had their lessons within the industrial school, most of their teachers came in from outside. One teacher in particular, Mrs O'Dwyer — whom the children named Mam the Wire — was kind to Terry. He never remembers her hitting anyone, and yet she had no difficulty controlling her class.

Like the other boys, Terry talks about the miserable food. He makes the comparison between the meals his mother gave him at home before she died and those in the industrial school. The family of two adults and six children were living at this stage on the income of their farm labourer father, earning just over £3 a week in the early 1950s. During the same period, the capitation fee paid by the State to the industrial schools in respect of *each* child was £1 and 4 shillings a week, which increased in 1952 to £1 and 10 shillings.

"At home, we used to get proper food — meat several times a week, vegetables, eggs, the lot. In Ferryhouse we never saw meat except a few sausages every so often. They never gave us vegetables — the cabbage water and two potatoes was our main meal. Even after my mother died, my grandmother fed us well. The food in Ferryhouse was a big change."

When Terry left Ferryhouse at sixteen, he went to work on a farm several miles from Clonmel. The farmer there was a relative of one of the Brothers at the industrial school. Terry spent four weeks picking the stones off a field. It reminded him of the time in Ferryhouse years earlier when the boys had to carry stones from the fields to build a grotto for the Brothers.

He was never paid on the farm and he couldn't stand the loneliness. He left after a few months and went home to his father. Some years later, he married and moved to Dublin where he now lives and works. During the 1970s, he went to visit the priest who was in charge of Ferryhouse during his own time there.

"I wanted to ask him why he had allowed such cruelty to go on in the school. He seemed to blame the Brothers under him — he told me his instructions to them were to get on with running the place, but if anything happened, they would carry the can. He also said that he did try to control them sometimes, and that you couldn't have done that job if you didn't love children.

But afterwards, I was thinking about this, and I kept asking myself what did he mean 'if anything happened'. Did he mean if a boy died or was maimed? Is that what it would have taken to stop them?"

Tom, St Kyran's Industrial School, Rathdrum (Sisters of Mercy), 1951–1959; and Artane Industrial School (Christian Brothers), 1959–1965

"I was about twelve, and I'd grown out of my shoes. When I asked for a new pair the Brother wanted to know why. The old ones looked perfectly okay, he said. I told him they were too small, and he hit me a belt across the face. Sent me flying. 'Now tell me the truth,' he said. I told him again, 'Because they're too small for me.' He hit me again, and asked me again, and this went on and on, and he kept hitting me. 'You're telling lies,' he said at last, 'Your shoes are not too small, you're too big for your shoes'."

When he was only eighteen months old, Tom was committed by the court to St Kyran's Industrial School for Junior Boys in Rathdrum, Co Wicklow. He has no memory of his parents. He now knows that he was put in because his mother deserted the family. But growing up, he had no knowledge of his family, or whether he even had one.

"What I remember most about Rathdrum was not so much the particular things that happened, but more an absence, an emptiness. I think I longed for affection, just to be held by someone. But I never was, or at least I don't ever remember anyone loving me.

I didn't get my first hug until I was seventeen. When that happened, it made me feel that I knew at last what I had been missing. But back then, I didn't know any different, I thought that this was the way the whole world lived, you know, that everyone grew up in orphanages, looked after by nuns.

But still I felt that there must be something more. From the age of about seven or eight, I used to know this song — I can't remember it now — but I used to put my name in a place in the song, and make up where I was from — there were mountains in the song, and a stream and a cottage. And they were mine, that was my home.

My very first memory is when I was about three, the nuns rubbed this white creamy stuff all over our bodies, and we were left lying there in the cold. There were lots of us, and the white cream was stinging like hell. I don't know why this was done, I just remember lying there in the cold.

When I was about five or six, it was one of my jobs to feed the babies. I'd be left on my own, and I'd have to feed maybe about five of them. They got a thing called goodie which is bread and milk mixed up. And I always remember being hungry myself, and for every spoon I gave them I'd take one myself. I still like goodie, I still eat it sometimes.

I remember at night I'd always be cold — never being cosy like you would nowadays, getting into a nice warm bed. They had plastic sheets on all the beds, in case you wet them. You would be lying on plastic, and you had plastic covering you. You just couldn't get warm.

There was one day I felt terribly humiliated — I needed to go to the toilet, and I ran, but I just didn't make it. So I wet myself. I think I was seven at the time. This was out in the yard, with all the other boys there.

This nun — I'd always been afraid of her — she took off all my clothes and she put a nappy on me. So I went away over into the furthest corner of the yard, just to get away from everyone looking at me. I can still remember feeling so ashamed.

There was another time there were loads of people gathered around the toilet in the yard. They were all very excited about something. I went over to see what was going on, and I saw a little lad, about four, and he was hysterical. There was this red thing, I suppose his rectum, hanging out from his backside, and a nun beside him trying to push it back in. At the time I didn't understand what was going on — I just remember the child screaming, and the red thing. It was frightening.

There was one thing, and I never understood why the nuns did it. They had a bit of an orchard, and one time when we were all in the yard, they started throwing apples over the wall, into where we were. And we were running for the apples, fighting for them, at least fifty or sixty of us. Most of us got an apple, some of us — the bigger ones — even got more.

But they were crab apples, which we didn't know anything about. And that night, every single one of us was sick. We were as sick as dogs, all going to the toilet all the time, many of us not even making it down to the toilet. God, we were violently sick that night. The nuns didn't pay much attention to us — you just got down to the toilet, and went back to bed, and that was it. I don't know if they knew that the crab apples would make us all sick. Maybe they did.

There was one nun who was nice. Sister Agatha. She'd give me a smile sometimes. And call me by my first name. She was the only one who'd do that. She made me feel special.

With the others, it wasn't that there was terrible cruelty, or bad beatings or anything. It was just the way they made you feel. Like they were doing you a favour. Like you were nobody.

I keep on telling my own kids that I love them very much, because I know the effect it can have on you, not being made feel that you're loved. I really missed out on that. I always kind of felt sad. Even thinking about it today, talking about it, makes me feel sad.

There was this visitors' room, and I used to sneak around outside the window and look in when some of the boys would have visitors. I never really had visitors. I remember one Easter Sunday — I would have been about six — looking through the window and seeing boys with their mothers and fathers giving them Easter eggs. And I used to wonder why no one ever came to visit me, or gave me an Easter egg. I felt so alone, knowing that I had nobody who loved me.

The only visit I ever got in Rathdrum was when I was about seven. At least, I think I was about seven — we never had birthdays or anything. In fact I didn't even know what a birthday was for years.

Anyway, this fellow came to visit, and he told me he was my brother and his name was John. I remember he gave me one and eleven pence, and a bag of sweets. I asked him was he going to take me out of there. He said yes, that he was coming the following Saturday to take me out. I was really excited — I had someone, a brother, he was mine. And I was getting out.

He never came back again, and I've never seen him since. Nobody knows where he is."

When the boys reached the age of ten, they were transferred to a senior industrial school. Most of the Rathdrum boys, including Tom, were sent to Artane Industrial School, run by the Christian Brothers. For many of them, Artane was a severe shock.

"From the very beginning in Artane you had fear instilled into you. I remember someone saying: 'You see that door over there? There's whips and hanging ropes and things in there, and that's what you'll get if you run away or get into trouble'.

When I went into Artane, it was around Easter time, and I had a friend in the village in Rathdrum, a girl who was in the same school — we used to go to the same national school as the local children.

This girl's name was Mary, and as soon as I went to Artane, she sent me a letter and an Easter egg. It would have been my first Easter egg. I never got them, never even saw them. I only knew about it because one of the Brothers told me an Easter egg had arrived for me, and I wouldn't be getting it. The same thing happened the following year, and they made sure to tell me that an egg had arrived and that I wouldn't be getting it. I suppose the Brothers ate the eggs themselves.

I'd been in Artane a few weeks when a Brother called me over and said: 'Do you see those two fellas over there? They're your brothers.' They were big boys, and they left soon after. We didn't have any contact, and I didn't see them again until years later.

One of my sisters came to see me in Artane once. I didn't know I had any sisters. I was told I had a visitor, and I went up and saw this girl I didn't recognise sitting in the visitors' room. She told me she was my sister, and we went for a walk for about twenty minutes. I never saw her again either. Never seen her since.

The main thing about Artane, and everyone will tell you this, was the size of it. It was huge. Hundreds of boys, all of us in short trousers, runny noses, shivering in the yard.

We'd get up real early, it would be dark, and we'd march down for Mass, and then march into the refectory for breakfast. Bread and dripping. There'd be a Brother blowing a whistle at meals — whistle and we'd all stand for grace, whistle and we'd all sit down. Whistle and we'd all march out again. You were always marching and lining up for inspection. It was all very regimental.

Early on, I had to sit at a table for meals with fifteen-year-olds. I suppose there was no room at the ten-year-olds' tables. Dinnertime, we'd get slurry — that's what we'd call cabbage and gravy. I suppose we got meat sometimes, but I don't remember it. There'd be a plate of usually rotten potatoes in the middle of the table. You had to be quick or you'd get nothing. More often than not, I'd get nothing. The bigger lads would have it all taken.

A bit later on, I remember we used to get bread and jam the odd time, and sometimes bread and margarine. In case you wouldn't get margarine with the bread at the next meal, you'd break bits off and stick them under the table. So that'd be there for you at the next meal.

There were two main groups in Artane. About half of us came from orphanages [as the junior boys' industrial schools were often called] and the others would have been sent in either from broken homes or for mitching from school. Maybe a small number were there for robbing or whatever.

There was always friction between these two groups. The orphanage lads used to get the worst of it. We were very naïve. The boys from the outside were much sharper, much more streetwise.

I think the Brothers gave our group a worse time as well. We were the more vulnerable ones, we had nobody to tell. Some of the other boys would have visitors at weekends, and could tell them what was going on. We had no one.

You'd get beaten all the time by the Brothers. The palm of my hand and my wrist were constantly swollen, permanently black and blue. I got so used to seeing them like that that I thought it was almost normal.

That was my right hand and arm. But there was this one time when a Brother came to the classroom and beckoned me out. I followed him, and we went into this small room and he locked the door. 'Hold out your hands', he said — there was no explanation. If you ever pulled your hand back when this Brother was hitting you, he'd give you a dig in the ribs.

Because I was so used to getting hit on the right hand, even though it was swollen, I was able to take the pain and hold it out. I think that annoyed him. 'Now put out the other one', he said. I couldn't hold out the left hand as well, I'd pull it back nearly every time he hit me. And each time I pulled my hand back he gave me an unmerciful punch in the ribs. I was doubled up. To this day, I still don't know why he did that, or what it was for. I just remember that all the time he was hitting me he had this smug grin on his face.

There was one Brother in school who'd put you up against the wall if you got something wrong, or didn't know an answer. Then he'd get take out his hurley and sliothar, and he'd hit the ball at you with his full force. Often, he'd miss, or you might duck. But he'd keep at it until he got you, and it really hurt when he did. I suppose that was entertainment for him.

It was hard in school, because you'd be thinking more about what they'd do to you than concentrating on learning anything. You were just afraid all the time. As well as school, everyone learned a trade, and I was put into the timber yard. The man in charge there was nice, but I never really knew what I was doing. I had no interest. I wanted the bakers' shop, but I never got a choice.

Not all the Brothers would beat you up, some of them were OK. But they never interfered with each other, not that I saw anyway. I think it was just accepted that they could do what they liked, and that no one would stop them, or even say anything.

At night it was bad. I often heard a Brother come into the dormitory in the middle of the night, and take some boy off up and out the door. You'd hear the screaming then and shouting and beating. There didn't seem to be any reason why they'd pick any particular boy. Just for kicks, I suppose.

There was another Brother that used to have a certain number of boys that he used to carry on with — sexual abuse, I suppose you'd call it now. He used to keep them at the top of the dormitory, beside his own room.

I was further down the dormitory, but he used to come down and sit on the side of my bed. We used to wear just a T-shirt in bed, nothing on underneath. And several times, he'd be sitting there pretending to talk to me and his hand would go down the bed.

I can't remember if he actually touched me, but I always felt uncomfortable, kind of afraid, and I knew that something wasn't right. Once in the middle of the night, I woke up to find that same Brother pulling back my bedclothes. I jumped up, and I think he got startled and he just left.

It was generally known that this Brother was abusing boys. I'd say that other Brothers knew. After a while of this going on, about four or five of us got together and we decided we'd tell the priest about it.

We were kind of afraid, in case the priest would go back and tell the Brother. We were really putting our lives on the line. I remember that when we told the priest, he didn't seem very surprised. Then about a week later, that particular Brother was gone. No explanations — he just wasn't around any more. And that was the last we heard of it.

It never occurred to me to run away. The lads from outside who had families, they were always escaping. But I had nowhere to go, or no one to run to. I remember once being called out of class and told to go after a lad from Benburb Street who'd run off. Myself and another fellow were the fastest runners in the place, so we were picked to chase him. We never caught him. The guards picked him up at his home, and brought him back.

One of the things I always looked forward to was being taken out by this family on a Sunday. Some local families would offer to take boys out, and I was picked to go with this particular family. They were very nice to me. I felt so proud going out and staying in their house on the Sundays they collected me. The lady, she was a saint. She was the one who gave me my first hug.

I've talked to them since about what Artane was like. But I didn't tell them while I was there. You just went out and came back. It never arose to tell them anything. And also, because I didn't know any different, I thought that all the beatings and the fear and everything else was just normal."

At sixteen, Tom left Artane — most boys were told to leave on the day of their sixteenth birthday. That was the day the State funding ran out. The family whom he used to visit got him a job in a pub down the country.

"The people there were very nice, but I just couldn't handle the whole thing. It was the shock, I think — from being locked in and never meeting people from the outside, to all of a sudden being with people, strangers, all the time, having to serve them behind the bar.

I was terribly nervous. I felt that I was always in the way, a total nuisance to everyone around me. It wasn't at all the fault of the people I worked for — they were very good to me, and what I learned from them has stood to me.

Even still, I'm always doubting myself. I don't really have much confidence. I suppose it's a kind of fear, the same fear that I had growing up all those years. Because I didn't really have a childhood. Not having been loved, never getting any affection, it does have a lasting effect. I really missed out on that, and I'll never get it back.

But I don't hate the nuns or the Brothers. The way I look at it is that people aren't born like that. I mean, who knows what they had gone through in their own lives. There but for the grace of God go I, as the fellow says. It was just the system, and they fitted into it. It was their job to show you who was the boss, and that's what they did. So I suppose that I've forgiven them. If I passed some of the bad ones on the street, I think I'd probably say hello to them.

But just as I think of that now, of seeing them on the street, I can feel the horror go through me ..."

Over the years, Tom has made contact with some of his brothers and sisters, most of whom themselves grew up in industrial schools. He has also met his mother. Tom still lives and works in Dublin.

Six

"Children in a Pitiable Condition"

A consistent theme in the testimonies of those who grew up in industrial schools is that of unrelenting hunger. Many survivors who had had the benefit of some years with their families remember being shocked by the contrast between what they were fed at home and in the industrial school. Many also talk about getting much better food on the days when visitors or the inspector would arrive. They also uniformly testify to the fact that the nuns and Brothers invariably ate much better than the children. There is only a small number of schools from which accounts of constant hunger have not emerged.

"The Department could have no graver charge against any school than that the children are not properly fed." Thus wrote P Ó Muircheartaigh, Department of Education Inspector of Industrial and Reformatory Schools in 1944. His holding of this position was to herald an extraordinary period of direct intervention by the Department in the schools.

The only other time that the State had shown any concern in the diet for the children, either before or since, was in the last century. For the first couple of decades after their establishment, the various inspectors of the schools appeared to have been reasonably satisfied with the food provided to the children. Artane Industrial School, in its early years, even brewed ale for those boys who required additional nutrition. Jane Barnes in her history of Irish industrial schools in the nineteenth century argues that as the century drew to a close, the inspectors started to voice serious concerns at the quality and quantity of the food received by the children.[1]

For example, George Plunkett O'Farrell, the Inspector of Reformatory and Industrial Schools, reported in 1889 that while the diet in the majority of schools was liberal, there were a number whose diet he could not approve of. In one particular school, he found that tea and cocoa with bread was given for breakfast, dinner and supper on three days of the week! The variation between the schools in terms of the quality and quantity of the food received by the children was to be a feature of the twentieth century, despite the fact that each school received identical funding for each child committed.[2]

Much documentation survives from the 1880s and 1890s which shows that the inspectors of the Irish schools, appointed of course by the British Government, took their job very seriously indeed. They appeared to be vigilant on behalf of the children, and did not mince their words when they discovered sub-standard care. John Fagan in the late 1890s described some schools in which the children were "dull, spiritless, ill-fed, ill-clad, subject to chilblains, stunted in growth of body and mind".[3] His reports on the schools were to cause a public outcry at the turn of the century, with the schools experiencing considerable negative publicity.

As already noted, the Department of Education files covering the early decades after Ireland's independence are almost non-existent. No inspection files exist for this period. The Cussen Report in 1936 showed a level of complacency regarding conditions in the schools. But in 1939, all that was to change.

In that year, two important appointments were made in the Department of Education. P Ó Muircheartaigh became Inspector of Industrial and Reformatory Schools, and Dr Anna McCabe was appointed Medical Inspector of the schools. Writing in 1964 in an internal report, Dr McCabe described her first impressions of the system: "I was simply appalled by the conditions in most of the schools." Referring to these conditions as "Dickensian", she wrote that she set about attempting to make improvements "particularly in the case of the boys' schools, which really were in a deplorable state".[4]

Both she and Ó Muircheartaigh spent the next six years working to eliminate some of the most severe malnutrition and neglect in the schools. They were savage in their criticisms of what they found. Their letters and reports contain some of the most direct and strongly worded language to be found anywhere in the Department's files.

They singled out the Sisters of Mercy as being particularly at fault in this area. While by no means all the children in the care of this order were starving, the Department focussed in particular on four of their schools. These were Passage West, Cappoquin, Rathdrum and Lenaboy (in Galway). Criticism of the children's food was expressed in several other schools, but seemed to undergo some improvement as a result.

Their overall analysis of conditions in the schools, particularly those managed by nuns, was that underfeeding was widespread, and that they were only satisfied with conditions in one school. In Dr McCabe's view, the general rule in the schools was the provision of what she termed a "bare maintenance diet, sufficient to keep children from losing weight but not enough to enable them to put on weight at anything approaching the normal rate."[5]

Perhaps the most trenchant criticisms of the management of the schools came in a memo from Ó Muircheartaigh to the Secretary of the Department of Education in late 1944. Describing the underfeeding of the children as "a serious indictment of the system of management of industrial schools by nuns", he said that it was "a state of affairs that should not be tolerated in a Christian community". He argued that: "If the children's parents subjected them to semi-starvation and lack of proper clothing and attention from which they suffer in some industrial schools, the parents would be prosecuted."[6]

It is clear from the Departmental files that Dr McCabe was initially cautious in her criticisms and preferred to issue verbal warnings to the managers, rather than commit her views to paper. However, when this had no effect, the Department became much more pro-active, culminating with its unprecedented insistence on the dismissal of three of the nuns running these schools. It was successful in only two of these cases.

The first school to be denounced by the Department for the condition of the children detained there was St Anne's at Lenaboy in Galway. In November 1941 a new nun, Sr Paul, took over responsibility for the school. She was described by the Department as "a miserly, ruthless old woman of seventy years who has as her objectives the reduction of the debt on the institution. She has been hardened by age and a lifetime spent in a Magdalen home". It was remarked that she had "no experience of children and has no sympathy with them". With "cold thoroughness" she reduced expenditure on clothes and food to the barest minimum. She sold the produce of the kitchen on the open market and there was also a suspicion that she was selling the children's tea ration. The Department recorded that two other nuns in the industrial school had complained about the treatment of the children, but they were removed and "replaced by two young novices who dare not challenge their superior's order".

Dr McCabe found the children in Lenaboy "looking emaciated, cowed, dirty and unhappy". Of those she weighed, only two had put on any weight in the period of a year, where they should normally have all put on up to six pounds. Dr McCabe investigated the diet of the children and found that it had been "reduced to almost starvation level". She ascertained that it consisted of "half a cup of milk a day, no tea, practically no butter or sugar, tiny portions of meat and vegetables, consisting largely of the unsaleable portions of the school's vegetable garden". Their staple diet she said consisted "mainly of cocoa, bread and dripping".

She also found that over two-thirds of the children were suffering from scabies, "many in a very aggravated condition, and many had other complaints necessitating treatment". The Department noted that these appalling conditions were but some "of the more obvious results of the regime of the new resident manager. One can only imagine the effects it must be producing in the hearts and minds of unfortunate young girls who must endure it during the most impressionable and formative years of their lives". Dr McCabe had found the children to be "cowed and frightened, shrinking when spoken to, like little savages". In late 1942, the Department demanded the resignation of Sr Paul, recommending that a "more humane member" of the community replace her. After some resistance from the Sisters of Mercy, this nun was eventually dismissed.[7]

Ó Muircheartaigh was to remark that "no lay women for example, could treat children as the former resident manager in Lenaboy did and escape imprisonment."

Two years later, another industrial school managed by the Sisters of Mercy was accused by the Department of starving the children. This was St Kyran's in Rathdrum, Co Wicklow. In a similar pattern to the Lenaboy school, it was found that the resident manager was unsuitable to the post and "in the short time that has elapsed since her appointment she has succeeded in lowering the standard of the school to new levels of wretchedness." However, Dr McCabe also noted that "semi-starvation seems to be a tradition" in the school, and that parents of the children had made a number of complaints. The Department took the view that the "condition of hunger and rags should not be tolerated a day longer".

The Department believed that nothing would be gained by sending a warning letter to the manager as she was in their view "a cynical heartless type of person who has no human interest whatsoever in the children". They recommended her immediate removal. In October 1944, the Minister for Education wrote to the Superior of the convent demanding that the manager be removed. However, the response of the congregation claimed that the situation had improved in the school, and that the manager "is devoted in her duties" to the children. Their explanation for the failure of the children to gain weight was that "the scales when tested after Dr McCabe's visit were found to be 3 pounds light".

In response the Department maintained their view that the "present resident manager is not a suitable person for the position" and refused to revoke the demand that she be removed.

Despite this, the Sisters of Mercy continued to refuse to dismiss the resident manager and sent a further letter to the Department, demanding that their interpretation of events be put before the Minister. In their letter they continued to deny that the children were starving, arguing "that the majority of children during the summer months, when they romp around much more than the winter, lose or at least do not gain weight is an accepted fact. The children in question had been romping and playing all day long for some weeks previous to the visit of medical inspector." They further stated that the weighing machine used was light by "5 and a half pounds", showing some inconsistency with their previous excuse, when the discrepancy was only three pounds. The view of Dr McCabe in relation to the alleged malfunctioning of the weighing machine was that it was "far-fetched". She reiterated her opinion that the manager was not a suitable person for the position. Despite the strong views of his officials, the Minister, Fianna Fail's Thomas Derrig, agreed to postpone his demand that the resident manager resign.[8]

Later that year, St Michael's Industrial School in Cappoquin, Co Waterford with seventy-five small boys came under the inspectors' spotlight. Described as "another school run by the Sisters of Mercy which has a long record of semi-starvation", the children were all under weight and looked "pinched, wizened and wretched and lamentably different from normal children". Once again, the inspectors identified the resident manager as responsible for the "deplorable and indefensible" conditions and demanded her immediate removal. This was Sr Mary Teresa Doran, and she had held office uninterruptedly since June 1927. Dr McCabe described her as a "ruthless domineering person who resents any criticism and challenges advice".[9]

The Department's attempts to remove this nun were bitterly resisted by both herself and the congregation of the Sisters of Mercy. She had herself explained the children's failure to gain weight as due to their "activity", which excuse was described by the Department as rivalling "Marie Antoinette's 'why don't they eat cake'". In desperation, it was suggested that an appeal to the bishop might have some effect.

Eventually, Sr Mary Teresa Doran was forced to resign. However, her replacement was little better. This was Sr Patrick, described by the Department as her second-in-command, and "a bit of a Martinet ... [and] unsympathetic to children". However, while Department officials suggested as an alternative "a young, active, sympathetic and kindly disposed towards children type of person", they did not get their way in this case.[10]

The conditions in the industrial school in Passage West, Co Cork also gave rise to grave concerns, resulting in Ó Muircheartaigh and the Secretary of the Department of Education travelling down to inspect it personally in late 1944. They arrived unexpectedly and went straight to the refectory where the dinner was set out. The dinner for the children "consisted of one big slice of bread and jam for most of the children, a few had an extra half slice." They went on to describe how they "watched the children come in and make short work of the bread with a tin cupful of milk, about half a pint. We were told that the rice which according to the dietary on the wall should have been issued did not arrive from Cork."

They challenged the nun in charge on the issue. "She kept up appearances for a while and then confessed to me everything I said was true, that things were worse than even I thought. One of her remarks was that she thought the children so badly nourished that their little legs were hardly able to carry them …. I pointed out the other two schools run by the order in Cork, Cobh and Kinsale, were at the very top of the list in the matter of food, whereas Passage West had become a kind of a byword. Rev Mother assured us that arrangements had been made to bring the diet fully up to the required standard and in future there would be no cause for complaint."[11]

Some years previously, this school had written to the Department demanding that more children be sent to them in order to increase their income. They had raised the spectre of proselytism to support their arguments: "I need not remind you that there are orphanages conducted by managers differing in faith from us. Many inducements are held out to guardians and relatives to have their children sent to them."

In the case of another industrial school in Co Cork, the Department took a series of steps which eventually resulted in its closure in 1950. This was the Baltimore Fishing School, unusual insofar as it was at the time the only industrial school not run by a religious order. It was under the management of a priest, who answered to a Board of Governors chaired by the Bishop of Ross.

A new manager took over in 1938. He was Fr John McCarthy, described in 1939 by Dr McCabe as a "young, keen man and anxious to improve conditions". By 1943, she had changed her opinion — the boys were "untidy and dirty looking, school badly kept .... I think the manager became a bit slack and needs a reminder about his responsibilities." She called in to visit the Bishop of Ross, Dr Moynihan, at this time, and told him of her concerns about the school, which then housed 180 boys between nine and sixteen.[12]

In 1944, Dr McCabe reported that she had observed that the bread being fed to the boys was "really mouldy". Fr McCarthy promised improvements. By 1945, she was saying that conditions remained poor, the boys were not being properly fed and were clothed in rags and went barefoot: Fr McCarthy, she said, "had all kinds of excuses". Again she went to the Bishop of Ross, the chairman of the Board of Governors, who told her he would do his best to improve the school.

By 1947, matters had not improved and Dr McCabe recommended the closure of the school, describing it as "easily the worst of all the schools and stands alone for inefficiency, slackness and neglect .... It is a most uncivilised place. There are no trades for the boys except the eternal net making .... It is a cheerless spot and I really sympathise with any child placed in this school." In a later report, she said "it is only by the greatest effort that I can get the boys any way fed .... I do not see any prospect for improvement. It has to be seen to be believed. Conditions are primitive and I am really sorry for any boy placed in such an institution."[13]

However, the following year, Fr McCarthy arrived to meet the Minister for Education in Dublin, demanding, incredibly, that more boys be sent to his school. He was armed with a letter of introduction from the Bishop of Ross, supporting his demand. The Bishop indicated to the Minister that "I shall regard as a favour conferred on me personally anything you can do for Fr McCarthy".

By this stage the Department had already decided to close Baltimore. Its responsibilities concerned only the boys who had been committed there by the courts, and the files contain much correspondence concerning the transfer of this group to other industrial schools. There are no references to the very large number placed there by the local authorities, the 'forgotten children' in care under the Poor Law system. Their fate remains a mystery.

This was to mark the end of this concerted period of Departmental activity with regard to the industrial schools. At no time since was it to become even remotely as concerned with the conditions experienced by the children in the institutions. Most of its activity had declined in 1945, when Ó Muircheartaigh ceased to be the inspector for the schools. The files do not indicate the reason for his removal or transfer from this position.

Close to the end of his tenure, Ó Muircheartaigh reported that:

> Dr McCabe and myself have conducted a strenuous campaign against this semi-starvation. On her inspections, she has attacked it in every school in which she found it and indicated the improvements to be made in the diet etc. I followed up the reports in all such cases with official letters, generally in strong terms. We have before us the task of uprooting the old idea that industrial schools children are a class apart and have not the same human needs and rights as other children and that they should be thankful for anything they get because it comes to them through Charity. There may have been something to this idea in the last century, but the present position is that from a material point of view running an industrial school on an aggregate grant of about 18/3 per head per week is a business proposition and the community should get value for its money. If the present deplorable conditions are to be abolished we must deal firmly with the more flagrant cases.[14]

Although Dr McCabe continued on in her role as Medical Inspector of the schools until the early 1960s, she appears to have played a more subdued role from 1945 onwards. Their work between 1939 and 1945 had resulted, for the first time since Independence, in an unprecedented spell of criticism of the system and of the deplorable conditions experienced by many of the children detained in these schools.

During the 1950s and 1960s, it is clear from the testimony of the survivors of the schools that conditions remained poor, with consistent accounts of hunger. However, the Department was no longer interested. Its response to a number of complaints was dismissive.

Litany of Complaints

In 1949, General Mulcahy, the Fine Gael Minister for Education, received a letter from Deputy Kennifick, a member of the Cork City Executive of Fine Gael. Kennifick said that their executive had received numerous complaints regarding the conditions in the Greenmount Industrial School managed by the Presentation Brothers. He claimed that for breakfast, the boys received only "a cup of black coffee and a couple of slices of dry bread" and that dinner consisted sometimes only of "potatoes and lemonade". In addition to inadequacy of the diet, he went on to say that a number of complaints had been made "regarding the verminous state of the children's clothes".

He concluded that there was little point in making official representations to the Brothers and "the only way to get to the root of all these complaints is to have some of the health and education authorities to visit the place without warning". However, when the Department investigated, having given prior notice of their arrival, they reported that there was no basis for the allegations.[15]

In 1959, Stephen Barrett, TD wrote to Jack Lynch, the Minister for Education, regarding complaints he had received about the conditions in the Upton Industrial School in Cork. In particular, Barrett said that he had obtained information that the children were underfed. Turlough McDevitt, the then Inspector, visited the school and concluded that the children were all healthy and well fed.[16]

Six years later, further complaints were received by the Department regarding Upton. In 1965, Senator Gus Healy, Lord Mayor of Cork, wrote to the Minister for Education saying that he had visited Upton on the 26th of January and that what he saw there "came as quite a shock". He claimed that the "boys were eating from battered tin plates and drinking tea from tin cups" and that he understood "that knives and forks are not used". He said that he had a good knowledge of conditions in children's homes in England and that the conditions in Upton would not be tolerated in any English district. He concluded his letter by claiming that the conditions he witnessed in Upton would not "be tolerated in a workhouse in bygone days". On receipt of this letter, McDevitt visited Upton and, following by this stage a well-established pattern of denial, rejected the complaints and stated that things had "improved immensely".[17]

In 1962, the Inter-Departmental Committee on Crime Prevention and Treatment of Offenders, under the chairmanship of Peter Berry, Secretary of the Department of Justice, discussed a number of complaints about the conditions in the schools.

At a meeting of the Committee on Tuesday 29th January 1963, Peter Berry mentioned a letter which had recently been received by the Minister for Justice. This was from the father of a boy in the Clonmel Industrial School, saying that when he and the boy's mother had visited their son in the school they found the conditions there were cold and miserable and his wife had been occasioned great distress. Inspector of Industrial Schools McDevitt told the Committee that the manager of the Clonmel institution (a Rosminian) was an old man who was really unsuitable for the position but that fortunately he would be retiring from the post in about eighteen months' time. The chairman suggested that perhaps something should be done in the interim if Education were satisfied that he was an unsuitable manager. It does not appear that any action was taken.[18]

This Committee also received serious complaints regarding the Artane Industrial School in 1962 from the school's chaplain, Fr Moore. However, Department of Education officials dismissed his complaints as exaggerated.[19] There is an extraordinary account from some of the survivors of Artane from around this time of a visit to the school by Dr Anna McCabe. The boys had been given chops for their dinner, a most unusual occurrence. When she entered the dining hall, they stood up and threw the bones of the chops at her. The former inmates describe this as their only way of attempting to protest at what they perceived as the sham of outside inspections.

The enormous divergence between the Department of Education's views and the reality on the ground in the schools can be seen throughout this period from the circulars which they were sending to the schools. These laid out the food which the children should be receiving:

> Each child should get as a minimum one pint of milk daily, the full ration of butter and sugar, four to six ounces of meat at each meal at which meat is served. It is desirable that the children's breakfast include an egg sausage rasher tomato and other suitable relish and that the dinner should be a substantial meal consisting of soup where practicable. Meat vegetables including potatoes to be followed by a dessert such as pudding, jelly, stewed or raw fruit, cereal etc. It would also contribute considerably to the health, happiness and good training of the children if higher standards in the table appointments and the preparation and serving of meals were aimed at generally.[20]

It is also abundantly clear that children were, by and large, dressed in ill-fitting, institutional style clothing. The absence of shoes for the children was noted regularly by Dr McCabe and she conducted a drive to ensure the children were adequately shod and clothed. In a slightly surreal incident, John Cohen who was the Secretary of the Football Association in London, visited Letterfrack on the 7th June 1959. While there he witnessed the boys playing football in their bare feet. He wrote to the Department of Education complaining about this and stated that when he questioned the manager of the school he was told that "the school had not got the money to buy any boots and the Irish authorities showed extreme reluctance to provide the money to purchase boots."[21]

This letter from Cohen caused considerable consternation and Oscar Traynor who was Minister for Justice was involved. Ulick O'Connor wrote an article about it in the *Sunday*

Independent under the banner headline "It Made Me Feel So Ashamed". There was a letter then from a J D Murphy to the Department of Education, explaining that "The day was exceptionally hot and the boys were playing with a light plastic ball. They requested permission to take off their sandals and they were allowed do so. Brother McKinney's remarks were not reported as said." It is somewhat ironic that more attention was paid to this matter of football boots than to almost every single one of the very serious complaints received by the Department of Education about the industrial schools.

It seems clear that from the time of the replacement of Industrial Schools Inspector Ó Muircheartaigh in 1945, the Department was principally concerned with the public image of the schools rather than with the actual conditions for the children trapped within the system.

Their attitude can best be summed up by the reaction to a letter from a former inmate of the Baltimore Fishing School, received in 1953. He had spent ten years at the school, and talked about "starving all the time, roaming the countryside in search of food ... There is somebody or bodies in the nation who are responsible before God for such past occurrence. What I really wanted to make known to you is that all that thing has made a mark on me that can not be effaced." He received no response to this letter. There is a note on the file from the then Inspector of Industrial Schools saying "I am still of the opinion that no useful purpose could be served by answering the letter. Even if we were disposed to reply, the only answer we could give him is that nothing could be done for him."[22]

John, Joe and Frank's Story, Baltimore Fishing School, 1940s

"There were rats everywhere, more rats than boys. Some of them were as big as cats. They probably had more to eat than we did. They'd scurry up and down the dormitory floor — the noise they made, you'd think they were wearing boots. Boys would be waiting for them when they came up out of the holes in the timber, and they'd hit them on the head. The rats really terrified me."

John's number in the Baltimore Fishing School in West Cork was forty-eight. The boys were called by their numbers — so much so, that John says he almost forgot his name.

He was born in 1934, the youngest of five children. The family lived in grinding poverty in Dublin's Cork Street. His father was an alcoholic, usually out of work. When he needed money for drink, he would get jobs as a cattle drover, earning 7 shillings (35p) a week. His family rarely saw any of his earnings.

John's mother received 7 shillings a week in State assistance. On this, and anything she could get from begging, she had to feed and clothe her young family.

By way of comparison, it is interesting to note that at this time, the capitation grant paid by the State for most children over six in an industrial school amounted to 15 shillings per week. (The grant for the under-sixes at that time was 7 shillings and 6 pence per week, and from 1941 that was increased to bring it into line with those over six.)

When John was three, his father died, killed he thinks by his mother who was driven to desperation by his drunken ways. He has a memory of seeing his father lying on the floor, with his mother standing over the body with an iron frying pan in her hand.

The children were immediately split up and sent to various institutions. John ended up in St Philomena's, Stillorgan, an orphanage run by the Daughters of Charity. He remained there for the following eight years, funded by the local authority by way of a capitation fee. He did not see his mother again until many years later.

"I don't blame my mother for handing us over to the State. I think she just couldn't cope any more. I missed her, but I didn't really miss my father. He had never shown us any love. I remember we were all crying when we were taken away, my mother as well. I suppose she must have thought we'd be better off with the nuns.

My first impression of St Philomena's was that it was lovely. It was in a very high-class area of Dublin, and it was so clean and beautiful and shiny. I settled in fairly quickly, but I was soon to learn that it had a cruel side to it.

They had a special punishment for children who wet the bed. I think they really believed we did it on purpose just to defy them. They would hold you up by your hands and feet, naked, and duck you into an ice-cold bath of water four or five times. You'd be blue in the face and gasping for air. It was lay staff who used to do these drownings to us. The nuns never beat me.

We'd be forced out of bed in the middle of the night and made sit on rows of potties for up to an hour. I used to try and stay awake so I wouldn't wet the bed. There'd be children crying in their beds, knowing they were going to get a drowning in the morning in the freezing water. And remember that in this dormitory, we were all under five years old.

If you got into trouble during the day, you were beaten at bed-time. You had to raise your nightshirt in front of the whole dormitory, and you'd get about six strokes of a big cane on your bare backside. Then you'd have to kneel for ages on the cold floor until they told you to get into bed.

In bed you had to display the sign of the cross — all night you had to lie on your back in that position. If you moved, you'd be woken up with a beating, often with one of the staff hitting us with her big pair of scissors."

Joe was also in St Philomena's at the same time, and he too was moved on to Baltimore. He was put into the care of the State at the age of four, when his parents separated. In St Philomena's, he remembers, his number was 36; in Baltimore he was known as Number 37. His experiences are similar to John's.

> "The food in St Philomena's was OK. We used to get enough. I only remember one really bad beating. I was about seven, and I got these blisters on my legs. One of the nuns gave me a terrible hammering for not telling her about them. She beat me with a stick, all over my body, even on my legs with the blisters. My leg got all swollen and I was brought to hospital. I told them in the hospital what had happened about the beating. I don't know if they believed me, but from then that nun never hit me again."

While St Philomena's catered for both boys and girls, the nuns kept them rigidly segregated. At ten or eleven, the boys were sent away to Senior Industrial Schools (for boys from ten to sixteen years old).

Many of the St Philomena's children, including John and Joe, were dispatched to the Baltimore Fishing School in West Cork. There were on average 180 boys there at the time, most of them from junior industrial schools run by nuns. John was delighted to be leaving St Philomena's.

> "We got the train down, and the journey took most of the day. It was getting dark when we arrived [there was a station platform in the Baltimore school grounds], but there was still enough light to make out all these boys dressed in rags, no shoes or socks, being beaten around the place by this old man. He had a big stick and he was hitting them on the head and on the back.
>
> I started to cry. I was completely terrified. The old man was beating the boys to get them out of our way, so we could get into the building. It was like a nightmare."

Joe also remembers this elderly man.

> "He was the night watchman. He was the only adult on duty at night. There were priests around during the day, but

they slept in their own separate house. The watchman would go round at night, rip the bed clothes of some boy, and start walloping him with his stick. There was no reason for this. It would happen to several boys each night, and you never knew when it would be your turn."

The Baltimore Fishing School was the only industrial school in the State to be under the direct diocesan control, in this case the Diocese of Ross. It was staffed by priests from the diocese, and there were usually only two assigned to the school at any one time. The teachers in the school were all lay people, whose salaries were separately paid by the Department of Education.

The other unusual feature of the Baltimore School was the pervasive filth in which the boys lived. While children in other industrial schools were made slaves to keep the premises almost obsessively clean, the Baltimore boys did none of this. They describe conditions of almost unimaginable squalor.

Frank arrived at Baltimore in 1940. He never knew his parents. Until he was seven, he had lived with a foster family in Sandyford, Dublin. He thinks that an inspector decided that he was being neglected in the foster home, and so he was moved to St Kyran's Industrial School, Rathdrum, run by the Sisters of Mercy. He has no bad memories of his time in Rathdrum, recalling that the nuns were kind. However, he does remember that they constantly told the boys that they should never ever talk to a girl.

When he was eleven, he was moved again, this time to Baltimore. He describes his first view of the school as "looking like the end of the world to me". One of his abiding memories is of the head priest sitting in the refectory with a gun, shooting rats. Frank's number was 165.

"The toilets were a total disgrace. They were only cleaned about once every three months when the governors and the bishop would visit. There was stuff [excrement] everywhere, all over the floor. At night you'd slip in it — there were no lights and it was pitch dark. There was no toilet paper.

The boys all had worms of all sorts. We were covered in lice, our clothes would be crawling with bugs. We were constantly itching, we'd call it the 'ire'.

We be given a bath every so often, over 100 boys using the same bath water. They put a type of sulphur in the bath, and Jeyes Fluid. It would burn your skin. We'd all queue up to get into the bath, and you'd see lots of boys black and blue all over their bodies with the beatings. The priest on duty would just sit there, reading his prayer book — he paid no attention to the state of us. I don't know if he even noticed."

John was still wetting the bed when he arrived in Baltimore.

"I remember on the train down that I was nervous wondering if we'd still get beaten and drowned for wetting the bed. I needn't have worried. They didn't care if we wet the bed. You just lay in it for months. The sheets were made of a heavy calico material, like sail cloth. They were filthy and sodden all the time. They'd only be washed about once every three months, when the bishop came to visit.

But what sticks out in my mind above everything else was the hunger. We were starving all the time. Compared to this, St Philomena's seemed like heaven.

We'd get a crust of bread in the mornings and a mug of cocoa. Never any butter. Often your crust would be gone because someone had stolen it. We stole food from each other, from everywhere all the time. Sometimes we'd get a thin gruel, and it would have rat and mice droppings in it. But we'd eat it all the same.

That had to keep you going all day. I don't remember getting any lunch. At 5.30 we'd get our last and only meal — a few potatoes in a watery stew, with a crust of bread. We'd get meat one day a week, delivered from Skibbereen, but often it would be rotten and have to be thrown out. Those weeks, we just did without meat.

We'd scavenge around, looking for food. We'd steal mangles and turnips from fields. We ate grass, berries, barnacles along the sea shore. If we escaped down the town, we'd beg for bits of bread from the boats in the harbour. The Spanish sailors were always very good to us, they'd sometimes even give us bits of fish in a soup.

I remember a visit from a Scottish priest once — he was a singing priest. He was so shocked by the conditions and the state we were in that he went straight out and bought us a feast of food out of his own money. It was the only decent meal that I had there in six years."

Joe also recalls the kindness of the people.

"The locals were good to us. If we asked them for bread they'd give it to us, if they had any. But they were poor as well. I think they knew what was going on, but they didn't dare speak out. The power of the Church, I suppose. That's the only thing I criticise them for, that they didn't report what was going on in the school."

Frank: "We were like snarling dogs, the way we fought among ourselves over food. We used to be called 'the marauding children'. Our clothes were ragged. We never had any shirts, underpants or coats. Just shorts and pullovers. We were also really small for our age.

I think the local people felt sorry for us. One time when a few of us robbed an orchard, the farmer complained to the priest that 'they're only doing this because you don't feed them'. The priest beat us all the more for that."

John: "If you were caught begging, you got a terrible beating. A special stage was set up, in front of the whole school. You were put across this stage, your pants pulled down, your hands held in a vice grip, and the priest gave you about ten lashes with a cane. There were often fifteen or twenty boys lined up for a beating like this.

Sometimes the priest would work himself up into a rage, and shout with every stroke 'You are nothing but bastards and beggars and analogous to pariahs.' For some reason, this has always stuck in my mind."

Frank: "They got so worried about us escaping, that at one stage they had us all lining up for parade every hour. The whistle would blow, and you'd have to run like crazy to line up and be counted. If you were even one minute late, you'd be walloped across the legs with a stick.

The priests and the teachers used to eat at the top table, in front of us. They had lovely food, the best of everything. You'd nearly faint from the smell of it. As soon as they left the table, we'd descend on it, fighting for the scraps.

Our drinking water was in a trough outside the kitchen. It was filthy, full of slime with a scum on top. There was an old tin mug on a string beside it. They only cleaned it out about once every nine months."

John: "When boys died, they were buried in an unmarked plot in Taulagh cemetery. We're convinced there's other boys buried up in one of the fields close by. And during our time, there was a big commotion when they sealed up the well.

As a punishment, boys used to be put into the well, and have to stay there for hours clinging to the ladder on the side so they wouldn't fall down into it. If your hands went numb with the cold, you could fall off and drown. We still don't know why they sealed up that well. All us boys were convinced that someone had died in there, but no one ever explained anything to us.

In school we were beaten all the time. Most of us came out not being able to read or write — you couldn't learn anything with the fear. We used to be beaten everywhere, even on the soles of our feet, because for most of the year we had no shoes or boots.

One teacher had a punishment called 'the aeroplane'. The boy being punished would be held up on the shoulders of two other boys. His pullover was wrapped around his head to stop his cries being heard. His shorts were pulled down and used to tie up his feet. Then this teacher would beat the boy with a big strap often till he bled. We had an absolute terror of 'the aeroplane'. One boy was beaten so badly that he collapsed and was taken away. We never saw him again."

In addition to the pervasive violence, the former inmates of the Baltimore Industrial School also report that some of the boys were sexually abused. They all knew about one teacher who molested boys in the dormitory — "you'd see him with boys under the blankets at night". None of them make any allegations of sexual abuse against any of the priests who ran the school.

At this time, the town of Baltimore itself was a thriving fishing port. The school's ostensible purpose was to educate boys in the arts of boat-building and fishing. When founded in the last century, the school even had its own fishing fleet of up to eight boats. However, by the late 1930s all activity in this area had ceased, and in practice, the boys' training was non-existent. John used to be put in the net loft, as it was called.

"All we ever did was repair some nets. There were big net mending machines in the net loft, but they never worked when we were there. We used to have to patch the nets by hand. And if you didn't do it right, you'd get the belt of a stick. I suppose the school was paid for this work, but we never got anything for it."

On leaving the school at sixteen, Frank, John and Joe each in turn went to work as farm labourers with local farmers. They never received any pay. Frank worked for over four years with no wages in the belief that that was the arrangement made between the farmer and the priests at the school.

In later years, some of the boys began to search for their families, who had never been allowed to visit them in Baltimore. Whenever they had asked about their parents, the priests said they had died.

Joe, however, did find an aunt of his years later, and also discovered the whereabouts of his parents. But he blamed them for abandoning him to his fate, and decided that he didn't want to meet them again.

Frank went searching for his roots in the early 1970s. He found that his parents had not been married, and he managed to track his mother to the Regina Coeli hostel in Dublin for homeless women, run by the Legion of Mary. The staff there refused to give him any further details about her. They just told him that she had taken to the drink. To this day, it is a source of deep sadness to Frank that he has never been able to find anybody belonging to him.

Ten years ago, John eventually found his mother after a long search. An old neighbour from Cork Street, where he had been born, had an address for her in England. When John met her, she was dying of a brain tumour. But he had a precious three weeks with her before she passed away.

All three men still live in the general area of the school in West Cork. The school itself closed in 1950, with the remaining boys being transferred to the industrial school at Upton in Co Cork.

Now, like St Michael's Industrial School in Cappoquin, the building is used as a guest house. It is ironic that the two institutions with probably the worst record for starvation of their young inmates should now be transformed into places of hospitality. But John is determined that the Baltimore boys should not be forgotten.

"I spent years trying to understand why those people were so cruel to us. Why did they hate us so much? I think maybe they got some sort of perverted pleasure out of seeing us suffer. I have lived with the scars all my life. I know it sounds strange, but even to this day I cannot rest easy unless I have a loaf of bread in the house — not necessarily to eat it, but just to know it's there."

Tom & Pat Sheehan's Story, St Joseph's Industrial School, Killarney (Sisters of Mercy); St Joseph's Industrial School, Glin (Christian Brothers), 1945–1955

"We were so hungry we'd eat the dilisk [seaweed] along the strand at Glin. We'd eat haws off the bushes, and leaves on hedges as well, but it was mainly the dilisk. You'd have to sneak it up — if the Brother caught you, you'd get a hiding. It tasted very salty, but it wasn't too bad. It probably saved our lives."

Tom and Pat are brothers, born two years apart. They are first cousins of Frank McCourt, Pulitzer Prize-winning author of *Angela's Ashes*. The Angela of the title — Frank McCourt's mother — was Tom and Pat's aunt, their father's sister.

In 1945, Tom and Pat's parents both died of tuberculosis within eleven months of each other. The two boys, then aged six and eight, were sent initially to the boys' section of St Joseph's Industrial School, Killarney, run by the Sisters of Mercy.

Pat: "When we were in Killarney, we got a big box of chocolates one time from our grandmother, who was also the McCourts' grandmother. Even though we had to be sent away, she still cared about us. I firmly believe that she was the main reason that the McCourt boys didn't end up in Glin Industrial School. Because they could very easily have. But it was Angela, their mother, and the grandmother who kept that family together.

But the grandmother died very shortly after she sent us those chocolates, and for us that was really the end of the family. Our Aunt Aggie visited us the odd time, and we were allowed out during the summers to stay with our Uncle Abe, but we never really had much of a sense of family."

Both Tom and Pat have few complaints about their time in Killarney. The food was adequate and the nun in charge was kind to them. They remember, however, that some of the lay women working there used to beat them.

For many years, the Killarney Industrial School was unique in that it accepted both boys and girls. The boys section was small, catering for only about forty, all under the age of ten. There were over 200 girls, who were kept rigidly segregated from the boys.

When Tom and Pat reached the age of ten, they were each in turn transferred to St Joseph's Industrial School in Glin, run by the Christian Brothers. They were to find conditions in Glin dramatically different. It was big, with about 220 boys, ranging in age from about six to sixteen. What both brothers talk about most is the hunger.

Tom: "We were just always starving. For breakfast, we got two slices of bread and dripping. Your dinner would be some kind of watery stew, hardly no meat, and a few potatoes if you were lucky. Supper, you got Indian meal, horrible lumpy yellow stuff. Around 1948, they phased out the Indian meal, and gave us gruel instead. It was a bit better, but not much.

I used to climb over a little wall and go to the ash pit, where they burned the rubbish. I'd root around in there and often find bits of vegetables that I could eat."

Pat: "The only time you ever saw an apple was when you robbed an orchard. At night you couldn't sleep because your guts would be rolling about so badly from the hunger.

In the winter, you'd be freezing. We never had coats or jackets. Just short pants, shirt and jumper. They'd leave us out in the yard until eight o'clock at night, then we'd have to go in and have a wash before bed. The water was always freezing — we never had hot water for anything. So you'd be in bed, shivering, and it could take you till half-ten or eleven o'clock before you could get a bit warm. I'd be down under the blanket squeezing my feet to try and warm them up. And this was night after night, all winter long.

If you ever complained about anything, you'd be hammered. So you just never opened your mouth. The one thing that saved my life was my brother Tom, when he was working on the farm, managed to slip me a turnip from time to time. I'd hide it, and wait until everything was quiet at night in the dormitory. Then I'd eat the turnip under the blankets. To my ears the sound of my teeth crunching the turnip was deafening. I was terrified eating them, but I was very, very grateful for those turnips."

Tom: "When I was fourteen they put me working on the farm. That was a bit better, because you could steal the animals' food. It was my job to look after the pigs, all sixty or seventy of them. I'd have to clean out the sties, and I'd prepare their food as well — loads of boiled potatoes. But I made sure that I was Number One Pig, I fed myself first. The truth is that the pigs were better fed than the boys.

The Brothers had a great big farm there. Some of the stuff, the potatoes and a few vegetables, would be used to feed the boys. But most of it was sold. The pigs would be sent into Mathesons for butchering, and the cattle were sold at the fair. They had about twenty cows, and the milk would be sent to the creamery. So it was like a commercial farm. The boys all worked on it for free, so I suppose they made a bit of money out of it.

The also kept hens, about twenty of them. The eggs were strictly for the Brothers — they'd have one in the mornings or maybe a fried egg with their tea. We only ever saw an egg at Easter. You'd get one as a treat on Easter Sunday and that was your egg for the year.

The egg store was a kind of hut, and it was where boys would sometimes be taken for beatings from the Brothers."

Neither Pat nor Tom has any memory of anyone coming from outside to inspect the school.

Tom: "We always knew the Brothers could do what they liked. There was no one to stop them. They could kill you, and no one would know.

I remember one Brother punched a boy in the refectory, in front of everyone, and knocked him out cold. He accused him of smoking and just knocked him flat.

I got a kicking one night, I was about ten. This Brother pulled me out of my bed and punched and kicked me all over the place. The only explanation was that he thought I was playing with myself. But he never really said why.

We never saw any sexual abuse. But there was definitely sadism there. Maybe they got pleasure from that."

Both Tom and Pat say that they have survived the experience of Glin. Neither feels that it damaged them unduly. Tom is married and lives in Limerick. Pat emigrated for many years, and has now also returned to Limerick.

Seven

The Child Labourers

There are two overwhelmingly consistent aspects of the testimony emerging from the experience of industrial schools. The first relates to the enormous workload of the young inmates in maintaining the buildings, grounds and farms of what were generally very extensive complexes. The second is the almost universal lack of proper education provided for the children in these schools. These two factors were of course related, and there are several references in the Department of Education's files to a certain anxiety that the children's work might possibly be interfering with their education.

There was from the very earliest stages a strong emphasis within the schools on their industrial nature. The 1868 Rules and Regulations were to establish the pattern which remained essentially unchanged for the following one hundred years. Under the heading "A Spirit of Industry to be Cherished", these rules stated that the children should be "constantly employed, and that they are taught to consider labour as a duty, to take kindly to it, to persevere in it, and to feel a pride in their work".

Industrial education was to take up six hours out of each child's day, as opposed to only three hours for what was called scholastic education, which was defined as reading, writing and arithmetic. The industrial education for boys consisted of farm and garden work, and whatever handicrafts could be organised. Girls were trained in "needlework, machine work, washing, ironing, cooking and housework".

The new Rules and Regulations issued by the Department of Education in 1933 changed very little. The exhortation to cherish a spirit of industry was removed, and the balance between industrial and literary education was shifted slightly for those children under the age of fourteen — they had four-and-a-half hours in ordinary school as opposed to three-and-a-half hours of industrial training. Given the fact that they were also supposed to have at least three hours of recreation each day, and that they all attended Mass on a daily basis, it is hard to see when they had time to eat their meals. Children between fourteen and sixteen only had to be in school for three hours a day, combined with six hours of industrial training.

It can be seen from this that the daily lives of children were in fact highly regulated by the State. However, what happened in reality was generally very different. The following timetable from Artane Industrial School during the 1940s shows how far the schools had strayed from the rules:

Timetable for weekday:
6.30: rising
7.15: Mass
8.00: breakfast
8.30: polishing boots inspecting of clothes, etc
8.50: dormitories and washing delf, etc
9.00: boys over 14 years go to trades
9.40: boys between 7 and 14 go to morning school until 11.40
11.40: recreation
12.00: trades, bands, cleaning of various departments
12.30: boys who have no set occupations go to school
2.00: dinner
2.30: recreation
3.00: trades, drill and recreation
5.00: boys between 7 and 14 go to school until 7.15
Boys between 14 and 15 and a half go to school until 7.15
Farms boys from 5.30 to 7.15
Trades boys from 6.00 to 7.15
7.15: supper
8.00: all in bed.

This showed that the rules were being flagrantly breached in several areas — specific recreation was allowed for only twenty minutes a day (the rules specified a minimum of three hours for the under-fourteens), and many of the fourteen to sixteen-year-olds were only receiving just over one hour of ordinary schooling a day (the rules stipulated not less than three hours). This timetable was submitted in accordance with the regulations to the Department of Education. There is no record that its officials even noticed the discrepancies, let alone sought to remedy them. Artane was, after all, the showpiece of the system, an extraordinary operation which prided itself on being totally self-sufficient. Its motto, proudly emblazoned on its letterhead, was "Success is the Reward for the Perseverance in Industry".

Artane's vast army of 800 boys worked the school's 290-acre farm of prime land, tended its herd of up to forty cows and assortment of other farm animals. It had facilities for example for up to one hundred pigs, and butchered its own meat on the premises. Well into the 1960s, no labour-saving machinery had been purchased for the farm — with so much free child labour, the Brothers presumably felt there was no need. Many boys worked in the school's trade workshops, which catered for all of the institution's requirements, making and repairing clothes, boots, bedding, furniture and so forth. The school also made money through the sale of both farm produce and goods made in the workshops by the boys.

There was also, of course, the famous Artane Boys Band. It was not the only school to have a band — several of the other senior boys industrial schools organised a band and taught selected boys to play an instrument. This was more out of a belief that learning to play music in a group instilled disciplined behaviour into the children than for any recreational value it may have had.[1]

The Artane Boys Band was by far the most successful of these. It was run as a commercial operation, with the Band engaged and paid to play a large number of venues each year throughout the country, culminating with its performances before major GAA matches in Croke Park. The Band was regarded by Artane boys as the best place to be. Because they appeared so often in public, punishments for this privileged group were not so severe, as they could not be visibly marked or damaged. They wore bright, shiny uniforms, and they led a considerably more exciting life than those stuck on the farm or in the workshops. Some boys did manage to make successful careers in music based on their musical training in the school.

But for those children in Artane not either lucky or musical enough to be in the band, the daily grind of labour was relentless. In 1962, Department of Education files show that almost 100 boys were employed full-time either on the farm or in the kitchens, laundry and workshops. This included five boys working in the Brothers' kitchen. This was at a time when the entire population of the Artane school had dropped to around 400 boys. That one quarter of this total — boys between the ages of seven and sixteen — were engaged in full time labour in the 1960s is remarkable.[2]

Artane did employ and pay the wages of adult instructors in the various workshops, and a number of men were also hired to work on the farm. The Brothers frequently used the cost of these employees to argue for increased State funding. Whenever they were asked by the State for a breakdown of their expenditure and income, they always maintained that any profits accruing from the farm were none of the State's business. Despite their extensive use of free child labour on the part of those placed in Artane by the State, the Brothers consistently maintained that their vast farm was a private venture using their own private property.[3]

All of the child labour in industrial schools operated under the guise of training. However, as the Cussen Report pointed out as early as 1936, many of the so-called training areas were in fact more geared towards the needs of the school than for any employment the children might subsequently be able to gain. In all the boys' schools, carpentry, boot-making and tailoring featured prominently — these supplied the major needs of the schools themselves. Farm work provided both food for the inmates and the religious, and also supplemented the income through sales for the institutions. However, despite the Cussen Report's recommendations that training be more closely tailored to good employment opportunities, the schools effected very little change, and continued to use the children's labour for their own needs until the system was disbanded in the early 1970s.[4]

Even for those trades in which the boys were trained, very few ended up gaining employment in those areas. The trade union movement did not recognise industrial school training for the purposes of apprenticeships. Many of the unions operated as closed shops, and perceived industrial school training as a threat to the standard mode of gaining entry to the particular trades concerned. Consequently, for many boys their years of toil in the schools proved of little value to them in adult life.

In terms of the girls, their workload consisted mainly of domestic labour around the schools. This also masqueraded as training, since many of them were destined for a life of domestic service, working as maids for well-off families around the country. The schools rarely employed any outside cleaning staff, and all of this work was undertaken by the industrial school children.

As many of the girls were often housed in large complexes, which could include a primary school, a private secondary school and a convent for the nuns, the amount of work involved in cleaning was very considerable. Generally, the nuns did none of their own cleaning. It was the children who scrubbed the convent areas and the nuns' rooms, in addition to all the other buildings.

In one case, in St Joseph's Industrial School in Cavan during the 1960s, one of the tiny number of girls given the privilege of attending secondary school was forced, at the end of her classes, to clean the entire secondary school building from top to bottom, including washing out the toilets. In another, St Augustine's Industrial School in Templemore, the inmates essentially became the servants of the girls attending the up-market boarding school which the nuns had opened on their complex in the town. A woman who grew up in the industrial school in Birr, Co Offaly, run by the Sisters of Mercy, spent so much of her childhood peeling potatoes for over a hundred people each day that she talks about how it has left her all her life with an abiding hatred of potatoes.

Boys in St Joseph's Ferryhouse, Clonmel, run by the Rosminians, remember that in the early 1950s the priests and brothers decided they wanted a new grotto to the Blessed

Virgin in the grounds. In addition to their normal work on the farm, boys of nine and ten were sent out to the fields to dig rocks out of the earth with their bare hands and then drag them the long distance to the grotto site. One man vividly recalls all the blood, sweat and tears of the children that went into the building of this shrine, which still stands in the grounds of what even to this day remains open as an industrial school.

The nuns, in particular, were highly exacting in their standards – girls and young boys had to endlessly wash, wax and polish all woodwork in the institutions including floors until, as they put it, you could see yourself in them. Little ones as young as seven years of age were involved in this daily grind, with the slightest inadequacy being brutally punished. One of the most vivid images described by former inmates is that of rows of girls, on their hands and knees polishing long corridors or washing yard areas, with a nun walking behind them carrying a stick or strap to make sure they all moved in unison and missed nothing.

Many of the institutions kept their lawns manicured in this way – a long line of children, bent over, moving slowly across the grass plucking each blade by hand. Survivors of Artane and Goldenbridge Industrial Schools in particular have vivid memories of this practice. Hay cutting and stacking was done by the children, their feet often cut and bleeding from having to walk on the hard stalks without shoes. In schools which were close to bogs, the inmates spent long days in the back-breaking work of cutting turf. In the summer they were given little to drink, some having to take the water from bog holes, and they had nothing to protect them from the sun. In the winter, they froze out in the fields or the bogs – their clothes were often threadbare, and they had no coats or gloves.

During the holidays, the children were employed in money-making schemes for the schools. In Goldenbridge and several other places they spent hours making rosary beads for sale, churning out hundreds of sets each week. In Ballaghaderreen the girls made St Patrick's Day paraphernalia for export to the USA. In Templemore they produced the cords for scapulars. In Athlone, they spent hour after hour putting stuffing into mattresses.

Many of the industrial schools were in fact little more than forced labour camps for children. Working the children so hard saved the considerable expense of having to hire outside help — many survivors speak of their work in the schools' laundries as having been particularly heavy in this regard. Up till the 1960s, many of the schools had no machines, and the laundry was washed by hand. In an institution catering for up to a hundred or more individuals, this was hard physical labour for the children involved.

Although their detention usually lasted until they were sixteen, their schooling generally ended when they were about thirteen or fourteen, and they were put to work full-time in the institution. Some survivors even remember being taken out of classes as young as ten years old to wash, cook and clean for the nuns and the other children. Another major job was caring for the babies, with some institutions having upwards of forty or fifty of these at any one time. The girls who worked in these nurseries were expected to get up during the night to feed and tend to the infants, many of whom were only a few months old. Needless to say, this had a disastrous effect on their school work.

In general terms, the schools placed no great emphasis on mainstream education. While the children were expected to attend primary school classes — indeed obliged to, by law — it seems clear that this was often regarded as being of secondary importance when compared to the labouring tasks assigned to them. While it is impossible to arrive at any exact figure, it is clear that the numbers of children who emerged unable to read or write from these schools is significantly large. Many of them remember school as a time of terror, where they were beaten and humiliated for the slightest mistake. In schools where they mixed with local children from the community outside, the 'house' children were often put at the back of the classroom and singled out for particularly harsh treatment. It is not surprising that so many of them were unable through fear and neglect to learn to read and write.

That the educational standards in industrial schools were so low, however, is remarkable when viewed in the context that both of the religious orders who dominated the industrial schools system — the Christian Brothers and the Sisters of Mercy — prided themselves for their achievements in educating the children of the nation.

However, it would appear that for a particular class of children, these orders did not regard education or even literacy as being particularly important. Ultimately the thrust of the education in industrial schools was to prepare these children to know their place in life. For boys, this meant labouring jobs in building or on farms. Girls usually ended up in domestic service. Without even the most basic education, most remained trapped in a cycle of poverty all their lives. They were never prepared by the religious for anything other than a life of menial labour and servitude. In this way, the Catholic Church maintained the rigid class distinctions within society, with industrial schools children firmly kept at the bottom of the pile.

The Christian Brothers and the Sisters of Mercy between them also ran most of the secondary schools in the country. Until 1967, when free secondary education was made available to all, these schools were obviously fee-paying. However, the orders had a number of scholarship schemes for needy children. These were generally not available to industrial schools children.

In 1951, the Department of Education became briefly concerned with the education of children in industrial schools. A circular was sent to each school, asking for information on the numbers allowed to further their education beyond primary school. It referred to the desirability of such education for "clever children", and hoped that more schools would afford this opportunity to their children. The Department was prepared to extend the period of the capitation fee support for such children until the age of eighteen. However, they would have to remain detained in the schools until that point.[5]

The replies received are instructive. In Artane, with its 800 boys, the Head Christian Brother said that he could find only one boy suitable for secondary education, and was hoping to make the appropriate arrangements in the near future. The nun in charge of St Martha's Industrial School in Monaghan said that "with regard to secondary school education, we have in the past found the experiment unpractical". It should be remembered that these were the Sisters of St Louis, who ran a number of up-market schools for the daughters of the middle classes, including one on the very same complex as the industrial school in Monaghan.

The manager of St Anne's Industrial School for girls in Booterstown, Dublin, said that "I wish to state that up to this, there has been very little thought given to that subject." This nun, a member of the Sisters of Mercy, went on to say that her girls were very well-educated in all forms of domestic work, and continued, "As the difficulty of finding good maids is so acute at the moment ... I think it is well to cater for this demand." Once again, the order ran a secondary school on the premises, some of whose pupils have only the vaguest memory of the industrial school children, who were kept rigidly apart.

The nun in charge of the Cobh Industrial School said that none of her girls were currently attending secondary school, but that she had offered the opportunity that year to two girls: "They declined the offer as they are near the end of their detention period."

As a result of the Department's 1951 circular, it became fully aware of just how dismal the figures for those in secondary education were: only one boys' industrial school, St Joseph's in Tralee, and twelve girls' industrial schools allowed a tiny number of their inmates the privilege of a full education. The Inspector of Industrial Schools added a note to this summary of results:

> In some schools I have noticed reluctance on the part of management and school staff to send on illegitimate children for a secondary school course and some managers and members of the teaching staffs of those schools were surprised when informed by me that illegitimacy was not a barrier to entry to the civil service or the teaching profession.

However, the Department made no serious effort to improve matters. Correspondence in 1952 concerned a complaint received by the Department that "talented boys" in Glin Industrial School were not able to avail of any education beyond the age of twelve. Department officials did not even deny this. The Inspector wrote: "All these problems ... would be solved if the Directors of these institutions followed a programme of 50% economic work for the institutions and 50% formal education. I think we should aim at that." There is no reference in the files to any attempt made by the Department to put this into practice.

However, over ten years later, the Department's attention had been drawn to the deplorable state of education in the Letterfrack Industrial School, run by the Christian Brothers. This catered for boys from as young as five or six up to sixteen. Commenting on the state of the place, a Department official reported that (underlining in original): "It is possible that the Christian Brothers have not made the best possible staff available in Letterfrack. Presumably, many Brothers do not care to work in Letterfrack." This official went on to describe the conditions that had pertained in the school for many years:

> Among them were (1) a most unsuitable school building; (2) defective lighting; (3) unsuitable furniture; (4) inadequate teaching appliances; (5) some weaknesses in teaching power; (6) difficulties in formulating suitable timetable arrangements owing to a clash with institutional domestic requirements; (7) pupils, particularly senior pupils, having to undertake tiring physical work in the afternoons due to shortage of paid labour in the institution; (8) depressing surroundings, classrooms were occupied by the pupils in the evenings .... improvements under the heads 1 to 8 in the preceding paragraphs are, if not essential under all heads, desirable.[6]

The appalling neglect of the education of children in Letterfrack had a cruel irony to it — many of its inmates were detained there for non-attendance at school, and the purpose of their committal was to ensure that they received an education.

The Letterfrack institution appeared to have been run almost as a business. Its letterhead listed the services it had on sale. "Orders Received in Tailoring, Bootmaking, Carpentry, Bakery, Cartmaking, Smithwork. Also Wire Mattress, Hosiery, Hearth Rugs, Motors Repaired, Petrol & Oils Supplied." While it employed some local staff, most of this extraordinary list of goods and services were produced as a result of the boys' labour.

When the Letterfrack school finally closed in 1974, the Secretary of the Department of Education sent a glowing letter of profuse thanks to the Provincial Leader of the Christian Brothers. The Department, he said, was deeply appreciative of the great care given by generations of Brothers to the boys of Letterfrack.

As recently as 1968, a man wrote to the Department of Education expressing concern at the apparent lack of secondary schooling for the children of the industrial school in his own town. He had come in to contact with some of these children when he had taken two into stay with his family as a holiday for a few weeks during the summer. He wrote in an almost apologetic manner that while he didn't in any way want to detract from the great work undertaken by the nuns, he was concerned at the lack of educational opportunities provided for these girls to prepare them for adult life. The relevant nun wrote to the Department, saying that these particular girls were only fit for domestic work. He himself eventually received an extraordinary response from the Department of Education. It said that it was important in this context that he understand that "the average level of intelligence of the children in industrial schools is understandably considerably below that of the average pertaining outside".

Turned Loose

For many of the children, release from industrial school at the age of sixteen was not to mean an end to their abuse. Having lived for so many of their formative years cloistered away in such a highly unnatural environment, they were disastrously unprepared for life outside the institution. They had no concept of their rights, or that they even had any. Many were ignorant of the most basic necessities of life, such as dealing with money, public transport or even feeding themselves. As they had not previously had any contact whatsoever with the opposite sex, this was an area completely new to them, which often led to tragic results. Most knew nothing of the facts of life. They were in short institutionalised. The only preparation some received for life outside the walls was a short lesson in how to use a knife and fork, and in the case of girls occasionally a few oblique and highly confusing instructions from the nuns that they were to stay away from men.

The vast majority of girls were placed by the nuns in domestic service jobs. Families looking for servants knew to contact the local convent, and a girl would be sent to them. If there was not a suitable girl from the local institution, one would be sent for from another convent. Effectively, the nuns operated probably one of the largest placement agencies for domestic servants in the country.

Many of the girls experienced lives of virtual slavery with these families. They speak of working non-stop often from six in the morning until midnight. While in most cases they lived in with the families, many were not allowed to join them for meals, having to eat alone in the kitchen.

During the 1940s, 1950s and even into the early 1960s, girls working with these families were paid only about £1 a week, in addition to their board and lodging. Some received no payment at all, and were afraid to object as the threat of being sent back to the nuns was ever present. Thousands of these girls saved as much as they could for the fare to England, and escaped. Many found that they were considerably better treated and paid in Britain for similar work.

Sadly, a number of the girls from industrial schools became pregnant outside of marriage while still in their late teens or early twenties. With a profound ignorance of the facts of life, many speak of simply not understanding how it was that they had become pregnant. They knew nothing of sex, and often mistook physical contact with another person for the kindness and affection they had so lacked as children. They were almost universally abandoned by the fathers of their children, and they often ended up back with the nuns, either in Mother and Baby homes or in Magdalen laundries. Many of their children completed the cycle by being placed in industrial schools.

The Magdalen laundries had always held a terror for many of the girls from industrial schools. They were often threatened with being sent there as children, and in some cases they even shared the same complex with a Magdalen laundry. There were some children whose mothers lived and worked in the adjacent laundry, but the nuns kept them rigidly apart, in the extraordinary belief that such a mother would be a bad influence on her child. Tragically, while the mothers often knew that their children were nearby, the children themselves were usually kept in ignorance of this.

Brigid, who grew up in the Good Shepherd industrial school in Limerick, told her story to the Channel 4 documentary on Magdalen laundries in Ireland — *Sex in a Cold Climate*. She remembered that the children were warned on fear of the severest punishment never to speak to or even look at any of the women working in the laundry part of the complex. The nuns used to tell them that these women were sinners and devils.

Brigid was caught speaking to one of the "Magdalens" when she was only about eleven. The woman had asked her for news of her daughter, who was in the industrial school in the next building with Brigid. The mother had not seen her child since she was a baby. Brigid had offered to bring this girl up on top of a low roof so that her mother could see what she looked like now. But before she could organise this, a nun saw her speaking to the "Magdalen", and dragged her away by the ear. Brigid's head was roughly shaved by this nun, who then beat her savagely with a piece of rubber piping. Brigid said that she could barely recognise her own face, she was so badly marked, "and this was just for talking to a 'Magdalen'".

The threat to lock up industrial school girls in these laundries was carried through in a number of cases. The laundries were commercial operations run by the nuns, and needed labour. They constituted a useful dumping ground for those children whose continued defiance of the nuns labelled them as "uncontrollable". However, that wasn't the only reason a girl could be doomed to a life of effective slavery in a laundry. Reports from Goldenbridge in Dublin and from the industrial school in Ennis (both run by the Sisters of Mercy) say that some girls were consigned to laundries for the only reason that they were regarded as pretty, and consequently "at risk". There was also a significant number of girls who on leaving an industrial school at sixteen were sent by the nuns directly to work in a Magdalen laundry. It seems clear that these girls were used as a ready source of free labour for these laundry businesses — the nuns did not pay most of the women working there.

This practice continued until the late 1960s, when the Kennedy Report was to discover that there were then about seventy girls between the ages of thirteen and nineteen confined within Magdalen laundries. The Report described it as "a haphazard system, its legal validity is doubtful and the girls admitted in this irregular way and not being aware of their rights, may remain for long periods and become, in the process, unfit for re-emergence into society. In the past, many girls have been taken into these convents and remained there all their lives."[7]

The boys of the industrial schools were not subjected to this type of continuing incarceration on leaving. They also were sent out grossly unprepared into the world once they had reached their 16th birthday, and the Government grant ran out. A very large proportion of them entered employment as farm labourers — jobs often arranged by the Brothers, who organised in this area a placement service similar to the nuns' agency for domestic servants.

Here also, the boys were aware of the constant threat that they would be sent back to the industrial school if they gave cause for complaint to their employers. In fact, it was an empty threat — no industrial school would have taken them back as they had no financial assistance to take children above the age of sixteen (unless to further their education).

The boys, equally unaware of their rights as the girls, were in many cases disgracefully treated by their employers. These were generally small to medium-sized farming families, who grossly exploited the youngsters from industrial schools. Many of the victims speak of being under-fed, having to sleep in barns, and worked like slaves from dawn until dusk. Often they were paid substantially under the minimum amount set out by law. In some cases they received no pay at all. These boys had no idea of their rights. Very often, their life working on farms was not dissimilar to that in the industrial school. Some who worked for no pay say that at the time they thought that they were not being paid because of an arrangement which existed between the industrial school and the farmer.

One case of gross exploitation was brought to the attention of the Department of Education in 1947 by the Leader of the Labour Party, William Norton TD, in the Dail. He told the House about a boy from an industrial school hired by a Co Leitrim farmer who was paying him only five shillings a week. The child had to sleep in a barn, and eventually contracted pneumonia, spending three years in hospital. The Joint Committee of Women's Societies and Social Workers was also very concerned about this issue, and wrote to the Department to ask what arrangements it had for inspecting the conditions of employment for boys and girls from industrial schools.[8]

The Department, of course, had no such arrangements. All it had done was to send a circular to the schools in 1944, drawing their attention to the minimum rates of pay the boys should receive as farm labourers. This circular pointed out that it was an offence for anyone to under-pay the boys working on farms. It asked the schools to ensure that the children were being adequately paid. However, many of the boys report that under-paying or no pay at all remained commonplace until the 1960s.

It is somewhat disturbing that so many survivors of industrial schools report such an extent of exploitation by their employers. These employers were in most cases ordinary middle-class families, farmers, merchants, shopkeepers and professionals. There were of course some exceptions, families in which the industrial school boys and girls were kindly treated, rather than forcibly being made to feel inferior. Nonetheless, the treatment of these children by middle-class Ireland for much of this century is something in which that class can take no pride.

Crime

The vast majority of children from industrial and reformatory schools went on to live ordinary, law-abiding lives, doing their best to overcome the disadvantages of their upbringing. However, a small minority were to become involved in crime, and to end up in and out of prison. The notorious Dunne family in Dublin, who effectively controlled the first major importation of heroin onto the streets of Dublin in the early 1980s, were one of the most famous examples of this. No fewer than eight of the boys of their very large family had spent several years in industrial schools as children. One of the brothers, Hubert Dunne, had died in St Patrick's Upton at the age of twelve, drowned while swimming. During the 1970s and 1980s, a significant percentage of the country's prison population was made up of those from industrial schools, although no figures on this have ever been compiled. However, it must be emphasised that this was always a tiny proportion of the vast numbers of children who had grown up in that system.

Some of the children also ended up homeless, living on the streets. Some others became prostitutes, which was a source of great concern to the Legion of Mary in the 1950s. Its founder Frank Duff wrote in 1950 to the Department of Health, showing a rare understanding of the root of the problem: "one out of three of the street girls dealt with in our hostel, No. 76 Harcourt St, are ex-industrial school girls …. A formidable proportion of the men resident in the Morning Star are of that same class, the ex-industrial school child. Therefore the action of any society which deliberately breaks up the union of child and mother is one to be seriously viewed and if at all possible checked."[9]

Betty's Story, Pembroke Alms House Industrial School, Tralee (Sisters of Mercy), 1951–1964

"For years I felt a hatred of Ireland and of everything Irish. It's only in the past five years or so, since I went back on a few visits, that I realise that there are some nice people in Ireland."

Betty was two years and three months old when she was the subject of a court case. It was 1951, and she was the child of a single mother from Listowel. The judge ordered Betty to be detained at the Pembroke Alms House Industrial School (known locally as the Balloonagh orphanage, or Nazareth House) in Tralee, run by the Sisters of Mercy.

Her entry in that school's register makes for interesting reading. Under the heading "With what Charged", it states "Destitute and illegitimate not being an orphan: her mother unable to support her".

Betty was ordered by the court to be detained at the Tralee school until she was sixteen years old. But in a mysterious sequence of events, for which she is still seeking an explanation, she ended up being moved from one convent to another. "I didn't escape from the nuns until I was nearly twenty, and I was lucky to get out then," she says now from her home in England, where she has lived for almost thirty years.

The industrial school for girls in Tralee had on average fifty children detained during the 1950s and 1960s. Located on the edge of the town, it was directly across the road from St Joseph's Industrial School, otherwise known as the Monastery, and run by the Christian Brothers.

Betty remembers her time in Tralee with horror. Her number was 985.

"Things were so bad there that I set fire to myself at one stage. One particular nun used a strap, and she whipped me almost every day of my life. You'd be screaming for mercy, but it didn't make a bit of difference. I was locked in cupboards regularly. Every day she'd say to me: 'You're an imbecile, you're a nobody'.

There was one time I was sick, and I vomited. I cleaned it up myself, and then I went and hid. I suppose I was about eleven. I was feeling really ill, but I was too scared to tell anyone. So I climbed into a small narrow locker and pulled a coat over myself and fell asleep.

That evening, the nun found me. She was furious and she dragged me out and made me go out to the shed and start stacking a huge load of turf. I was still sick, and must have fallen asleep again. I was woken up by her strap across my back. She whipped me and whipped me with that leather strap.

That evening going to bed, I felt all sticky. It was the blood from the beating earlier. A lay woman in charge of the dormitory found me that night and took me out of bed to wash the blood off my back and bathe the cuts made by the strap.

My grandfather used to visit me the odd time. He'd get very upset to see me in there. You see, his wife — my grandmother that is — had died in childbirth. My mother was only very young when this happened, and she ended up in the Tralee industrial school herself for a number of years. She used to visit me about once every two years. I think that she hated the place too."

One of Betty's jobs was to keep the fire going in the institution. It was here that she decided to commit suicide. She was thirteen years old.

"I remember that I really did want to kill myself. I wanted to make sure that I'd go quick, so I tucked my dress into my knickers, thinking that the fire would burn me better that way. I still have the burn marks on my upper legs and on my side. Another girl threw a bucket of water over me and that put the fire out.

I don't remember getting any medical attention for the burns. They never sent me to hospital or anything. But I do know that every time I cried with the pain, the nun threatened me with the strap."

In 1964, a little over a year after her suicide attempt, Betty was moved to Cork, to St Mary's, a Magdalen laundry run by the Sisters of Charity. There was no explanation for the move. Betty was only fourteen years old.

She is still trying to find out how it was that she was transferred, while still a child, to work for another order of nuns in what was effectively a laundry sweatshop. This was in spite of the fact that the court had ordered that she remain at the Tralee Industrial School until she was sixteen.

> "In the Cork laundry, we had to sleep in little cells, and they locked us in every night. There were no toilets in the cells, just a pot, and we'd have to slop out each morning when they'd unlock our cell doors. It was really degrading.
>
> There was one time the nuns accused me — falsely — of stealing another girl's sweets. They locked me in a punishment cell for three day and nights. They kept the light on all the time, and fed me on bread and water. They tried to break me, but they never did."

Also working in St Mary's laundry in Cork was Patricia, a girl even younger than Betty. Patricia had been transferred down from Lakelands Industrial School in Dublin, another Sisters of Charity institution. She equally had no idea why she had been sent there. The two girls became fast friends.

> "The work in the laundry was endless. In theory they paid us two shillings and sixpence (25p) a week, but we never saw it. They would enter it into a book for you, and they would deduct money as punishment, so you never really saw any of it. We didn't know we had rights, we knew nothing about rights. It's hard to believe nowadays just how ignorant we were."

Betty worked in the laundry for almost three years. When she was seventeen, she ran away. She managed to get a job in the kitchens of a local hospital, where she received her first pay check. The hospital was run by the Sisters of Mercy, and Betty believes that they got in touch with their fellow nuns in Tralee and found out about her background.

"I was only there a few months when the Gardai arrived and said I had to go with them. They brought me to the Good Shepherd convent [another Magdalen laundry] in Cork. One particular Garda told me not to run away again, or I'd end up somewhere worse. I didn't know what was going on. I was totally confused.

The first thing that happened in the Good Shepherds was that they changed my name. And the new name they gave me was the same name as the nun in Tralee who had been so cruel to me. Can you imagine that? Did they know? Why did they do that?"

Betty refused to answer to the new name they had given her. After only three months there, the head nun called her in and told her she wasn't settling in well. She was to be transferred the next day to another Good Shepherd laundry, this time in Waterford. But this last move was to be her salvation.

A kind nun there took pity on her, and told her that if she worked for a year, she would get her a proper job outside. This nun was as good as her word, and a year later Betty was finally able to begin her life in the outside world.

She went to Dublin, and shortly afterwards emigrated to England.

"All my life I've tried to educate myself. I've done lots of courses, trying to make up for what those nuns took away from me. I'm doing an degree course at the moment through the Open University.

Some days I'm alright. Like today, I've been able to tell you all this without breaking down. But if I'd been talking to you yesterday, I'd have been in floods of tears. Yesterday was a bad day."

Martin McMahon, St Joseph's Industrial School, Ferryhouse, Clonmel (Rosminians), 1955–1966

"One Brother had a pellet gun, and he used to take pot shots at the boys. He'd get them in the legs. He did this a lot, until another Brother threatened to wrap the gun around his neck if he didn't stop."

Martin was born in 1950. When he was five years old, his father died, and his mother started drinking. There were nine children in the family, and six of them were put into care. Martin and three of his brothers went into St Patrick's Industrial School in Kilkenny, run by the Sisters of Charity.

"I ran away once. I missed Mammy. I spent ages looking for her, and eventually discovered her in the cinema. She kept me with her for one night, and then the Guards came and brought me back to St Patrick's."

Martin has no complaints about the nuns in St Patrick's. He remembers frequent visits from family members — they were keeping an eye on the boys, he felt.

At ten years of age, Martin was transferred to St Joseph's, Ferryhouse in Clonmel, an industrial school for senior boys run by the Rosminian order. In 1999 the Gardai were investigating several allegations of abuse against members of this order in the Clonmel school, in their industrial school at Upton in Co Cork, and in St Joseph's School for the Blind in Drumcondra, Dublin.

When Martin entered St Joseph's Ferryhouse at the age of ten, he encountered a pervasive atmosphere of violence.

"My first memory of Ferryhouse was when we were out for a walk, my older brother Larry put me up in a tree, and I couldn't get down. All the boys walked off, and I was stuck up there for hours. A nice Brother found me eventually, and helped me down.

But when we got back, another Brother grabbed me and beat me badly. And I thought to myself: 'Another six years of this, how am I going to cope?'"

They beat me for wetting the bed — they'd hit me with a stick or a strap and force me under cold showers, every single morning for six years. They never let me see the film on Saturdays as a punishment — I'd get a cold shower and be sent to bed. At least fifty of us wet the bed. We were known as 'the sailors'. At one stage, they took all the springs off the sailors' beds, and we had to sleep on hard boards. I suppose the springs were getting rusted.

I bit my nails, and I was beaten every single day for that. Your clothes torn or dirty, you'd be beaten. In the dormitories, if one lad did something, like if they found a book under his mattress, they'd beat every boy in that dormitory. It was just endless — beating, beating all the time.

There was one time I wiped my mouth with my sleeve, and this Brother told me to go to the office and wait for him. He said I had stuck out my tongue at him. This was about nine in the morning, and I waited there until 4.30, just standing there, no food or anything. I was weak with the hunger.

The Brother arrived at last and he beat me all over my body with a strap for about fifteen minutes. I remember seeing a pile of hurley sticks in the corner, and thinking if I could only reach out and get hold of one of them and hit him back. But I was too weak to make it. When the Brother had finished beating me, I was bleeding all over. He gave me an orange and told me not to tell anyone about it.

I had to go to the nurse, who put iodine on the cuts. She asked me and I told her who beat me. I don't know if anything happened as a result. I was kept out of sight in bed for ten days as a result of that beating.

We'd sometimes go for walks up the mountains, and I remember once two boys came down dead. They were two first cousins, about thirteen and fourteen years old. They took their own lives, that's what we all thought. They just couldn't stand it any more. I knew them well. Their faces keep me awake at night."

Like so many others who grew up in industrial school, Martin was not taught to read or write. He never sat any exams, and at fourteen was put out to work on the school farm. He describes getting so little food that he was constantly hungry.

"The place was known in the town as the monastery, and I suppose everyone thought it was fine. Sometimes people would visit — I remember they used to throw coins in the air and we'd run and gather them. They didn't know about the fear.

But we did have some good times as well. During the summer, they'd send us down to a holiday place they had at Woodstown in Waterford. That was a happy time. I don't want to run the school down for everything. They were careful as well in Woodstown not to mark us too badly with the beatings, because we went swimming in public places and people might notice the bruises."

At sixteen, Martin left the school to work on a local farm. It was 1966, and he was paid only ten shillings a week. He had no holidays, no days off. He worked seven days a week from dawn until late at night.

"Because I had no education, I didn't know my rights. The farmer said I'd be locked up if I escaped, and I didn't know any better. They never gave me my letters, and so I never even knew when my favourite Aunt Maggie had died. She had sent us presents, been like a mother to us. And I didn't even know she was dead. I'll carry the pain of that till the day I die.

After about three years with that farmer, I couldn't stand it anymore, and I did escape. But the Gardai found me and brought me back. Eventually I got away from that farm, and got various jobs on other farms.

I've been in and out of psychiatric hospitals since. But it doesn't do me much good, it doesn't take the pain away. It's the way they cut me off from my family that hurts so much.

All my life I've tried to tell people what happened to me. I've been to the newspapers and everything. But it didn't do any good — no one was interested. But I think maybe it's changing now, and that gives me some hope."

Margaret's Story, St Joseph's Industrial School, Cavan (Poor Clares), 1950–1967

"I try never really to think about my childhood. I don't go down into the dark reaches of where I don't want to go. And I'm sure there's an awful lot of stuff down there. Because I did go to a psychologist once to try and see what could be done. I couldn't really take the strain of that first session. So I never went back and I don't really want to go back. I think sometimes the cure is worse than the illness."

Margaret was born in Aughrim, Co Wicklow, the second youngest of nine children — five boys and four girls. When she was eighteen months old, her mother came downstairs one morning and put a note on the mantelpiece. On it she had written "goodbye", and she then left the house, never to return. The consequences of her mother's desertion of the family were disastrous. Margaret did not see her mother again for over thirty years.

"It's been said in the area around Aughrim that my father did try to keep the family together after our mother left. And the neighbours had agreed to take a couple of us here and there. But the Government wouldn't allow it. We were all taken to court and the family was split up. Myself and two of my sisters were sent to the industrial school in Cavan. Some of my brothers were sent to Artane and one to the home in Rathdrum. I didn't even know I had brothers when I was growing up.

The first thing the nuns did when I went in was they took away my soother. So my mother, my father and my soother all went in the same day. I got very sick, and so did my sister who was a year older than me. We got so bad that it came to the stage that we were both anointed. They didn't think we were going to make it. Our older sister, who was about twelve, was made to stand at the end of the bed and watch us being anointed. We looked like skeletons we were so ill, and the nun said to my older sister, 'This is what will happen to you if you don't do what you're told.' My sister still talks about the terror of that to this day sometimes when I see her.

My main memories are of the feeling of black. Well, black and white, black and white — that was the uniform of the nuns. There was no affection, no cuddles. You were alone. And then fear, just fear and aloneness.

My father never came to visit, and my sisters — well, I hardly knew the older one, she was only there a few years. With my sister who was a year older, we were never really allowed to be close. We did things completely separately. The nuns didn't like you to get close to anybody, you were punished if you did. Sisters, friends, it didn't matter. I don't really know why. I suppose it had something to do with religion, you know, your body is the temple of the Holy Ghost, and you must never touch another person. I mean, we all played together and that, but there was always that adultery, this feeling of wrongness. You had to be pure — that's a word that came up an awful lot. So this purity, whatever it was, we all had it. We were all wonderfully pure.

You'd be beaten for anything and often for nothing. The nuns had a huge big black leather strap, very thick, about an inch-and-a-half, maybe two inches thick, with a lot of tight threads. It always left a big mark on you like criss-crosses on your arms. That was used quite frequently. And then if they didn't have that, they would use branches of trees, sticks, legs of chairs, whatever came to hand.

As well as that, they'd often make you wait a long time for your punishment, threaten you with it for ages. And you'd wait in terrible fear — you didn't know why they were doing this to you, and you didn't know why the beatings were so severe. The punishments just didn't fit the crime. I found it personally very difficult to watch others being beaten, I would take the punishment for them. I'm not a violent person, I never was and I don't think I ever will be, and I can't bear to see anybody getting hurt. Sometimes the nun would be hitting girls and they would just stand there. And some of the others and myself, we would cry for them.

Because they wouldn't cry, to be brave they wouldn't cry. So we would cry for them.

I remember one night somebody was talking in the dormitory and we were all made to stand in the corridor in our bare feet all night. And it was cold. One nun said, 'You'll all be getting it in the morning now.' And we stood in the corridor, terrified, what in God's name are they going to do to us in the morning? We weren't allowed to talk in the corridor, and all night we stood there, shivering, in our little nightdresses.

In the morning the nun came and put each of us across her knee in turn and slapped us on our bare behinds. Even the bigger girls, fifteen and sixteen years old. Just to humiliate us all. But some of the girls kept running to the end of the line. And when the nun eventually got to them, they wouldn't let her. There was another nun there who tried to help her to get these kids across her knee, and I remember some of the girls saying, 'You won't do it to me, you won't do me', and we were screaming for them, egging them on. I remember one of the girls actually tore at one of the nuns and her veil came off. This was really bad, but we were sent out then so I don't really know what happened to the girls who wouldn't go over across the knee. I think there was about three of them, and we really admired them.

I'm not sure what age I was when this happened. I think I was quite young, but age is a big thing for me — the day was so the same, so boring that one had no sense of time really. And also I never had a birthday. The first I knew of my birthday was the day I made my confirmation. Because you had to have a baptism certificate to make your confirmation, I was handed this piece of paper, and on it was my birthday. So that's how I discovered when my birthday was.

There was another episode I remember when this elderly nun told us all to line up. She had two huge big rectangular boxes of Lemons sweets. And she told us all to put our hands in the box and take a big handful. This was wonderful, amazing, and we all did, and some of the cleverer girls put them up their sleeves, but I never thought about that. As soon as the two boxes were empty, she put them down on the table and said 'Now you can put them all back'. We were kind of flabbergasted. But we all dutifully put all the sweets back. There was a younger nun in the room — she was sitting at the sewing machine — and she said to her 'Why did you do that?' And the older nun said 'I just really wanted to make fools of them'. That was the only time I ever heard of one nun questioning another about a punishment. During the physical punishment, they usually backed each other up — one nun would be giving the beatings and another would be there and would never stop it, would never say 'Take it easy', would never say 'Do you not think that's enough'.

I don't know why they hit us so much. It was probably an awful lot of frustration on their own part. You know, young women being sent in to be nuns when they didn't have a vocation. Some of them may have had vocations, but I'd say most of them didn't. It was a great thing for a family to have a nun or a priest, and probably pressure from the parents made a lot of young girls become nuns. They hadn't fulfilled their emotional desires or sexual desires. They hadn't used any of the emotions they're supposed to use, so they got frustrated and took it out on us, on little children. And they weren't trained. They had no idea how to look after children. No idea whatsoever.

For instance, when I was a bit older I was in charge of the babies for a while. I try not to think about it, but those kids, babies really, when they wet the bed, they were taken out and put into cold showers. That's one of the things that I don't think about because to me that's inhuman, I mean I can't take that. All I can see when I think of that is the children now, my own children now and how could anybody do that to a young baby? Only when I'm talking to you now do I think about it. But I don't go round thinking about it because I would be crying every day walking up and down the street. So it doesn't come to the surface, and it's better off.

The nuns had a terrible thing about wetting the bed generally and wet sheets. They used to drape them over the children, and the kids would have to walk around with the wet sheets on their heads. There was one little child there that I really loved. She was about two or three and she was terrified of wetting the bed, and I was terrified of what they'd do to her if she did. So every night she'd knock on the glass partition opposite my bed and call my name and say she needed to go to the toilet. We were both so terrified that we'd stay awake, often till maybe two in the morning, until she knocked on the glass and I brought her to the toilet. I couldn't sleep until I knew she was safe and comfortable in her bed.

I really loved that little girl. One of the first things I did when I left was to save up from my wages of ten shillings a week and buy her a present. It was a little blue check pinafore and a little yellow jumper to go under it. It cost one pound and ten shillings, £1.50. I couldn't wait to go back to the orphanage and give them to her. Everyone said she looked gorgeous, she was a beautiful little girl. And as soon as I left, the nuns took the clothes off her and she never saw them again. But even that few minutes of me seeing her in them was enough.

I lost touch with her, and I think she's in a mental hospital now to tell you the truth. Because she just wasn't a well child, you know, and they didn't treat her well. She was devastated when I left as well, it destroyed her. But I couldn't do anything about it. So in a way maybe I actually hurt her more by caring for her.

Nobody had shown me any love when I was small. But when I was much older, a new nun came to the school, and I liked her because she actually called me by my first name. I thought this was wonderful. She was a very decent woman, she was a nice nun and we'd never come across a nice nun before. But I kind of kept it to myself, I didn't really know what to do. You couldn't tell a nun you liked her — they'd suspect and accuse you of all sorts of things.

No one ever talked to us about sex, or even about periods. The first time I got them, I think I was in school and I noticed that I was bleeding. I went back into the orphanage and climbed into a little cupboard beside the music room and I locked myself in. This was it. We were always being told that the devil would come and get you. And this was it — I had done something wrong and the devil was coming to get me and I was hiding. I stayed in the cupboard for hours and hours and hours and I prayed and I prayed and I prayed, but it didn't stop. And I had to go to school, and I'd take off my pants and I'd wash them and put them on the radiator until they were dry.

It was just unbelievable terror, and thank God it only lasted for three days the first time. It went away, and I thought the prayers had worked. In future, I was going to be good. I knelt down and I said rosaries. I think I'll go to heaven, I said so many prayers on that day. But then it happened again.

I mentioned it to one of the bolder girls, because she knew everything, and she said 'That happens everyone', just like that. I couldn't believe it. The relief of knowing that they had it as well — because the fear came from the time one morning when we got up and one of the girls had blood on her nightdress. We all laughed at her, we didn't know what was happening. That girl was taken out of the room by the nuns and murdered. Physically beaten, and this was going to happen to me, I was going to get beaten, and I was hiding. I would have quite happily died on that day, just never have come out of the cupboard again. But I had no choice. It was just sheer terror.

And the facts of life, that was a joke. One of the nuns brought me into a room and she said: 'Say the Hail Mary.'

And I went down to 'Blessed is the fruit of thy womb...'

'Stop. Where's your womb?' 'I don't know, Mother.'

'Do you know the part of the body where you go to the toilet?'

'Yes, Mother.'

'Do you know the part of the body where the man goes to the toilet?'

I said 'Yes, Mother' even though I didn't know. I mean where was I ever going to see anything like that? I'd seen a baby boy alright, but not a man.

And she said 'Well, you join those two together and you make babies, and if a man ever puts his hand on your leg, slap his face.' And that was it, she told me I could go. Now she may as well have told me cabbage was green. It made no sense to me.

We'd be warned when we were changing the nappies of the baby boys. You were never encouraged to cuddle or even hold the babies at all, and you changed them very firmly and very fast, especially the boys. I remember one of the girls was looking at this boy baby, you know, how this was a different child, and she was murdered. Oh, really slapped and beaten, just because she took a little bit of extra notice of the baby boy. She had done nothing wrong, it was just a moment of curiosity, and she was murdered for it.

I don't think we were very healthy because some of the girls used to get terrible boils on their ankles and their shoulders. They'd be sick and generally very run down. An inspector used to come, and we'd be trying to hide the boils. We'd all strip down to our underwear and line up for the inspector. The nuns would have put powder on us to cover any bruises. We always thought this was so the inspector wouldn't see that we'd been beaten. They always seemed to know when the inspector would be coming, and they'd have us prepared.

Even though we weren't too healthy, we used to think the food was alright. We got porridge for breakfast, some sort of meat most days for dinner, and bread and jam at teatime.

It wasn't a lot of food, not much protein, and there was no variation — it was just the same all the time. But we used to try and make up for it — we'd eat the leaves off the trees, off the hedgerows. We called it cheese. We used to eat handfuls and handfuls of this cheese, and it didn't seem to do us any harm. We used to eat sorrel as well. We used to think it was sad because the cows peed on it. But it didn't bother us, it was very bitter.

The other thing we'd do was to make chestnut water. We'd collect the conkers, not the brown bit in the middle, but the green outside part, and we used to let that go brown.

And we used to put that into water and we would shake the bottle, we'd get bottles from somewhere, and the water would turn brown. Then we would strain it and the nuns would actually give us the sugar to put into it and we drank that as lemonade. That lemonade and the cheese is probably what kept us alive and kept us going.

The orphanage had its own farm, and there were chickens and cows and pigs, but we didn't get any of the meat from it. I don't know where it went. We didn't get the eggs either. The nuns would always get the eggs.

All the girls loved to get the job of working in the nuns' kitchen, because they had the most wonderful, wonderful food. Poverty, my ass. They had roast lamb, they had roast beef, they had two vegetables, they had potatoes, they had dessert. Sponge cakes with custard. They ate like queens. And they had gravy, they used to have gravy with their meat. I thought this was the best thing since sliced bread. Wonderful stuff.

We used to eat out of their pigs' bucket. The food out of their pigs' bucket was just fantastic. They used to get chops, and the bones would be in the bin, and we'd be watching out for the girls bringing out the bin to the pigs and we'd stop them and take any meat that was left on the bones.

The only time things were different was on Christmas Day and Easter. They looked after us on Christmas. The priests would come in and we'd have turkey. The older girls remember getting presents and having to give them back the next day, but that had stopped when we were there. Our presents were small, like maybe a tennis ball or something, but at least we got something. And we'd get a few sweets and the same at Easter. Once we even got a chocolate Easter egg. So things weren't all bad. It was all we knew, we had nothing to compare it to, and we made the best of it.

Summers were better than winters because we could get out more, and there was a lot less praying and religion. One time, they brought us to their convent in Omeath for a week's holiday, and we had a great time. So, I'm not saying everything was bad, because it wasn't. It's important to point that out too, you know.

School wasn't too bad either. I suppose it was an escape from the orphanage. The national school was part of the same grounds, and the nuns ran it too. So we never actually went out to school, but girls from the town would come in.

We were never allowed to mix with the girls from outside. We were always separated. We never really became friends with them. It wasn't encouraged at all. Some of them actually thought that we were better off than them. You know, that we were safe, we had a house. But some of them as well used to go round the yard in a circle singing 'God help the poor orphans, they're not normal'.

We got punished at school alright, but it was different. There wasn't the same fear at all. You usually knew what it was for, and it was limited to slaps on the hand with a cane. It was sore alright, but it kind of meant you were normal. Not like in the orphanage — it was different, just different.

I tried to keep out of trouble. I wasn't one of the rebellious ones, and so I didn't get too many beatings, either in school or in the orphanage. I kept my head down and did my own thing emotionally, and I'm probably one of the survivors. And because I kept my head down, they thought I was more intelligent than I was, and they sent me to secondary school.

This was pretty unusual, but they still never encouraged me — 'she's only from the orphans,' they'd say. They always made me feel really really low, always at the bottom end of the scale.

All the outside girls were better than I was. I mean they had their uniforms — I had to go and fight for everything I wore. If my tights got torn I was physically abused for it by the nuns. I was afraid of my life to let anything happen to my uniform because I couldn't get another one and I would suffer the consequences if anything did happen. And I used to have to try to get my homework done, feed the babies, help the other kids with their homework and it was just all go all the time.

I'd be afraid to ask for anything. When I had to write essays, I'd make my writing tiny so that I'd use less paper. I was always worried about running out of space, out of paper. And as a result I couldn't write what I wanted to write because I didn't have the space. Cookery was very, very difficult, cookery was the worst. They'd tell me to go away when I'd look for the ingredients we were told to bring in. My poor partner was stuck with me, and she'd have to bring in most of the stuff. I'm sure that girl has never forgiven me, but there was nothing I could do about it. It was just humiliating.

There was a fancy dress parade and competition that we had once in secondary school. I went to one of the nuns and said 'What will I dress up as?'. We had no such things as costumes or anything. So she said to me 'You can go as a scarecrow.' And I said 'What will I wear?', and she said 'You can go as you are.' She wrote the word 'SCARECROW' on a piece of paper, and when it came to my turn, I walked around the yard in my uniform with the piece of paper saying SCARECROW stuck to my back. The girls kind of just looked at me and probably thought, 'the poor orphan'. I must have looked a holy show, because I wasn't a pretty girl. I was very plain — which was good in a way, because you didn't stand out, you could stay out of trouble easier. But anyway, I was plain, and my front teeth stuck out because I sucked my thumb until I was fourteen years old. I sucked my thumb and rocked, rocked constantly, well into my teens.

One of my jobs was minding the babies. I remember one time when I was about fourteen or fifteen, two tiny babies, a few days old, came in. I used to have to get up during the night every four hours and feed these two babies. I remember I used to pin the sheet down, something told me just to pin the sheet down at night-time because you know the way babies move around and move their little hands, and they could smother themselves.

And one night I got really really tired. I was so tired I couldn't study. I would be up at twenty-past-six every morning to go to school. And up half the night feeding the babies. So I said to the nun one day, I said I need a night off, I just need to do some homework. I think I had exams coming up. The nun put another girl in charge of the babies and the following morning one of the babies had been smothered by the sheet going up over his head — he had pulled it up in the night. It wasn't the girl's fault — she had no experience and I hadn't told her that you must put a pin in the sheet. I never forgave myself for it. After that, I looked after the babies myself as much as I could.

I also had to clean the school. When classes were over I'd have to stay back and wash the floors, clean the sinks, wash out the toilets, clean up the sanitary towels and the whole thing. I mean this was all after a day in school. And everyone in the school knew that this was my job, that I cleaned the building every day. I was never paid or anything, it was just unfair.

One evening I said it to the head nun, I said 'Listen, I'm not doing this any more.' I lost the run of myself completely. I actually got really bold. And I got expelled. I got put out of school because I wouldn't clean the building. That was the end of school. I was about seventeen and I'd just done my Inter Cert.

I always felt that they gave me an education for their own sake, and not for mine. They did it to be able to say that one of their girls went to secondary school and got her Inter Cert. But never to be able to say to me 'You're a great girl for going to secondary school and well done to this and well done for that.' No, it was for their benefit I went and not for mine.

In a way, I kind of resent them for it. Because it made me the outsider with the girls in the orphanage. They all thought I was the clever one. But I wasn't any better than them, and I never wanted to be any better. So, I had no place in society, and I still feel that I don't fit in any category. They took that away from me and that's what I miss most in my life. I have no sense of place.

I left the orphanage when I was almost eighteen. When I was going, one of the nuns said to me: 'You have a brother, he used to write to you, and these are his letters.' He had been sending me letters, and I kind of said, well why didn't you give them to me? And they told me it was because he was in prison, or in Artane (Industrial School). He'd stolen something, they said. That was the reason I got, that it was because he wasn't a good person to know.

I don't think I ever really got over the shock of leaving the orphanage and having to deal with life on my own. There are times I would still prefer the regime of the industrial school. When things are really bad I want to go back, back to the regime where you were fed at certain times, you went to bed at certain times, where it was neither bad nor good. It might be what people would call wallowing in self-pity, but I can't help that.

I hear some people saying now that I should be grateful to the nuns, and I can understand them saying that. But I will never be grateful. I will never forgive my mother for what she did. I will never be grateful to the nuns for taking away every ounce of confidence that I ever would have had. They were just rearing us because they had to. And because in their eyes our mothers were no good, or were prostitutes, or were this and that and the other. And we were made suffer for our mother's sins. They never gave me an education — I gave myself an education. All they did was put me in a classroom. I can't understand how anyone could thank them.

But I would think of myself as a survivor. And as someone who helped others through their time there. Some of them still talk about the times I did their homework for them, or when I used to sing to them in the dormitory. That's important to me — the fact that I might have made a difference and helped even just a couple of them to have a nicer day the odd time. And I think it's that that has helped me too to be a survivor.

The last thing I want to say is that I've always wanted to thank this girl who was in my class, her name was Cahill. I had never got anything for my birthday, and I happened to mention to her one day that it was my birthday, just to have somebody to tell. She said nothing, but the following morning she brought me in a present. It was a bottle of Tweed perfume and Tweed powder and four bath cubes. That bottle of perfume and the powder brought more pleasure to all of the girls in that orphanage than anything that I've ever had in my life since.

It was just magnificent, it was gold dust. She must have spent a lot of money on it, and I never thanked her enough. I couldn't, I didn't know how. I didn't know how to let her know how important this was, and all the girls would have a little spray. And I'd be spraying them all going out in the morning going to school. It was just the most wonderful, wonderful thing."

Some years ago, a letter appeared in the paper — a mother was searching for her children after thirty years. This, as it turned out, was Margaret's mother. The media became interested in the story, and press photographers recorded the family reunion. But the relationship between Margaret and the mother she didn't remember was not good, and today they have little contact. Margaret has three children and lives in Dublin. She is now beginning to build a singing career for herself, at last making use of the talent she never had a chance to develop.

Christina's Story, St Vincent's Industrial School, Limerick (Sisters of Mercy), 1944–1956

"There was one time I was sick in bed in the dormitory all day. And I heard this other girl getting a terrible beating from the head nun. I thought it would never stop — it was making my stomach feel sick to hear it going on. Some time later, the same nun came back and she came over to me for a chat. She had brought some cake for me. This nun was very fond of me. I suppose she was sorry that I had had to listen to the other girl being beaten."

Christina's mother died of TB when she only four. Her father was in the British army and had lost contact with the family. Christina and her older sister were sent to court in Newcastle West, where they were committed to St Vincent's Industrial School in Limerick, run by the Sisters of Mercy — simply known as The Mount. Christina remembers being in court — she had a great time playing with the other children there.

"It was the local priest who brought us in his car. I really enjoyed the trip. When we arrived at The Mount, the first thing the nuns did was change my name. They had too many Christinas, I think.

We were met by a kind nun, who gave us a doll to take to bed with us. It was a lovely thing to do, but the next morning the doll was taken away, and I remember being so disappointed. They cut my hair as well that morning — I had lovely long curly hair. But I was let grow it after that. If you had curly hair, you were safe. The girls with straight hair used to have to get it cut short.

As soon as I went to school I made friends with a young nun — she was a postulant. She was my saviour at times in the place. She really cared about me, and you need that growing up.

The school was in The Mount, we didn't go outside, but local girls came in. They were the day girls, and we were called the house girls. I was very lucky, because the head nun liked me. There was one time two of us from the same class were sent to her for punishment because we got our spellings wrong. She slapped the other girl, but she didn't touch me. I don't think the others were too happy about the way I'd get off punishments, and the teachers didn't like it much either. But I was just glad to escape.

So I led a charmed life until primary cert. And then she just dropped me. I failed my primary cert — I was no good at the maths. And she just cut me off. It was like she couldn't be bothered with me any more.

I felt completely useless after that. I lost all my confidence. I could see her treating other girls much better than me. I didn't know whether to like this nun or to hate her. It was very confusing, I was just all mixed up inside.

But she wasn't a bad nun. She had brought a lot of new things into the place. We had a radiogram which she'd put on at the weekends, and sometimes we'd dance waltzes. And she bought books for the school, we could all take out books and read as much as we liked. Christmas there was lovely as well. They really made an effort to make it a great day.

The food wasn't too bad, either. I don't remember being hungry, and we used to get meat a couple of times a week. At Christmas we used to have turkey. We only ever got the brown meat, and I never really liked it. I only discovered when I left that there was white meat on a turkey. I suppose the white meat went to the nuns, or to the staff working there. They got different food to us. They used to get a fry every morning, and we'd get porridge.

I remember it was strange when the inspector would come. We'd all be lined up in our best clothes — the nuns always knew when she'd be coming. She was a fine-looking woman, all made-up, quite stout and very glamorous. And she used to joke to us, saying 'You get a fry for your breakfast, I suppose', and we'd all shout back 'Oh, yes'. At least, I think it was a joke. Because we never got a fry. It was all very strange.

Bad things did happen in the place, though. There was one child who always wet the bed, and I remember seeing her being made to stand in the dormitory with the sheet wrapped around her head. At the time it didn't mean anything to me. It's only much later you begin to wonder about things like that.

The big threat if you were bold was that they'd send you to the Good Shepherds, who had a big Magdalen-type laundry in Limerick. And some girls were sent there. We'd never see them again.

I think some people tried to blot out the bad times. My friend doesn't want to talk about it at all, even though her husband tells her that she should, for her own good. But as far as I was concerned, nothing really bad happened to me.

They let me go on to secondary school, but I couldn't really study properly. I felt that I was no good because of what had happened over the primary cert. There were always a few girls from The Mount who were allowed a full education. In my time, I suppose there were about ten of us. So that nun really did make an effort.

I just went as far as my Inter Cert. I was seventeen when I left. I felt they didn't know what to do with me. They didn't seem to want me to go into domestic service. I'm not sure why — maybe it was because I had an aunt who was a nun in the Mercy order. Eventually I wrote to my cousins in Dublin, and they said I could stay with them.

But when I was leaving The Mount, no one said goodbye to me. It was a bit sad. I just kind of slipped away. No one made any fuss, or had a little goodbye for me, or anything. I felt it was like I didn't matter any more.

I didn't spend long in Dublin. I decided I wanted to be a nun. So I went across to England, and became a Dominican novice. The Dominicans had come to visit us in Limerick, and I liked them. But I knew even then that I was only doing it because I was institutionalised. I just wanted to be part of another institution. I couldn't really deal with ordinary life."

Christina spent only eighteen months with the Dominicans before returning to Ireland. Shortly afterwards, she married. She now has two children and lives in Dublin.

"I left that place feeling totally inadequate. I think I've made up for it now, but a few years ago I became very angry with that nun who just dropped me after I failed the primary cert. I sat down and wrote her an angry letter. I never sent that letter, but at least I think I got it out of my system."

Eight

"A Disgrace to the Nation"

In 1946, those running industrial schools in Ireland were to receive a most unpleasant shock. They were subjected to unprecedented public criticism, and from one of their own — a priest.

Monsignor Edward Flanagan's visit to Ireland in 1946 was something of a milestone for the country. Feted wherever he went, he attracted large crowds to his public meetings. He was treated like a film star, and indeed he was the next best thing — a hit Hollywood movie had been made about his life and work.

Boys Town, which opened in 1939, featured Spencer Tracy and Mickey Rooney, two of Hollywood's biggest stars at the time. The film was hugely popular, particularly in Ireland, and Spencer Tracy won a Best Actor Oscar for his portrayal of Fr Flanagan.

The movie told the story of the founding of Boys Town in Nebraska, a residential child care centre catering for boys of all creeds and colours. Fr Flanagan had battled against the odds to open this centre, which received no financial support from the US Government.

Though in fact Irish, from Ballymoe in Co Galway, Fr Flanagan had spent all his adult life in the United States, working with homeless and delinquent boys. He was an enlightened priest, far ahead of his time in terms of his approach to child care. His slogan — "There's no such thing as a bad boy" — summed up the policy of Boys Town, where physical punishment of the children was not permitted.

Fr Flanagan was horrified to discover the widespread use of severe physical punishment in industrial and reformatory schools (and in prisons) in Ireland. In a statement issued to the press at the end of his visit to Ireland in July 1946, he described these institutions as "a disgrace to the nation".[1]

He had given a series of public lectures in cities around the country. His packed audiences invariably included senior members of the Catholic Church. In Limerick and Waterford, for example, the local bishops were in attendance.

He used the opportunities provided to elaborate on his own child care philosophy — to love, support and encourage the children in his care. But he also contrasted the approach of Boys Town USA to the attitudes towards children in care in Ireland. Addressing a packed audience at the Savoy Cinema in Cork, he stated: "You are the people who permit your children and the children of your communities to go to these institutions of punishment. You can do something about it, first by keeping your children away from these institutions." These remarks brought prolonged applause from the audience.

The Irish Government, however, was not quite so ecstatic about Fr Flanagan's criticisms of its child care institutions. Fianna Fail's Gerry Boland, the then Minister for Justice, responded angrily. In Dail Eireann, on 23rd of July 1946, he accused Fr Flanagan of using "offensive and intemperate language" concerning "conditions about which he has no first-hand knowledge".

Sean Brady TD asked the Minister if he was aware of American press reports that Fr Flanagan had stated that "physical punishment, including the cat-o'-nine tails, the rod, and fist, is used in reform schools both here and in Northern Ireland".

Minister Boland answered that he was indeed aware of these statements. "I was not disposed to take any notice of what Mgr Flanagan said while he was in this country because his statements were so exaggerated that I did not think that people would attach any importance to them. When, however, on his return to America, he continued to make statements of this kind, I feel it is time that someone should reply."

It is a somewhat telling point that the Government only felt the need to respond to Fr Flanagan's very serious criticisms of its institutions when that criticism was given coverage outside of the country.

In fact, the American coverage of the controversy was a source of great outrage to James Dillon TD, later the leader of Fine Gael. He referred in the Dail to how "Monsignor Flanagan turned up in this country and went galumphing around … got his photograph taken a great many times and made a variety of speeches to tell us what a wonderful man he was and of the marvels he had achieved in the United States. He then went back to America and published a series of falsehoods and slanders."

The Ceann Comhairle interrupted at this point: "That is rather severe language."

Unabashed, Dillon continued: "when a Catholic Monsignor uses language which appears to give the colour of justification to cartoons in American papers where muscular warders are flogging half-naked fourteen-year-old boys with cats-of-nine-tails, I think it is right to say in public of that Monsignor that he should examine his conscience and ask himself if he has spoken the truth … If he finds that the substance of what he is alleged to have said is grossly untrue, then he should have the moral courage to come out in public and say so, and correct in so far as he can, the grave injustice he has done not only to the legislators of this country, but to the decent, respectable, honest men who are members of the Irish Christian Brothers."

When Fr Flanagan replied to these attacks, the issue turned into a substantial controversy. "As a result of my denouncement of the penal institutions in Ireland," stated Fr Flanagan, "I have made statements that caused the people in authority to feel rather uncomfortable." While in Ireland, he said, he had in fact visited several reform schools and prisons. He had also paid a visit to Artane Industrial School, often described as Ireland's Boys Town.

Fr Flanagan also stated that the use in these institutions of "severe physical punishment for the inmates is hardly in keeping with the high ideals of a Christian nation …. I do not believe that a child can be reformed by lock and key and bars, or that fear can ever develop a child's character …. If trying to help the forgotten boys of reform schools and prisons, whether it be in Ireland or in the United States, is intemperate and offensive, I'm afraid I'll have to plead guilty."

A vigorous correspondence on the issue continued for several months in the letters pages of several newspapers. Most of the letters were favourable to Fr Flanagan. However, there were several more traditional views expressed. P O'Reilly, for example, wrote the following to the *Times Pictorial* of 7th September 1946: "Through original sin children are naturally vicious little savages, and it needs a rigorous discipline with fear as a wholesome deterrent to mould them into decent citizens."

The following week, also in the *Times Pictorial*, TR Kearney violently disagreed with this view. Calling P O'Reilly "a particularly disgusting type of prig", he went on to condemn his letter as bearing "the stamp of a bigoted lout, and that judging by the opinions expressed therein, the only youthful being which could, with benefit to itself, be entrusted to his care is a baby gorilla."

Even such luminaries as Maud Gonne MacBride contributed to the exchange of letters, although hers (to the *Times Pictorial* on 12th October 1946) was mainly confined to the poor conditions in Irish prisons. She did however add: "One would like to know more of actual conditions in the borstals, reformatories and industrial schools to which these juveniles are being sent, for the 'Father of Boystown' warns us that some of these institutions are unsatisfactory and need to be changed."

However, the tide appeared to turn in the Government's favour when the *Irish Press* printed an editorial on the controversy (16th October, 1946). That paper accused Fr Flanagan of having behaved "in an entirely irresponsible manner". His criticisms, the paper said, were based on hearsay only, and were "so reckless and so far removed from the truth that nobody in this country is likely to pay much attention to them."

In private correspondence during February 1947 to one of his many friends in Ireland, Fr Flanagan wrote: "I am not sorry that I have opened up this discussion. It seems that people over there are afraid to come out and discuss things in which the government has something to say, because of fear."

In private, he was also far more direct about the nature of the Irish industrial schools system, describing it in February 1947:

> ... the institutionalization of little children, housed in great big factory-like places, where individuality has been, and is being, snuffed out with no development of the personality ... and where little children become a great army of child slavery in workshops, making money for the institutions which give them a little food, a little clothing, very little recreation and a doubtful education.
>
> How can those people become inspired with religion when they think with their more adult minds back over the years where they had been child laborers?... How in the name of God could a man like Mr. Boland [the then Minister for Justice] justify his stewardship of these helpless little children throughout the little island of Eire when he is face to face with all the information that has come out through the papers since last July — criticisms which I so justly made. All he has done is deny them and try to put me in a bad light with the church and otherwise by trying to strike at my character.

Fr Flanagan's views on the Irish hierarchy and its role in child care are interesting. Once again in private correspondence he wrote in 1947: "Since nearly all of the [Irish] people are Catholic, the hierarchy has to be very careful not to offend the people in power .... But the church should protect the welfare of these children. It should keep a vigilant eye on those who are in charge of these institutions and should visit them most frequently and not make these visits occasions of wining and dining."

At this stage, Fr Flanagan had been provided with very detailed information on the beating of a boy by Christian Brothers in Glin Industrial School in Co Limerick — this boy, still bearing the marks of the whip on his back "was one of the few to escape after such beatings so that their mistreatment might be exposed". (This is the remarkable case of Gerard

Fogarty, and is detailed later in this book.) Flanagan had made a brief reference to this case in one of his public statements, and it had given rise to the cartoon in *American Weekly* of a grotesque cleric beating a small boy, so vividly described in Dail Eireann by James Dillon.

Fr Flanagan appeared to have held rather a dim view of the Christian Brothers for some time. Again in private correspondence he writes:

> We have no Christian Brotherhood here at Boys Town. We did have them for five years but they left after they found out that they could not punish the children and kick them around ….
>
> Your great country that is sending forth missionaries into foreign lands … might well learn to begin at home to do a little missionary work among the unwanted, unloved, untrained and unfed children, who are suppressed and have become slaves because of the dictatorial policies of those in power. What you need over there is to have someone shake you loose from your smugness and satisfaction and set an example by punishing those who are guilty of cruelty, ignorance and neglect of their duties in high places. We have punished the Nazis for their sins against society. We have punished Fascists for the same reason …. I wonder what God's judgment will be with reference to those who hold the deposit of faith and who fail in their God-given stewardship of little children?

What emerges so powerfully from Fr Flanagan's private correspondence is his overwhelming sense of outrage at the mistreatment of children in industrial schools in Ireland. All of his life he spoke out passionately against the physical punishment of children. He perceived the beating of a child as being, without exception, destructive, and motivated by a combination of revenge and ignorance — "flogging and other forms of physical punishment wound that sense of dignity which attaches to the self. The result of such negative treatment is that the boy comes to look upon society as his enemy. His urge is to fight back."

Fr Flanagan struggled with the difficulty of reconciling the Catholic nature of Irish society with apparent disregard for the conditions being endured by the children locked away in institutions. In a public statement in October 1946, he said that "the good people of Ireland can be trusted to do what Christian charity demands if they know the facts. The problem is to get the facts before them." However, four months later, in February 1947, he wrote sadly that "I don't seem to be able to understand the psychology of the Irish mind".

Fr Flanagan was, however, determined not to give up. Throughout 1947 and into early 1948, he was preparing for a return visit to Ireland. This was in spite of his considerable international commitments — he had been appointed by President Harry S Truman to advise on the needs of the world's homeless children in the aftermath of the Second World War, which involved him in extensive travel around the world.

In the middle of all this, he had already written to the Irish Government requesting permission to visit a substantial number of penal institutions for both adults and children in the country. He anticipated arriving in Ireland during the summer of 1948.

But he was never to make that visit. On the 13th of May 1948, during a field visit to Berlin and its homeless children, Fr Flanagan suffered a major heart attack and died the next day. He was only sixty-one.

His untimely death effectively marked the end of this controversial public debate surrounding the care of children in industrial schools. Almost twenty years were to elapse before the issue once again came into the public arena. In that twenty years, roughly 15,000 children served out their time in industrial schools throughout the country, enduring conditions which had changed little from those condemned by Fr Flanagan in 1946.

"The rod is badly needed"

There was one other lone voice at the time questioning the system of detention in industrial school. This was District

Justice Henry McCarthy of the Dublin Metropolitan Children's Court. Like Fr Flanagan, he too was regarded with hostility by Justice Minister Gerry Boland.

McCarthy was a thoughtful man. In 1945, he had written advocating a more humane way of dealing with children in need of care. While not specifically critical of the nature of industrial schools, he was concerned at the large numbers of children effectively treated as prisoners. "It is always with the greatest reluctance", he wrote, "that I commit any child to an Institution, because ... they cannot supply to a child the loss of its natural home .... Day after day, Courts are obliged to remove children from their homes only because their parents, who idolise them, and who are entitled to the joy and solace of their companionship, are unable, through no fault of their own, to keep them from destitution. Surely this should not be tolerated in a State which has enshrined so eloquently its Christian principles in its Constitution."[2]

McCarthy was an advocate of the more frequent use of the Probation Act for children appearing before the courts. He remarked on its great success in many cases, but complained about the fact that for the whole of Ireland there were only four probation officers dealing with children. With a view to reforming the entire area of children and the courts, he proposed to Government the setting up of a committee to examine the area.

However, behind the scenes, the Government knives were out for him. They were deeply suspicious of his attempts to find alternatives to locking up children. Department of Education files contain an extraordinary letter from Justice Minister Gerry Boland to his opposite number in Education, Thomas Derrig.[3] Boland recommended adopting Justice McCarthy's suggestion to set up the committee, and then use it to hang him. In this letter (dated 21st May 1947), Boland added "I am aware that you (like many others) think Mr McCarthy too lenient. Here is our opportunity to urge more drastic action upon him with facts names and dates. This is a course to which he cannot object because he has himself invited it and I think that the advice of such a committee might be sought with advantage in about six months time as to how far Mr McCarthy is at fault, how far, on the other hand, he is the victim of circumstances and what changes ought to be made, e.g. caning as a regular customary punishment in the case of larceny, burglary and house breaking."

Boland added a post-script to this letter, saying that he had just received correspondence from a Fr Counihan SJ of the Commission on Youth Employment. According to Boland, Fr Counihan strongly advocated the caning of young delinquents — "the rod is badly needed for the under-16 offenders". It is a clear indication of Minister Boland's general outlook that he recommended that Fr Counihan should immediately be invited to serve on Justice McCarthy's committee. Whatever happened to that committee remains buried in the Department of Justice's files, not all of which are available.

Richie's Story, St Joseph's Industrial School Ferryhouse, Clonmel (Rosminians), 1951-1956

Richie was eleven years old when he was detained at St Joseph's, Ferryhouse. For years as an adult, he never thought about his time there. But during the 1970s, he heard a radio programme about the Christian Brothers, and it brought it all back to him. His wife arrived home to find Richie in tears.

He cried for a week, he says, remembering what had happened to him at the Clonmel Industrial School. The nightmares returned. As he talks about it again now, he frequently breaks down in tears and cannot continue. But he is determined that his story be told.

"My big mistake was when a gang of us broke into the grounds of a house belonging to the local judge. We didn't know he had tropical birds, and some of them got loose. We were caught, and when I was up before him the following week, he remembered me. He sentenced me to five years in Ferryhouse.

I was no angel. I didn't go to school, and I used to rob apples and biscuits because we were hungry. But when they put me into Ferryhouse, they said that my parents weren't fit to look after me. That was a lie. And compared with the way we were looked after in Ferryhouse, it was an evil thing to say.

My mother came to visit me once, but she got so upset about the place that she never came back. There were twelve of us in the family. We had good parents, but they just didn't have anything to give us.

What I got in Ferryhouse was five years of beatings and starvation. You were beaten for no reason, so there was no way to prevent it. If they caught you smiling for instance they'd beat you. You could be just walking in a corridor, and one of them would come up and say 'you're in the office, three o'clock'. That meant you were going for a beating — they'd mainly beat you in the office.

One particular Brother used to beat me all the time. He'd also come into the dormitory in the middle of the night and drag me out of bed and into the showers. I'd have to stand there under a cold shower for maybe an hour. And this might happen a couple of times in a night. I never knew why he was doing this.

I told in confession once — I was about twelve — that I was going to kill this brother with a scissors. I worked in the barber's shop, cutting boys' hair, so I could easily get a scissors.

Immediately after that confession, they moved me to another area, so the priest must have told on me. But confessions are supposed to be secret. Anyway, I didn't kill that Brother, though sometimes I wish I had.

You'd still have to be up at six the next morning for Mass. Most days, I'd be working in the fields for hours after school, but you didn't get any extra food for this, although you were almost literally starving.

What you got was porridge with bread and dripping in the morning, two potatoes in cabbage water for lunch, two slices of bread for tea and that was it. I was out in the fields from the age of eleven, in all weathers, winter and summer.

At one stage, we had to build our own outdoor swimming pool. The boys did the hard manual labour, dragging in all the materials. Our little hands would be bleeding from the work — blood and tears went into that swimming pool.

But when we swam there, it was great — except for the beatings. There was a place around the back of the pool where the Brothers would bring boys to beat them, and then straight back into the cold water so the bruises wouldn't show as bad.

In my case, it was the beatings that did the damage. I wasn't sexually abused, though I do remember one priest asking me if I wanted to put my hand in his pocket and feel his snake. I know now what he meant, but at the time I didn't have a clue."

Many Ferryhouse boys have vivid memories of one particularly traumatic incident. It happened in 1953. Three boys had run away, and when they were caught, the whole school was gathered to witness their punishment. This included boys as young as four years of age.

"The three lads were marched in wearing nothing but wet swimming togs. This was so it would hurt more, and so the bruising on their backsides wouldn't be as marked. Each of them was spread over a table, with Brothers holding them down. Then another Brother beat them with a thick leather strap.

The head priest told us that this is what we would get if we even thought of running away. The beatings went on for about an hour, the boys were screaming and roaring. One of them fought back, and they beat him all the more.

There was one lad, very religious and very good at reading, used to read the Bible and all, and won prizes. One day he was sent down to the office, though he hadn't been in trouble. And when he came out a few hours later, he didn't believe in religion any more. Whatever they did to him in there changed him forever."

Richie left Ferryhouse unable to read or write. Shortly afterwards, he emigrated to England, where he worked in a succession of jobs, including a stint with the merchant navy. He married and has two children, now grown up. Richie and his wife returned to Ireland several years ago, and now live in Waterford.

"I don't believe in religion or in God. There just can't be a God to let people do those things to young children. How could any God allow children live in a hell like that for so many years.

You never really forget the brutality. You can put it to the back of your mind, but it comes back at you, especially the nightmares. I've heard people say that was just the way things were in those days, and I get very angry. But I have to control my temper. Those Brothers, they never had to control their tempers. I don't know how they can live with what they did to us on their consciences."

John's Story, St Joseph's Industrial School, Glin (Christian Brothers), 1945–1952

> "I remember they made these fellows stand in the yard in the rain for hours. No one was allowed talk to them. It was a bit like a concentration camp — the boys, with their heads totally shaved, falling on the ground unconscious, passed out from exhaustion. They were just left lying there where they fell. All they had done was to try and run away."

John was born in Limerick in 1937. Eight years later, his mother died in childbirth. She was only twenty-nine. She had already had five children, but three had died. Only John and his older brother Patrick were left. When their mother died they were all alone — their father had already disappeared.

> "Soon after my mother died, I remember the Guards came for me and one of them brought me up to William St Barracks. He cycled up with me on the handlebars of his bike, I was that small. Then I had to go to court, and appear before the judge. He sent me to Glin. I felt like I was classed as a criminal straight off, just because my mother had died."

John already knew all about Glin. Not only had he been threatened with it if he didn't behave, but his brother, Patrick, was already there.

> "About a year-and-a-half before my mother died, Patrick was up around the town hall. He would have been about ten or eleven years old. He was doing handstands on the window sill of the building — something we all used to do — but this time Patrick's feet went backwards, straight through the window, breaking the glass.
>
> Everybody knew it was only an accident. But it didn't matter. Patrick was hauled off by the Guards. He was up in court, and got convicted for what they called 'criminal damage'. He was sent to Glin, where he served seven years.
>
> Patrick was what you'd call a slow learner, he was mildly mentally handicapped, I suppose. But even that didn't matter. My mother went down to the court, and begged and

pleaded for him to stay at home. They weren't interested. They made him serve his time.

Glin was a fairly miserable place. We were always cold and hungry, and the Christian Brothers would beat you for anything. If they didn't like your face, they'd beat you. They used to hit me on the wrist, I had the marks of it for years afterwards. They just got away with it — there was never anyone to stop them."

John remembers one particularly bad beating. Each boy was supposed to change his shirt and socks every Saturday. One Saturday, John forgot to change the socks.

"This Brother spotted me, and he gave me such a beating there and then. And the next morning when he saw me, he dragged me into the boot room, and beat me all over again. There was nothing I could do to stop him.

I didn't learn much in school. So they put me out to work in the piggery. You'd have to stay up all night when the sow had her bonhams [piglets], to stop her rolling over and crushing any of them. If the Brother came in the morning and found any of the bonhams crushed, he'd beat the living daylights out of you.

But we did have funny incidents. There was one time one of the pigs wouldn't stop roaring, so this other boy picked up a stick and started beating the pig to make it stop. He literally beat the pig black and blue.

When he realised what he'd done, he knew he'd get into terrible trouble if the Brother spotted the bruises on the pig. He went off and found a bucket of whitewash which he poured over the pig. So you had this totally white pig wandering about the yard. But then didn't it start to rain, and the pig became all streaked. We all just fell around laughing. I don't think the Brothers ever found out.

Looking back, I'm not really too bitter about Glin. But what gets me is that just because my mother died they sent me through the courts and treated me like a criminal. That was wrong, but they did it to hundreds of us."

John (highlighted, see p.136) with a group of
Baltimore boys, all age 14/15.

Dormitory in Baltimore Fishing School, 1944, where John (above) was terrified of the
rats scurrying up and down the floor.

Classroom in Baltimore Fishing School, 1945.

Fr Edward Flanagan
during his visit to
Ireland in 1946.

Fr Flanagan and actor Spencer Tracy during the filming of the movie *Boystown* in 1938.

AN CHUIRT DÚITHCHE
(THE DISTRICT COURT)

CHILDREN ACTS, 1908 TO 1941

Henry M ~~Order of~~ Detention in a Certified Industrial School

napp N.S.P.C.C. Wexford Complainant | District Court Area of *of Cahnam*

Patrick Joseph Doyle Defendant | District No. *24*

(1) Insert here the appropriate recital from Part II of the District Court Rules, 1942. (No. 2).

WHEREAS (1) *Patrick Joseph Doyle, who appears to the Court to be a child under the age of 15 years of age (having been born, so far as has been ascertained on the 19th day of May 1951) at who resides at Spawell Avenue, Wexford, in the County of Wexford, has been found having a guardian who does not exercise proper guardianship.*

(2) Delete the word "borough" where not required.

AND WHEREAS THE COUNCIL OF THE SAID COUNTY (2) BOROUGH HAS BEEN GIVEN AN OPPORTUNITY OF BEING HEARD.

AND WHEREAS THE COURT IS SATISFIED THAT IT IS EXPEDIENT TO DEAL WITH THE SAID CHILD BY SENDING HIM TO A CERTIFIED INDUSTRIAL SCHOOL.

AND WHEREAS THE RELIGIOUS PERSUASION OF THE SAID CHILD APPEARS TO THE COURT TO BE CATHOLIC.

IT IS HEREBY ORDERED THAT THE SAID CHILD SHALL BE SENT TO THE CERTIFIED INDUSTRIAL SCHOOL AT *St. Michael's Cappoquin, Co Waterford* BEING A SCHOOL CONDUCTED IN ACCORDANCE WITH THE DOCTRINES OF THE CATHOLIC CHURCH, THE MANAGERS WHEREOF ARE WILLING TO RECEIVE HIM TO BE THERE DETAINED UNTIL,

(3) Insert date up to but not including which detention is to continue.

BUT NOT INCLUDING (3) THE *19th* DAY OF *May*, 196 *7*

AND IT IS FURTHER ORDERED THAT

RESIDING

(4) Insert "parent of" or "person legally liable to maintain."

AT THE (4)

THE SAID CHILD SHALL PAY TO THE INSPECTOR OF REFORMATORY AND INDUSTRIAL

(5) Insert "during the whole of the time for which the said child is liable to be detained in the school" or "until further order."

SCHOOLS A WEEKLY SUM OF SHILLINGS (5)

THE FIRST PAYMENT TO BE MADE ON THE DAY OF

19

GIVEN UNDER MY HAND, THIS *14th* DAY OF *August*, 19 *55*.

JUSTICE OF THE DISTRICT COURT ASSIGNED TO SAID DISTRICT.

A799 Ji (mt) 44.5.5.000.9/35. Flext 201.

Gerard Fogarty in 199[
(see p.210).

St. Joseph's Industrial School, Glin
(now demolished).

Limerick Borough Councillor Martin McGuire (see p.210) making a presentation to
Kennedy (early 1960s).

Children at Pembroke Alms House Industrial School, Tralee, 1960s. Geraldine (see p.369) is on the far right.

...dine (right) and friend, Pembroke ... House Industrial School, ...e, 1960s.

Terry, age fifteen (see p.110).

...ng at St Joseph's Industrial School, Ferryhouse, Clonmel, 1950s.

Artane Industrial School trade workshops, 1905.

The Juvenile Workshop at Artane Industrial School, 1905.

boys on parade, Artane Industrial School, 1905.

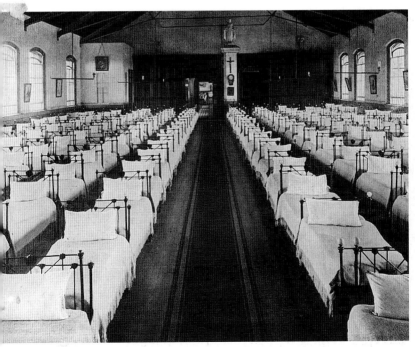

e of the five dormitories at Artane Industrial School, 1905.

Donough O'Malley, Fianna Fail Minister for Education 1966–1968.

(photo courtesy Independant Newspapers)

Justice Eileen Kennedy of the Dublin Children's Court.

Richard Mulcahy, Minister for Education 1948–1951 and 1954–1957.

Thomas Derrig, Fianna Fail Minister for Education 1932–1948.

John still lives in Limerick. He returned to Glin several years ago, just before the industrial school building was knocked down. He photographed it from all angles, just so that some record of the place would survive.

Nine

"Beating the Devil Out of Them"

Some of the most overwhelming testimony from those who grew up in industrial schools relates to how they were beaten by the nuns and Brothers in charge of them. It is one of the most relentless aspects of the way in which these schools were routinely run.

The argument has been made in defence of the schools that such physical punishment of children was commonplace in Ireland during most of this century. This is indeed true — excessive assaults on children did occur frequently within the general community, which accepted a level of violence against its most defenceless members which would horrify today's more enlightened society.

However, the industrial schools remain unique for the sheer scale and sustained nature of their physical brutality. Even judged by the context of the times, the excessive violence within the schools shocked many of those outsiders who witnessed it. The Department of Education's archive contains complaints about several incidents of cruelty against the children in State care. Its response to these was invariably to refuse to believe them.

However, contrary to what one might be led to believe from the testimony of former inmates of the system, there were in fact specific rules governing punishment in industrial and reformatory schools. The very earliest set of these dates from 1868. They list the type of punishments permitted to be used: "forfeiture of rewards and privileges, reduction in quantity or quality of food, confinement in a room or lighted cell for not more than three days, and moderate personal correction .... No other forms of grave correction to be allowed unless approved of by the Inspector." The rules insist that all serious misconduct and punishments be entered in a special book kept for that purpose. In the case of food reduction, the minimum permitted was listed and specified. However, "moderate personal correction" was not defined.

One interesting paragraph, which was to remain constant in all sets of rules for the following hundred years, reads as follows: "The Manager must, however, remember that the more closely the school is modelled on a principle of judicious family government, the more salutary will be its discipline, and the more effective its moral influences on the children." It is interesting to note that even in the last century, there was a clear view that inflicting any kind of corporal punishment on children in institutions was undesirable, and to be used only when all else had failed.

A new set of rules was issued by the Department of Education to the schools in 1933. This repeated the injunction to base discipline on "judicious family government", saying that if this is done, "fewer occasions will arise for resort to punishment". While these particular rules did go considerably further in defining types of physical punishment allowed, there remained a certain lack of clarity. For instance, "moderate childish punishment with the hand" was permitted, but once again, there was no definition of moderate. "Chastisement with the cane, strap or birch" was allowed, but in no case could it be inflicted on girls over fifteen. For girls under fifteen, "it shall not be inflicted except in cases of urgent necessity, each of which must be at once fully reported to the Inspector". The rules then proceeded to state, rather ambiguously, that "caning on the hand is forbidden", without indicating whether the use of another implement on the hand is permitted, or on what parts of the body caning is allowed.

A circular sent by the Department of Education to each industrial school in 1946 went even further. Punishment, it said, "should be confined as far as possible to forfeiture of rewards and privilege obtained by good conduct". It stated that corporal punishment should be used only as a last resort. "It should be administered only for grave transgressions, and under no circumstances for mere failure at school lessons or industrial training. Corporal punishment should in future be confined to the form usually employed in schools, viz. slapping on the open palm with a light cane or strap .... Any form of corporal punishment not in accordance with the terms of this circular is strictly prohibited. Any other form of punishment which humiliates a child or to expose him or her to ridicule before the other children is also forbidden. Such forms of punishment would include special clothing, cutting off girl's hair as a punishment, exceptional treatment at meals etc."[1]

The circular concluded with what could perhaps be interpreted as a greater concern for appearances than for the unfortunate children under detention. It sternly enjoined managers to "recognise that any instances of improper treatment or punishment in certified schools tends to cast an undesirable reflection on the schools generally."

In the rules and regulations published as part of the Kennedy Report in 1970, all reference to specific types of punishments has been removed. However, the stricture to enter details of serious misbehaviour and resultant punishment into the special Punishment Book remained, as did the rule that all punishments should be administered by the manager of the school, or in his/her presence by an appointed deputy.

The daily reality for the children in industrial schools differed wildly from that prescribed by the rules. Survivors describe a wide range of weapons used to beat them on all parts of their bodies — whips, cat-o-nine-tails, leathers, belts, straps, canes, sticks, tree branches, chair legs, hose pipes, rubber tyres and hurley sticks. Many of the leathers used had been reinforced by having pieces of metal or lead sown into them — a task the children themselves were often forced to perform. One former inmate remembers a Brother who used to freeze his leather in order to make it harder and consequently more painful. Children were also directly kicked and punched on all parts of their bodies by both nuns and Brothers. They were stripped naked for beatings, and many were routinely humiliated in a wide variety of ways in front of other children. The shaving of heads continued as a commonplace punishment into the late 1960s. The small inmates were beaten for everything and for nothing — very often they had not the slightest idea why it was that a nun or a Brother was hitting them. Violence was an intrinsic part of the culture of these institutions — its aim and often its effect was the systematic and thorough destruction of the will of each and every boy and girl at the mercy of those who orchestrated this campaign of terror.

It is abundantly clear that the Department's rules were not taken even remotely seriously by the religious orders running the schools. It is also evident that the Department itself paid equally little attention to them. Punishment books were seldom properly kept, and there is no record on file of one ever having been either examined as part of the routine inspection process, or having been sought by the Department in the context of a complaint made. It is also highly unlikely anyone believed that all "personal correction" was carried out only by the head of the school, or in his or her presence by an appointed deputy. In fact, the complaints files show clearly that this was not the case.

As early as 1940, the Department of Education showed an awareness of the severe nature of the Christian Brothers, who ran most of the industrial schools for boys over ten years of age. In a report submitted by the Department to Taoiseach Eamon de Valera on the proposal to transfer the State-run Borstal institution in Cork to religious management, there are revealing remarks about the respective merits of the various religious orders involved in custodial care for children.[2]

In assessing which order might take over the management of a new Borstal for the detention of sixteen to twenty-one-year-olds, a Department official reported that "I do not think that either the Christian Brothers or the Presentation Brothers would be suitable. The former because they are too strict and the latter because their discipline is too lax." It must be remembered that at this time the Christian Brothers were responsible for five industrial schools, detaining over 1,500 children below the age of sixteen. It is remarkable that the Department of Education had no apparent concern about this order's "strictness" in dealing with much younger children — perhaps because smaller boys were much less likely to strike back and cause major problems for their keepers.

It is clear from the Department's files that it rarely bothered to inquire into any matters associated with discipline, being generally content to leave matters in the hands of the religious orders. Its officials were moved to action only when presented with the most incontrovertible proof that brutal beatings had taken place. This proof did not often present itself, and even then the action taken was grossly inadequate. There is not one single shred of evidence that any member of a religious order was either warned, disciplined or removed by the Department for physically abusing a child in an industrial school.

There is, on the other hand, considerable evidence that the religious sought to conceal the evidence of beatings. A number of the survivors of industrial schools talk about badly marked children being hidden during the inspector's visits, or having bruises covered with talcum powder to conceal them. Some of the religious, particularly the nuns, confined their beatings of the children to parts of the body which wouldn't show up in a cursory examination. The Brothers tended to be less careful — this is probably one of the reasons why the formal complaints of brutality to the Department of Education mainly concern boys.

It is reasonable to assume from this that the religious were aware that the extent to which they were beating children in industrial and reformatory schools was wrong. (One notable exception is the extraordinary admission by the manager of Daingean Reformatory, which is detailed later in this chapter.) No argument about the standards of the times can possibly be applied here. This begs a number of very serious questions about the nature of the religious themselves. It is evident from the testimony of former inmates that by no means all of them behaved brutally towards the children. But it is a common theme that the "good" nuns and brothers never interfered with or protested about the activities of their more violent colleagues. This remains a crucial issue, which has so far not been in any way addressed publicly by the religious orders themselves. It can be argued that central to this issue was their own highly authoritarian internal structures combined with the overriding importance of the vow of obedience. It appears undeniable that in this context the necessity for obedience within the orders superseded any thought of acting in accordance with individual conscience.

As to the very large numbers of religious who beat the children so often that it can only be assumed they took some pleasure in it, this is a much more difficult pattern of behaviour to explain. However, a number of factors could have contributed to it. Firstly, it is clear that working in the industrial schools was regarded within the religious orders as far less prestigious than their other activities. Consequently, there are several references to the fact that it was undertaken in many cases by the less able members of those congregations, some of whom even disliked being associated with the schools.[3] It is reasonable to argue that the inevitable frustrations associated with this were likely to have been taken out on the children.

Secondly, as elaborated in Chapter Twelve, the children in industrial schools were not valued, and were clearly viewed by the religious as being inferior and in need of punishment to correct the "evils" of their backgrounds.

Thirdly, the industrial schools were invariably understaffed. The Department of Education rarely expressed any view as to the desirable number of adults who should care for the children. The religious orders, particularly the nuns, keen to cut their costs, often assigned only two or three of their members to care for very large groupings of children. The need for the behaviour of the inmates to be highly regimented in this context was clearly a contributing factor to the way in which they were brutalised.

On the occasions when the Department's officials could not ignore the evidence of their own eyes, they did raise the matter with the religious, usually in the form of a mild and often apologetic query. But black eyes and broken jaws were explained away as being the fault of clumsy boys colliding with individual Brothers. It is greatly to the discredit of the Department that it so readily accepted these unlikely explanations. A number of examples of this are given in the following pages, and in the knowledge that we now have about the savagery of these schools, they make for bitter reading.

It is clear from the testimony of the survivors that the nuns and the Brothers were equally brutal. Both were physically stronger than their victims, and the injuries inflicted on both boys and girls were equally great. In terms of the Department of Education's files, however, the vast majority of complaints relate to the beatings of boys by Brothers. Very few complaints were made on behalf of girls within the system.

This underlies an important difference between boys and girls committed to industrial schools (see Chapter Two). On the whole, girls tended to be committed at a much younger age, and to lose complete contact with their families. On leaving at sixteen, most were placed by the nuns in jobs far from their homes, as domestic servants living in the houses of their employers. They remained cut off from those most likely to intercede on their behalf, and suffered in the main in silence.

The boys, however, tended to be committed when older, and consequently more of them retained a level of contact with their families. For instance, many more boys than girls were detained for non-attendance at school, and when released returned to their families. Also, many more boys than girls tended to attempt to escape from the schools. Some of the best documented cases of abuse are in respect of boys who escaped, sometimes with the marks of their beatings still visible on their bodies.

The Gerard Fogarty Case — "Shock the Public"

"It is only by chance that once in the history of these institutions did a boy escape in the condition in which he was presented to me." Thus wrote Martin McGuire, Limerick businessman and local representative, to James Shiels, Manager of the Theatre Royal in Dublin on 5th July 1946 and a conduit for sending messages to Fr Flanagan of Boys Town in the US.

The boy was fourteen-year-old Gerard Fogarty, a detainee at Glin Industrial School in Co Limerick, run by the Christian Brothers. The "condition" referred to was the visible evidence of a flogging with a cat-o'-nine-tails which had severely marked his back and arms.

The case gave rise to a remarkable exchange of letters between Martin McGuire and the Department of Education. There is, astonishingly, no trace whatsoever of this voluminous correspondence in the Department's own files. They retain no reference of any kind to the case of Gerard Fogarty, which was even mentioned in the daily press. It gives a tantalising glimpse into the kind of material that is suspiciously missing from those files.

However, an almost complete record of the case was uncovered in Fr Flanagan's archive in Nebraska. The documentation had been sent to Fr Flanagan in 1946 by Martin McGuire, through the good offices of James Shiels. McGuire's hope was "that Fr Flanagan will use it to the best advantage to shock the public, the Minister for Education and his Department, into the grave responsibilities which must rest upon them for these conditions".

Over a half century later, Gerard Fogarty still lives in Limerick. Now sixty-nine-years-old, he shares a small cottage with his dog. He vividly remembers the events of the summer of 1945.

> I ran away from the place that summer. I just wanted to go home and see my mother. I missed her all the time. I made it home, and they hid me for a while. I suppose I was on the run, really. But the Guards caught me after a few days. They had been watching the house. They called the Brothers, who came up and brought me back.
>
> The next day, I was sent for by the Head Brother. I came to his office, and he roared at me to take off all my clothes. As soon as I was totally naked, he took out this stick which had several leather thongs on it. He gripped me by the hand, and he started laying into to me with the whip. He gave me at least twenty lashes. I was crying and trying to get down on the ground, trying to curl up and get away from him, but I couldn't because of the grip he had of my hand.
>
> That evening, they brought us down for a swim [Glin is on the River Shannon estuary], and I had to get into the salt water, even with the cuts on my back. The pain of that was terrible.
>
> I couldn't sleep that night, and so I slipped out and ran away again. It's thirty-two miles from Glin to Limerick city, and I walked all the way, keeping to

the fields. I knew they'd be searching the roads for me. I think it took me about twelve hours.

By the time I got home, the bleeding on my back had stopped and the blood had dried into my shirt. I must have been a terrible sight. My mother nearly tore the hair out of her head when she saw me.

That same day, Wednesday 1st August 1945, a delegation of almost 100 men, women and children arrived in the offices of Martin McGuire Ltd, which were in Francis Street, the same road where the Fogarty family lived. McGuire was a big mill owner in Limerick and Independent member of the city's Borough Council.

The crowd was made up of neighbours of the Fogartys, and McGuire was their local representative. They brought young Gerard with them and told him to take off his shirt and show Martin McGuire the marks on his back. The crowd was clearly angry — they were demanding action.

Martin McGuire shared their outrage. He called in local doctor John Holmes, who examined the boy, and certified in writing that Gerard had "wheals — about 2 to 3" long" on his back and arms. These marks, Dr Holmes wrote, were "such as would be produced by a leather thong".

Gerard remembers his father taking time off work to bring him around to various offices. "I was very upset at the time, there were so many people looking at me and asking questions. I was terrified that the Guards or the Christian Brothers would catch me again and take me back to Glin. That would have meant another hiding, and I knew I just couldn't have taken it."

However, Martin McGuire acted quickly. On the 3rd August, just two days after Gerard's escape, McGuire wrote to the Minister for Education, Fianna Fail's Thomas Derrig. He described in stark terms Gerard's flogging at Glin, and proceeded to ask a number of questions:

- "If a form of punishment so described by this boy is proscribed by law in certain cases in Industrial Schools.
- If the recipient of such treatment is compelled to be stripped or partly stripped of his clothing.

- If the use of a whip with a number of leather thongs is prescribed and permitted.
- If the report from Glin Industrial School agrees with the statement made to me by young Fogarty.
- If it does not, in what respect does it differ."

Shortly afterwards, Dr Holmes sent a copy of his medical report on Gerard Fogarty's injuries to the Department of Education. Over six weeks later, the Department had still not responded, and McGuire sent a sharp reminder.

Then, on the 29th of September 1945, the Secretary of the Department of Education finally replied. "I am directed," he wrote, "by the Minister for Education to say that he has had full enquiries made into the circumstances of the case and has taken appropriate action in connection therewith." That was all. The letter had answered none of McGuire's highly pertinent questions.

McGuire immediately wrote back, reiterating his queries and stating that this was a matter of "grave public importance". He also asked for details of the "appropriate action" taken.

The response McGuire received to this letter was remarkable. The Secretary of the Department wrote: "The Minister for Education desires me to inform you that he does not feel called upon to give you the information you have asked for in the matter [i.e. the Fogarty case] unless he is supplied with evidence as to your right to obtain that information and is given an assurance as to the purpose for which it is required."

McGuire responded: "My position as a Public representative entitles me to the information requested. I seek the information requested for the purpose of confirming the allegations made to me, which if correct should be ventilated in the interest of the public."

As this high-level correspondence was continuing, its subject, young Gerard Fogarty, was still at home. To his enormous relief, no one had come to forcibly take him back to Glin. "Martin McGuire was great," he says now. "I'm sure that he squared it with the Guards so that I didn't have to go back."

Gerard had originally been sent to Glin for not attending school — "mooching", as it was called in Limerick.

I just couldn't settle in school. But it was a real shock when the Judge in court said Glin. I was only barely eleven, and I thought I might just get a warning or something. But I was taken away immediately from the court, and they held me at the Garda station until a Brother arrived up to collect me. I was crying all the way in the car, I was really devastated, but the Brother never said a word to me, not a single word.

At Glin, you got hidings from the Brothers all the time. They'd give you a box in the head for nothing. I know young fellows who went deaf later because of the beatings on the head.

They'd be watching you all the time. If a group of us gathered in the yard or anywhere, they'd come over and break us up. I think they were afraid we'd be plotting something.

There was one Brother who picked up a boy in the class one day and threw him out the window. Just threw him straight out, glass breaking and everything. This classroom was on the first floor, so the boy could have been killed. As it was, he had some bones broken. But it was like the Brothers didn't care, that they knew no one could touch them. Another time, the same Brother picked up another lad and flung him up against the blackboard. There was definitely some sadism in them.

I never learnt anything in Glin. They locked me up there to make me learn, and then they never taught me anything. It didn't make any sense. And they made my mother pay some money each week to keep me there. All I wanted to do was go home.

On 12th October 1945, Gerard's mother received a letter from the head Brother of the Glin Industrial School. He wrote: "The Minister for Education has informed me that he has granted the discharge of your son Gerard …. Hoping he will be a success and give you complete satisfaction."

This was most unusual — Gerard still had over a year of his detention period to run, and cases of children not serving out their full sentences were rare. Also noteworthy was the absence of any reference from the head Brother to the circumstances surrounding Gerard's beating or his dramatic escape.

Meanwhile, Martin McGuire continued to pursue Thomas Derrig, the Minister for Education. On 5th January 1946, he received a letter from the Minister. Somewhat mysteriously, he inserted the following note into the file: "Letter of 5th January 1946 withheld from this file as the contents were given to me at the direction of the Minister for Education for my confidential information." This letter unfortunately remains missing from the file. Martin McGuire died in 1964, and a search among his remaining papers did not reveal the missing letter. Inquiries to the Department of Education were similarly unproductive.

However, there are some clues as to the contents of the missing letter. McGuire himself responded to it by writing the following on 12th April 1946: "I am now fully convinced that nothing short of a sworn inquiry into this case will satisfy the public conscience … I shall deem it my duty to lay the relevant information in my possession before a Tribunal set up by the Minister." McGuire also asked for a general inquiry to be held into the running of all industrial schools.

In his letter to James Shiels (Manager of the Theatre Royal), asking for the file to be forwarded to Fr Flanagan of Boys Town, McGuire wrote that the information contained in that file "has been admitted as being substantially correct".

In other words, it is reasonable from this to surmise that the Minister for Education admitted in the missing letter that the whipping of Gerard Fogarty by a Christian Brother with a cat-o'-nine-tails did indeed occur.

On 26th April 1946, the Minister for Education summarily dismissed any notion of holding either a sworn inquiry or a Tribunal to investigate these or any other matters. The Secretary of the Department wrote: "The Minister is satisfied … that he is in possession of all the facts concerning the punishment inflicted, and in these circumstances he considers that a sworn inquiry as suggested by you is unnecessary and would serve no useful purpose."

Martin McGuire was clearly incensed by this. On 9th May 1946, he wrote to the Department of Education: "In my opinion the useful purpose of an enquiry would be to put the public in possession of the facts which the Minister and his officials and a few others only now possess. As the Minister refuses to give the necessary publicity, I am compelled to take other steps so that it may be procured."

McGuire goes on to say that he now feels free to reveal the contents of the letter of 5th January 1946 — the missing letter. And at that point the correspondence with the Department of Education comes to an end.

What McGuire then appears to have done was to send the material to Fr Flanagan. McGuire's letter to James Shiels on the subject is revealing. "You have some knowledge of this case," he writes, "and I recall you saying to me some time ago, that you were approached by a prominent public man, who asked you to use your influence with me to drop this case. To your credit you used no such influence with me."

He described the Fogarty case as "this most degrading reflection on our system of detention of juveniles", and he went on: "These conditions will exist as long as Industrial Schools … remain closed boroughs to the public."

There is no doubt that Fr Flanagan's knowledge of the Fogarty case served to spur him on in his determination to continue the campaign to highlight the brutal treatment of children in Ireland's industrial and reformatory schools. He referred to it briefly in one of his public statements, made in October 1946, which was covered by the Irish newspapers.

However, there the matter lay. A hint as to why there was no further publicity is to be found in Fr Flanagan's file of correspondence. Walter Mahon Smith, one of Fr Flanagan's contacts in Ireland, wrote to him in November 1946, saying that "as regards the Glin case none of the Daily papers would investigate or publish this". Walter Mahon Smith was the author of the book *I Did Penal Servitude*, which dealt with the time he had himself spent in prison. He had long been a passionate campaigner for prison reform.

The refusal of the main newspapers to investigate the Gerard Fogarty story, despite such a wealth of documentary evidence to substantiate it, does very clearly show the nature of self-censorship of the times. To print such a story in detail would have meant seriously implicating not just the State, but also the Christian Brothers, and by extension the entire Catholic Church. The evidence seems to show that such a course of action was unthinkable.

"What still makes me more angry than anything else," says Gerard Fogarty, "is that they got away with it. I did nothing, nothing at all. All I wanted was to go home and see my mother again. The part that gets me is why were they beating us like this, because I was certainly not the only one that got whipped. You know, even after all this time, I still wake up at night thinking about it, trying to work out why ...?"

Killing the Messenger

It is noteworthy that in not a single case of those which remain on file with the Department of Education did its officials show any evidence that they believed the nature of the complaint. In fact, a somewhat shocking pattern emerges of assassinating the character of those making complaints.

A case in point is a complaint made in 1949 about the conditions and treatment of the boys in Greenmount Industrial School in Cork[4]. This school took boys from the age of ten, and was the only institution of its kind to be run by the Presentation Brothers. A member of the Cork City Executive of Fine Gael wrote to the then Minister for Education and his party colleague, General Richard Mulcahy, complaining about his knowledge of the poor food and living conditions being endured by the boys at Greenmount (see Chapter Six).

Dr Anna McCabe, the Department's Medical Inspector for Industrial Schools, went to Cork to investigate. Her report indicates that the housekeeper employed at the school had also reported ill-treatment of the boys to the Gardai. She had claimed that they were taken out into the yard, stripped naked and beaten.

Dr McCabe reported that she had each boy undressed and found no signs of ill-treatment. She added that the housekeeper had a "decided grudge" against the school and had been dismissed from her post. Dr McCabe concluded that the school was well-run and that all complaints against it were unfounded.

A complaint about the treatment of boys at St Patrick's Industrial School Upton in Co Cork was similarly dismissed. Upton was run for boys over ten years by the Fathers of Charity, also known as the Rosminians. The complaint was made in 1959, when two men who took an interest in the boys had a meeting with local Fine Gael TD Stephen Barrett. They told him about the poor food for the boys at Upton, and objected to a curtailment in visiting times to only once a month. They also alleged ill-treatment. Barrett wrote to the then Minister for Education Jack Lynch: "They say that a leather strap is being used to punish the boys and that it is used fairly often." However, he added a rider saying that this allegation "is purely hearsay, and that some of it in my view is obviously exaggerated, to say the least of it".

Once again, Dr Anna McCabe investigated. She dismissed the complaint saying that "the boys in this school are very well fed and cared for. I have no comments to make on this letter as I consider it a grouse".

The resident manager of Upton, when asked for his response, was equally dismissive, calling the complainants "grousers". He wrote to the Department, saying that the leather strap "is used very rarely, and when used only according to the prescribed rules". He added that the strap had been used only three times in the previous three months.[5]

The former children of Upton Industrial School have recently formed a support group among themselves. With over 100 members, they say that the violence and brutality they suffered in Upton at the hands of the Rosminians was savage. The testimony of Christy (see page 275) also bears out the routine nature of beatings and assaults against the boys of Upton.

Dr Anna McCabe is a central figure in terms of the Department's summary dismissal of so many of these complaints. While she had taken a most active part in pursuing the religious managers for starving the children in their care during the 1940s, she did not match this with a concern about physical abuse.

The Department of Education files contain a long hand-written note from her, written in 1964, when she had held her position as Medical Inspector for twenty-five years. In it, she looked back over that quarter century, giving a long list of improvements for which she claimed some credit.[6]

In this she refers briefly to what she calls "corporal punishment", saying that "this was very prevalent when I first visited the schools, beatings of children being quite commonplace. In addition there was a form of sadism displayed by the close-cropping of girls' hair and the shaving of boys' heads. All of this has been virtually eliminated with the exception of the unforgettable recent example of the nuns in Bundoran." (This incident is detailed later in the chapter.)

This shows firstly that there was a clear view within the Department of Education that violence against children had existed in the industrial schools, and most importantly that this was wrong and needed to be stopped. However, in stating that it had in fact been stopped, the Department was guilty of at best serious gullibility, and at worst a gross dereliction of its duty. The overwhelming testimony of survivors categorically shows that severe beatings of children continued to be routine, systematic and obvious within these institutions.

There is only one case which could be found on file where Dr McCabe herself drew attention to a case of suspicious physical injury. In 1943, during her routine inspection of St Joseph's Industrial School in Letterfrack, Co Galway, she happened to spot a boy with a black eye. On inquiry, she was told it was the result of a blow received by the child for talking in class. The Department wrote to the manager of the school, which was run by the Christian Brothers, asking if this was in fact the case. If so, the letter continued, the Department is to "request you to forcibly forbid correction of this kind in the future as it is extremely dangerous and undesirable".

The Christian Brother in charge of the school wrote back after a delay of over a year — they had apparently changed their minds as to the cause of the child's injury. "The Brother, while remonstrating with his class, happened accidentally to strike the boy, who stood behind him, with his elbow on the face .... The Resident Manager regrets the occurrence indicated and has no doubt that there will be no recurrence of a like nature." No further action was taken by the Department with regard to this case.[7]

"Look out for window dressing"

Dr McCabe continued dismissing complaints of brutality during the 1950s. One of the most interesting of these once again concerned Glin Industrial School in Limerick, run by the Christian Brothers. On 12th September 1950, a letter was sent to Richard Mulcahy, the then Minister for Education, from an individual employed as night watchman at Glin. It was heavily marked "in confidence". He said that by drawing the Minister's attention to conditions at the school, he would be doing a great work of charity.[8]

He wrote about the poor food and clothing for the boys, and went on to say that "everyone employed at this school are free to have a smack at the boys, including the Brothers who appear to be indifferent to all this …. The whole place and system is very very bad. I know that the Brothers can scrape out of <u>any</u> difficulty, but I know from personal experience that if you could arrange surprise visits night and day you could see for yourself. I could never have believed that such could exist in a Catholic country. I know there is a good deal of window dressing to deceive the eye of the visiting official, but I learned that the boys are warned not to complain."

As a result of this letter, Dr McCabe visited Glin. She reported that she had a long chat with the Christian Brother in charge, and she told him about the letter. She went on to say in her report that "I really could find no grounds for the complaint in the school. It is well run, and the boys appear well and happy. The Manager told me that the night watchman had been dismissed for insubordination, and seemed to want to injure the school."

However, the night watchman was not prepared to leave it at that. Six weeks later, he wrote again to the Government, this time to the Minister for Justice, General Sean MacEoin. "I may tell you, Sir, that I never expected to find in a Catholic country like ours the awful bad conditions insofar as the poor boys are concerned. Only that I had spent six months seeing them for myself, I never could have believed such conditions could exist, especially as this institution is under the care of our Irish Christian Brothers, who are so reputed for teaching, etc. When I took up employment there last March, I found the poor children there in a very nervous state due to harsh treatment at the hands of the former nightman ... the children have no redress whatsoever and are just like convicts."

He went on to make specific references to particular Brothers beating the children with leather straps, and to recommend that special attention be paid to the nature of those employed as night watchmen in the schools. "The children are at the mercy of the nightman during the night .... And Glin school can tell some queer tales about night men .... Do your best, Sir, and look out for window dressing, and bear in mind that the children are afraid to complain to any visiting official and you cannot expect much help from them. God bless you, Sir."

General Sean MacEoin took this letter very seriously indeed. He personally wrote to the Minister for Education, Richard Mulcahy, saying that "if what he [the night watchman] says is even in general true, it reveals a serious state of affairs .... My correspondent seems to be an intelligent and well-meaning type of man, and I feel his letter demands some type of investigation. I had an idea that corporal punishment was abolished in these industrial schools, and that the inflicting of any punishment was strictly regulated. To get these boys young and treat them rough could have very bad consequences for society." General MacEoin asked that he be informed of progress in the Department's investigation of this matter.

There follows an internal report of the investigation, dated March 1951. The Department privately accepted many of the criticisms of the boys' living conditions. However, it states that there was "no evidence of harshness or cruelty on the part of the staff on the boys". Officials of the Department had reported that they were "absolutely satisfied that it would not be in character for ... any of the Brothers to treat the children unkindly". However, later in the same report and in direct contradiction, it is stated that "there may be some slight grounds for a charge of occasional severity".

There then follow in this same internal report a number of revealing comments as to the character of the complainant. There appears to be some surprise at his literacy, with the remark that "his turn of English is unusual in a night watchman". The internal report adds that he "is a rather well-meaning person of rather unreserved character".

The conclusion of this was, predictably, that the complaint was dismissed out of hand. The internal report recommends "taking no further notice of any missives he [the night watchman] may forward." There was a reference to the desirability of more frequent inspection visits to Glin, but there is no record of these ever having taken place. There is equally no record in the file of any response ever having been sent to the night watchman by the Department of Education. However, revealingly, there is a hand-written annotation on the letter from the Minister for Justice demanding an investigation. Signed by an official of the Department of Education, it simply says "No action required".

"An affair at Glin"

Thirteen years later, the Department of Education's attention was once again to be drawn to Glin. This time it was almost by accident. On the 1st of May 1963, an official at the Department was clearing arrears of work for another staff member who had been ill for some months. He came across a routine notification that a boy from Glin had been admitted to hospital in Limerick. Each school was by law required to notify the Department whenever a child was removed from an industrial school for any reason.

Noticing that facial injury was the reason given for the hospitalisation of the boy, the official sent off an inquiry form to the manager of the Glin school, asking the cause of this injury.[9] Three days later, he was contacted by no less a person than Brother Moynihan, the Provincial Leader of the Christian Brothers, who wanted to meet him to discuss what the Provincial called "an affair at Glin". They met on Saturday the 4th of May 1963. What had prompted this urgent and unprecedented step by the Christian Brothers was, according to the official, anxiety about a combination of "the Bundoran incident and that the [Department's] enquiry was the result of a Dail question".

The Bundoran incident referred to was the shaving of the heads of eight girls who had escaped from St Martha's Industrial School in the Co Donegal town, run by the Sisters of Saint Louis. This had happened on the 31st of March 1963, and had been plastered across the front page of *The People*, a British newspaper, under a banner headline of "Orphanage Horror". It was the cause of acute embarrassment to the Government, who had believed that such punishments were no longer inflicted. However, it is clear from survivors' testimony that the practice was routine in several schools, normally being reserved for those who attempted escape.

In the wake of this — and unknown of course to the public — a Department of Education official went to Bundoran to meet the Mother General of the Sisters of St Louis, who was senior to the nun managing their industrial school. Her primary concern was to find out what action the Department intended to take as a result of the head-shaving incident. Incredibly, the official assured her that "the Department was unlikely to take any action of a disciplinary nature". In his report on their meeting, he wrote that he had "allayed her anxiety as best I could regarding punitive action by the Department".[10] It appeared that everyone had conveniently forgotten that the shaving of heads had been specifically and expressly forbidden by none other than the Department of Education itself, in its own rules concerning punishments laid down in 1946 and sent to each school.

It was by coincidence only one month after this highly publicised event that the "Glin affair" had arisen. When the Provincial of the Christian Brothers' arrived with such haste into the Department of Education, he sought to explain the nature of the facial injury of the boy at the school who had ended up in hospital for nine days. The official whom he met at the Department reported that the Provincial said that it was a broken jawbone, which had occurred when the child "was being punished by a Brother for calling him an objectionable nickname. Brother Moynihan was not sure whether the injury was the result of a blow from the strap, or from collision during punishment."

The official asked for the name of this Brother. The Provincial refused to give it, but told him that the Brother had since been transferred elsewhere. The official assured the Provincial that the Department's interest in this affair had not in fact been prompted by outside interest.

This official's report on the matter concludes: "there is the possibility that the coincidence of the official query and the Bundoran inquiry may have flushed a bird which otherwise might have lain concealed. In the interests of all concerned an investigation of the accident or assault is recommended. The nature of the injury and the circumstances under which received demand this action."

The form sent to Glin was returned to the Department a week later, with the cause of the boy's injury stated as "facial injury accidentally caused in the administration of punishment". The boy had spent nine days in hospital, and was apparently recovering well.

A month later, the Christian Brother at the centre of the affair wrote to the Department: "As requested from our recent interview re. the above mentioned boy, I emphatically deny that I struck this boy on the face for a very insulting remark he made about me. I fail to understand how this false charge has been made against me. Therefore I have nothing to add to our recent conversation in St Joseph's Tralee on the 31st May."

That was the end of the matter. Any further thoughts of "flushing a bird" were never again to resurface within the Department.

And the location to where this Brother had been transferred in the wake of this episode — it was St Joseph's Tralee, which was of course another boys industrial school run by the same order.

"Atrocities"

Barely a year after this incident, the Department received a letter from a former inmate concerning the industrial school in Tralee. It related to his period spent at the school, a total of seven years during the 1920s and 1930s: "I noticed a great number of atrocities by the so-called Christian Brothers against the boys, i.e. beatings and floggings in the most perverted way, as if Christ was not present on the altar as a boy as well as a man. I believe such pagan methods are still used against boys who get beatings and run away. … I hope that the truth of what I saw during my time as a boy … will put an end to this degrading practice of naked beating which is nothing short of homosexuality, and that a Christian method will be used and not degraded pagan methods of keeping order."[11]

Despite the fact that this letter clearly referred to continuing practice, there is no record anywhere in the Department's files that it was even responded to, let alone investigated.

With further reference to the school in Tralee, a complaint was received in 1968 from the father of a boy who alleged that his son had had a strap wrapped around his neck as punishment for absconding, and pulled so tight that the child's neck was "in an awful condition". He said that he could bring as witness two other boys who would testify as to the condition of his son's neck.[12]

This complaint came by way of a letter from Fine Gael TD Stephen Barrett, the same TD who had written to the Department ten years previously about ill-treatment of boys at Upton Industrial School. The letter was in fact sent to the manager of the Tralee school, and copied to the Minister for Education, Brian Lenihan. It also detailed further allegations of brutality, namely "that one Brother put the young fellow's neck between his (the Brother's) legs whilst another Brother held his hands behind his back and that he was punished whilst in that position. When John came home, the parents said that John had a black eye …. The parents are obviously intent on ventilating this matter, and I told them I would make every effort to have it privately investigated …. I hope you appreciate my view that it would be a bad thing to let this story be propagated without at least taking some steps to discover the real situation and that is why I write to you."

Minister Brian Lenihan promised an investigation. The head brother of Tralee wrote back promptly, categorically denying that the boy received any excessive treatment. However, he did say that "It is true I used a leather strap as the instrument of correction. I used it on his bottom because I maintain that that is where nature intended it should be used in such circumstances. There is no question of the strap having been put around his neck."

The matter ended with a letter from Brian Lenihan to Stephen Barrett TD saying that the Department agreed with the head Christian Brother's account of events, and dismissed the complaint as unfounded. The Minister added that the boy himself had withdrawn his allegations and now "bears no resentment towards the Brothers for their treatment". The child, of course, remained under detention at the school, and one can only speculate as to what transpired to have made him change his mind in this way.

A revealing insight into the minds of officials within the Department of Education can be found a report about Artane Industrial School compiled in 1962. This was on foot of complaints made about conditions for the boys by the school's chaplain, Fr Moore. These were dismissed out of hand by the Department.

The report is written by the then Inspector of Reformatory and Industrial Schools, Turlough McDevitt. Its findings are dealt with more thoroughly in Chapter Fourteen. However, its section on discipline makes for interesting reading. It begins by referring to complaints about the treatment in industrial schools, which it says "are not infrequent, but from experience I would say that the majority are exaggerated and some even untrue."

The Inspector goes on to refer to a specific case where a mother had brought her child into the hall of the school, alleging

> ... that he had been beaten on the head and on the buttocks by [named Brother]. Fortunately Dr McCabe [the Medical Inspector] was in the office the same day and on uncovering the bandaged head she diagnosed the injury as ringworm. The child had bruises on his body but in the subsequent investigation [named Brother] claimed that they had been made in a rough and tumble fight with other boys and the balance of the evidence favoured the Brother's case.

His report then discusses the suitability of this Brother as a carer for young boys, and examines his methods of punishing the children:

> His policy of deprivation of privileges because of misconduct and acquainting the culprit of the reason is basically sound, but he explained that successful application of this policy was not always possible owing to the ages of the boys, some of whom didn't care if say the privilege of watching television or going home for a few hours on Sunday was withdrawn. He felt that having withdrawn privileges and still being faced with insubordination he had no alternative but to punish moderately with the leather on the hand in certain cases. He stated that he probably used the leather about twice a week.

The report had no doubt but that this Brother acted "with sincerity and firmness but without harshness". The Department of Education officials suggested that perhaps some training in psychology might help the Brothers in their work with the children. The Superior of Artane replied "that the question had never been examined by the Order".[13]

There is probably more testimony from survivors of Artane than from any other single industrial school. From no where else is the evidence of a sustained policy of routine and savage beatings (combined with sexual abuse and rape of the boys) so compelling. This evidence remains consistent from the 1930s up until the school closed in 1969, following a fire on the premises. The above case illustrates the extraordinary level of ignorance of the reality of daily life in the schools that existed in the Department of Education.

Naked Humiliation

All of the complaints detailed in this chapter were omitted from a list eventually provided to the Kennedy Committee, after it had repeatedly requested the information. That Committee had been established by the Government in 1967 to examine the entire industrial and reformatory school system (see Chapter Fifteen). Its Chairperson, District Justice Eileen Kennedy of the

Dublin Children's Court, wrote to the Department of Education on the 4th April 1968, seeking details of *all* complaints received over the previous five years, and how these complaints had been dealt with.

Over a year later, the Department had still not responded. Justice Kennedy sent a sharp reminder on the 5th May 1969. It reads:

> My Committee is concerned at the failure to obtain replies to enquiries made to your Department affecting your Reformatory & Industrial Schools Branch. These include:
>
> 1. Letter sent in April '68 asking for details of complaints made to your Dept re. Industrial Schools, and how they were dealt with. Reminder sent last April ('69)
> 2. A letter sent in June '68 regarding Daingean, reminder sent last March.
> 3. A complaint made by the ISPCC regarding an alleged incident of excessive corporal punishment at Artane Industrial School. The ISPCC brought up this matter at a meeting with the Committee.
> 4. An enquiry made by a member of this Committee in his official capacity in connection with an incident at Marlborough House Glasnevin.
>
> While it is appreciated that in certain cases, enquiries could be protracted ... this hardly justifies the failure to obtain any kind of a reply.

This correspondence is most important, particularly as it is virtually the sum total of what survives in the Department of Education's archives about its dealings with the Kennedy Committee. The report of that Committee was published in 1970, and was scathing in its criticism of the system, and by extension of the Department of Education's central role in regulating it. It is remarkable that virtually all of the files associated with that Committee have disappeared without trace.

However, the above correspondence does give a tantalising clue as to the nature of the relationship between the Department and the Kennedy Committee. To put it mildly, the

Department did not appear over-anxious to assist the Committee in providing it with information sought.

When the Department did finally — well over a year later — respond to Justice Kennedy's request for information, the details provided were highly skimpy. There was a summary of only five complaints — all of them dismissed out of hand:

- In 1965, a father complained that his son had received twenty slaps from a Christian Brother in Artane. The Department decided this was unfounded, saying that "the parents had a record of trouble-making".
- In 1966, a mother alleged that her son was not being properly looked after in St Joseph's, Ferryhouse, Clonmel. The Department concluded that he was suffering from severe chilblains, which he had had on admission.
- In 1967, a stepfather had complained that his step-daughter's education was being neglected in St Michael's Industrial School, Wexford. The Department stated that this was found to be untrue.
- In 1968, a father complained that his two daughters in St Dominick's Industrial School, Waterford, were not receiving proper care or attention. The allegations were refuted by the manager, and the Department stated that the father was of bad character.
- In Lakelands Industrial School in Dublin, a mother complained that her daughter was in poor health. This was denied.[14]

With regard to the complaint made by the Irish Society for the Prevention of Cruelty to Children (ISPCC), it, too, was refuted. It had been alleged that two boys at Artane Industrial School had been severely beaten all over their bodies by the Christian Brothers for being out of bounds — one of them was beaten in the dormitory in full view of other boys, the other in the school grounds. One of them had been punched in "the private parts" by a Brother.

The Department of Education did accept that the boys had been "slapped", as it described it, by a Christian Brother. However, the strong implication in its report was that the boys had deserved it. Furthermore, true to form, the Department sought to blacken the character of the person who had made the complaint — she was the foster mother of one of the boys, and the Department told the Kennedy Committee that she "is reported as being of an irresponsible nature".

The only other surviving clue as to what the Kennedy Committee discovered about the beating of children within the system comes from a report made by the representative from the Department of Justice on that Committee. His report of the Committee's visit to Daingean Reformatory caused consternation within several Government Departments.[15]

Daingean was run by the Oblates of Mary Immaculate. Its manager, Fr William McGonagle OMI, was during the 1960s the Chairman of the Association of Resident Managers of Industrial and Reformatory Schools. He had been described by Department of Education officials in glowing terms just one year before the eventful visit to Daingean by the Kennedy Committee. An internal memorandum to the Minister Donough O'Malley stated in 1967 that "Fr McGonagle in particular is not only a man dedicated, but a man of vast common sense and goodness".

Exactly one year later, the visit of the Kennedy Committee to Daingean occurred on the 28th of February 1968. Some of its members had begun asking Fr McGonagle about his arrangements for discipline at the school. The report of the Department of Justice official was cited in Dail Eireann in May 1999 by the current Minister for Education Micheal Martin. It continues:

> Both of the doctors on the Committee then put a number of questions to Fr McGonagle about the circumstances associated with the corporal punishment of the boys. He replied openly and without embarrassment that ordinarily the boys were called out of the dormitories after they had retired, and that they were punished here on one of the stairway landings. The boys wore nightshirts as sleeping attire when they were called for punishments. Punishment was applied to the buttocks with a leather. I put the only question that I asked in respect of corporal punishment at this

juncture. I asked if the boys were undressed of their nightshirts when they were punished. Fr McGonagle replied that at times they were. He elaborated some further remarks to the effect that the nightshirts were pulled up when this was done. This remark was subsequently commented upon by the Committee members in private discussion. The point was made that when boys were punished with the leather they could hardly be expected to remain still and his struggles were likely to enlarge the state of his undress, and the likelihood that a struggling boy could be struck anywhere on the naked body could not be excluded. Some other Committee members asked why he allowed boys to be stripped naked for punishment, and he replied in a matter of fact manner that he considered punishment to be more humiliating when it was administered in that way.

The information on what happened as a result of this extraordinary disclosure is unclear. The authors of this book were not permitted to examine any documents in the Department's archive since 1969 — the Department was acting in accordance with the National Archives Act governing the release of State papers, which sets out that archives under thirty years old are not normally released for examination.

However, Micheal Martin read what he had managed to unearth into the record of the Dail on the 13th of May 1999. He identified the Daingean visit as "the only significant occasion on which the [Kennedy] Committee seems to have confronted the abuse of children". He proceeded to explain that District Justice Kennedy had written to the Department of Education on the matter and received no satisfactory response.

The Minister went on to say that while assurances had been given about the closure of Daingean, "assurances about the punishments stopping seem only to have been given as a result of significant disputes, the exact details of which do not seem to be documented."

The one exception to this is a letter from Peter Berry, the then Secretary of the Department of Justice to his opposite number in the Department of Education. In this letter, he pointed out that his Department's representative on the Kennedy Committee had signed the final Kennedy Report only on the basis of assurances that the Daingean punishments would be stopped. The Report had omitted any references to the flogging of children while naked.

The letter contained the following revealing remarks:

> To sign a report which made no reference to the situation about punishment in Daingean would, in the absence of evidence that the practice had ceased, be to appear to acquiesce in a practice which is indefensible, and for the continuance of which the Minister for Justice could not avoid some official responsibility arising out of his having registered Daingean as a suitable place of detention under the Children Acts.

Even more revealing, according to Minister Micheal Martin, was what followed from a man who was the most senior official in the Department of Justice:

> On the other hand, to make any reference, however oblique, to this particular method of punishment in Daingean would be likely to lead to a disclosure of the situation and, in this way, to cause a grave public scandal.

Micheal Martin commented on this by saying that "this episode demonstrates, I believe, the need for everything to be out in the open. I have no doubt that there are many other such incidents in official records and that official neglect and ignorance was commonplace."

Tip of the Iceberg

It is clear from the records in the Department of Education that Minister Micheal Martin is indeed correct in his analysis of the past behaviour of that Department. That they were probably only aware of a fraction of the brutality that existed in the industrial and reformatory schools was the result of their own neglect. What the files on complaints show is a combination of complacency and solid determination to dismiss out of hand those few complaints that were made by a handful of courageous individuals who refused to remain silent.

One extraordinary absence from the Department's records relates to the deaths of children in detention. Under the 1908 Children Act, the schools had a legal duty to investigate all violent or sudden deaths of children in their care. They were obliged to furnish the State with the reports of these investigations. The published annual reports for the Department of Education up to the mid-1960s do contain figures for these deaths, and their causes. Consequently the information was centrally compiled on a yearly basis. However, these files do not exist in the Department's archive.

There are a number of accounts from survivors of deaths of children under suspicious or unexplained circumstances. The *States of Fear* documentaries contained accounts from some of these. One was from Barney O'Connell of the death of a boy in Artane Industrial School. Barney had been detained there during the 1950s, and this child had fallen forty feet to his death through an internal stairwell. The boy fell past Barney, who was on the stairs, almost touching him as he passed. It is an image which he cannot forget, he says, and he will not rest until he receives a proper explanation for the boy's death. The Christian Brothers have stated that a boy did indeed die in this manner in Artane during the 1950s, but that it was an accident resulting from the children's' exuberance following a visit to the circus. Once again, no records whatsoever exist on this case in the Department of Education.

Following the broadcast of *States of Fear*, RTE received a letter from a woman in Australia. She had heard about the programme, and wanted to tell us about the experiences of her husband, who had only recently died. There was not a day went by, she said, that he had not spoken about his time growing up in the Tralee Industrial School. He and his brother had been committed there during the 1940s. His brother had started wetting the bed, and was receiving appalling beatings from the Brothers, which her husband had often had to witness. During one such episode, a Brother picked up the boy, then only ten years old, and rammed his head against a wall. The boy died from his injuries, with his brother (the man in Australia) there watching. His wife felt strongly that the story of these two young boys should be told — it was what her husband would have wanted, had he lived to see a time when he would have been listened to.

Sheets in the Wind

There is no reference in the Department's archive to the universal and systematic cruelty meted out to those children who wet their beds. A very large proportion of those detained in industrial schools appear to have been afflicted in this way. This is not at all surprising — bed wetting in children has long been associated with anxiety and trauma, and it would be difficult to find a more stressful environment than that of an industrial school.

However, it was regarded in all cases by the religious who ran the schools as a deliberate flouting of their authority, and was dealt with in the severest manner. There are numerous accounts of the ritual beatings and floggings of bed wetters each morning at breakfast. In some cases, this took place in front of the other children, in others the bed wetters were forced to queue up outside the manager's office to await their beating. Some survivors speak of being beaten in this way every day of their lives until they left the institution at the age of sixteen. Sometimes they were made wear their wet sheets on their heads, and paraded around the school to shame them. Some children used to have their faces rubbed in the wet sheets. They were often forced into freezing cold baths or showers, even in the middle of the night, in an attempt to cure them of what was perceived as wilful defiance of authority. The endless suffering of this particular group of children is almost unimaginable. They were trapped in a vicious circle over which they had not the slightest control — the more savage their beatings, the more they wet the bed; the more they wet the bed, the harder their punishment.

Possibly the most vindictive such punishment was described by boys from St Joseph's Industrial School, Letterfrack in Co Galway, run by the Christian Brothers. Children who wet the bed there were forced to run around the cold stone yard for hours, holding their sodden sheets above their heads until they dried. The problem in Letterfrack, however, is that it rains for most of the year. That made no difference — the boys were still made to run around with their sheets aloft, trying to dry them in the rain.

One explanation has been advanced for the extraordinary level of savagery directed at children who wet the bed. The drying of sheets and mattresses could indeed have posed serious practical problems in Ireland's wet climate for large institutions that had a shortage of replacement bed linen. On a superficial level, it could be plausible that anxiety over this might have led the religious to over-react. However, it is interesting to note that in Western Australia, with its dry, sunny climate, the Christian Brothers and the Sisters of Mercy behaved in an identical manner towards those children who wet the beds in the many orphanages they ran in that part of the world. It is thus far more likely that bed wetting was so severely punished because the religious viewed it as a continuous expression of deliberate disobedience on the part of the children.

Had there been even a modicum of vigilance on the part of the Department of Education, they would have spotted this unavoidable evidence of severe disturbance on the part of so many children within industrial schools. However, there exists hardly a reference to it in the files. It was, in fact, the Department of Health which stumbled upon it, almost by accident, in 1967. This Department had no role in the industrial schools, although it had repeatedly expressed the view that they were an undesirable way of dealing with children in need of care (see Chapter Thirteen). In 1967, however, following the death of a boy from meningitis in St Joseph Industrial School, Ferryhouse, Clonmel, they were sent a report from the local health inspector, who had decided to examine conditions in case of a possible epidemic.

Department of Health officials were clearly appalled by the report they received on Ferryhouse. It had recorded that forty-three out of the one-hundred-and-ninety-two boys detained there were habitually wetting their beds at night. This had correctly been interpreted as a sign of great distress among the boys — it was described in the report as evidence of "social malaise". The Department of Health Inspector for Boarded-Out Children said that "this shocking report confirms some unofficial information that I have had over the years concerning Ferryhouse .... From what I have heard the ill-treatment of the boys could do with investigation also. One person who spoke to me about this matter was an inspector of the ISPCC. It is scandalous that only the death of one of the boys has led to the conditions there coming to light."[16]

The Department of Health recommended that the twenty-three boys who had been placed in Ferryhouse by the local authorities should be immediately transferred elsewhere. They could have no say in the future of those committed through the courts, as this was entirely a matter for the Department of Education. Once again, no record of any of this could be found in the Department of Education's archive, which contains no general inspection records whatsoever on the Clonmel school before 1969.

"Dirtbird"

Marlborough House in Dublin, known officially as The Place of Detention, was the only facility for locking up children which was run directly by the State. Under the control of the Department of Education, it was used for children on remand, for those serving sentences of up to one month, and for boys whom industrial schools had refused to admit. During the late 1950s and 1960s, its Superintendent was a lay person appointed by the Department of Education, and his wife was the Matron. Its staff had been recruited from among men claiming benefits from the unemployment exchange office.

It is clear from Department of Education files that the children here were just as brutally treated by some of the lay attendants as those detained in the religious-run industrial and reformatory schools. The first official reports of brutality at Marlborough House start in 1956. Under the headline "Claims He Was Hit With Stick", the evening papers of the 7th of March 1956 carried a report of the dramatic events of that day in the Dublin Children's Court. An eleven-year-old boy had announced in court to Justice MacCarthy that he had been beaten while on remand in Marlborough House. The boy was facing charges of causing damage to a roof.

The newspaper reports continued with a quote from the boy:

> 'I did not like Marlborough House,' he said. 'I had to march around a field bigger than the room and if I tripped over the sticks on the ground they would make me get up and they would start hitting me with a stick.'

When questioned by Justice MacCarthy, the boy named two staff members as being responsible for the beatings. "I shall have them down here," the Judge said.

At that point, the officer in charge of the case interjected: "I don't imagine that the punishment was very severe." The Justice responded: "You don't imagine, but you were not there."

Another boy questioned in court by the Justice corroborated the allegations of the first boy. He also said that he had been beaten at Marlborough House. However, Sergeant M Byrne said that all this was a surprise to him. He was not aware that there were any punishments used in Marlborough House.

Justice MacCarthy remanded the case for fourteen days, at which time he ordered that the Superintendent of Marlborough House should appear before him.

What then transpired, according to Department of Education files, was that a number of statements were made by inmates and staff at Marlborough House, refuting the claims of beatings. The statements from the boys include similar remarks to the effect that all the staff are kind to the children and that "we all get plenty to eat while we are detained here"[17].

The Superintendent duly appeared before Justice McCarthy a fortnight later, and presented these statements to the courts. When asked by the Justice how he punished misbehaviour, he said that the boys were separated. Justice McCarthy then dismissed the complaints of ill-treatment as being in the boys' "fanciful imaginations".

Also in 1956, there was a letter to the Ministers for Justice and Education from a man complaining about the treatment of his son at Marlborough House. The child was only eight years old, and was serving a one month sentence for stealing sweets and lemonade from the Mount Pleasant Lawn Tennis Club. His father had discovered while visiting the boy that he had been hit hard on the head by another, much older inmate — a seventeen-year-old awaiting trial for murder. The father said that he informed the Superintendent, and went on to say that "I think my child has paid his penalty and I ask you to return him to my custody."

There follows a statement from the Superintendent. He accepted that the older boy had indeed struck the eight-year-old, but said that it was only "a slight tip". The Department of Education investigated and reported that the child's allegations were "greatly exaggerated, and were nothing more than would happen anywhere where a group of boys lived together." The small boy at the centre of all this remained to serve out his time in Marlborough House.[18]

An incident occurred in 1968 which was not so easy to dismiss. A probation officer reported in writing to the Department of Education that he had personally witnessed:

> ... a brutal beating of one of the inmates (a boy from Sligo, I was informed) by an attendant .... This beating consisted of numerous punches with his clenched fist which reduced the boy to a whimpering mass. The concluding portion of this incident was witnessed by the Matron, and the complete incident took place in the presence of all the inmates at the time. May I say that I considered this a savage, uncontrolled beating accompanied by expressions from the attendant in which I could plainly hear 'dirtbird' mentioned on quite a few occasions.

His report also included a further incident of brutality. The parents of a boy had complained to him:

> ... that while detained at Marlborough House during October he was hit with a lamp on the lips, arms and other parts of the body by [attendant]. I was informed that he had made no complaint at Marlborough House because he was afraid of

[attendant] and because he was convinced he would
not succeed in any complaint he made.

This report was investigated five months later by the
Department of Education. The boy from Sligo who had been so
savagely beaten was by then in a psychiatric hospital in the
Midlands. He was interviewed, and confirmed that he had been
beaten. The only conclusion drawn by the Department,
however, was that he was a difficult and violent boy. He was
fourteen years old at the time.

As regards the boy who was beaten with a lamp, they
concluded that it was probably true, "but he has exaggerated
his account". The Department pointed out that the particular
attendant against whom these allegations had been made had
worked for the Oblate Fathers in their Reformatory when it was
in Glencree, and that "they found him very satisfactory".

The internal report on this matter concluded: "Under the
present circumstances, the attendants perform their task of
keeping the boys disciplined very well. In the case of [named
attendant], I think he should be advised to exercise restraint
when provoked but deserves praise for his interest in and
kindness to the boys."[19]

The Kennedy Committee had become aware of these
incidents, and had repeatedly demanded information on them.
When it was eventually provided, the Department merely
stated that "the attendant undoubtedly contravened the
regulations governing the treatment of the detainees at
Marlborough House."

This was, however, only one among a deluge of complaints
at the time about treatment of boys at Marlborough House. In
May 1969, a fourteen-year-old complained in the Children's
Court before Justice Kennedy that he had been beaten while
detained there by an attendant who was drunk. She ordered the
matter referred to the Department of Education.

In another case the same month, the Clerk of the Children's
Court wrote on her behalf to the Secretary of the Department of
Education about allegations made in court "by a juvenile of
maltreatment in Marlborough House at the hands of [named
attendant]... he (the boy) appeared before the court this
morning with a black eye .... Justice Kennedy was anxious that

you be made aware of her increasing apprehension concerning the proper treatment and care of children and young persons in Marlborough House. She takes the view that the present complaint is deserving of investigation." There is no record of any such investigation.

The Department's files also contain a statement from a welfare officer in February 1969, reporting that she had been told by both a thirteen-year-old boy and his father that the child had been "walloped" by an attendant in Marlborough House. There is no record on file of any response to or investigation of this complaint.[20]

While the Kennedy Report described this facility as "deplorable", and recommended its immediate closure, it made no reference to the beating of boys detained there. Despite its recommendations, Marlborough House was to remain open for a further three years, with children continuing to be detained there until 1972.

The Fallout

Since 1996, and the shocking revelations of brutality contained in the television documentary *Dear Daughter*, there has been a steady increase in the numbers of former inmates of industrial schools taking legal action against both the religious orders concerned and the State.

Dear Daughter concerned the experiences at Goldenbridge Industrial School in Dublin of Christine Buckley, who grew up there during the 1950s. She had suffered horrific abuse, and descriptions were also given of the systematic ill-treatment of other children by the Sisters of Mercy, who ran the school. These included children being routinely and savagely beaten, having boiling water poured over them, being locked in a furnace room, being forced to stand all night on a corridor as punishment, and very young children being made to sit on potties so long that in some cases their rectums collapsed.

The programme produced an enormous response, most of it horrified at the deeply shocking nature of the abuse outlined. However, there followed a few months later another programme on RTE, which looked at Sister Xavieria, the nun at the centre of the Goldenbridge allegations. This was made by

Prime Time, RTE's Current Affairs flagship programme. It contained interviews with the Fine Gael TD Jim Mitchell and a retired official from the Department of Education who sought to defend Sr Xavieria, the Sisters of Mercy and Goldenbridge Industrial School against the allegations made. It also contained a long and memorable interview with Sr Xaveria herself in which she denied the allegations of excessive brutality against her.

Much of the response to this *Prime Time* programme centred on the nature of memory, or more particularly on the matter of different people's memories of the same or similar events.

On the programme, two sisters were interviewed who had diverging memories of one of the particular punishments used. This underlies a very important point – namely that some people have relatively benign memories of growing up in industrial schools. Christina's story of her experience in Mount St Vincent's (Limerick) as told in these pages, is one such account.

It is clear that some children, particularly in those schools run by nuns, were picked out for better treatment, and did not in general share the experience of abuse of their not so fortunate peers. In some cases, this fact was used as an argument to undermine the accounts of maltreatment from those who did suffer abuse. This was an unfortunate aspect of some of the debate which followed the broadcast of both *Dear Daughter* and the *Prime Time* programme, and one which many survivors single out as having been particularly hurtful.

The Goldenbridge survivors had been the first group to reveal so publicly their experience of an industrial school, and consequently bore the brunt of the Catholic Church's attempts to discredit the accounts of their childhood.

In the wake of *Dear Daughter* the Sisters of Mercy hired a media consultant to attempt to limit the damage to the order. A spokeswoman for the Mercy Sisters was quoted at the time as saying: "We need to look at [the issue of] recall and how hurt manifests itself and how complications such as the hurt of family rejection work." She called for more psychological and psychiatric work to be done on how the effects of family rejection inter-related with both painful memories and imagination.

Three years later in the wake of the documentary series *States of Fear*, the testimony of severe abuse in industrial schools is now so overwhelmingly consistent that the false or unreliable memory line of argument is no longer seriously being put forward.

In terms of the legal cases being taken by survivors for civil damages resulting from physical abuse, all are being vigorously contested by the religious orders. It is likely that the Statute of Limitations may prove a serious obstacle to their success. This limits the period in which a civil case for damages can be brought to court — most cases must be taken within three years of either the incident having occurred, or within three years of the individual reaching the age of twenty-one. An exception is made if the plaintiffs can prove a disability which prevented them filing suit within the three-year period.

The Government in June 1999 announced that it intended to legislate to extend the concept of disability under the Statutes of Limitation to all those who experienced sexual abuse as children. However, it did not make similar provisions for those who were physically abused, saying merely that it would refer this matter to the Law Reform Commission.

The firm distinction made by the Government between these two forms of abuse has been greeted with considerable anger by many of those who spent their childhood in industrial schools. They have always believed there to be a strong connection between abuse of a physical and sexual nature, and many of the boys in particular experienced both simultaneously at the hands of their carers. It is one of the points they will be arguing most strongly before the Commission to Inquire into Childhood Abuse when that body begins its hearings.

Catherine's story, St Joseph's Industrial School, Dundalk (Sisters of Mercy), 1937–1953

"I can remember being beaten when I was only three. I had a head of natural curly hair, and nobody was allowed have curly hair, it had to be straight. One nun used to beat me just because of my hair. Whenever she'd be around all the other girls would tell me to hide, because every time she'd see me she'd call me in. 'Did you curl that hair last night?' she'd shout at me. I hadn't, of course. It just curled by itself. But she'd pull my hair straight, and she'd beat me around the room on the face, head, body, legs, arms, anywhere, with a long bamboo cane with a handle on it. I'll never forget the swish of that cane coming towards me. She'd shut the door so that no one would hear me scream when she was beating me."

Catherine was born in the workhouse or county home in Dundalk in 1937. Her mother was unmarried and had been thrown out of her home when her family discovered she was pregnant. Her boyfriend, who was Catherine's father, denied that the baby was his. Her mother tried to keep Catherine with her, but she was unable to afford to pay someone to mind the baby when she went out to work. When Catherine was six months old, her mother brought her to Dundalk's industrial school, run by the Sisters of Mercy.

"My first real memory of my mother is when she came to visit me when I was about five or six. She had married by this stage and had her own family. She sat on one end of the couch and I was on the other end, and I was afraid of her. I kept pulling away from her.

She was asking me were the nuns good to me, and I couldn't tell her that they weren't, that we were being beaten. She might say something, and then I'd get it worse when she was gone away and they had me at their mercy. I remember the nun coming down, and saying to my mother 'I think it's time for you to go'.

There were other children there whose parents were married, and when they came to visit they could stay as long as they wanted. But it was because my mother wasn't married when she had me that they treated her like she was a nobody. She only came to visit me about once a year.

One of things I remember was crying with the cold. In winter in the afternoons, we'd all huddle together in a long shed, with no door and little square windows. We had pigeon holes where we kept our overalls. We were dressed in rags, patches on top of patches on top of patches. We'd bunch up together in this open shed to try and keep warm. All we had was a jumper and skirt. We never had a coat. I remember having chilblains from my ankles up to me knees, and I'm not exaggerating. We knitted from about five years old, making our own stockings and jumpers.

During the winter we all wore our clothes in bed — it was the only way to keep warm. We had no heating at all. There were huge big fire places all over the building, but they never lit fires in them. I remember being brought to a doctor in Dublin because I had a club foot, and he remarked on how cold I was. He warmed up my feet in front of an electric fire. The teacher with me told one of the nuns about this and she beat me and beat me, just because I was cold. This nun, we used to call her the Witch, but even that was too good for her — she was like a devil in nun's clothing. When she'd be walloping me, froth used to come out of her mouth.

She beat me so badly that I actually had a nervous breakdown as a child. Every Friday we used to sing hymns. I was standing up on a bench in the back row one day, when suddenly everything went away on me. I was there and I wasn't there, it's hard to explain. And I jumped down and started screaming that I couldn't see anything. I was about eight or nine.

They brought me down to the local doctor, and I heard him saying something about Ardee. I knew there was a mental home there, and I remember thinking, oh no, that's where they're going to send me. I couldn't tell him about the beatings because the nun was there, and I knew I'd be beaten to a pulp if I opened my mouth. I remember pleading with the doctor not to send me away. He came in to see me about once a week after that. He wanted me to tell him why I was always crying, why my eyes were always swollen. But I couldn't say a thing because we were never alone — there was always a nun there, so I'd just look at the floor. I kept getting these turns, like blackouts, and I'd be shoved into one of the parlours and I'd cry and cry for hours. And then I'd eventually fall asleep on one of the hard benches. When I'd wake up I'd be fine.

It was definitely the beatings and the fear of those nuns. There were two in particular, and I used to fall to pieces at the very sight of them. The Witch as we called her would pick on the girls who didn't have parents, or who were illegitimate. If you had parents you were okay. We got the worst of it. I wet the bed until I was fourteen, and I was beaten into a pulp for it. But I was only wetting the bed out of fear of the nuns.

We were constantly starving. In the morning, we got cocoa, bread and dripping. Then at half twelve, during the lunch hour in school, we'd be marched into our dining hall, with its big long tables and benches. We got two potatoes and soup. We never got meat — only the big girls were allowed meat. You might try and swap something like a hairclip for an extra potato — you'd give your life for a hairclip so you'd have something to swap. When you got big, you were moved up to the top table and the nun would give you a little bit of meat.

The place was over-run with mice. They used to put black sticky stuff onto bits of wood around the place, and the mice would stick to it and not be able to get away. And we'd be eating our dinner with maybe twenty-five mice sitting there looking at you, and squealing to get away. But we'd nearly eat them, we were that hungry.

The pantry where they kept the bread was crawling with mice. We'd see them running all over the bread we were going to eat, and we'd have to pick their droppings out of it. But none of us got sick from that.

The dining hall was down in the basement. When you looked up at the windows you could see the legs of people walking past on the street. An odd one would look down, but most of them kept going. People wouldn't want to look anyway — they just passed by.

At half three, when we got out of school, we'd be herded into the shed in the yard and they'd bring out a big tray of bread and everyone would grab at it. If you were small, you got nothing. I remember being about five or six, and I was down on the ground eating the crumbs left by the others, and somebody gave me a kick. But I didn't care, I was just desperate to get those crumbs. Even to this day, I go around picking up crumbs everywhere. I can't stop myself.

At half-five in the evening, we'd be all marched down again for tea, which was a plate of porridge. That's all, every tea time without fail.

It was a mini concentration camp — it's the only description I can make of it. We would have been better off to be put in a chamber and gassed. We wouldn't have had to suffer, and that's the truth.

I remember the inspector coming very well — Dr. McCabe was her name. Once a year she arrive to examine us. The preparations for her visit would go on for ever. We had to be spotless and the place had to shine. It was she who said I had to go to Dublin for the club foot.

When I was eleven, I went to hospital for the operation. I loved it there. Compared to the orphanage it was heaven. People were kind to me. It was coming up to Christmas, and a man and a nurse came round asking us all what we wanted Santa to bring us. We had heard about Santa in the orphanage alright, but we knew he didn't come to us. He came to children outside, but we had done something wrong so he stayed away from us. We'd put out our stockings just in case, but they'd be empty on Christmas morning, unless your friend might have put a holy picture cut out of a magazine there for you.

When I woke up on Christmas morning in the hospital I couldn't believe it — there were so many presents. Colouring books, a story book, pens, soap. It was just marvellous. While we never got presents in the orphanage, they did give us a nice day on Christmas, to be fair to them. We'd be sick with the excitement over what we were going to eat. At Christmas dinner we got a delft plate and a lovely mug with pictures on it and a beautiful knife and fork. They'd disappear then for another year. Priests and loads of other nuns used to come into the orphanage for a visit, so they had to put on a good show. We got turkey, Christmas pudding, the works. We'd be so sick with the excitement, though, that often we weren't even able to eat it. We'd try and wrap up bits of food and stash them under our pillow for the next day. Because you always knew that the next day would be a hungry day.

We were always frightened of men. We were told that they'd attack us, so if a man ever came near us we'd scream, we'd be so nervous. We were terrified of everything really. When we got our periods we were terrified. Everybody used to hide it, keep it secret. We knew the bigger girls had a secret but we didn't know what it was. I got mine when I was just over fourteen. The nun gave me three home-made towels, as hard as nails. We had to wash them out ourselves and you'd be trying to hide them so no one would see they were yours. We never heard the word period. We used to call it 'that'. We'd say 'she has that'.

There were nuns teaching us in the national school, which was part of the complex. Some of them were nice, and were very good teachers. One of the nuns in the school knew how I was being beaten by the other nun in the orphanage, but she couldn't do anything. I think she was afraid. They had a secondary school, St Vincent's, on the complex as well. I was all set to do the exam to get in, but the nun who used to beat me wouldn't let me do it. She blocked me, so I never had a chance.

At sixteen you had to leave, and the nuns put you into jobs. It was all housework, slaving in other people's houses. Three days after my sixteenth birthday I was sent out to work. I was only told on the day, and then out I went. I wasn't even given the time to say goodbye to my friends. I had been almost sixteen years with many of them. I didn't realise that I'd never see some of them again. The nun who had been so cruel to me said 'Off you go now, and don't do what your mother did'. And all the way on the bus to Dublin to the house where I was to work, I was asking myself what on earth had my mother done. I didn't know."

Catherine worked in domestic service with a family just outside Dublin for many years. She is now married with two children and lives in County Dublin. She maintained contact on and off with her mother. She even managed to track down her father. He died recently, still refusing to publicly acknowledge her existence.

Tessie's Story, St Augustine's Industrial School, Templemore (Sisters of Mercy), 1950–1963

"At Christmas, we'd hang a sock at the end of our beds. We'd heard somewhere that other children used to get presents from Santa in their stockings. But Christmas morning, we'd look in the socks and they were always empty. That happened every year — Santa never left anything in our stockings."

Tessie was born in the county home in Thurles in 1947. Her mother was a single parent, and Tessie went into St Augustine's, the industrial school in Templemore run by the Sisters of Mercy, when she was about two years old.

"I used to think I'd be in there all my life. I thought that in the world there were small people and there were big people, and that I was one of the small people, and that's what I'd be for ever. I used to ask myself, 'why didn't God make me a big person?' Big people didn't seem to get bashed about as much.

I had to go to a dentist a few years ago, and he asked me, 'who broke your jaw?' I didn't know that my jaw had been broken, but when I thought back I remembered my mother telling me about an incident that happened in the county home where I was born.

I was maybe six months old, and she was trying to feed me some baby rice. Apparently I wouldn't eat it, and if I did I'd just vomit it back up. This nun used to come in and collect it up and feed it back to me. But she got annoyed one day and walloped me on the face, sent me flying across the room. Maybe that was when my jaw was broken.

My first memories of St Augustine's are not very clear. I remember seeing loads of girls down on their hands and knees scrubbing the yard, and a nun standing over them beating them on their backs.

Some of the older girls used to be in charge of us babies. If we wet the bed they'd beat us with a shoe last — a piece of wood in the shape of a shoe but with a spring and a handle on it.

They used to put us to bed, and they'd give us ten seconds, and we'd have to have our eyes closed. They'd go round banging on our pillows, and anyone who even blinked would be taken out and dragged around the floor. If you opened your eyes, they'd beat you. They used to lock us in cupboards under the stairs as well.

The food wasn't too bad — I don't remember being hungry. Except at Mass. We had to go to Mass every day before breakfast — we'd be up at six in the mornings. And at Mass there would be girls fainting all the time. Just falling over.

The big treat at Easter was you'd get a boiled egg. But the cook — she was cruel and used to beat us badly — she'd always give one of us the dummy egg. This was made of wood and is what you put under the hen to make her lay.

I was given the dummy egg for several Easters in a row, and I'd be hammering away at it, with all the other girls eating up their lovely eggs. And that was all you got. You'd have to wait another whole year to have a chance of getting an egg again. It was so cruel.

At Christmas, the nun would bring out a box of dolls, and we'd all get one to play with. But a week later, the doll was taken off us and put away for the next year.

I got some very bad beatings from nuns when I was there. I stuck out my tongue at one of them once — I suppose I was about eleven. It's hard to remember ages, because we never had any birthdays, so you never really knew your age.

Anyway, this nun saw me sticking out my tongue and she flew at me with her leather belt, and she beat me, beat me, beat me, until she was out of breath. When she got her breath back she started at me again. I was down on the ground crawling around to get away from her. It felt like it went on for ever.

At least with that nun I knew what it was for. But this other nun called me into a classroom once. There was a group of us in the corridor with our rags waiting to start cleaning. I was about eight or nine. I remember that we were happy and laughing for some reason. I think it was coming up to summer holidays.

This particular nun came out of the classroom and she called me in. She had a big stick, and she just beat me around the room with that stick. Hitting me everywhere, with her full force. I must have blacked out because I don't remember it ending, or how I got out of the room. The other girls thought she was going to kill me. I never knew why she beat me like this — I think it was maybe because she saw that I was a bit happy.

That nun remembered that beating. I went back years later when I was married, and I brought my children, just to show them that I had done well, you know. They gave us high tea, and this same nun came over to me and whispered, 'Tessie, do you regret the beatings?' And even then I was afraid to say anything.

There was another girl there, Kitty, and she was beaten so badly that they had to hide her when the inspector came. Kitty wet the bed every night, and it was the cook who beat her that time. The roaring and screaming coming from the room was something terrible. They just hammered poor Kitty all the time. I think they broke her nose once.

I remember the inspector coming. There was a woman who used to come sometimes as well. They'd just walk in and walk out, wouldn't really talk to us or anything. There was one time we were in school and we were sent for and given new clothes, new underwear and shoes, because the inspector was coming. Usually when he came the girls would get to go to the pictures, but they usually wouldn't let me go.

Things got a bit better when the nuns opened up the boarding school there. I suppose they didn't want to be seen beating us so much. I was about twelve. The boarding school was for well-to-do girls, and what happened was that we basically became their servants.

There were over eighty of them. We'd set the tables for their meals, and then clear up after them. I was kept out of school on Mondays and Tuesdays to wash their underwear and socks by hand. And do the ironing. We'd also clean their dormitories and wax the floors.

Another thing we had to do was gather up the boarding girls' sanitary towels and burn them. That wasn't so bad I suppose, compared to the girl whose job it was to wash the nuns' sanitary pads. They wouldn't even wash their own.

They got in the heating when the boarders came, and it was my job to look after the furnace. It was man's work really. I'd have to shovel a big heavy load of anthracite from the shed into a wheelbarrow, take it to the furnace and then shovel it in. I did that twice a day.

And I did the potatoes as well. I had to scrub six huge bucket loads — enough to feed the whole school. I'd scrub them out in the yard, in freezing water, and leave them lined up outside the kitchen.

We didn't get any education as children — we were just educated to scrub. One of the girls went back later and asked the nuns why didn't they educate us. And the nuns said that it wasn't the policy.

School was mental torture anyway. We went to school with the 'outside girls', the ones from the town. One nun who taught us used to make fun of us in front of the other kids. 'Look at the orphans,' she'd say, 'all they're going to be good for is going round with sacks on their backs begging.' It's no wonder I never learned to read or write at school. Years later, when I went to get my eyes tested, they told me I needed glasses from when I was a child."

Tessie's mother used to visit her from time to time at the industrial school. She herself worked for the nuns, as a cleaner in the local hospital, formerly the county home.

"The nuns always told my mother that I was bold — they never said a good word about me. And they always told me I was no good and would turn out like my mother.

She was eighty-two when she died, and was still in the same hospital. She had letters and photographs and lots of stuff, but when she died the nuns burned it all. I have two brothers whom I've never seen, and her papers might have had some information about them. But now everything is burned, and I'll never be able to find them. That hurts me more than anything else."

When Tessie left St Augustine's at sixteen, the nuns got her a job in the kitchens of a Dublin hospital, also run by nuns. At seventeen, she became pregnant after meeting a man on her day off. She had been told nothing of the facts of life. She ended up in St Patrick's Mother and Baby home on the Navan Rd, and her baby, a boy, was taken for adoption. He returned to find her recently, and they are delighted with each other.

"I've always been open with my own children about my past. They knew all about the orphanage and everything from when they were small. I didn't want to have to pretend that I'm something that I'm not.

You see, years ago I was going with a gorgeous fellow, and he asked me to marry him. I was thrilled, and I told him about my background at that stage. And when I told him, he said it was all off, that he couldn't bring me home to meet his mother.

So for years I felt I wasn't good enough for anyone, that everyone else was better than me. I often feel that I'm not normal, that there's something missing out of me. That's one of the things that stays with you from the orphanage. I don't know if you ever leave it behind."

Ten

The Evil Within:
Child Sexual Abuse

Perhaps the most shocking revelations to emerge from the industrial schools in recent years relate to the sexual abuse of children, especially boys, in their care. It is now clear that this abuse was widespread, constant and spanned a number of decades, from the earliest reports in the 1930s up to allegations from the 1980s.

The Gardai have been brought in to investigate allegations related to almost all of the industrial schools for boys over the age of ten in the country. Almost 150 religious Brothers have been implicated, over eighty-five per cent of them Christian Brothers and the remainder made up of Rosminian priests and Brothers. The schools involved include Artane, Salthill, Letterfrack and Tralee (Christian Brothers) and Clonmel and Upton (Rosminians).

To date charges have been laid against eleven Christian Brothers relating to allegations of child sexual abuse in the Artane, Salthill and Tralee schools. They have pleaded not guilty and are awaiting trial. One Rosminian Brother has been convicted for the sexual abuse of boys in St Joseph's Ferryhouse, Clonmel, in the late 1970s.

The largest child sex abuse investigation ever undertaken by the Irish police is in relation to Artane Industrial School. At the time of writing the Gardai at Clontarf station in Dublin have taken more than 300 statements from former inmates alleging sexual and physical abuse against up to 100 current, former and deceased Christian Brothers. This makes it one of the biggest child abuse police investigations ever undertaken internationally. The attitude of the order has been to encourage anyone who suffered abuse to come forward and make a statement to the Gardai.

All this is taking place against the background of an avalanche of child sexual abuse cases generally within the community. While most sexual abuse of children had always taken place within their families, much public attention has been focussed on the abuse by clerics. Prominent cases concerning Fr Brendan Smith, Fr Sean Fortune, Fr Ivan Payne and Fr Paul McGennis have received enormous publicity, creating in the public mind a somewhat unfair connection between priests and paedophilia. The slowness of the Irish hierarchy to acknowledge the problem and the clear pattern that existed of moving abusing priests from area to area have served to seriously undermine the credibility of the Catholic Church in this country.

Given the public pronouncements by the Catholic Church over the decades on matters of sexuality, it is hardly surprising that there should be such a focus on the members of their own clergy convicted for sexually molesting children. The Church's defence has been that they, together with the State authorities, were ignorant of the issue of child sexual abuse until very recently. It is a general claim that it was only from the early 1980s that professionals became aware of the phenomenon of child sexual abuse and only much later were guidelines developed to respond appropriately to the issue.

However, it is interesting in this regard to examine the evidence in the trial of Fr Paul McGennis, convicted in 1997 for sexually abusing two young girls during the 1960s, one of them a patient at the time in Our Lady's Hospital for Sick Children in Crumlin. It was stated in court that a file had been discovered during the investigation indicating that Fr McGennis had sent pornographic photographs of children to be developed in England in 1960. The staff at the processing laboratory became concerned and alerted the British police, who contacted the Gardai. The Gardai immediately got in touch with the Archbishop of Dublin, John Charles McQuaid.

According to a statement issued by the Dublin Archdiocese in July 1997, what happened next was that Archbishop

McQuaid interviewed Fr McGennis, "and arranged for him to have treatment which was considered successful at the time".[1]

It is clear from this that not only was the Archdiocese of Dublin fully aware as far back as 1960 of the sexual abuse of children by priests, but it also had put in place some kind of treatment mechanism and clearly some means of assessing this "treatment". Far from ignorance of the problem, this seems to indicate that they not only knew all about it, but had developed a *modus operandi* for dealing with it.

The defence of ignorance of child sexual abuse has also been widely used by many statutory authorities and child care professionals. For example, in what became known as the West of Ireland Farmer case (the appalling sexual and physical abuse of four of the six McColgan children by their father Joseph McColgan from the late 1970s to early 1990s), the team of professionals who investigated the case concluded "that a genuine incredulity of sexual abuse existed initially and may have persisted at senior social work management level and with the family general practitioner".[2]

Dr Harry Ferguson, an expert witness for the Health Board in the McColgan case, argued in an article in *The Irish Times* that "the McColgan children were subjected to sexual abuse at a time when our understanding of such crimes was less advanced than now", and that "the tragedy is that the case spanned a period when awareness of serious physical and sexual abuse was only beginning to develop".[3] Ferguson's article drew a strong rebuke from Alan Shatter TD who argued that "judged by the standards of the time, the health board's failure throughout the period of the McColgan children's childhood is inexcusable and should be seen as nothing but gross negligence".[4]

Sr Stanislaus Kennedy, a well known member of the Irish Sisters of Charity, also took this line of defence in an article in *The Irish Times* in May of 1999.[5] *States of Fear* on RTE had reported from a statement made to the Gardai by Sr Stanislaus in 1995 in connection with their investigation into the sexual abuse of boys in St Joseph's Industrial School in Kilkenny.[6] Referring to a complaint made to her about one of the child care workers at the school, which was run by her order, she said: "I picked up on it that he might have been sexually abusing them [the children] as well."

Sr Stanislaus' statement related to events in the mid- and late 1970s. Subsequent to *States of Fear*, she was interviewed on RTE radio, and shortly afterwards wrote in *The Irish Times* clarifying her position. Referring to the sexual abuse of boys at the industrial school in Kilkenny, she wrote that "at the time I did not know this, nor did I even suspect it. I was a young nun and the term 'sexual abuse' had not, as far as I know, even been coined — it was certainly never discussed even among childcare professionals".

Sr Stanislaus was, at that stage in her late thirties, and a central and enormously important figure in child care in Ireland. She had been one of the leading advocates of the need for the training of child care workers, and was instrumental in developing the first such professional training course in this country. This was the Diploma in Residential Child Care based in the School of Social Education in Kilkenny, which had been established in 1971. Sr Stanislaus was co-director of the course throughout the 1970s.

It is true that the specific term "child sexual abuse" was not explicitly used in Ireland at this time; rather terms like incest, un-natural practices, or carnal knowledge were in more common usage. But there can be no doubt that those charged with the responsibility for protecting vulnerable children had been aware for many years that children were both potential and actual victims of sexual crimes.

From the mid-1960s, child sexual abuse had become the subject of major international discussion. The Kennedy Report referred to the issue in its bibliography in 1970. Perhaps the earliest example of this awareness was the establishment of a committee as far back as 1930 to examine The Criminal Law Amendments Acts (1880-85) and Juvenile Prostitution.

This committee, under the chairmanship of William Carrigan KC, was asked to consider whether the criminal law amendment acts as related to sexual crimes required revision. Its report was received in August 1931. However the Department of Justice decided that "having regard to the statements made in the report as to the condition of morality in the Saorstat, it would be unwise to publish it on the basis that Commissions on matters of this kind are rarely helpful".[7]

The Department went on to say that:

> "In this country, decent people — the vast majority — feel that sexual offences should be punished vigorously. The desire is sincere, but vague. Commissioners are tempted to play up to this vague desire in order not to be outdone by the general public in the zeal for morality. Consequently, the reports of such commissions are liable to be too drastic, lacking judgement and unworkable in general, the report of this commission is no exception to the rule."[8]

Not only was the report kept secret, but the Oireachtas debates on the matter took place in private committee, and they also were not published. The Department of Justice argued that "it would be far better if a bill dealing with the matters reported on by the commission could be passed into law without public discussion in the Dail. A judge or two, a lawyer or two, a well-balanced priest or two, an experienced police officer, meeting in private, all sharing the Catholic view on the moral gravity of sexual offences, could give the Government much helpful advice".[9]

The most significant aspect of the work of this committee was a fascinating memorandum prepared for it by the then Garda Commissioner, General Eoin O'Duffy. Remarkably, O'Duffy stated that:

> Immorality in the individual or community is undoubtedly the forerunner of crime, and the latter can invariably be described as the effect of the former. In the country a careful examination of our most heinous crimes reveals the fact that in the majority of cases, the depraved career of the perpetuator originated from his immoral instincts, or from association with persons of this class. The outlook of many of our people, even in rural areas, has changed within the past ten years, and the morally depraved who then would be exorcised from

society are now regarded as rather clever and interesting. An alarming aspect is the number of cases with interference with girls under fifteen, and even under thirteen and under eleven, which come before the courts. These are in most cases heard of accidentally by the Garda, and are very rarely the result of a direct complaint. It is generally agreed that reported cases do not exceed fifteen per cent of those actually happening.[10]

His next statement echoes reactions to some sentences handed down by the courts to persons convicted of child sexual abuse in the 1990s:

For the fifteen per cent of cases which do come to notice, legislation does not provide punishment sufficiently salutary to discourage the commission of an offence, which, unless checked will very fatally strike at the rudimentary fundamentals of society. Worse still, Judges have not been imposing the extreme penalties allowed. To impose a sentence of six months on, or to fine a ruffian who destroys the innocence of a child under thirteen is farcical.[11]

He gave some further evidence of the type of offences that the Garda became aware of in the first six months of 1930:

During the years 1928, '29 and '30, JCD aged twenty-seven years committed sodomy with PT aged eleven years, and committed acts of gross indecency with three other boys aged about fourteen years; Between 1/5/29 and 4/2/30, one PK aged forty-two years had carnal knowledge of his daughter, MAK aged sixteen years; On 12/8/30 and on three previous occasions, TK aged thirty-eight years, committed sodomy with his son JK aged ten years.

The Criminal Law Amendment Act, 1935 was the eventual outcome of this Committee's deliberations. It allowed for the imposition of a term of penal servitude for anyone convicted of having carnal knowledge of girls under fifteen years of age.

Thus, from the early 1930s, there is clear evidence that both the Gardai and the Department of Justice were fully aware that adults could and did sexually abuse children. To say that in the 1960s and 1970s people in Ireland, particularly those who worked in the area of child care, had no knowledge of child sexual abuse suggests a level of ignorance clearly not shared by the authorities of either State or Church.

The earliest public inklings of what we now know to be the widespread sexual abuse of children in the industrial schools came in the early 1960s. Peadar Cowen, a former Clann na Poblachta TD during the 1940s, raised the issue of the sexual abuse of children in the schools in a pamphlet entitled "Dungeons Deep: A monograph on prisons, borstals, reformatories and industrial schools in the Republic of Ireland, and some reflections on crime and punishment and matters relating thereto". In it he argued that:

> There is a tendency to hide from the public knowledge of any incident of unnatural practice in institutions to which children are committed by the courts. Fortunately these incidents are infrequent, but when they do occur the citizens ought to be told. Only by knowing can they take a helpful interest in the welfare of those children for whom they, too, have a moral responsibility. On one occasion an official of an institution to which boys were frequently sent by the courts was convicted of grave offences on boys there. The case should have got publicity so that citizens could satisfy themselves that adequate steps were taken by the authorities for the protection of the children afterwards. It was wrong to hide it.[12]

The way in which anything controversial to do with the industrial schools was hidden is graphically described by Brian Quinn, a former editor of the *Evening Herald*. In a letter to *The Irish Times* following the *States of Fear* programme he described how he witnessed:

... one of the worst of the Christian Brothers [Br Joseph O'Connor, director of the Artane Boys Band] break into the office of the manager and demand that a court case that mentioned Artane should not be used. Before the manager could lift a phone he [O'Connor] would push open the editorial door to tell us the manager had instructed that the case be dumped. He got away with this just one more time. On the third time of demanding, the manager, who was most honourable and dedicated to ethics, said no, as he was not going to interfere with the editors any more on behalf of Artane.

Quinn concluded that:

... those requests should have alerted journalists to start inquiries into what was happening in Artane. That we did not is a heavy burden. Journalists of that time were trapped in a carefully designed plot that mixed lies with official evasion and ecclesiastical terror. Nevertheless, I for one, believe that we allowed cowardice to rule.[13]

An important question relates to what the Christian Brothers knew of the sexual abuse of children by members of their order. Within their industrial schools in Ireland, sexual abuse is described by survivors as being common knowledge. In Artane, the children referred to it as "badness" — they had no other words to express what was being done to them. However, while many children knew which Brothers were abusing, and which boys were being abused, the sexual abuse itself generally took place behind closed doors and with no witnesses present. While there are some accounts of boys being abused in open dormitories, showers and classrooms by Brothers, these are less common.

The Christian Brothers' refusal to allow access to their archive (on legal advice, they now say) makes it difficult to ascertain precisely the extent of knowledge of abuse at senior levels within the order. However, a fascinating and revealing clue to this has emerged in Australia.

Australian society was rocked in the late 1980s and early 1990s by a series of revelations of horrific sexual and physical abuse of boys in Christian Brothers orphanages, particularly in Western Australia. It transpired in some of the subsequent court cases that the Christian Brothers knew of the sexual abuse of children by their members within their institutions as early as the mid-1930s. But what is even more interesting about this is that they communicated this knowledge in writing to the order's headquarters, which were in Dublin.

In a letter to the Superior General of the order in Dublin in 1935, one Australian Christian Brother wrote prophetically on the issue of child sexual abuse within the order: "If we do not take a determined stand with regard to this matter we are bound to have numerous scandals in the near future." Another letter from an Australian Brother on the same issue showed an even greater concern: "The weakness being a deplorable one and scandalous in the extreme, the ever-present possibility of publicity being given to the incident gives abundant cause for the most serious concern." A third Brother, writing during the early 1940s seemed primarily concerned with public exposure: "As long as outsiders do not become aware of these things we may hope for better times after the War."

Perhaps the most graphic letter arrived in Dublin in 1948 and concerned one particular Brother who had been sent for rehabilitation following his sexual abuse of children, but had continued to offend. As the letter to the Superior General in Ireland said: "generally the dog returns to his vomit especially where the Second Vow is concerned".[14] Throughout the correspondence, there is no record available as to how the Christian Brothers' leadership in Ireland responded to this avalanche of information on sexual abuse by the members of their Australian congregations, many of whom were of course themselves Irish. These responses are now locked away in the order's archives in Rome, assiduously concealed from public view.

Much of the information on this correspondence comes from Dr Barry Coldrey, himself a Christian Brother working in Australia. He was commissioned by the congregation to write a history of its involvement in the provision of institutional care for children in Australia. In his book *The Scheme*, Coldrey says that at times savage physical abuse and fairly widespread sexual abuse occurred in these institutions.

Coldrey cites further evidence of knowledge of child sexual abuse within Christian Brothers' institutions amongst the senior members of the congregation. Statements such as "shameful betrayals of trust with reference to boys", "terrible question of interference with boys", "he must never be in contact with the young" all reveal that clear and precise knowledge of such abuse existed.[15]

Damning as Coldrey's book is, more dramatic events were to follow. In the mid-1990s, it was revealed that Coldrey had in fact written a second book. When he had finished the manuscript of *The Scheme* and was waiting for the book to go through its publication stages, he wrote what became *Reaping the Whirlwind: A Secret Report for the Executive of the Christian Brothers - Sexual Abuse from 1930-1994*. This was a confidential report for the then Superior-General of the congregation, Colm Keating. Despite its confidential status, *Reaping the Whirlwind* found its way into the Australian legal system, and was cited as evidence in many civil cases against the Brothers and the Church.[16] In this report, Coldrey admitted that "that the situation in the orphanages was worse than the impression given in *The Scheme*". He also uncovered evidence of "sex rings" in two of the orphanages operated by the Brothers in Western Australia.

To give some sense of *Reaping the Whirlwind*, we reproduce here an account of the sexual abuse of one young boy, given by a survivor of the notorious Bindoon Orphanage in Western Australia:

> I settled into Boys town, Bindoon, and worked very hard under Brother Keaney but was singled out by several Brothers for special attention and often found myself in very unsavoury situations where I was given jobs away from the other boys and was subjected to a Brother taking all his clothes off and all my clothes off and he (Angus) tried to penetrate me for a long time until the lunch bell rang. I was told not to say anything and it won't happen again. The

Brother would give me a job; and this other one would turn up. He told me I was doing something wrong, took my pants down and belted me with the strap and told me I would get the same till I learned to do exactly what he wanted me to do. The climax came on one day when all the boys were to go to the Bindoon Show. This Brother was going with them, so I made an excuse to stay behind, so one Brother told me to feed the hay to the cattle, and clean up the dairy. I nearly died when the Brother turned up behind me with no clothes on... he ordered me to remove my shorts ... I was scared and he grabbed me and threw me onto bales of hay and raped me. I was crying as he kept trying to push his penis into me . . .

Brother Keaney, mentioned in the above testimony, was born in Rossinver, Co Leitrim in 1888. He emigrated to Australia in 1912 and after working in a number of jobs, joined the Christian Brothers in 1916. He was a well-known figure in Western Australia. Liking to describe himself as 'Keaney the Builder', the orphanage he ran at Bindoon was literally built from scratch by the children, who were mainly child migrants sent out from the UK. A significant number of these had been born to Irish mothers in Britain, and placed in orphanages throughout the UK. Australian journalist Alan Gill in his definitive history of the child migration schemes to Australia has argued that "Claims of physical abuse perpetrated by Keaney are so numerous that, even if only ten per cent were true, he would be quite unfit for any form of contact with children".[17]

Keaney is also reported to have committed acts of savage sexual abuse on several boys. One survivor describes his methods:

Keaney had a special stick which had — and I'm an ex-army man — a bullet on the end of it. Now if you know a 303 bullet, the bullet goes inside a casing like a shell, but the shell casing has got rivets on it. And what he'd do with this stick after he'd hit you, he'd give you a quick thrust up the rectum and give it a twist and that would withdraw your lower bowel out of your rectum and that happened to me once. He must have thought he hurt me pretty badly, because he inspected me some time after that.[18]

In the late 1960s, some years after Br Keaney's death, the Bindoon Orphanage was re-named Keaney College in honour of this Brother. His bronze statue dominates the courtyard of the building, with his hand resting on the shoulder of a small boy.[19]

It is interesting to note that no child migration scheme ever developed directly from Ireland, despite the attempts of the Christian Brothers to persuade the Irish Government to send children to their institutions in Australia. In 1938, Br Louis Conlon, manager of the Tardun orphanage in Western Australia, wrote to the Taoiseach, Eamon de Valera, inviting the Irish Government to participate in and provide financial assistance for a child migration scheme to Australia. Conlon visited Ireland to promote his cause and received some media attention. However, on the 17th of August 1938, Conlon was told by the Cabinet Secretary that the Government would not sanction such a scheme. It was thought that de Valera did not approve of such forced emigration as the solution to Ireland's problems.[20] Irish children in industrial schools were thus spared having transportation to Australia added to their other miseries of hunger and abuse.

A House of Commons Report established to investigate the Child Migration Scheme from Britain to Australia was published in 1998. It noted that "the worst cases of criminal abuse in Australia appear to have occurred in institutions run by agencies of the Catholic Church, in particular the Christian Brothers and the Sisters of Mercy."

The Committee went on to say that:

It is hard to convey the sheer weight of the testimony we have received. It is impossible to resist the conclusion that some of what was done there was of a quite exceptional depravity, so that terms like 'sexual abuse' are too weak to convey it. For example, those of us who heard the account of a man who as a boy was a particular favourite of some Christian Brothers

at Tardun who competed as to who could rape him
100 times first, his account of being in terrible pain,
bleeding and bewildered, trying to beat his own eyes
so they would cease to be blue as the Brothers liked
his blue eyes, or being forced to masturbate animals,
or being held upside down over a well and threatened
in case he ever told, will never forget it.[21]

The Christian Brothers Canadian orphanages in Newfoundland and in Ontario have also been the subject of investigations
of child abuse.[22] In attempting to explain the existence of
violence and abuse in institutions managed by the Christian
Brothers, Dr Coldrey has written that such allegations must be
placed in their historical and institutional context:

> The Institute's recruitment was heavily rural in
> Ireland, and from the respectable working-class
> world-wide. Institutional youth had regularly
> suffered acute deprivation before their admittance, a
> deprivation at which the Brothers could only guess
> because courses in child care were very much a thing
> of the future — the 1960s, not the 1880s. The Brothers
> were normally trained as primary teachers, not as
> child care professionals. In institutions Brothers and
> boys had one another's company around the clock.
> The work was especially tiring and stressful;
> recreation away from the institution was rare;
> holidays few; and the boy's moods and reactions
> differed from those with a stable family background.
> Bedwetting among the younger inmates, the result of
> basic insecurity and poor toilet training, was a
> pervasive problem, and no solution appeared to offer
> itself except primitive aversion therapy. It was likely
> that stress would lead to violence.[23]

In more recent work, Coldrey has highlighted the very thin
line that exists between physical and sexual abuse in such
institutions. He says that the fact that so many children were
stripped before they were beaten suggests a sexual element to the

punishments inflicted on them. He points out that the beating of naked children was often a precursor to sexual abuse.[24]

Barry Coldrey remains a Christian Brother, living in Australia. He is an established scholar, with his doctoral thesis on 'The Influence of the Christian Brothers on Militant Irish Nationalism' having been published as the book *Faith and the Fatherland* in 1988. However, it appears that his more recent work in discovering the extent of child abuse in Australian institutions has not proved popular with the order. According to his own web page on the internet, he says that "My mission as an 'agent secret' for a section of the Roman Catholic Church ended unromantically in February 1998 when I was handed my redundancy papers, nor was the handshake golden."

The Christian Brothers in Ireland have issued an apology (in March 1998) to those who were sexually and physically abused as children in their care. However, they have not given any indication that they have detailed knowledge of the fact that their own members had been sexually abusing children for at least the previous sixty years. Neither have they answered the crucial question as to how it was that the sexual abuse of boys was so concentrated within the industrial schools. While it is likely that the closed nature of these institutions was undoubtedly a factor, what remains to be discovered is whether the order had a policy of transferring into the schools those Brothers whose activities had given scandal within the wider community.

There was a frank acknowledgement in 1982 of how the Christian Brothers dealt with their members who had 'problems'. In papers prepared for the Christian Brothers International Spirituality Conference in Dublin, it was acknowledged that "in the past, a common practice was to shift men who had problems — alcoholic, social, psychological — from community to community as a substitute for dealing with the issues".[25] This is a phenomenon not unique to the Christian Brothers — it was the accepted way in which the Catholic Church internationally dealt with child sexual abusers among their clergy. However, it does give some hint as to a possible reason for the extraordinarily widespread nature of the sexual abuse of boys within Christian Brothers' industrial school.

While the vast majority of cases in this area relate to the sexual abuse of boys by male religious, there are some accounts of girls within industrial schools being abused by priests who came to visit. Brigid from the Good Shepherd Industrial School in Limerick has one such account in the 1950s of a priest who abused her as a child during confession. She was too terrified to tell anyone, knowing that it was unlikely that she would be believed.[26]

There is also one reported account of sexual abuse by a nun. Paddy Doyle, in his book *The God Squad*, describes the physical and sexual abuse he suffered as a very young boy at the hands of a Sister of Mercy in their industrial school in Cappoquin, Co Waterford. He had been committed to the school at the age of four during the 1950s, when both his parents had died. He describes the sexual abuse as "causing me to squirm and writhe involuntarily. When it had passed I sobbed uncontrollably, frightened at what had happened."[27]

In a separate matter, the case of Nora Wall, formerly Sr Dominic of the Sisters of Mercy, and Paul McCabe was heard before the courts during 1999. They have now been found completely innocent of all charges. They were accused of the rape of a young girl at the Cappoquin Industrial School during the late 1980s. They had been tried and found guilty, but the verdict was quashed as unsafe at the request of the Director of Public Prosecutions. The case itself and the subsequent complete exoneration of Nora Wall and Paul McCabe of all charges attracted enormous publicity.

Meanwhile, the orders implicated in the sexual abuse of children continue to vigorously contest the large number of civil cases being taken against them in the courts by the victims of that abuse. New legislation amending the Statute of Limitations to allow victims of sexual abuse to take cases based on incidents which occurred more than three years ago is likely to have a significant impact on this area. Furthermore, with a number of criminal charges pending against Christian Brothers and with the testimony to be laid before the Commission to Inquire into Childhood Abuse, it can safely be said that we have heard only the beginning of one of the darkest and most disturbing aspects of this country's recent past.

Barney's story, Artane Industrial School (Christian Brothers), 1949–1958

"When I went in there, the first thing that happened was they took away my name and gave me a number. Mine was 12,847. Everything I owned in the school from that time on was numbered 12,847. It was on my boots, it was on my bib, it was on my blankets, it was on my towel, it was on my brain."

Barney's mother died when he was seven years old. His father was a sergeant major in the army, posted all over the country, so Barney and his eight-year-old brother John were sent to Artane Industrial School, run by the Christian Brothers.

"Coming from a home into that place was like the difference between day and night. My family lived in the inner city of Dublin. Everybody knew each other, all the families had served in the armies together. Many of them had died in the Great War and on Flanders fields. My granddad died in the Dardanelles, fighting the Turks. We came from a place that was full of real people, mothers with children, old folks, young people, babies in prams outside getting the sun. Going into Artane, it was frightening seeing that awful, ugly, gigantic building. It was always cold, always wet, damp, grey, never anywhere to shelter from the cold and the wet.

The first thing that hit me was the food. There was hardly any of it, and because I was so small, the bigger boys would often steal my food on me. Three days a week we got a kind of pea soup, and four days we got a slice of corned beef type meat about the size of your two smallest fingers. And that was the same for the nine years I was there. We were all of us hungry all the time.

My brother John died when he was only forty-three. He was overweight and he had a heart attack. He just couldn't stop eating, and we always put it down to the fact that he never got enough as a child, and that's just the way it affected him. He always looked out for me in the school — he was my hero. One of his jobs was to look after the furnace, and when the kitchen waste would come down to be burnt, John would always get a few scraps and put them in his pocket to give to me. Things like apple skins, sometimes with bits of coal dust stuck to them from the furnace, when he'd picked them out of the fire.

I remember eating grass. They'd have about 200 of us out in the field, making us pull the grass by hand to get it cut. And we'd eat big handfuls of it. Some boys used to steal food from the animals on the farm. They'd get mangles, which is a type of turnip, and they'd eat them and swap bits of them for maybe a comic or something.

At Easter we'd get two eggs, just boiled eggs, one on Easter Sunday, and another on Easter Monday. The Brothers told us that that one was to celebrate Irish independence. I don't know from what we were celebrating independence. It certainly wasn't from cold or hunger or fear or deprivation.

We were so hungry that some of the boys broke in and stole the Holy Communions, you know, the bread. And everyone got kind of arrested on the parade ground, right where you were, and you had to open your pockets. Everything you had, you put on the ground. And they got some of the boys with the communion wafers and they beat the living hell out of them, they beat them beyond a pulp. So, there were funny things, but they were brutal.

They ruled by fear. Fear of the strap and the leather. Some of the Brothers would hit you with a rubber tyre from a baby pram, and it would go right up your arm. One Brother hit me so hard with this that the back of my hands would bleed, the blood would be oozing out.

A few years ago, my hands started going numb, and I couldn't hold anything. This was very serious because I was a carpenter and I needed my hands. So I went to a doctor and he arranged for me to have surgery. After the operation, the surgeon asked me how I had injured my hands — he said that the only time he had seen injuries like mine was a Korean karate expert who used to chop blocks with his hands.

I explained to him how the Brothers used to hit us in Artane for all those years, day after day with heavy leather straps, and he said that must be it. It formed a bony overgrowth which was strangling the nerves inside. And of course, we got hit on both hands, and if you didn't hold them out you were walloped across the face, on the legs, the back, anywhere. They were vicious, vicious beyond any reason. Some of them were sadistic — that's the only word for them. There was absolutely no one to stop them, and they'd beat you until they were literally spent.

Some of the boys were so badly beaten they used to suffer from what they call head staggers, like when boxers get punch drunk. I remember one boy used to stand there banging his head against walls for hours. Some boys lost an eye or a finger. One Brother had a hurley stick and he used to fire a sliothar at you, and that really hurt. They were some of the cruellest, most sadistic, unbridled people I have ever met.

It still scares the living hell out of me when I think of the boys screaming, and I can still hear it. I was so terrified in Artane that I developed a very bad speech impediment. When I was there I saw a boy hanging by the neck — a suicide. I saw another boy go out on a beam over the stairs. He was about twelve and was in his nightshirt. Something awful must have happened to him because he was frightened to death. He kept screaming 'If you touch me, I'll jump', and it was a sheer drop of over forty feet below him.

Artane was worse than a prison. At least in prison people get better fed, and they were certainly more humanely treated than we were, because in prison they're adults. And people from the outside come to visit, there are committees and so forth. But we were only children, we had nothing. No one gave a damn about us. I never saw any inspectors coming in, no one ever looked at me or talked to me.

Anyone who ran away got a horrific beating, and their heads were shaved. So you were bald, and you had to stand facing a wall for days and days. Sometimes you were chained to a tree, or tied to what we called the lamppost in the middle of the grounds. And if someone ran away, the whole school would be punished. We wouldn't be allowed margarine for maybe a week, and we'd have to eat the bread dry. And of course when you got the boy who ran away, you gave him a good kicking. He got a terrible time.

Brother Joseph O'Connor — we called him Joeboy — kicked me so badly one day that he damaged my hip. We were marching down to the trade shops and he just kicked me, in front of maybe 200 boys. I ran and hid in a hole, and he came after me and stomped down hard with his foot on my hip. I was in a terrible state. The teacher in the carpentry shop where I worked let me sit down for the rest of the day. Later that evening, when we were in school class, at Angelus time we all had to get up to pray, but I fell down. I couldn't stand, I felt my hip give out. The Brother in charge asked me what was wrong, and I told him about the kicking I got. He put me over his shoulder and carried me down to the infirmary, which was about a quarter-of-a-mile away. And that's the single best, kindest, most decent thing a Brother ever did for me in Artane. Since then I've walked with a limp on and off. The hip would just give out from time to time. It was permanently damaged.

Joeboy was in charge of the band, the famous Artane Boys Band. It was the gleaming jewel of the place. He hated me because I only stayed in the band for two weeks. I didn't like it. Joeboy had it in for me, and he was the most evil person I ever met. He was wicked beyond words. Some boys who were in the band liked him because he got them extra food and they had uniforms and went on trips. But he had a temper that was beyond control, and he was an evil child abuser. He had a lust that was totally abnormal.

I was in his class once — he taught school as well as the band — and I had said or done something, and he put me out on the line, at the edge of the classroom. Then he told me to take off my clothes. And right there in front of the whole class he sat down on the bench, on the desk with his foot on the bench where the boys would sit and write, and his other foot on the ground. He opened his cassock and put me across it and put his left hand under my private parts. He was squeezing me and beating the living hell out of my bare backside. He was foaming at the mouth, jumping and bopping. He was having a sexual orgasm in front of the whole class of boys. And I wasn't the only boy he done. It just hurts you to be degraded in such a manner. He didn't even have the goodness to bugger you in private. He was a bastard. And yet he would march around there on parade with the band like he was King Tut. He was evil.

He did things to me that I couldn't even tell my wife about, they were so shameful. One of the things he'd do when he'd be sexually molesting you was that he'd be trying to choke you as well. He'd be foaming at the mouth during it. Some of the things he did I can't even talk about now. It's too painful.

And yet many others suffered the same fate as me, or even worse. Especially the young boys from the convents in the country who had absolutely nobody. If something happened to them, even if they had disappeared, nobody would have missed them."

Brother Joseph O'Connor died about ten years ago. Because of his activities with the Artane Boys Band, he was a well-known figure in Ireland. He had been frequently interviewed on RTE television, and in 1976 the *Trom Agus Eadrom* programme, presented by Liam Ó Murchú, featured a special tribute to him and his work with the band. One of his victims has described how when he heard that Brother O'Connor was dying in Dublin's Mater Hospital, he went down and waited around the hospital until O'Connor was dead. He then went in to take a look at the body. He describes how he had an overwhelming need to actually see him dead. This man tells of being tied to a bed and raped at the age of eleven. He testifies to having had his head pushed into a drawer, and the drawer closed tight on his neck as he was being raped by Brother O'Connor. In account after account from survivors of Artane, Brother O'Connor's name is one of those repeatedly mentioned in the context of sexual abuse. Barney's experiences at his hands have scarred him for life.

"Sometimes we'd talk to each other about all the abuse. But we didn't know the words for rape or buggery or masturbation. We used to call it 'badness'. We'd say Brother

X was doing 'badness' with so and so. Sometimes when the Brothers had their pet boys they'd give them a bar of chocolate. You might get a share of it, and the boy would tell you what had happened.

Some of us told the priest in confession about how the Brothers were abusing us. I told the priest once, because I thought it must be a sin. But nothing came of it.

But not all the Brothers abused us. Some of them weren't too bad. But they never seemed to report what was going on. I think they had a responsibility to us. I mean stuff like that couldn't happen in the army or in prisons. But for us it was a daily occurrence, it was just a regime. And it was on a gigantic scale. The thing that reminds me of it is a film like *Schindler's List*. It really was like a concentration camp for children.

I still wake up with nightmares. Many of the boys in Artane do. Many committed suicide very young. The thing that affects me most is the boy who fell to his death right in front of me. He was being chased and he fell over the banisters, a drop of forty feet. He touched me as he fell, passed right in front of me. I can still hear his scream. I went looking for his grave, just something to identify him, but I couldn't find anything."

Barney emigrated to the United States some years after leaving Artane. He worked as a carpenter for many years, ending up as a buildings inspector for the City of Los Angeles. He returned to Ireland for a number of months during 1998 — he was determined to see justice done for the thousands of victims of Artane Industrial School. He was one of the first survivors of the school to speak out publicly about the horrific sexual abuse he had suffered.

"Children are a country's most precious asset. But not in Ireland. We were treated like we were unwanted, something to be hidden, to be ashamed of. There's so much shame, not just the shame of a person who was raped, but the shame of a nation that allowed it to happen. It made Ireland into the child molesting capital of the world. Shame on us."

Christy's Story, St Patrick's Industrial School, Upton, Co. Cork (Rosminians), 1963–1965

"It was fear of the beatings that made me keep quiet about the sexual abuse for so long."

Christy was born in 1949 in Cork city, the second of a family of four. His father left the family shortly after he was born – Christy would not meet him again until he was eighteen years old.

"Life growing up was rough. My mother was on home assistance and I would often rob food and bring it home. I only went to school a couple of times a week. I was a bit wild, and we had no home life really. When I was fourteen, I got caught for stealing apples out of the English Market. I was sentenced to two years in Upton. Two Gardai brought me from the court to the Bridewell and then out to Upton."

Upton is a tiny village about thirty miles from Cork city. It is dwarfed by the huge industrial school and farm complex of St Patrick's, which was run by the Rosminian Order of priests and brothers.

The Rosminians were also known as the Institute of Charity, or sometimes as the Fathers of Charity. They were the second largest provider of residential child care for boys over the age of ten, next only to the Christian Brothers.

The Gardai are investigating allegations of both physical and sexual abuse in all three of the child care institutions run by the Rosminian order. So far, over forty former Upton inmates have made statements alleging physical and sexual abuse at the school. These concern a total of fifteen Rosminian priests and brothers, both dead and alive. As the complaints keep coming in, the Gardai expect that their investigation will not be concluded for a number of months.

"My first year at Upton I went to ordinary classes. I couldn't read or write going in there, and when I came out I was just about the same. They didn't really bother much about me. I taught myself since, but my writing and spelling still isn't great. We'd have classes from 9.30 till 3.30 and then from 3.30 till 6.30 I used to work in the shoe workshop.

The beatings started very soon after I went in. There was one particular Brother who was very bad, he was the worst Brother for giving out brutality in Upton. Other Brothers beat me as well, but this one — Brother O'Brien — was vicious. He's dead since, died in 1969.

There was one time, I'd been there a couple of months, so I was about fourteen and a half, and I was watching television with the other boys. It was after tea, about half-seven. I needed to go to the toilet, and I asked Brother O'Brien for permission. He said no.

I began to get a pain in my stomach and I couldn't hold the water in any longer. I went in my trousers. I wasn't far from Brother O'Brien and when he saw the wet on the floor, he got up off his chair and smacked me right across the face and I fell backwards.

Then he told me to put my two hands down by my sides. He hit me so many time across the face with the palm of his hand, left and right, that I lost count. I had bells in my ears. He then told me to go to the office where he took his big, thick leather strap off the wall. It was always hanging on the wall. He lashed me about twenty times on each hand, ten up and ten down.

Then he told me to drop my trousers, which I did. I was afraid of my life. I had to bend over and tip my toes – these were called 'benders'. Brother O'Brien gave me somewhere between fifteen and twenty-five lashes on my backside – I lost count. The pain was terrible. I was crying and screaming and kept pleading and telling him I was sorry for wetting myself. But it didn't make any difference. All he said when he'd finished was 'up to bed'.

I couldn't sleep. I just lay there, asking what did I do wrong. All I had wanted to do was to go to the toilet. I kept tossing and turning – it was too sore to sleep on my back. When I got up in the morning, the sheets had blood all over them. The blood came from the marks on my backside, but I never told anybody. I was afraid it would get back to Brother O'Brien.

I got another beating for sending a letter to a girl I met at home – they had let me go for a few days' holidays. I asked another lad to write the letter for me, since I couldn't read or write. Then I managed to post it without anyone seeing me while we were off on one of our long walks.

But the letter never reached the girl. A few days later, during dinner in the dining hall, Brother O'Brien came over to me and asked me did I write a letter to a girl without his knowledge. I said no, which was the truth. I wouldn't tell who wrote it for me, because then that boy would have got a beating as well.

So, there in front of everybody, Brother O'Brien hit me so hard with his right hand across my left ear that I fell against the wall. Then he told me to put my hands by my sides. He just kept hitting me with both his hands on my head and face. It went on and on – I thought my head was going to explode, I was in so much pain.

After that, he told me to go to the office, and he beat me with the strap. My hands were bleeding, and then I had to bend over. I think he only stopped because he ran out of energy.

Some of the lay staff there weren't much better. They'd hit you as well, with sticks or planks, or whatever came to hand. One of them had beaten up another boy and the police were called in. This was around December 1964.

A number of boys, including myself, were called in to make statements about this lay staff member. There were two Guards and the head priest in the room during the interviews. I told them that this staff member had beaten me as well, and I signed the statement.

But it was all just covered up. The man kept his job, and he took it out on all of us afterwards. But those files and those complaints have to be around somewhere still."

Christy was also sexually abused while at Upton. The abuse started almost as soon as he arrived and continued for the next eighteen months. The Brother who abused Christy is still a member of the Rosminian Order.

"I woke up one morning to find this particular Brother – we'll call him Brother X– sitting on my bed with his hands under the blankets inside my underpants playing with my private parts. This went on for two or three minutes, and then he'd go away again.

He kept this up for around twelve months. Most times I'd be awake, but I used just close my eyes and pretend to be asleep. I was afraid to say anything, because I'd just get another beating. If he wasn't at me, he was doing it to someone else. It was common knowledge what was going on in the dormitory.

He'd never speak when he was abusing us, but when he'd finished, he always say 'Rise and shine'.

Things got worse when I got sick with a sore throat and a fever. I went to the nurse, who put me in one of the spare rooms up close to where the Brothers slept. My first night in there I was woken up by someone coming in and lying beside me on the bed. It was Brother X, and he started abusing me. He was pushing himself against me. When he'd finished, he just left, never said a word.

The abuse would last about five or six minutes. It was the same for every night I was in that room. Most nights when he'd gone I just cried myself to sleep. I kept asking myself why is he doing these things to me. I knew that what he was doing was wrong. But I knew that he'd hurt me if I tried to stop him.

When I turned fifteen, I got a job in the building trade in the school. For a while I was working near the boiler house, mixing sand and cement. Brother X called me into the boiler house, and sexually abused me in there.

This happened a total of three times, and then I cracked up. I told him that it had to stop. He said that if I ever told anyone about it 'I would be sorry the day I was ever born'. But I didn't care anymore. I went to a priest and told him what Brother X had been doing to me for the past eighteen months.

I was crying and upset, and also I had a speech impediment. The first thing the priest did was smack me across the face. Then after a minute or so he went and sat down and called me over and sat me on his knee. As I told him what Brother X had been doing to me, I felt him pushing against me and breathing heavily. I think he was trying to do the same thing.

But after a few minutes, we both got up, and he went to get some sweets out of the drawer. As he gave me the sweets he said that I wasn't to tell anyone about what had happened to me, that it would be our little secret.

After that, Brother X never interfered with me again. The priest must have spoken to him. And I kept that 'little secret' for thirty-four years. It's only now, when all this stuff is coming out in public, that I have been able to talk about it.

It's affected me all my life, what happened at Upton. It affected me in my marriage, and my speech impediment is now much worse than it was when I was a young fellow. I think it's because of what I suffered. Things are improving a bit now, but still every so often I get visions of Brother X. He has a lot to answer for."

Eleven

Sisters and Brothers

In the context of looking at the role and behaviour of the religious orders in child care in Ireland, it is important to have some sense of their origins and their own internal organisation. They themselves have been noticeably reticent in recent years in seeking to explain how it was that so many of their members were either involved in or colluded with the abuse of children in their institutions.

The makers of *States of Fear* had asked for access to the archives on industrial schools of the Christian Brothers and the Sisters of Mercy, who between them catered for up to ninety per cent of the children in the system. The authors of this book repeated this request for the purposes of their research — no access was granted in either case.

It is difficult to understand the consistent refusal by the religious orders to open up their archives for the purposes of valuable study. It is possible that they contain material which the orders might find embarrassing. However, it is surely beyond time for society to be able to form a complete view of the past, to which the archives of the religious orders would provide a most important and informative addition.

There were in total twelve orders running industrial and reformatory schools in Ireland for the greater part of this century. The major providers of boys' schools were the Christian Brothers, although the Fathers of Charity (Rosminians), the Oblates of Mary Immaculate and the Presentation Brothers were also involved. For the girls, the Sisters of Mercy ran the vast majority of schools, and also ran most of the facilities for boys under ten years of age. Also involved in running girls schools were the Sisters of the Good

Shepherd, the Irish Sisters of Charity, the Daughters of Charity of St Vincent de Paul, the Sisters of St Clare (Poor Clares), the Sisters of Our Lady of Charity of Refuge, the Presentation Sisters and the Sisters of St Louis.

The treatment of children within the industrial and reformatory school system was universally harsh, regardless of the religious order involved. The Christian Brothers and the Sisters of Mercy have been singled out as being particularly severe, but in truth this is only because they were the two largest providers of care. Members of all the orders running industrial schools were responsible for abusing and neglecting the children they detained. One of the great difficulties for a population today beginning to come to terms with this is how to reconcile such abusive practices with the avowed religious, caring and charitable public image of these congregations.

Sisters

The Sisters of Mercy were responsible for the running of two-thirds of all the industrial schools in the country. Founded in 1831 by Catherine McAuley, they together with several other congregations of nuns provided the Catholic Church with workers willing and able to achieve direct contact with large sections of the population through the provision of a range of social services. Their Rules, published in 1863 stated that the order:

> "... besides attending particularly to their own perfection, which is the principal end of all religious orders, should also have in view what is the peculiar characteristics of this congregation: i.e. the most assiduous application to the education of poor girls, the visitation of the sick, and the protection of women of good character."[1]

These nuns were seen as a key group in terms of the Catholic Church's changing role in Ireland during the middle of the nineteenth century. Up to the early part of that century, it was a disorganised Church with few of its members adhering to its rules and rituals, particularly in the west and north of the country. Over 100 years of suppression had left it fragmented and weak.

However, from the 1830s it set about a thorough reorganisation. Its most powerful impetus was the sectarian warfare being waged with other Churches for the souls of the Irish people. The Catholic Hierarchy decided that a major drive was required in order to counter the effects of proselytism. Its move into the provision of social services such as education, health and child welfare was seen as a crucial part of its strategy to combat "souperism". From the 1850s, it was the nuns from the various congregations, particularly the Sisters of Mercy, who were to provide the foot soldiers in these sectarian battles.

The great success of the Catholic Church's overall strategy could be seen by the beginning of the twentieth century. It had an almost complete domination of the provision of social services to the population, even though these were often funded directly by the Treasury. It had become a highly centralised, disciplined organisation. Attendance at Mass and adherence to the rituals of the Church were virtually universal amongst the Catholic population, and earlier folk beliefs had been eroded. Irish Catholics had, in essence, become Romanised.[2]

During the middle decades of the nineteenth century, the Catholic religious congregations experienced phenomenal growth. Only fifty years after they were founded, the Sisters of Mercy alone had established 168 convents in Ireland.[3] (By 1950 there were over 1,500 Sister of Mercy convents worldwide.) Overall, the population of nuns in Ireland had grown from 120 in only six orders in 1800 to a remarkable 8,000 nuns in thirty-five orders and congregations in 1900.[4] (This explosion of vocations was not, of course, unique to Ireland. Both France and England experienced similar growth — by 1880, there were an extraordinary 200,000 religious in France alone.[5])

The main reason for the dominance of the Sisters of Mercy in the fields of education, health and industrial schools in Ireland was the fact that their rules allowed them to come under the direct control of the local Catholic bishop. It was the bishops who had the ultimate say over who was to provide services within their dioceses, and they preferred to be able to maintain the maximum control over these. Many orders were organised to be answerable only to a mother superior or internal central authority, and consequently could not come under the direct control of the bishop. The Sisters of Mercy, however, were highly accommodating to the local bishops, as can be seen from their Rules:

> This Religious congregation shall be always subject to the authority and jurisdiction of the Bishop of the Diocese, and the Sisters shall respect and obey him as their principal Superior after the Holy See. If on account of his many avocations he should not have leisure to attend immediately to the direction of the community, a Priest shall be appointed by him on whose prudence, piety and experience he can depend to govern and direct under him and to whom he will give the necessary faculties. Nothing of importance related to the House or community shall be undertaken without the consent of the Bishop.[6]

Well into the 1960s, the local bishops were to maintain an interest in the industrial schools in their dioceses. Many children have vivid memories of the arrival of the bishop and his entourage on visits. The nuns were always described as being devoutly respectful, the children warned to be on their best behaviour and the institution spotless. Even tiny children knew to kiss the ring. However, there is no record of a bishop ever having commented unfavourably on any of the industrial schools under his control, even during the 1930s and 1940s when in many schools the children were visibly starved looking.

This control of services by the Sisters of Mercy is evident to the present day in towns all over the country. Almost every major population centre has a Mercy complex dominating the geography of the town. Usually prominently positioned either on a height or in the centre of towns and cities, they were built to be imposing manifestations of Church power. Behind their somewhat bleak Victorian facades, they usually contained several separate units — often a secondary school, primary school, industrial school and nuns' convent were grouped together on the same site. In some locations, a Magdalen laundry was also included. In this way, they effectively controlled the lives of women and girls from all classes within their localities.

There has been much speculation in recent times that perhaps so many of the nuns were cruel to the children in their care because they themselves were frustrated, having possibly even been forced to enter a convent by their families. There is no evidence to support this view. In fact, quite the reverse. Unlike for instance the Christian Brothers, most nuns entered a convent when they were much older, usually over the age of eighteen. Most had received a full secondary education, and the religious life gave many of them a status unequalled in almost any other area. In Ireland up to the 1970s, it was difficult for women to achieve any degree of social standing in their own right as a result of their work. To become a nun was a highly respected calling within society, and gave many women an outlet for their considerable professional skills. It also gave them a degree of power almost universally denied to other groups of women at the time. It is the way in which they used, or even abused, that power which is now being so deeply questioned by society.

One of the ways in which the Sisters of Mercy in particular exercised this power was actively to perpetuate the class system in Ireland. They maintained a rigid distinction and indeed segregation between the children of the poor in their industrial schools and those from mainly middle-class families in their fee-paying secondary schools.

Even within their own order they had two levels of nuns. What were known as the lay sisters came from poorer families, were not required to pay a dowry on entry, and provided much of the menial labour in the convents — cooking, cleaning and sowing for the superior choir nuns. These came from better-off backgrounds, had to pay a dowry, and were not required to undertake domestic tasks.[7] Although the distinction between these two classes of nuns was supposed to have been abolished following Vatican II, many orders in practice continued to maintain it until well into the 1970s.

The children in the industrial schools were aware of the differences between these two ranks of nuns. They generally have fond memories of many of the lay sisters, who invariably worked in the kitchens or laundries often alongside the children. They received many small kindness from them, such as an extra bit of food now and then, or help with their chores. The children perceived a common ground with these lay sisters — many of them say now that, looking back, the lay sisters were as intimidated by the superior choir nuns as were the children themselves.

Within this rigid authoritarian structure of the nuns themselves may well lie an important clue as to why such widespread abuse of the children was allowed to go unchecked. Patricia Burke Brogan, a former Mercy novice, speaks revealingly about the crucial central importance of the vow of obedience in the lives of the nuns. Now an internationally renowned playwright and artist, she left the order in the late 1950s after a short time spent in their Magdalen laundry in Galway. She was so shocked by the way in which the women there were treated that she felt she could no longer remain part of a body of women responsible for this:

> What defined you as a good nun was that you obeyed the rules. There were the three vows — poverty, chastity and obedience. But if you were obedient, that covered everything. The only way I can explain it to myself now is that the order was a kind of institution in itself and we were all institutionalised within it. There was a God of fear at the top, and then you had a Reverend Mother, a figure of fear, and the top always sends the messages down. And that it was sort of a reign of terror instead of a reign of love.
>
> It was supposed to be about conscience and love, wasn't it? But here we are dealing with conscience as obedience. What was wrong was defined as anything that broke the rules, that's what you had to tell the confessor. It wasn't a social conscience the way we understand it now. It was more of a religious

conscience, which is a different thing, and is about obeying the rules.

I suppose I was a bit of a rebel from the beginning. I had joined the Mercy order because I wanted to work with the poor. I was very committed to this, and wasn't interested in any of the better-off orders. As a novice, I was put into the kitchens to work. I didn't mind that, I liked cooking. But one of the first things I noticed was that all the time the best quality food, the best cuts of meat for instance, were always put on the top table for the most senior nuns. The novices got the rest. I suppose with my sense of social justice, I felt the unfairness of this. I didn't object or anything, I just happened to mention it to one of the other novices. She reported me — it's in the rules that you have to report everything to your superiors. The following day I was moved out of the kitchen, and put to cleaning the sacristy. It didn't particularly upset me, but it did wise me up a bit.

But the major break came when I was sent into their Magdalen laundry to stand in for another nun who was sick. I was only there a week, but the ground seemed to go from under my feet. I was shocked at the sense of injustice of it. I asked questions about it. I wondered why these women were locked away, and I was told that if they were let out they'd be back pregnant again in a few months. Then I asked about the fathers, were they locked up too, but I didn't get any answer to that.

I'll never forget the way the women looked at me, like I was a gaoler, and I suppose I was. I was the one who had the keys and who locked them in. I tried to talk to them, but it wasn't any good. I was very, very upset by it. That was when I decided to leave. I didn't want to be a gaoler, that's not why I had entered the convent.

I went into a crisis of vocation. They kept telling me it would pass, that it happened to everyone, that if I just carried on and obeyed the rules everything would fall into place and I'd make a great nun, or even a great Mother Superior! It was very hard to leave, and it took me over a year before they would let me go, but eventually I did get out.

Patricia Burke Brogan vividly illustrates the great difficulty of speaking out within such a rigidly authoritarian structure, which held obedience as its primary virtue. For a Mercy nun, even the slightest flouting of authority was a major sin, an admission of failure in maintaining the vow of obedience. This was a crucial feature of Mercy congregations not just in Ireland but all over the world, where severe abuse of children has been extensively reported by survivors of their institutions in Britain, Australia and Canada. As Patricia Burke Brogan says: "This wasn't the real Church — it was just an institution. Total unquestioning obedience like that is a very dangerous concept. If you close your mind and you don't allow questions to be asked, the danger is very great that abuse of that power can happen."

Her play, *Eclipsed*, deals with the lives of women in a Magdalen laundry. It is a remarkable piece of work, funny, human and piercingly tragic. It has however only received limited performances in Ireland. But abroad it has been hugely successful, and has been staged all over the world to enormous acclaim. Written in the early 1980s, it was the first public exposure in this country of the cruel and inhuman nature of Magdalen institutions. It is also an outstanding piece of theatre.

Two other Irish-founded orders of nuns were also significant providers of industrial schools for children. The Irish Sisters of Charity were founded by Mary Aikenhead in 1815. They did not expand at the same rate as the Sisters of Mercy largely because they remained autonomous from control by the bishops, and answered only to their Mother Superior. During the twentieth century, they ran several fee-paying secondary schools, a number of Magdalen laundries, together with industrial schools in Sligo (Benada Abbey), Roscommon (Ballaghaderreen), Dublin (Lakelands, Sandymount) and two in Kilkenny (St Patrick's for boys and St Joseph's for girls). The

Presentation Sisters, founded by Nano Nagle in 1775, ran only two industrial schools, both for girls and both in Co Tipperary.

A flavour of the Irish Sisters of Charity approach to the children in their care is to be found in a letter written by two nuns working in the order's institution in Ballaghaderreen. This was sent in 1946 to Fr Flanagan of Boys Town. They asked for his advice on punishments for children, on what to do with those who were "stubborn", and on how the rule of silence should be applied to children in their care. In return for his thoughts on these matters, they said "we will get the children under our care to pray for your wonderful work".

Fr Flanagan wrote back a somewhat stern reply. He emphasised the importance of love above all else, saying that in its absence systems become inhuman. He advocated kindness and understanding in terms of dealing with minor infringements of the rules. He added, rather severely, that "I hope that you and I have no misunderstanding about this punishment business. We punish by denial of privileges, not physically. Let's not talk about punishment at all, Sister, let's talk about ... training by example rather than preaching". As Mary's story on page 319 of this book shows, the Sisters in Ballaghaderreen paid scant heed to Fr Flanagan's admonishments.

There were a number of other significant female orders in the industrial schools area, who had originated in France and had expanded to Ireland during the nineteenth century to assist with the drive to provide social services. Most noteworthy among these were the Sisters of the Good Shepherd.

These nuns were effectively the gaolers of the system. In addition to their vows of poverty, chastity and obedience, they took a fourth, somewhat chilling vow to "employ themselves in the instruction of the penitent girls and women who submit themselves voluntarily, or shall be forced, by legitimate or competent authority, to submit themselves, to the guidance of the religious of this congregation, to be converted and to do penance".[8]

Unlike many of the other orders, the Good Shepherds had no point of contact with the more general population. They were not involved, for instance, in the running of ordinary schools or healthcare. Their primary function was to provide incarceral facilities for children in their industrial schools and reformatory, and they did the same for women through the very large Magdalen laundries in a number of towns and cities in the country.

They ran a series of enormous complexes, completely isolated from the general communities in which they were placed. Their compound in Limerick city was one of the most remarkable of these. Lavishly built in 1848, at a time when the country was only just emerging from the Great Famine, it housed an industrial school, a reformatory for girls, a huge Magdalen laundry, a convent building for the nuns, and a church which can only be described as a miniature basilica, complete with ornamental dome and gilt decoration.

The compound was designed in such a way as to maintain complete separation between these groups — a remarkable feat of architecture as they all had to gather together for daily Mass. A system of covered tunnels linked each of the buildings, and each separate institution had its own tunnel which led to its own particular cordoned-off area of the church. The separation of the various groupings in the church was absolute — the children and the women couldn't even see each other. After Mass, each group, including the nuns, would go back along its own particular tunnel or corridor, to its own segregated building.

When one realises that some of the Magdalen women's own children were detained in the adjacent industrial school, this isolation of the groups assumes deeply tragic proportions. A similar practice obtained in their operation in Sunday's Well in Cork city. Former inmates report that occasionally some of the women would shout across the huge partitions in the church on the premises to see if indeed their children were still there.

The only point of contact with the local communities was when people arrived to hand in their laundry to be cleaned by the Magdalen women. In Limerick, when the Good Shepherds sold the buildings a few years ago to the Institute of Technology, it was the first time that people living across the road were able to go in and take a look around. They report being amazed by the size and wealth of the buildings under whose shadow they had lived all their lives.

The other Good Shepherd complexes in New Ross and Waterford were similarly characterised by their enormous size and great wealth. The laundry operations were clearly highly profitable. Using the unpaid labour in most cases of well over 100 women, it would have been hard for them to be otherwise. It must be remembered that this was at a time when people did not have domestic washing machines, and the provision of commercial laundry services was a lucrative business.

Accounts from the Good Shepherd convent in Cork show an average profit on the laundry operation of the equivalent in today's money of £100,000 a year during the 1950s and 1960s. They illustrate that the nuns spent much of this on themselves, paying out enormous sums for instance to decorate of their internal chapel. Money spent on the maintenance of their imprisoned and unpaid workforce was minimal.

The Good Shepherd Industrial School in Cork, (St Finbarr's), was also the home of "Little Nellie of Holy God", the only inmate in the country ever to have been accorded the signal honour of being buried in the nuns' graveyard. She died in 1908 at the age of about six, by all accounts a saintly child. The people of Cork developed a special devotion to her, and many used to visit her grave every year. She was held up as a model to the children of the industrial school, who were encouraged to pray to her.

Looking at the more recent behaviour of the Good Shepherd nuns, there is one point which should be made in their favour. When the Magdalen laundries closed during the 1970s and 1980s — as much from the advent of the domestic washing machine as from the changing social climate in Ireland — the Good Shepherd order continued to provide accommodation for the many women who were so completely institutionalised that they could not have survived outside of the convent environment. Some of these women are still alive, and continue to be supported by the nuns in often purpose-built housing complexes, purchased and constructed from the money accruing through the sale of the Order's valuable property.

Other orders of nuns imported mainly from France to provide social services include the Daughters of Charity of St Vincent de Paul, who operated a number of orphanages in Dublin and an industrial school for young boys in Drogheda; the Sisters of Our Lady of Charity of Refuge, who ran an industrial school for girls and two Magdalen laundries at High Park in Dublin's Drumcondra, and in Sean McDermott St; the Sisters of St Clare, known as the Poor Clares, an enclosed order who had a girls' industrial school in Cavan; and the Sisters of St Louis, who founded a reformatory for girls in Monaghan, which was turned into an industrial school in the 1903, and later moved to Bundoran during the 1950s.

Of these European-based orders, the Poor Clares were to become engulfed in controversy surrounding their role during the tragic fire in their industrial school in 1943, when thirty-five of the children were burnt to death. In correspondence with the Department of Education during the 1950s, they were given to describing their industrial school as "the only orphanage in Free Ulster"! The Louis nuns in Bundoran were to become infamous after the publicity surrounding the episode in 1963 when they shaved the heads of eight girls who had escaped.[9]

The Sisters of Our Lady of Charity of Refuge ran the largest Magdalen laundry in the country, in their convent at High Park in Dublin. In addition to "fallen women", ex-prostitutes and single mothers, they also catered for "women perceived to be in danger of losing their virginity". In this context, the nuns had stated that "until the penitents forget the past, nothing solid can be done towards their permanent conversion".[10]

In 1993 these nuns received a barrage of hostile publicity when it was revealed that they had exhumed the bodies of 133 Magdalen women, buried in two mass graves on a part of their land which the nuns wanted to sell. The bodies had been cremated and reburied elsewhere. The order was in financial difficulty, partly as a result of some dealings on the stock exchange which had blown up in their faces. They had invested in GPA shares whose value had been wiped out, with a loss to the sisters of roughly £110,000.[11]

This callous treatment of the remains of so many women who had spent their entire lives working in the order's laundry was to produce a public reaction of shock and revulsion. Shortly afterwards, in an attempt to properly commemorate the lives of all the Magdalen women in Ireland, a plaque in honour of their memory was unveiled by President Mary Robinson. It stands today in Dublin's St Stephen's Green.

As the industrial schools system began to contract during the 1960s, culminating with its effective disbandment in the early 1970s, the religious orders engaged in a spirited defence of their work with children. They were critical, for instance, of what they perceived as the scant regard paid to their long involvement by the Kennedy Report in 1970. Spearheading this movement was Sr Stanislaus Kennedy, who was one of the keynote speakers at the major conference on child care in Killarney in 1971, organised by the Catholic Church.

She engaged in a spirited defence of the record of the orders in this area on almost theological grounds. She spoke of the great value of celibacy in this regard, saying that "in the context of child care, consecrated virginity adds a dimension far more important and more positive than freedom from the 'distractions' of married and family life." Because of the "gift" of celibacy, she said, "the needs of the children whom we receive under our care may be answered in a unique way by the consecrated religious."

She referred to the fact that nuns engaged in this work were not isolated but operated within a community of religious. One of the advantages of this, she added, is that "each member of a community has a responsibility to prevent other members becoming neurotic and unchristian through lack of love".

A further argument she used to defend the continuing role for religious in the child care system centred around a child's need for "a sense of permanence in the person who cares for them. The very fact that the religious is someone whose commitment is for life and that the service which is inherent in her vocation is a life-long, and not a transient one, should give to the children that feeling that the loving care they receive is no passing thing."[12]

It is interesting to look at this specific point in the context of remarks made by the Catholic Parents Guild in the early 1960s to the Department of Education. They complained particularly about the policy within religious orders constantly to move nuns from school to school, saying that this "lack of continuity in staffing is a defect which militates seriously against the children's welfare". They singled out none other that Sr Stanislaus' order, the Sisters of Charity, as being the worst offenders in this regard. Even Sr Stanislaus herself acknowledged that things were perhaps not all they should be in this area.

Brothers

The most significant order in the provision of industrial schools for boys was the Christian Brothers. They ran schools for senior boys (between the ages of ten and sixteen) at Artane, Salthill, Letterfrack, Glin and Tralee. The latter four were all called St Joseph's, presumably after St Joseph the Worker.

Founded in 1802 by Edmund Ignatius Rice, the order was to achieve an overwhelming dominance in the provision of education for boys in Ireland. Like the nuns, the Christian Brothers also underwent an enormous growth spurt during the nineteenth century. In 1831, they had only forty-five Brothers, which had shot up to almost 1,000 by 1900. By the 1960s, there were 4,000 Christian Brothers in Ireland.[13]

The expansion of this order worldwide was a remarkable success story. By the mid-twentieth century, they had thirty houses in England, five in Gibraltar, seventy-five in Australia, twelve in Canada, eighteen in the United States, eighteen in India and ten in South Africa. This was in addition to their ninety-five houses in Ireland, the home country, and up until the 1960s the international headquarters of the order. They were one of the largest male teaching orders in the world, imposing their own brand of Irish Catholicism on generations of boys across the globe. However, during the 1980s and 1990s, stories of horrific abuse began to emerge from many of those who had grown up in their orphanages, particularly in Canada and Australia. These were an uncanny mirror of the experiences of many boys in their industrial schools in Ireland.

Founded originally for the purposes of educating poor Catholic boys, they promised to vow "poverty, chastity, obedience, perseverance in the Institute and Gratuitous instruction of poor boys". During the nineteenth century, they were to remain outside of the State-run national school system, determined to provide separate education specifically for Catholic children. They were an important part of the Catholic hierarchy's campaign for segregated education. While initially established under the control of the bishops, this changed as the order grew, and it was decided to give control to their own Superior General. It was a development which caused friction in the Diocese of Cork, where Bishop Murphy insisted on retaining control over the congregation, resulting in a split and the formation of the Presentation Brothers. These ran a single industrial school in the country — Greenmount, in Cork, for boys over the age of ten.

In the context of the Christian Brothers' later severity towards the boys in their schools, it is interesting to note the words in 1820 of their founder, Edmund Rice, in this context. "Unless for some faults which rarely occur, corporal punishment is never inflicted." Some years earlier, in 1814, the Christian Brothers had claimed that they managed their pupils more through love than fear, and that they had removed "as much as possible everything like corporal punishment from their schools, a plan which is found to answer the best purpose in the formation of youth". When the strap was introduced from Paris in the 1820s, its use was carefully regulated — "it was not to be given on a boy's writing hand and was normally to be one slap only".[14]

However, as the order grew, the Christian Brothers were to develop an awesome reputation for physical violence against their pupils, whether in general or in industrial schools. While brutality was to become an integral part of their teaching and control strategy, it is clear that this was the subject of some considerable internal debate. Fintan O'Toole in his book *The Ex-Isle of Erin* has written revealingly on the subject. In a circular to all the members in 1861, the then Superior General Michael Riordan advocated trying to win the trust of boys by force of personality rather than by "the humiliating alternative of enforcing submission by coercive measures". He went on to say:

"The subject being of too painful a nature for lengthened detail, we prefer to throw a veil over its naked deformity; but nevertheless we cannot omit strongly exhorting you to exhibit and practice towards these poor children that paternal tenderness and solicitude peculiar to God's chosen servants."

The internal debate about methods of discipline continued into the twentieth century. In 1930, the Superior General JP Noonan advocated the complete banning of corporal punishment. "Abuses have arisen; and they will recur, I fear, as long as our regulations give any authority for the infliction of corporal punishment. Let us aim at its complete abolition in our schools, and anticipate legislation which would make its infliction illegal." A bare ten years later, the Department of Education felt that the Christian Brothers were unsuitable to run a Borstal institution in Ireland because their discipline was known to be "too strict". It is clear both from the experiences of the general male population in Ireland, and particularly those who went through industrial schools, that the Superior General's exhortation had little practical effect.

The Christian Brothers themselves tended to come from lower middle-class rural backgrounds. For many, entry to one of the order's training seminaries was the only way to get a full education at a time when all secondary schools were fee-paying. Strictly speaking, the Brothers were a congregation rather than an order. The distinction was essentially theological – congregations took simple vows as opposed to the solemn vows taken by the orders. But crucially, the congregations were regarded as being socially inferior to the orders, and the backgrounds of their respective members tended to mirror this divide. (In the case of the female religious, the Sisters of Mercy were also a congregation rather than an order).

There is no doubt that the means of their recruitment and training contributed in no small part to the harshness of the Christian Brothers. However, this is an area on which very little has been written, and very few Brothers have spoken. One insight came from a radio interview on the Gay Byrne Show in 1986 with Tony, a former Christian Brother. Saying that the Brothers were popularly described as "baby snatchers", he spoke of how he was recruited like many others at the age of twelve. He was essentially cut off from his family and community, and went full-time into the training college at Baldoyle in Dublin:

> It sounded good to join up, I admired my teachers, and I'd be getting an education .... But from the first day, they'd start indoctrinating you. I've three children and I wouldn't have allowed them to make that sort of decision at twelve. You missed everything that was good about family life.
>
> When I was thirteen, we went to Bray, and then to St Helen's, Booterstown, when you got the collar. I thought it was the best day of my life. You were brought up very hard, as a monk rather than as someone who was going to be let loose on the world. You made up for what you lost by the spiritual side of it.
>
> From the first day in, the Brothers were very conscious of modesty, morality. There were people who as soon as you got into the place start giving you indications that they fancied you, and how they would go about it. They used to catch your little finger, and fingers together meant you had a special friend in the Brothers. Now very few of them lasted the pace. The Brothers were very quick, very observant, and anyone who was seen in any way to fraternise too familiarly was immediately brought to the office and he had his case packed the next day.
>
> Because you were going to be together for so long, seven years, they took great steps to make sure that familiarities wouldn't develop. For example, on a Sunday when we were all put out marching in our long black coats, and black hats, the same three wouldn't be allowed go walking together any Sunday. They'd change who you were sitting beside in your desks as well. So they were very conscious of the fact that it was there. Lots were put out for over-familiarity. I mean some did get through, and [the abuse] caused havoc, absolute havoc. They did try to

prepare people for it and try to be observant, but no society is perfect.

Tony left the Christian Brothers at the age of twenty-two. He never worked in an industrial school, but taught instead in the mainstream system. He found the fact that he was expected to administer corporal punishment to his pupils particularly unacceptable:

> I was unforgiving in retrospect for any form of corporal punishment. We were ignorant men, we knew nothing about child psychology. I remember picking up a book about psychology, about dealing with people and this was a whole new world — you could actually learn about this?

The breaking point for Tony was when he discovered that a boy in the class he was teaching had had no food for two days. Tony brought him up to the monastery and gave him something to eat. "The Head Brother said to me, 'we mustn't make a habit of this', and that was it. I didn't want to live with men who don't have that feeling."

While the Christian Brothers are now in significant decline, they maintain ownership and control of much of the educational infrastructure in Ireland. Together with the Sisters of Mercy, these two vast teaching orders continue to have a major influence on the shaping of young Irish minds.

Two other male orders are important in the provision of industrial and reformatory schools in the country. The Institute of Charity (Rosminians) ran two such schools: St Patrick's at Upton in Co Cork, and St Joseph's Ferryhouse in Clonmel. They had been founded in 1828 by Antonio Rosmini, an Italian philosopher and priest. Like many of the female congregations, they also had a two-tier system of recruitment, with a membership of both priests and brothers. The Rosminian priests would generally have come from a better-off background than the brothers. In their industrial schools, the usual pattern was to have a priest in charge with a staff of brothers under him. Reports of severe physical and sexual abuse have emerged from both of the industrial schools run by this order.

The Oblates of Mary Immaculate initially ran two boys' reformatory schools in Ireland, St Kevin's in Glencree and St Conleth's, Daingean in Co Offaly. St Kevin's closed in 1940. They were a French order, and had been founded in 1816. Martin Cahill, the infamous Dublin criminal known as the General, referred to the Oblates as the "mad monks down in the bog"[15]. He had spent several years in the Daingean reformatory as a child, convicted for larceny offences. On his release, he wrote a letter to the Oblates thanking them for their help, and promising to mend his ways. In this one case at least, their attempts at reform were to have little effect.

The Oblates articulated their aims in reformatory schooling during the 1950s:

> The aim and purpose of this school is to instruct boys in religion and develop their moral sense …. However, reformation can only begin when the boy has adjusted himself to a more or less normal outlook and has become receptive of instruction and amenable to discipline.

By the Oblates' own admission during the 1960s, this discipline meant taking a boy from his dormitory, stripping him naked, holding him down and flogging him with a leather strap in one of the stairwell areas of the school. Many former inmates of Daingean have spoken of the extraordinary levels of violence against children within the institution. But no Oblates Fathers have been as forthcoming.

Hugh is a former Oblate priest, who left the order in 1958. Just before leaving, he was dispatched to work in Daingean for a year. Now working as a barrister in England, what he saw in St Conleth's Reformatory School was to leave a lasting impression on him:

> The members of the order working in Daingean were all programmed with an extraordinary level of violence. It was the only way they ever dealt with the boys. It's a miracle that there weren't murders or

riots. The brothers and priests were completely hated by the boys. Most of the boys ended up totally disturbed.

There was one time two of the lads escaped. They were no angels. They were eventually caught in Britain, and they were brought back. They had their heads shaved and a Brother brought them into the boxing ring and literally pummelled them unconscious. I don't know how they weren't killed. A doctor used to come and go, but I don't remember anyone ever being sent to hospital, no matter how severe the injuries.

You'd hear the younger ones screaming during the night, the twelve- and thirteen-year-olds. There was a night watchman who used to patrol the dormitories with an ash plant on his shoulder. You'd see him constantly bringing down that stick onto a boy in a bed with his full force, about five or six times.

There were an awful lot of priests and brothers there in my time. I really don't know what they were all doing. The place was horrific. It wasn't even Dickensian, it was pre-Dickensian. The priests were unimpeachable, they beat the boys with complete impunity. No one ever interfered. They were a total law unto themselves. They didn't have a remorseful breath in them. It was the closest thing I've ever seen to an SS prison camp. The kids were just kicked and bullied and beaten and starved, all the time.

It is interesting to compare this perception of Daingean with the rules for the institution as drawn up by the Oblates and ratified by the Department of Education. While they proscribed a long list of behaviour, they remained highly vague as to the nature of any penalties. The enormous gulf between how the priests and brothers wished to be perceived and the brutal reality behind the high walls of Daingean was best summed up in the introduction: "Obedience to authority and the rules laid down brings happiness, improvement and contentment to both staff and boys."

Ed's Story, St Joseph's Industrial School, Kilkenny (Sisters of Charity), 1966–1978

"I rang the door at the convent, and I remember telling the nun in charge that David Murray was in my bed last night. She gave me her knuckles across the back of the head. She says now that she doesn't remember it. But I remember it like it was today, me in short trousers looking up at her face and telling her what he was doing to me. And to this day she still denies it."

Ed was put into care when still only a baby. His family was from Kilkenny, but his home situation was unstable and he was placed initially in St Patrick's, an industrial school for small boys, run by the Sisters of Charity in the town. It closed in 1966, and a group of over thirty boys, all aged between four and six, were transferred to St Joseph's Industrial School, also run by the same nuns in Kilkenny. This school had previously only accepted girls. There they encountered Teresa Connolly, the first person in the home to sexually abuse some of them. She was tried and found guilty of this abuse in early 1999.

"From my point of view, St Joseph's wasn't too bad for the first few years there. Teresa Connolly was pretty bad, but there was a nice nun there who used to take me on her knee and talk to me. She was great.

But from the time I was about eleven, the place turned into hell on earth. That's when the nuns brought in David Murray to look after us. He was a complete pervert. He'd bring a group of boys to the cinema and you wouldn't be allowed to wear underpants. He'd put a coat over your knees and he'd play with you right there while the film was going on.

Then you'd go back to St Joseph's, and he'd be in someone's bed. I'd say he abused some boy every night of the week. He'd rub some sort of cream on your ass, and then he'd stick his penis in you. There was a group of about six of us in particular that he was raping — we used to talk about it among ourselves, but there was nothing we could do. He was in complete charge of us and the head nun didn't want to know.

Sometimes he'd have us strip to our underpants and have fighting matches with each other and he'd be feeling us up all the time. He'd be doing the same in the showers."

In 1975, David Murray left St Joseph's to work elsewhere in the child care system. During the course of the Garda investigation in 1995 into his crimes, Sister Joseph Conception O'Donoghue, the resident manager of St Joseph's, made a statement to the Gardai saying that she did in fact realise that in her own words "something serious was wrong". A number of complaints had been made to her about Murray at this stage. She stated that she had reported her concerns at the time to the Department of Education.

However, the Department denies that it was ever aware that children in St Joseph's were being abused during the 1970s, and that it had not been so informed by Sr Conception. David Murray was sentenced in 1997 to ten years in prison for the gross sexual abuse of several boys in St Joseph's. He had also repeatedly raped his two foster sons.

Murray's replacement in St Joseph's was Myles Brady. He remained for just under a year. In 1997, he also was charged with the sexual abuse of boys at the industrial school, and sentenced to four years — he has since died in prison.

It was about Brady that a complaint was made to Sr Stanislaus Kennedy, working at the time for Kilkenny Social Services on the same complex as St Joseph's. A child care worker told her that Brady was abusing the children. No direct action was taken, and Brady continued his abuse for a further six months. The child care worker resigned in protest, telling Sr Conception in writing that for the boys in St Joseph's the situation was "highly undesirable and unsafe".

Eventually, when another complaint was made to Sr Conception, she took action. She reported the matter to the Gardai. Myles Brady was at the time on a visit to Dublin. Sr Conception accompanied by a Garda went to Dublin and together they confronted Brady, as she described in her Garda statement of 1995. "He never returned to St Joseph's after that. I never gave him a reference afterwards." Despite this apparent involvement by the Gardai at the time, there were no charges laid against Myles Brady. As with David Murray, the child victims of these two paedophiles had to wait over twenty years to see justice done. Ed still lives with the consequences of the brutality of Myles Brady.

"Brady was an alcoholic — we used to call him 'whiskey breath'. He was one of the most violent people I've ever met, and I've met some very violent ones. He'd give us terrible beatings. I remember picking broken teeth out of my mouth after he'd punched me. I've a mouthful of false teeth now because of what Myles Brady did to me.

He pulled my arm so far up my back one time that he broke it. He was a complete animal. When I had to go to hospital he told me to say that I got my injuries falling down the stairs. I had to get nine stitches down the back of my head once after he hit me with a hurley stick. I got a beating almost every day of the week. It was just the policy.

He didn't care if we went to school or not. He didn't care about anything. There were about seven or eight of us from St Joseph's in the local De La Salle secondary school. We were sent down the back of the class, and we got extra beatings from the Brothers. I never once saw a boy with a mother and father getting a beating like they'd give us.

The nuns used to send us out to local families at weekends and some of them were awful. There was one family, though, who were really nice to me. They didn't want a permanent child, just a weekend kid, but they were very good to me. I still keep in touch with them. But most of the time the nuns kept moving me to different families. Then, when I was about fourteen, they decided I was a problem child.

They sent me up to St Michael's in Finglas, which was an assessment centre. I think they were trying to get rid of me because they couldn't look after me. St Michael's was a place for young offenders, pretty much a prison, but I thought it was great. I felt safe there because there was nobody getting into my bed to rape me. You'd have a guard with you when you went anywhere. I really felt safe. I could have a shower in a cubicle, and I wouldn't have David Murray around looking at me or trying to wash my back.

I was only there six weeks. I cried when they brought me back to St Joseph's, to all that pain and abuse and torment. I wanted to stay in the prison, but they wouldn't let me.

I have no happy memories of my childhood. I don't remember a single good day. I should have had Christmas and birthdays. Now I'm like a little boy around Christmas time — I put trees and lights all over the place. I suppose it's to make up for what I lost.

When I look at the lads now in my group, about four of them have committed suicide. There's one in a mental hospital. Some of the others are homeless, living on the streets. I've been in and out of prison all my life, never for anything violent or sexual though, mainly for robbery and drugs. I've never really been able to have a stable relationship. When I was married, my wife was always saying to me 'You're hiding something'. I couldn't tell her for years about what had happened to me in St Joseph's.

We broke up, but I have my son around now. He's grown up and he's brilliant. But even today I still sleep with the lights on. I'm afraid of the dark, and often I'm up sleepwalking. A lot of the time I can't sleep at all, and I was told to take tablets. I just hate going to bed.

About six years ago, the Gardai from Kilkenny came and found me. They were investigating David Murray and Myles Brady. It was a great relief that it was finally all going to come out in the open. I began to settle down a bit after that. I haven't been in jail since, and some of the Gardai shake my hand when I meet them because I've managed to stay out of trouble for so long. I'm back working now, and beginning to get my life together.

I blame St Joseph's for all my years in prison. They ruined me, just destroyed me. If the nuns had looked after me properly maybe I'd be a Grade A chef today — I love cooking and I'm good at it. But I never got a chance. The nuns employed these men who raped us and beat us as much as they liked. No one interfered, even though they knew it was going on.

The only one who was in any way decent was that nice nun who used to sit me on her knee when I was little. I kept in touch with her, and she used to come and visit me when I'd be in prison. I think that maybe she knew a bit about what was happening, but she couldn't do anything either. The nuns would be afraid of the more senior ones — you'd see them all nervous whenever the head would appear. They probably felt there was nothing they could do either.

This nice nun was the only person I ever trusted as a child. But I knew when I'd tell her things that happened that I'd be hurting her. Now, whenever I see her, all she does is cry. The whole thing just broke her heart. I think that all of us connected with what happened in St Joseph's ended up as broken people in one way or another."

Twelve

Pity the Poor Orphans:
How the Children Were Perceived

One of the most enduring legacies of the industrial schools was the sense of shame they instilled in the minds of many who grew up there. It has dogged the survivors of the system, often for their entire lives. Even some of those now in their eighties continue to feel that society looks down on them because of their upbringing. There are still many, particularly those living in small rural areas, who while they were happy to have their stories told in this book, felt that to fully reveal their own identities would expose them to hostility within their communities.

This reveals two important aspects of the industrial schools system. Firstly, the general popular view of these children was that they were mainly either criminals or born out of wedlock. Consequently, they quickly learnt to hide their origins, and there are those who even today feel unable to tell their partners or their children about where they themselves grew up.

Secondly, there was the fact that as children, they were constantly told that they were no good, that they had been rejected, and that it was their own fault that they had ended up in industrial schools. This was such a persistent aspect of the schools that many of those who emerged from them actually believed it, and tragically in some cases continue to suffer today from an enormous lack of self confidence.

Occasionally in their adult lives, many attempted to reveal to those around them some limited aspects of what had happened to them as children. That they were universally not believed served to reinforce their isolation and the sense that they were themselves in some way responsible for the way in which they had been abused by their carers — nuns and Brothers who were held by society in the highest esteem.

It was not only society at large that had such a disastrously inaccurate understanding of the nature of industrial schools and those detained within them. The victims of this system themselves equally had no clear view of how it operated. Most of them believed all their lives that they were objects of the charity of religious orders. This is what they had been told by the nuns and Brothers who raised them, and they were instructed that they should be grateful to them and to God for this. Many survivors speak of the guilt they experienced when feeling anger, rather than gratitude, towards those nuns and Brothers, and even towards God. Had they been aware that it was in fact the State, and not the Catholic Church, who paid to maintain them in the schools — that they as children were funded as of right and not out of charity — they might well have been able to develop a very different view of their undoubted worth and value within society.

Children of Charity

The charity myth was so pervasive that many well-meaning local people believed it their duty to assist the industrial schools, or 'orphanages' as they were more euphemistically called, in their area. Former inmates speak with great gratitude of local communities organising summer outings or parties at Christmas. Both the buildings and the children always looked their best on these occasions. The premises were spotlessly clean, and the children well-dressed and happy looking. From the point of view of those who had contact with the industrial schools in this way, nothing appeared amiss. They were not to know that it was the children themselves who had slaved to polish every corner of the building until it shone, that any fruit or flowers on display would be immediately removed after the event, that the children only ever wore those nice clothes when visitors were around, and that any presents the youngsters were given, at Christmas or Easter for instance, were very often taken away from them as soon as their benefactors had left.

It was partly this two-faced nature of the institutions which allowed them to exist unchallenged for so many decades. While people clearly pitied the unfortunate children, they preferred to believe the superficial evidence presented to them that things were perhaps not so bad for the small inmates after all.

Many people, however, do have memories of the 'orphanage' children which did disturb them. The people of Galway noticed that the children from St Joseph's Industrial School in Salthill, run by the Christian Brothers, used to go swimming on one of the poorest beaches in the area, that which was closest to a sewage outlet. They rarely appeared near any of the better swimming spots. People living close to this school also vividly remember hearing the screams of children at night, and simply not knowing what to do about it. This is also reported for Daingean, the tiny village in Co Offaly which housed the country's only reformatory for boys. People there talk about the same sense of paralysis as to what, if any, action they could take.

The people of Dun Laoghaire have vivid memories of the children from Carraiglea Park Industrial School, also run by the Christian Brothers, being taken for their weekly walks. They describe being able to hear them before they saw them — the sound of over 100 pairs of hobnail boots hitting the pavement in unison as they were marched around, military style. A well-known comedian who often entertained school groups has said that the hardest audience he ever played was the children from Glin Industrial School in Country Limerick, another Christian Brothers institution. They never once even smiled, and watched the entertainment nervously as black-clad Brothers patrolled the hall.

There is also the indelible memory of the boys of Artane Industrial School brought to the occasional GAA match in Croke Park, carefully policed by Christian Brothers, and confined in what people describe as a cage-like area. Spectators used to sometimes throw them sweets or cigarettes — almost like feeding the animals in the zoo. The boys, however, were delighted to get out and grateful for anything thrown to them.

The publicity surrounding the 1963 incident in Bundoran involving the shaving of girls' heads in the local industrial school also had a deep impact on the local community. The phrase "a Bundoran haircut" entered the local vocabulary, and children all along the border counties were threatened with this if they misbehaved.

The practice in industrial schools of bringing the children out for a walk once a week, usually on a Sunday, is one which has often been remarked on. In towns the length and breadth of the country, they were highly visible on these occasions, marching two-by-two in a long file, with a nun or a Brother at either end. Many people remember the children looking different from the norm, being abnormally subdued and docile.

People in the general community would also have been aware of the industrial school children in many of the local primary schools. In several towns, these schools were run by the Sisters of Mercy and were part of the complex which also housed an industrial school. In class, the local towns children mixed with what were often referred to as the 'house' children. In very many cases, the industrial school inmates received considerably harsher treatment than did children from the outside community, and this would generally have been well-known.

Another point of contact with the general population was the fact that many families took in industrial school children for a holiday during the summer. This was usually for only a week or two, but the children were often visibly miserable on having to return to their industrial school. With a few notable exceptions where they were abused by these families, most former inmates speak of these holidays as being the happiest times of their young lives. They were often amazed by the quantity of food served to them — what would have been considered normal meals by these families. RTE television carried an extraordinary interview with one such young boy in the early 1960s who had spent time with a family in the Kilkenny area — he listed at great length, and in palpable awe, all the different types of food he had been given to eat during his stay. He remarked with pride that he was even provided with a knife and fork to eat his meals with, something he clearly had never experienced before.

There was one town where the community was brought into close contact with its industrial school in the most tragic way. This was in Cavan, in 1943, when St Joseph's Industrial School, run by the Order of the Poor Clares, burnt to the ground, killing thirty-five children and one elderly woman.

When the alarm was raised in the town, several local people went to help. Some managed to gain access to the building but were so unfamiliar with its layout that they couldn't even find the light switches, let alone the dormitories where the children were dying. The Poor Clares were an enclosed order, with no outsiders allowed access. There was much criticism around this time as to their suitability for the care of children.

An inquiry was held into the fire, under the chairmanship of senior counsel Joseph McCarthy. It effectively exonerated the nuns of any negligence. This was in spite of the fact that it was concluded that many of the children could in fact have been saved had proper action been taken. It appeared that a crucial fire escape door was kept locked, and although it could have been unbolted from the inside, everyone seemed to believe that in fact a key was required to open it. Consequently, the fire escape proved useless in the face of the fire. According to Mavis Arnold's and Heather Laskey's excellent book on the Cavan industrial school and fire, *Children of the Poor Clares*, the primary concern of the nuns was to ensure that they and the children should not be seen in their nightclothes by the outsiders. This wasted crucial time during which it is likely the children could have been saved.

The inquiry's report paid tribute to the nuns, the staff and all the local people involved in the rescue. The one group glaringly omitted was a small number of girls from the industrial school whose heroic actions had saved several of the younger children. According to Arnold and Laskey's book, the inquiry team was even hostile in its questioning of these girls. Their treatment by the inquiry showed clearly that they had not merited the same respect as every one else involved in giving evidence.

The secretary to the inquiry was one Brian Ó Nualláin, better known by his pseudonyms of Flann O'Brien and Myles Na Gopaleen. He was then a civil servant in the Department of

Local Government. While attending the inquiry in Cavan, he composed the following limerick:

> In Cavan there was a great fire;
> Joe McCarthy came down to inquire
> If the nuns were to blame
> It would be a shame
> So it had to be caused by a wire.

It is also revealing to examine the Department of Education's files on the Cavan fire. For such an enormously tragic event, they are remarkably scant. The bulk of the documents deal with how likely the Department was to be sued as a result of the disaster. The inquiry team's report had strongly indicated that the Department should have been much more rigorous in its inspection of fire safety precautions. However, Department files show that they concluded that as there were no known parental addresses for ten of the dead children, and most of the others had been committed at a very young age, the State was unlikely to face compensation claims. There is no record in the Department's files that it ever did.

It is interesting to note that in the Department's file on the Cavan fire, the dead children are referred to by their numbers. The practice of assigning a number to each child in an industrial school was almost universal. In several schools, the children were called only by their numbers, with their names never being used. This practice tended to die out in the 1960s.

Official documentation also commonly used the numbering system. Lists of numbers appear in Department of Education files under the heading "the following for dental treatment" — often names are not mentioned. An entry in one file, for instance, refers to "glasses needed for 977". While the numbering system might have had certain practical uses in dealing with such large groups of children, former inmates testify strongly to its dehumanising effect on them. Many believe that the use of numbers served to reinforce the view that they were inferior and consequently made it easier for nuns and Brothers to beat and abuse them.

Even in death, industrial school children were treated differently to others. The victims of the Cavan fire were buried in a mass grave in the town graveyard, marked only by a small metal cross. No date or names were marked on the cross, only an inscription which read "In Memoriam to the Orphans who died in St Joseph's Industrial School, Cavan. May They Rest in Peace. Amen". The impression was clear — these children did not exist as individuals, but only as a group to be prayed for. During the 1980s, this cross was replaced with a headstone. All reference to the industrial school or the fire was removed. It merely said "In loving memory of the Little Ones of St Clare. R.I.P. Children pray for us".

Without doubt a more fitting tribute to those young lives lost so tragically in the Cavan fire is to be found in the lines of Austin Clarke, the third poem of whose *Three Poems About Childhood* is about that fire:

> Martyr and heretic
> Have been the shrieking wick!
> But smoke of faith on fire
> Can hide us from enquiry
> And trust in Providence
> Rid us of vain expense.
> So why should pity uncage
> A burning orphanage,
> Bar flight to little souls
> That set no churchbell tolling?
>
> Cast-iron step and rail
> Could but prolong the wailing:
> Has not a Bishop declared
> That flame-wrapped babes are spared
> Our life-time of temptation?
> Leap, mind, in consolation
> For heart can only lodge
> Itself, plucked out by logic.
> Those children, charred in Cavan,
> Passed straight through Hell to Heaven.

Children of No Value

There was one constant theme that continuously informed the way in which industrial school children were treated. That was the clear perception from the religious that they were in some way less valuable and less worthy than other children. Much of this view was shared by society in general, and gives a unique insight into the nuances of the very rigid class system which operated in Ireland during this century. The fact that the children themselves were in no way responsible for their condition in life did not appear to mitigate the view that they were less deserving than children from better-off backgrounds, and were consequently treated accordingly. Nowhere was this more true than in the harshness reserved for the many so-called illegitimate children within the system.

It is not possible to give accurate figures for the numbers of such children in industrial schools. Statistics were never properly compiled by the system, although the schools admission forms for each child did have a heading marked "illegitimate". However it is clear that they were always in a minority within the industrial schools.

Across the board these children were singled out for particularly severe treatment, and were invariably those who were confined to menial cleaning and washing duties, particularly in the girls' schools. The Department of Education's discovery in 1952 that many of the nuns actually believed that illegitimate children were barred from employment in the civil service gives some indication of the extraordinary depth of prejudice against these children that existed in the minds of the religious. The Department hastened to disabuse them of this false notion.[1]

One such group spread across the schools was that of black or "coloured" children, as they were called. A number of them have spoken out prominently in recent years about their experiences in industrial schools — Christine Buckley in St Vincent's, Goldenbridge, Sharon Murphy in St Joseph's, Clifden, and Kevin Sharkey in St Joseph's, Salthill. During Sharon's time in Clifden in the 1960s and 1970s, there were a total of eleven other black children there. She describes how they generally did not experience racism within the school, but rather were singled out for comment by the locals whenever they went into the town.

The Department of Education commented on these children in 1966, saying that:

> ... their future especially in the case of girls presented a problem difficult of any satisfactory solution. Their prospects of marriage especially in this country are practically nil and their future happiness and welfare can only be assured in a country with a fair multi-racial population, since they are not well received by either 'black or white' .... It was quite apparent the nuns give special attention to these unfortunate children who are frequently found hot tempered and difficult to control. The coloured boys do not present quite the same problem. It would seem they also got special attention and that they were popular with the other boys.[2]

Not only were these remarks racist, they were also inaccurate. Many of these so-called "coloured" children now testify that they received no such "special attention" — they say that they received the same beatings and abuse as most of the other children within the system.[3]

It does seem that, in general, girls (whether black or white) born to single parents were more harshly treated in this regard than boys. While all the orders of nuns who ran industrial schools were guilty of this, several accounts point to the Good Shepherd Sisters as being especially hard on the so-called illegitimate children in their care.

Many single mothers who gave birth in Mother and Baby homes gave up their babies to the religious orders running these institutions. While some were informally adopted, a high proportion ended up in industrial schools. They had been given up so young that contact with their mothers was very often permanently lost.

However, there was a significant number of single mothers who did try to keep their children with them. This was no easy task, and a combination of pressure from their families and communities, and a genuine belief that the child might be better off, often resulted in committal to industrial school for the infant. In many of these cases, the mothers did manage to maintain some contact with their children through visits, which usually were allowed only once a month.

However, the industrial schools made no attempt to facilitate these visits. The mothers were often treated disdainfully by the nuns, and this was usually in front of their children. Many former inmates report that their mothers were not even allowed inside the building for visits, which had to take place outdoors regardless of the weather.

This was particularly hard, especially as in many cases the mother was herself paying for the upkeep of her child or children. These 'parental monies', as they were known, are one of the more mysterious aspects of the system. In Dublin, there was a specific official of the Department of Education assigned to this task, known as the 'Parental Money Collector'. Elsewhere in the country, the money was collected by the local Gardai.

The Parental Monies scheme illustrated a particular attitude to the parents of children in industrial schools — namely that they should be in some way penalised for being unable to bring up their own children. This was very much part of the rationale of the times — that people who were either single parents or who were simply poor were the architects of their own misfortune. Amounts extorted in this way by the State from parents varied during the 1950s from 2/6 to 10 shillings a week per child, a substantial sum for many who could ill-afford it. Many young single mothers, especially those in domestic service, would have been fortunate to have been earning over £1 a week at this time. A most unsavoury aspect of the scheme was the implicit threat to expose anyone who was not paying up regularly. While there is no documented case of this ever having happened, the fear of exposure and consequent public humiliation (especially for single mothers) was clearly sufficient to ensure compliance.

This was entirely a State-run scheme, with no connections to any other body. While the money was collected by the Department of Education, there is no record as to how it was spent. It is probable that it went into central exchequer funds;

there is certainly no record of it ever having been used directly to improve conditions for the children concerned. The amounts collected were by today's standards not large — an average of £9,000 a year during the 1950s and 1960s.[4] When calculated as a comparison with average wage levels at the time, this amount is equivalent to about £500,000 today. It must, however, be remembered that it was in all cases collected from the very poorest members of society.

It was not only single mothers who were badly treated by nuns and Brothers while attempting to visit their own children. Widows, widowers and those fallen on hard times were also dismissed as being unworthy of even the most basic facilities in which to talk to their children. Former inmates report children seen huddling in doorways or under trees with a parent, trying to shelter from the rain. In some cases, parents were unable to continue to accept the humiliation, and stopped visiting their children.

This attitude to the children's families was starkly at odds with the frequent public utterances of the Church and State concerning the fundamental importance of family and family values to a Christian Irish society. It is clear that the families of a particular class of people, those who lived in poverty, were of less value and less importance in this context. Consequently, not only was no effort made to keep industrial schools children in contact with their families, in fact the direct reverse was the case — those families were often actually broken up and torn apart.

While the bulk of this hostile attitude to family came from the religious orders, there is no doubt that the State colluded in it. Many children were deliberately committed by the courts to industrials schools hundreds of miles from their homes. This was a highly effective means of cutting off all contact with their families, as the expense of travelling to visit was an effective barrier for very many of their parents.

When, as often occurred, large families of children were committed to industrial school at the same time, sisters and brothers were invariably split up. But, often, even a group of sisters from the same family would be spread across a number of different schools, and would completely lose all contact with each other. There are endless stories of people only discovering in middle age the identities of siblings they never knew they had. Geraldine, whose story appears in these pages and who grew up in the Sisters of Mercy industrial school in Tralee, had a total of seven brothers and sisters, spread across no fewer than seven different industrial schools.

Even when sisters (or brothers) were within the same industrial school, they were not encouraged to view themselves as family. There are numerous cases from girls' schools of sisters being forbidden to have any contact with each other. Some of the saddest cases are those of brothers having been placed when very young into different junior boys' industrial schools, and ending up in the enormous Artane school from the age of ten, never knowing of each others' existence. The Christian Brothers apparently felt no need to inform them that they had family members in the same school.

All of this served even more to isolate the children, to make it clear to them that they were completely alone, and that no one either would or could help them. It was one of the arsenal of tactics used, particularly by nuns, to break the children's spirit and so shape them for their place in life — namely as docile servants in the houses of the middle-classes, a large number of whose female members had of course been given a full and complete education by the very same nuns.

In cases where this had not worked, and a girl managed to maintain a sense of individuality, frequently expressed as defiance of the nuns, she was very often perceived by them as being either unreformable or insane. For those who refused to conform to the draconian discipline of the industrial schools, there was always another institution used as a threat — a place even worse than where they were already. Boys were threatened with Letterfrack or Daingean, girls with being sent to Magdalen laundries run by the Good Shepherds.

The girls knew that if they ended up in this type of laundry, it could be a life sentence for them. Children from a very early age had an enormous fear of such places instilled in them. They knew less about psychiatric hospitals, but there is testimony from a number of women who were sent as children to be detained in these facilities because they were considered by the nuns to be uncontrollable.

It is interesting to note that while Magdalen laundries or psychiatric hospitals were used as threats for those in industrial schools, children in the often fee-paying orphanages had a great fear of being sent to those same industrial schools. Girls in St Joseph's Orphanage on Tivoli Road in Dun Laoghaire, run by the Daughters of the Heart of Mary, remember being told they would be sent to Goldenbridge Industrial School in Inchicore if they misbehaved. Children in St Vincent's Orphanage in Glasnevin, which was for middle-class orphaned boys, were threatened with Artane Industrial School. It seems clear from this that everyone within the child care system at the time was aware of a hierarchy of institutions.

For the more general society, the threat of incarceration of errant children was also a reality. The primary factor here was one of geography. Each locality was acutely aware of its own facility for locking up children. Boys in Cork feared being sent to Upton, for girls it was the Good Shepherds. Boys in the Midlands were terrified of Daingean, in Limerick it was Glin and in Galway it was Letterfrack. In Dublin, Artane was used as the local demon to frighten children. These threats had teeth — the places were known to be unpleasant, and were considered useful in this context. However, it is likely that people did not draw any precise connection between making the threat and a detailed awareness of just how terrible conditions were for the children in these institutions.

What all of this paints is a picture of a society which was vaguely aware of the iniquities of the industrial schools — one which simultaneously both knew and did not know just how badly treated the children were. Even if the unthinkable were true, and revered nuns, priests and Brothers were treating the child inmates with cruelty, the population lacked any mechanism for dealing with this. All attempts to denigrate the Catholic Church were viewed with extreme hostility, and those few individuals who did so often paid a heavy price. Irish society in this regard has certain similarities with Germany during and after the Second World War and the question of what ordinary Germans knew about the Nazi concentration camps.

Much has been written about the culpability or otherwise of the German people for the Holocaust. There has always been considerable dissension within that country as to the exact level of general awareness of the death camps. The only reasonable answer lies, as in Ireland, in the peculiar phenomenon of people both knowing and not knowing at the same time, or perhaps more precisely, knowing enough not to probe any further. Even had people in Germany possessed detailed knowledge of Nazi atrocities, what action could they have taken in a climate where dissent was so ruthlessly punished.

While the respective scales of the crimes are obviously significantly different, both Irish and German society shared a similar pattern of denial. Both were afraid to acknowledge that terrible events were occurring within their communities.

Somewhat the same analogy can be made with any number of countries where gross injustices have been perpetrated against vulnerable minorities within them. What Ireland shares with many societies around the world is a dangerous reality: once a group of people is isolated as being in some way inferior, the general population becomes less concerned with how they are treated, even in the face of evidence of cruelty and abuse. In Ireland's case, the thousands of victims of industrial schools bear witness to a society unwilling to question its own comfortable certainties out of a fear that those beliefs might turn out to have been built on sand.

Mary's Story, St Francis Xavier Industrial School, Ballaghaderreen, Co Roscommon (Irish Sisters of Charity), 1949–1961

"They used to call me 'red boy', as in the devil. When they were really angry they'd call me Satan. But 'red boy' was what I went by. Either that or my number, which was five. It didn't bother me. I didn't know any different."

Mary spent the first year of her life in St Patrick's Mother and Baby home on the Navan Road in Dublin. It was one of the largest institutions for unmarried mothers in the country, run by the Daughters of Charity of St Vincent de Paul. Many of the babies were left with their mothers for about a year, and then moved out to various industrial schools around the country. Mary was sent to the industrial school in Ballaghaderreen, Co Roscommon, run by the Irish Sisters of Charity.

"I never knew my mother. She never visited and I have no memory of her. It never really occurred to me that people would love children. We never experienced it — never had hugs or kisses or anything like that. It just never arose.

The routine from about the age of five was that we'd all get up at half-six, wash and dress and then go to Mass. The nun stood at the back of the church and if you coughed or moved, she would take your number. After Mass, when we went back, she would sit up on her high chair — we used to call it her throne — and she'd call out your number.

You'd have to go up, and instead of breakfast, you'd get a piece of black soap. You had to put it in your mouth, and keep it there all during breakfast. We had disturbed the priest during Mass, and that was the punishment.

From when I was about eight or nine, I noticed that I wasn't going to school a lot. The nun would say 'red boy, you do the dormitories!'. And I'd have to go off and clean them. It didn't bother me — I used to love polishing. But I couldn't read or write. My writing isn't too bad now, but I still have problems with the reading.

But when the inspector was coming, they'd always make me put on a uniform and sit in the classroom. They always knew when she was coming, and there'd be fruit put out in bowls around the place — they had an orchard in the grounds. We weren't allowed touch it, we never got any fruit.

But the food was alright. We got meat quite often, and we weren't hungry. They used even give us a few sweets on Sundays, unless you were on the list for being bold. I seemed to be always on the list.

The nuns would punish us with beatings. It wasn't just on the hand — in school we'd get hit on the hands, but you didn't mind that because you generally knew what it was for. But in the orphanage you'd be hit anywhere — legs, back, head, it didn't matter. They used the belt off their habit to hit us with. There was one nun who used to love to watch children fighting. She'd egg us on, encourage us to beat each other up.

One time when I was quite small I knocked against a door and it pushed against a nun. She grabbed me and belted me across the head and then she threw me down the stairs. They were hard stone steps. When I fell, I couldn't get up, so I was dragged by the hair down into the bucket cupboard, where they kept all the cleaning stuff. And I was locked in there.

I was afraid they'd forget about me in there, and it used to be full of rats. So what I did was sing at the top of my voice — all I knew were hymns, so I sang them all. After a long time, I heard the nun outside the door saying 'Get that red boy out of there'. But I couldn't walk, my leg just gave out from under me.

They brought me to hospital, and it turned out my leg was broken in five places. I told the doctor and nurses about the nun throwing me down the stairs. I always felt they kind of believed me, but that they weren't going to say anything to the nuns.

When I got out of hospital, that nun was afraid to do anything to me because she knew I had to go back to get the bandages off, and it mightn't look good if I was covered in bruises. She was clever enough, that one.

It's funny, you know, that I don't remember any pain with the leg. I suppose it's that we grew up with so much pain from the beatings that you just pushed it to the back of your mind.

I remember a girl once had impetigo and she was covered in sores and scabs. She got loads of attention. I'd be along the corridors polishing and I'd see her in a special room with fruit beside her, waiting for the doctor to come in every day to check on her.

So one night I rubbed my blanket on bits of my skin until it was raw and cut. I wanted to get what she had, so I could get the same attention. So they put me in the same room with her. But after a few days, my sores started healing and hers didn't. So the doctor said I didn't have impetigo after all.

They got it out of me how I had made the scabs, and I was sent to the bucket house again. After a while in there, I didn't mind the rats at all. I looked on them as my friends. They never touched me, and I remember one of them used to look at me — he had beautiful eyes.

I don't know why there were so many rats. The place wasn't dirty, and the nuns kept us very clean. They got cats at one stage to catch them. The cats were more vicious than the rats.

Another punishment was that they'd threaten to send for the handyman. I was terrified of him, and it was the only thing that would make me behave myself. He'd be called, and I'd be left in the room with him.

I suppose they expected him to beat me. I'd climb up onto the highest window in the room and shout that I'd jump if he touched me. The poor man — I think he was more frightened of us than we were of him. He never really did anything to me."

Mary has a clear memory of American couples arriving at the industrial school, and selecting girls to adopt. Sometimes there would be a short-list, and the children were interviewed. Mary was on the short-list once, but nothing came of it. She also remembers that children were moved out of the school from time to time. She never knew where they went. Until it was her turn, that is.

"One day when I was twelve, they told me to pack my case. They said I was going on my holidays. I asked where, and they said 'It's a secret'. I got a few new clothes, and they took me off in the convent car.

I ended up in Athlone in another orphanage, with the Sisters of Mercy this time. I didn't know why I was there, but I do remember them saying in Ballaghaderreen that I wasn't fit to be sent out into society.

I didn't last too long in Athlone. When we were at confession in the town, I stopped outside to talk to a man who was admiring the church. I delayed for maybe about twenty minutes behind the others.

There was uproar when I got back. They dragged me up to a small room and told me to stay there. Then the nun came up and there was a man with her — he was a doctor. 'Get up there on the bed,' the nun said to me. 'This man is going to examine you.'

'But I'm not sick,' I said. She grabbed me and held me down. The man opened his little case, and I'll never forget to this day what was in it. Just a pair of rubber gloves, and nothing else. So when he came over to examine me I gave him a kick between the legs, and down he went.

They left me alone then, locked in this room. I got nothing to eat that day, and the following day they took me to the station. Two Sisters of Charity met us there, and they took me to Dublin on the train. All the way up they kept telling me how bold I was, and said rosaries non-stop. I still had no idea what I was supposed to have done.

I was fascinated by the lights in Dublin. We got a taxi at the station, and I was wedged in between the two nuns again — I suppose they thought I might do a runner. The taxi brought us to Donnybrook, to the St Mary Magdalene asylum, where I was to be put.

They kept me in a little room there, and after a few days brought a man, a doctor I suppose, to examine me again. I lost the head, and wouldn't let him touch me. They kept referring to how I was going to have a baby, but I had no idea what they meant.

Then they put me working in the laundry there, and I met loads of past pupils of Ballaghaderreen. They were asking me when I was going to have the baby. I said I didn't know, that the nuns hadn't told me when they were going to give it to me yet.

You see, what I thought was that they were going to give me a baby to mind, and that this was the reason I had been moved to Dublin. I hadn't a clue about sex or boyfriends or anything.

You weren't allowed talk in the laundry, and the nun caught me one day. The next thing I knew, they were taking me to Grangegorman, to the mental hospital. I knew about Grangegorman — the nuns in Ballaghaderreen used to threaten us with it when we were bold. The Donnybrook nun kept telling me that I was mad, and I suppose that's why they sent me there. At this stage I was about thirteen or fourteen.

I spent about three months in Grangegorman. At first I didn't know how I'd survive, because they really were all mad in there. There was an awful lot of shouting and roaring. I kept very very quiet — I knew if I didn't, they'd give me an injection. So it wasn't too bad — they left me alone really.

I was sent back to the laundry in Donnybrook. But a Carmelite priest had taken an interest in me — he really was genuinely trying to help me. He organised that I be transferred to another laundry in Dublin — in Gloucester St, also run by nuns. And from there, he got me a job as a servant for a family down the country. So that's how I managed to escape."

Mary worked in various domestic service and cleaning jobs for a number of years. She is now married with two children, and lives on the outskirts of Dublin. She feels that she has survived her childhood experiences well.

"I don't believe in blaming individual nuns for what happened. I think that it was the system, that they had their rules and they went by them. We were like an army — the group was all important, and you had to toe the line. But they didn't break me — I managed to stay an individual, they never managed to take that away from me.

But I do blame them for not giving me an education, and for all the violence that went on. And I blame them for trying to break my spirit. But the way I look at it, God was good to me. I never lost my faith, I always separated religion from anything that had happened to me as a child. And I had a great patron in the Mother of Perpetual Succour. I think that because I was strong enough, she stood by me, and she rescued me."

Elizabeth's Story, St Brigid's Industrial School, Loughrea, Co Galway (Sisters of Mercy), 1951–1960

"From when I was little, we used to wash our own clothes. I remember I would take off my dry vest and petticoat and put on the wet ones, especially in the winter. They'd be ringing wet and freezing. I wanted to get sick so that they'd take me out of the place and put me in hospital. I'd have done anything to get out. But it never worked — I never did get sick."

Elizabeth was born in 1944 in Co Galway. Her mother, a widow with seven children, was having an affair with a married man who lived locally. Elizabeth was born as a result, and remembers that for the first seven years of her life she was kept locked away in a room in the house.

"I suppose it was the disgrace of having me, and her a widow for years. I think that's why I was kept hidden. When I was seven, I remember I got a little pink flowery dress, and a black car came for me and took me away. I never went back to that house again.

I don't remember my mother loving me or giving me hugs and kisses. She was a cold woman. She used to visit me once a month in the orphanage, and she'd bring me sweets, but I never remember a hug or a kiss.

I think the reason she came was to pay money to the nuns to keep me there. I never went to court, and I think the nuns told my mother that it was either go to court and have me put in, or else she could pay them to keep me. I suppose my mother wanted to keep it all quiet.

I was terrified when I went into the place first. There were so many children, so many beds, and so much noise. And I wasn't used to seeing anyone, having been locked away for so long.

School was a real problem for me. I hated it, I was no good at it. It was the local national school and was attached to the orphanage. All the local girls came in to it. But the teachers used to single out the orphanage children, saying we couldn't read or write.

I used to wet the bed, there were a number of us who did. The nuns used to make us go to school with the wet sheet on our head or wrapped around our waist. They'd make us stand on a desk at the back of the classroom with the sheet on you, so everyone would know that you were a bed wetter.

The punishments were brutal. You'd be hit all over, usually with a stick. I remember getting my head banged of a wall many times — the nun would hold my two ears and wallop my head, back and forward. You'd be punished for anything, even talking during meals which was forbidden.

There was one time my back was all sore and black and blue from a beating, and I asked my mother to take a look at it during one her visits. But she didn't do anything. 'You'll be alright,' was all she said. So you were on your own really. But the thing is we all thought that this was normal. We didn't know any better.

Even if the inspector had looked at us a bit harder, he'd have seen the lumps and bruises. But he never did. We'd just line up about once a year, and he'd walk down the line slowly with the nun, looking at us. Nothing ever changed.

I can't complain about the food. It was alright — we'd get meat quite often for our main meal, and we used to get eggs and that. But the work was very hard. From the time I went in at seven, there was endless scrubbing and cleaning and washing.

I remember we used to scrub the yard once a week. Loads of us scrubbing in a line on our hands and knees. And if one girl was a bit slower, the nun behind us would give her a belt on the back with the strap they wore around their habits.

There was a lay woman there who used to make me do things to her — I suppose today you'd call it sexual abuse. I was terrified of her and I just did what she told me. She had threatened to tell the nuns on me if I didn't do it. I never told anyone at the time, and I never knew if she did it to anyone else. But years later, I met another woman who was there and she told me it had happened to her as well. But there was just no one you could tell.

When I was twelve, I was taken out of school to work with the babies. That was the end of school for me. I still didn't know how to read or write. Even today I have problems, but my husband and children are very good to me, they help me if I need to write anything.

Four of us girls worked minding the babies. There were rows and rows of cots, all tiny babies in them. We did everything — we washed them, fed them, changed them. We washed their clothes and their nappies. We also had to get up to them in the middle of the night, so you rarely got a full night's sleep.

You learned never to get attached to any of them, because they were always coming and going. There was constant movement of babies in and out of the place. Most of the time we had about fifty of them there, so it was hard work.

I remember the day of my first period as clear as anything. I looked down at my legs and saw blood all over them. I had no idea what was going on, nothing had ever been mentioned about periods. So I went up to the nun and I said 'my legs are all bleeding'.

She told me I was lying, and she beat me around the place. Then she told me I'd be alright and she sent me away. They never gave us any pads or anything. I found a bit of a torn sheet and used that. But if my mother had been any good, she'd have brought me something to use.

When I was about fourteen, three of us tried to run away. We stole bread from the kitchen the night before and put it under our mattresses so it wouldn't be found. The next morning we stuffed it down our jumpers, and slipped over the wall on our way to Mass.

We walked and walked for hours, but we'd no idea where we were going. Sure, we'd never even been outside the gates. Eventually we got very tired, and our feet were sore, and we were thirsty. So we knocked on the door of a house to ask for a drink of water. And who answered the door only the priest who said Mass for us every morning.

He recognised us and he brought us in and made us a cup of tea and some lovely sandwiches. He left us alone for a bit, and then he came back with the Gardai. We didn't even get to finish the sandwiches. They grabbed hold of us, and put us into the car to bring us back. The nuns sent us to bed with no tea, and we got no breakfast the following morning either. They beat us as well, of course.

When I turned sixteen, I was told that I was going to Dublin to work. I remember being delighted, because I was getting out. I went around telling everyone. The following day, two nuns brought me to the train and one sat on either side of me all the way to Dublin. They never told me where I was going, or what the job was.

We arrived in this place with a big long avenue, and when we came up to the building my heart sank. All I could see was bars on the windows. We went in, and the nuns there told me that my name was being changed. I wasn't Elizabeth anymore, I was Magdalene. They gave me clothes to wear — a big long grey thing and an apron, and the next day I started work in the laundry."

Elizabeth had been brought to High Park convent in Drumcondra. It was the largest Magdalen laundry in the country, with well over 100 women working there. It took in laundry from all over the city, and especially from the large number of religious institutions in the close vicinity. The nuns there also ran their own industrial school for young girls. They were the Sisters of Our Lady of Charity of Refuge.

"We were never paid for our work in the laundry. And I spent over ten years there. Once a month a nun sent around a slip of paper and you were allowed put down four items that you needed, and they'd get them for you. They'd be things like a bar of soap, toothpaste, a pair of stockings and a few sweets or a packet of biscuits — it was one or the other, you weren't allowed have both sweets and biscuits.

We'd get up in the mornings at half-seven, and go to Mass. Then after breakfast we worked in the laundry. It was a big operation — they had lots of different sections. They had machines for the shirts, and different machines for coats. I was in sorting for a while, but because I couldn't read what was on the labels, they moved me back to ironing. There were heaps and heaps of washing, we were kept going all the time.

We weren't allowed to talk during our meals. At dinner, one of the women would stand up and read something religious right through the meal. There were women of all ages there, some of them very old. The older women were lovely — they used to help us a lot and teach us how to use the machines. And each year, there'd be a new batch of sixteen-year-olds.

They used to lock us in. I remember the big bunch of keys. I never thought of escaping anyway. I knew I'd just be brought back again, like the last time.

When I was in my late twenties — this would have been around 1972 or 1973 — they brought in a hostel, and allowed some of us to apply for jobs outside. I got a job in Guinness's doing the wash-up, and I stayed in the hostel at night. That was my first taste of freedom and my first wage packet. It was wonderful."

Elizabeth worked at Guinness's for a few years until she met her husband. She has two children, both grown up now, and she lives in Dublin. She never made a secret of her past — her family know all about her childhood and her years in High Park laundry.

She also tried to trace her mother and her family in Galway. She eventually found them, but they rejected her. One of her sisters told her that she was a "mistake," and that she should leave them alone.

A few years ago, Elizabeth did attempt to go for counselling, but she found that it distressed her too much to go into the detail of it all again.

"I'd love to ask all those nuns why they treated us so badly. Because they were reared themselves as children, they knew what it was like. And what about the ones who didn't beat us — why didn't they have the guts to speak out about it? I'd just really love to get a reason for it all. Maybe some day I'll find out."

Thirteen

The State: "None So Blind..."

On the 11th of May 1999, Taoiseach Bertie Ahern made the following statement. "On behalf of the State and of all citizens of the State, the Government wishes to make a sincere and long overdue apology to the victims of childhood abuse for our collective failure to intervene, to detect their pain, to come to their rescue." Less than a fortnight later, the Minister for Education, Micheal Martin announced the establishment of a Commission to Inquire into Childhood Abuse, chaired by Ms Justice Mary Laffoy of the High Court.

The apology and the establishment of a commission to investigate the abuse of children marked a dramatic acknowledgement by the Irish State of its role and responsibility in the provision of services to children.

For many years, the State's files dealing with its responsibilities to the children detained in industrial schools lay gathering dust in boxes dumped around the corridors in the Department of Education. In the late 1980s, an attempt was made to gather them centrally, and some years later they were transported to the Department's new offices in Athlone. There they remained, carefully locked away and left relatively undisturbed until a few years ago. Now, in the wake of the explosion of controversy and litigation surrounding industrial schools, they are among the most frequently consulted archive files within the Department. Hundreds of former inmates of the system have availed of their rights under the 1997 Freedom of Information Act, and are now demanding access to any records which the Department holds on their own individual cases. However, many of the Department's files are completely missing, and others contain gaps spanning several decades with no documentation available.

In total, five sets of archives survive in Athlone. The first of these consists of the registers for each school — rows of huge, dusty and ancient-looking volumes with hand-written entries for each child committed to the school. Only the most basic information is given on the children, such as names, dates of birth, dates and reasons for committal. The Department has now compiled an electronic database of these names. However, because not all the registers have survived, the database contains information on only 36,000 children, about one third of the total number committed by the courts since 1869. There are also a number of files giving more detail on about 10,000 children within the system. Neither these files, nor the schools' registers are open to public inspection, which is entirely proper as they essentially comprise confidential information on individual, named children.

The second category of archives are the Certification Files for each industrial school. Much of the information in these relates to the establishment of the individual schools over 100 years ago, and is remarkably detailed. In fact, it is generally the case that the level of detail available for the nineteenth century in these files is considerable greater than anything relating to the relevant decades of the twentieth century.

Thirdly, there are the Medical Inspection files — one for each school. However, these contain no information whatsoever prior to 1939. Each file begins with a report on the school from Dr Anna McCabe, the newly-appointed Medical Inspector, giving the findings of her inspection visits for 1939. While there is a considerable amount of detail on a number of schools during the 1940s, the information decreases to a bare trickle throughout the 1950s and '60s. The files contain standard forms for each school, to be filled out under the following headings; Condition of premises; Accommodation; Equipment; Sanitation; Health; Food and diet; Clothing; Recreation facilities; Precautions against fire; and General comments. For school after school, and year after year, these were all described as "adequate", "good" or "very good". From the mid-1940s, there was a noticeable absence of any critical commentary for the vast majority of schools.

The fourth set of archives contain the General Inspection files for the schools. Once again, these contain very little material prior to 1939. In many cases, they overlap with the Medical Inspection files, with no clear distinction between them. They also share the peculiarity of being quite detailed in a number of cases during the 1940s, and then becoming very sketchy during the '50s and '60s. The period for which the files are most detailed of course coincides with the six years from 1939 to 1945 when P Ó Muircheartaigh held the position of Inspector of Industrial and Reformatory Schools (see Chapter Six).

The final set of archives are the general policy files, relating to funding, correspondence and complaints, together with a number of files relating to St Conleth's Reformatory School in Daingean. These also contain very little material before the 1940s. The Department itself has no explanation as to why the files contain such significant gaps. Crucially, it is this set of archives which should include the working files of the only two committees established in the lifetime of the State to examine the industrial schools system. However, every single shred of material related to the Cussen Committee and its report in 1936 has vanished. In fact, based on the Department's files, one would not even be aware that such a statutory Committee had existed. This is in spite of the fact that the Department was heavily involved during the two-year period when the Cussen Committee carried out its examination of the system.

Equally, the working files of the Kennedy Committee, which reported in 1970, have also disappeared. Only a handful of documents survive, giving tantalising clues of the somewhat hostile relationship which appears to have developed between the Kennedy Committee and the Department of Education. The findings of that Committee were highly critical of the role of the Department within the system.

Death

Another glaring omission from the archive is the absence of files on the deaths of children in industrial schools. This is remarkable, as an official inquiry was mandatory following the death of any child in the schools. It is clear that such information was compiled on a yearly basis — figures and causes of death were published in the Department of Education annual reports. The numbers shown were small and the causes usually due to illness. Occasionally death due to an accident was recorded, although no further details were provided. One would expect to find files on this within the Department, however none appear to have survived.

There is, however, one tragic case, discovered in the middle of the Medical Inspection file for St Kyran's Industrial School in Rathdrum. This was for small boys and was run by the Sisters of Mercy. On the 31st of December 1947, Michael McQualter child number 999, died following a scalding when placed in an extremely hot bath by a fourteen-year-old domestic assistant in the school. Michael McQualter was only three years old. Dr Anna McCabe investigated the accident — she focussed her attention on the nuns and attached no blame to the fourteen-year-old domestic. She interviewed Mother Avallino, the Sister of Mercy in charge of the school, and produced a written report for the Department on the death of the toddler.

Dr McCabe recorded that Mother Avallino "did not appear unduly upset", and that she was much more interested in complaining about the inadequate funding for the school. She described the nun's reaction as "callous". She expected some expression of concern about the death of the child, but she reported that Mother Avallino was "more concerned with the possibility of trouble from the parents than with the suffering of this little boy, who she stated was a soft child who would be inclined to burn or scald easily".

Dr McCabe added that when she had mentioned the adverse publicity which the inquest on the little boy's death might generate, Mother Avallino replied that "the matter had been taken care of in Carysfort [the mother house for the Rathdrum convent] and there would be no report of the matter in the press". Dr McCabe concluded that the death of Michael McQualter amounted to "criminal negligence". However, the

Department of Education appears to have taken no further action on the matter.[1]

In addition to the absence of general files on the deaths of children, there are also a number of other peculiar omissions in the archives. Little survives of the correspondence between the Department of Health and the Department of Education on the 'Poor Law' children maintained in industrial schools, although much of this can be found in the Department of Health's archive. There is no reference whatsoever to the widely publicised criticisms of the system by Fr Edward Flanagan in the mid-1940s, and nor is there any mention of the well-documented case of the beating of Gerard Fogarty in Glin Industrial School (see Chapters Nine & Ten). Interestingly, the file on the Glin school contains more correspondence on the cost of transporting the children elsewhere when it closed in the early 1960s than on any other single episode in the history of the school.

Equally, there is nothing relating to the preparation of material for the Department of Education's published annual reports. These reports are generally uninformative. They contain only general comments on the operation of the schools under various rudimentary headings and they gave some basic figures on the numbers detained. By the 1940s, only a short note and some bare statistics appear, and from the early 1960s, even the commentary was dropped. This sharp decline in published information is not peculiar to the section on reformatory and industrial schools — it is a general feature of the Department's annual reports covering all of the areas within its remit.

The archives of the Department of Health contain some revealing material related to industrial schools. This Department had responsibility for children placed in the schools by local authorities, the majority of whom had been born to single mothers. A number of fascinating files survive on the inspections conducted by the Department of Health of industrial schools who applied to be certified to receive the local authority children. It is clear from these that the inspectors in the Department of Health were often more critical of the schools than their counterparts in the Department of Education.

For example, in 1940 the Department of Health found the industrial school in Ennis to be "very much overcrowded. The water supply is unsatisfactory, the sanitary arrangements are inadequate and the bathing facilities are inadequate". They refused to certify the school to accept local authority children.[2] This was of course in spite of the fact that it was registered by the Department of Education as a fully fit industrial school, and contained over 100 children at the time.

Similarly, in 1951, St Dominick's Industrial School in Waterford was inspected by the Department of Health. Their report noted that the school was certified by the Department of Education for 160 children, but as the inspectors considered the dormitories overcrowded, it was suggested that 140 children would be a more reasonable figure.[3] The Department of Education responded by saying that Dr Anna McCabe "who has been inspecting the school regularly since 1939 has always reported very favourably on the accommodation, equipment, condition of premises, care of the children committed, and the general management of the school". They requested that "favourable consideration" be given to the school's application to be allowed accept local authority children.[4] However, the Department of Health refused to budge on this issue.

One of the most remarkable aspects of the State's approach to child care was the enormous difference between the policies of these two Government Departments with responsibility for the area. The Department of Health stated repeatedly and publicly that maintaining children in their families of origin should be encouraged and facilitated and, if this was not possible, foster care rather than institutional care should be provided. In sharp contrast, the Department of Education believed firmly that institutional care offered many benefits and went so far as to prohibit the boarding-out of children from industrial schools in the 1940s. The third body with a role in the area — the local authorities — were primarily concerned with minimising their costs with regard to dependent children. They inclined towards institutional care, for which they had to pay only half the bill, as opposed to the full amount in the case of fostering.

The negligence of the local authorities in this regard was sharply criticised by the Department of Health Inspectors for Boarded-Out Children. Two of them were particularly active and outspoken – Miss Fidelma Clandillon and Miss Alice Litster were among the very few women who held senior positions within the civil service during the middle decades of the century. They condemned the local health authorities' behaviour towards those children for whom they had responsibility – it showed "a complete indifference to the fate of deprived children", they said.[5]

These Inspectors clearly identified the reasons why local health authorities dumped the children into industrial schools, rather than arranging to have them fostered:

> ... the children are not subject to inspection either at local or Departmental level, no reports on their progress are called for, and no records or case histories have to be compiled in relation to them; frequently not even a register is kept despite continuous pressure from the inspectors. Once admitted to a school, therefore, the health authority has no further trouble with a child apart from an occasional letter from the Department [of Health] inquiring why he has not been boarded out. The easy answer to this is that a suitable foster home is not available and there the matter rests.[6]

The result was that no one visited these 'Poor Law' children, their backgrounds were generally unknown, and their progress was not monitored. They truly were the "forgotten ones" of the system, in the words of Miss Clandillon.[7]

From as far back as 1905, Inspectors at the Department of Health had been critical of the industrial schools themselves. Stating that while the schools might turn out children who were "better disciplined and better trained", they did not provide "those somewhat undefinable adjuncts which go to make a 'home'. This point in the boarding-out system is, I think, too often overlooked, and yet it is one of the most humanising influences which can be brought to bear on the waifs and strays of our population with which the Poor Law has to deal."[8] The

Department of Education, with its primary responsibility for the industrial schools, never seriously allowed the question of "humanising influences" to concern it.

This contradiction between the stated objectives of the Department of Health and the practices employed by the Department of Education was noted in 1964 following a query from Kerry Co Council. The council was concerned at the high numbers of children maintained by them in industrial schools, and wished to find foster homes for them, a decision facilitated by their appointment of a local children's officer. Outlining the reasons why such fostering was prohibited, the Department of Education observed that:

> It seems strange that two Government Departments should be at variance on such a fundamental issue. I spoke to an official of the Department of Health and apparently that Department considers that a home, even a disrupted home, is preferable to an institution, however good. This Department's [of Education] decision of 1946 prohibiting the boarding out of children was based on justifiable fear that such a child might die in circumstances necessitating a public inquiry. A child boarded out from an industrial school under Section 53 remains the responsibility of the manager, and should anything untoward happen to the child the manager would be automatically implicated and the Minister indirectly implicated. The decision of this Department to prohibit boarding out was taken at a time when economic conditions were very bad and based on fear of inquiry rather than on what was best for a child.[9]

However, the Department of Education never made any serious attempt to revise its policy opposing fostering. It was only after the devastating criticisms of the Kennedy Report in 1970 that responsibility for child care was removed from Education, and given to the Department of Health, who immediately began implementing a policy of finding foster families for children in need of care.

There are various clues in the Department of Education's files as to why the State remained so committed to the model of institutional care for children. Its activity in this area clearly flies in the face of the cherished notion that in Ireland the State did not intervene in families. Much of the literature in this area to date has generally supported the interpretation of a non-interventionist State committed to upholding family values and the primacy of the family unit. However, this standard view may now need to be re-examined in the context of the sheer scale of the State's direct intervention in the lives of such vast numbers of families, through the committal of their children to industrial schools.[10]

The State's motivation for this was on a mixture of pragmatic, moral and political grounds. There was a clear awareness that to provide a proper alternative State child care system would have been very costly. Minister for Justice Gerry Boland graphically outlined the advantages of using Catholic Church institutions for this purpose. Writing in 1947, he stated that they:

> … can be located almost anywhere because men in the Religious Orders will readily forego, for the sake of their mission, amenities which the paid State servant with a wife and family will insist upon. Thus the Reformatory at Glencree was able to carry on very well despite its isolation, even before the days of the bus and the motor car, whereas it would not do even with these modern advantages as a Borstal institution. Lay staff would simply refuse to live in such a place without schools, without picture houses, without shops, without even a public house.[11]

On moral and religious grounds, the State also perceived considerable advantages to the religious-run industrial schools system. The Secretary of the Department of Education, writing in 1963, summed up this position:

> The Minister feels that the State is particularly fortunate in that industrial and reformatory schools are under the management of priests, nuns and

> brothers, since vocation and dedication play an all-important part in the accomplishment of the arduous task of shaping committed children into useful members of society.[12]

On political grounds, it was very clear that any attempt to wrest control of the system from the religious orders would have been met with the most serious resistance. While the religious congregations constantly demanded more money from the State, they repeatedly and successfully resisted attempts by the Government to have any influence over the industrial schools. Consequently, the role of the Department of Education was effectively reduced to that of funding the system, without having any major impact on it. In this regard, the area of industrial schools did not differ significantly from the more general schooling system, funded by the State but run by various bodies within the Catholic Church.

On the few occasions prior to 1970 when the Department did seek to effect any change in the industrial schools system, they were met with hostile opposition from the religious orders. For instance, the Department's attempts during the 1940s and 1950s to have an additional industrial school for boys established within easy reach of Dublin were met with failure. The thinking behind this was to allow boys from the city to be visited more frequently by their families — many of the Dublin boys sent to schools in the West of Ireland were effectively cut off from their parents.

Typically, however, the Department made no attempt to provide such a school itself. Rather, it pressurised the Christian Brothers to do so, offering to cover half the costs. The Brothers were unsure as to whether there was a need for such a school — they did not share the Department's view that boys should be located nearer to their families. However, the Provincial told the Department that "this particular type of work on behalf of neglected, erring or destitute boys makes a special appeal to us. I appreciate the compliment which you as Minister for Education paid the Christian Brothers asking them to undertake it."

In the late 1940s, the Christian Brothers purchased Oakley Park in Celbridge, Co Kildare with 156 acres of land for just under £20,000. However, they then insisted that the Department pay the entire remainder of the costs associated with setting up an industrial school on the site. The Department for its part believed that there had been an agreement with the Christian Brothers that they would share the costs between them, and that the Government grant had allowed the Brothers to purchase and have sole ownership of this valuable property. There then ensued a highly acrimonious correspondence between the two sides, with the Department accusing the Christian Brothers of dishonouring their agreement, and the Brothers hotly denying this.

In a revealing letter in 1951, the Christian Brothers wrote to the Department that:

> The Ministry for Education has written and acted since 1944 as the party giving help not the party receiving it, and now from the Department's latest communication the uninformed reader might be led to conclude that this new school was a good business investment due to yield rich dividends and that the Christian Brothers were striving to inveigle the Department to subscribing five-sixths of the capital while the Brothers proposed to draw all the dividends.[13]

This incident highlights two crucial points: firstly, the assumption by the State that any new facility for children should automatically be owned and managed by a religious congregation; and secondly, that in return for ceding ownership and control, the State expected a substantial investment in the project from the Christian Brothers. The option that the State should itself purchase, own and run such an institution never even arose. The school at Celbridge was never established, and boys continued to be dispatched often hundreds of miles away from their families.

The situation was made even worse when the Christian Brothers decided to alter the function of the Letterfrack Industrial School in 1954, and effectively turn it into a junior reformatory for the detention of boys under twelve convicted of either truancy or criminal offences. Letterfrack was one of the most remote and isolated industrial schools in the country, and this move substantially increased the number of boys detained there who came from the cities, particularly from Dublin. It did not appear to weigh with the Christian Brothers that visits to these often very young children from their families were virtually impossible — none of them would have had either a car, or the money for train fares, bus fares and the overnight accommodation that such a long journey would have entailed during the 1950s and 1960s. The Christian Brothers' decision in this regard was announced to the Department of Education, who simply acquiesced in it, and the courts then acted accordingly. It resulted in further misery for the children involved.[14]

A further example of the impotence of the State can be found in its attempts to establish visiting committees for the schools. These had been a feature of the prisons system for many years and provided the opportunity for some kind of independent assessment of conditions. However, the Department of Education took the view that the religious orders running industrial schools would not accept such outside examination. In 1963, the Inter-Departmental Committee on Crime Prevention (comprised of officials from the Departments of Justice and Education) strongly recommended the establishment of visiting committees for the schools. However, the Department of Education's official response was negative, saying that the religious orders who ran the schools "were very sceptical of the efficacy of visiting committees, being of the opinion that they could very easily constitute a grave nuisance unless the personnel of the committees were chosen with the greatest care."[15]

Also around this time the Catholic Parents Guild, the chaplain of Artane Industrial School Fr Moore, and members of the judiciary had all recommended strongly to the Department that visiting committees should be introduced.[16] However, the Department remembered the last time it had attempted to become involved in the management of the schools:

> It is well to point out that when it was proposed in 1951 that a committee composed of representatives from the Departments of Education, Social Welfare

and Finance should hold an inquiry into the schools, with the object of establishing a firm basis for an increase in grants, the School Managers Association was unalterably opposed to the carrying out of the enquiry.[17]

Despite considerable pressure, especially from the Department of Justice, no further attempts were made to establish visiting committees for industrial schools. Indeed, it appears that the Department of Education did not even bother to suggest it officially to the religious orders, so sure were they that it would be rejected.

The matter was raised again in 1966, in a letter from Brian Lenihan, then Minister for Justice, to his counterpart in Education, Donough O'Malley. Lenihan pointed out the Inter-Departmental Committee's recommendations on a number of areas, particularly with regard to visiting committees:

> Since we have heard no more I assume that Education have dragged their feet or that the school managers rejected the idea ... I think that a vigorous approach to the managers of the Industrial Schools individually or collectively would make it extremely difficult for them to maintain a negative attitude. If the Department of Education were willing to assign one energetic officer to the organisational work involved, I believe that the beneficial results could justify the effort a hundred fold.[18]

Donough O'Malley's ultimate response to this was the establishment of the Kennedy Committee to examine the entire system (see Chapter Fourteen).

Apart altogether from the matter of visiting committees, the Department of Education itself didn't even bother to fulfil its statutory requirement to inspect each industrial school annually.[19] The Inspector of Industrial Schools, Turlough McDevitt, informed the Inter-Departmental Committee on Crime Prevention in 1963 that frequent inspection of the schools was not a feature of the system. He said that there were a number of schools which he had never visited. When asked by the Committee had he ever, for example, inspected Lakelands in Sandymount, run by the Sisters of Charity, he replied that he had never visited it. The Committee strongly recommended regular inspections of the schools by the Department of Education.[20]

A further example of the Department disregarding its statutory obligations arose with regard to St Brigid's Industrial School in Loughrea, Co Galway, run by the Sisters of Mercy. When a young girl died there in 1961 as a result of illness, the Department of Health became involved. An official there reported a conversation she had with the Inspector of Industrial Schools (McDevitt again), who told her that he had never inspected the Loughrea school, and that it had not been visited for "a very considerable time". There is no reference to any of this in Department of Education files, but it is recorded in the archives of the Department of Health.[21]

"Crooked Souls"

The concern with visiting committees and inspections was on one level highly commendable. However, when viewed against the background of the State's own record in regard to the only institution for children directly under its control, a certain scepticism might be appropriate. In terms of its conditions and facilities, Marlborough House was one of the most shocking institutions in the State. No education, activities or recreation were provided for the children. The staff were recruited from the local labour exchange and had no training in child care. In 1955, the Department of Education's files indicate that the Superintendent of Marlborough House was then seventy-five years old, and that they proposed allowing him to continue in the position.[22] During the 1960s, there were numerous reports of serious physical abuse of the children by some members of staff.[23]

The building in Dublin's Glasnevin had been condemned as dangerous as far back as 1957 by the Board of Works. It wrote to the Department of Education urgently recommending its replacement with a new building, warning about "a grave risk of loss of life" were any part of the building to collapse.

Nonetheless, up to fifty children at any one time continued to be detained there for the following fifteen years.

The indefensible meanness of the Department of Education was illustrated when the Superintendent of Marlborough House recruited two artists to teach painting and drawing to the boys for a few hours each week. When he asked for the artists to be reimbursed for materials and paid for their work, the Department refused.

However, when it came to providing religious services and instruction for the boys, the Department showed no such parsimony. More correspondence in the files relates to this provision than to any other aspect of this disgraceful institution. The Department decided in 1960 that the practice of marching the boys out to the local church for Sunday Mass was "an unedifying public spectacle" which had been the subject of some public complaint. According to the Department, it also provided the boys with an opportunity to escape, "involving a chase through the streets". It was decided to provide the sum of £55 for materials to allow Mass to be said on the premises, and an allowance of £100 a year was paid by the State to the local parish priest for the purposes.[24] Outside of bed and board, this was literally the only provision of any kind made for the boys under detention.

On this and other matters, the Archbishop of Dublin John Charles McQuaid had taken an interest in Marlborough House. He was not happy that it should be left in the hands of the State. He had proposed as early as 1946 that it be handed over to a religious order, which had been agreed to by the Government during the 1950s. However, the Archbishop was unable to convince a religious order to run a children's remand home until the early 1960s.[25] The De la Salle Brothers, who had agreed to undertake the work, had to wait a further ten years before taking over the new remand centre. In a letter to the Taoiseach in 1966, the Archbishop showed his impatience:

> ... if I stress that I initiated this project at least nineteen years ago with the Department of Justice, you will realise my desire to save so many lives that could be saved. When I see such vast sums being expended on the roads of Dublin and the

> neighbouring counties, I may be pardoned in wishing
> that something could have been spent on
> straightening the crooked souls of very many youths
> in the past two decades.[26]

Meanwhile, during the decades of discussion between Church and State as to the ultimate fate of Marlborough House, children continued to be detained there in conditions of great misery. No attempts were made at improvements. It was a classic case of the State waiting to see what the Church would do and clearly unwilling to do anything itself.

Of all the Ministers for Education who held office during those years (see Appendix 2), only three appear from the Department's files to have taken a serious interest in the industrial schools — Thomas Derrig, Richard Mulcahy and Donough O'Malley. The others are barely even mentioned in the files.

The general neglect by the State of child care can be seen with great clarity in the case history of one individual boy. His story was brought to the attention of Minister for Education Donough O'Malley in 1967. This boy — we will call him Brendan — first came into contact with the system when he was nine years old. At eleven, he was sent to Letterfrack, where he served three years. Shortly after his release at the age of fourteen he appeared in court for larceny and what were referred to as "homosexual activities". At fifteen, he was sent to Daingean Reformatory for stealing. He ran away a number of times, and was eventually re-captured and sent to St Patrick's Borstal. Just turned sixteen, he wrecked his cell in St Patrick's and was dispatched to what was then referred to as the Dundrum Criminal Lunatic Asylum. This is where he was in 1967. The irony was that when Brendan was fourteen, he was seen by a psychiatrist who gave his opinion that "this boy would be seriously mentally ill in his early twenties unless he was provided with full psychiatric treatment".[27] Needless to say, Brendan never received any treatment: his ultimate fate is not recorded in the files.

He was just one victim of a State which so callously locked up children without making the least attempt to provide them with the help many of them so desperately needed.

Claire, St Anne's, Booterstown, Dublin (Sisters of Mercy), 1950–1966

"This may sound funny, but I always thought there was only one sex. I know we had the priest, but no one ever said, this is a man and that's a woman. I don't know when or how I realised that there were men and there were women. But then I used to say to myself, "Are the nuns a man or a woman?" I used to think if they're supreme, they must be something different. I know it's daft, but for years as a child that's how I used to think. "

Claire was one of six children. They had the same mother, but different fathers. The five older ones were put into industrial schools — three girls into St Anne's in Booterstown, the eldest boy into Artane, and a younger boy into St Kyran's Industrial School in Rathdrum. Their mother kept the youngest girl with her. Claire herself was put into St Anne's when she was nine months old. She remained until she was sixteen.

"In St Anne's, your name didn't mean anything. The nuns always called us by our numbers: I was forty-seven, my older sister Madeleine was twenty-seven and my younger sister was eighty-nine.

Our mother always said to us, 'You were never taken off me. I gave you up to make life better for you.' But now I'm not so sure. When I sent away for the documents, they said that we were taken from her because of the way we were being treated. The courts had her down as being destitute. I don't know really.

In one way it was great to have my sisters in the same place with me. But in another way, it was worse. I remember when it was their turn to be punished, beaten, it was terribly frightening. You couldn't do anything. I wouldn't cry out loud. Even now I don't cry out loud. The tears would just come down my face, and I'd just feel sad inside. It was bad enough when you were getting it yourself, but somehow it was worse seeing your own sisters being beaten.

My earliest memory — I would have been two or three — is that I was called one of the bold girls because I wet the bed. I was brought down to the laundry, put up on a big wooden table with a big galvanised bath on the table and a washboard beside it. And I was made wash my own sheets. I remember thinking, 'I'm going to fall into this' — I was so small.

Wetting the bed was a terrible fear. It went on for years, until I was at least twelve or thirteen. They'd wake us up in the middle of the night and put us into baths of freezing cold water. We'd be left there for ages, two to a bath, shivering in the dark. I'll never ever forget that, it left a terrible fear in me. I used try and use the heat of my body to dry the bed — I'd lie directly on the wet patch. But it never did any good.

I was very religious, very holy as a small child. I used to pray all night that I wouldn't wet the bed because I knew the whole routine, the beatings, would start again in the morning.

Oh God, you'd be hit for everything. We were hit with legs of chairs, that was the main thing. But they'd use blackboard pointers as well, really anything that came to hand. We used to call it 'getting flogged'. They flogged everyone. They'd say you were telling lies. But you weren't, but you couldn't say that. If a nun said you were a liar, then you were a liar.

There was this one nun who didn't like me. She beat me many times, and she would use her full force. My sister said that you could see pleasure in her face when she was beating you. I never saw that, but then I never looked her in the face. We all had marks from the beatings we got — it was just normal, everyone had marks, everyone got hit.

When you look back on some of the things we did, they were so trivial. The nuns wanted us to be so perfect, nothing out of place. I think that they were training us to be like themselves, to be little nuns. But we lived with a terror of doing wrong all the time.

One of my terrible, terrible fears — it still affects me now even as I talk about it — is the chair. It was in the dressing room, and I'd have been quite small. We would stand in a line, and one of the bigger girls in charge would call out someone's number. And there would be this chair. It was one of the wooden, upright convent chairs with the round wooden bars on the back.

Some of the older girls would make you sit back to front in that chair, and they would swing the chair around and then just let you go. And you just banged off anywhere. The floor and the hand-basins were hard marble, and it was terribly painful. There were nuns around when this was going on, they'd be in the room. But no one ever stopped it happening.

My mother used to come and visit us, but I never told her what was going on. I was afraid. My sister told her once about being beaten for wetting the bed and hiding the sheets. She'd been given an awful flogging for it.

So my mother challenged one of the nuns over that. But the only thing that happened was later that day, my sister got a bar of soap — the kind you scrub the floor with — she got that put down her mouth, and she had to keep her mouth closed over it. So the message was clear. You don't tell. And I never told. I never, ever told.

My mother came out on the third Sunday of the month which was visiting Sunday. She worked in laundries, usually in hospitals. She used to tell us that times were very difficult, she'd have to walk all the way out to Booterstown from Inchicore where she lived.

Maybe she didn't, maybe she was lying, but this used to upset me so much that I used to clean out the nuns' kitchen every week and get sixpence for it. An old woman who worked for the nuns used to do it, but sometimes she'd pay one of the girls to do it for her. I'd save up the sixpences and give the money my mother so she wouldn't have to walk out, she could get the bus.

Our mother used to take us out for a few weeks during the summer. It was like holidays, I suppose. Your belongings would be left up on the stage in a brown paper bag. If your number was on a bag on the stage, that meant you were getting out. I had this huge wish — I really really wanted a case. It would make me a bit special, to have a case instead of the brown paper bag.

So this is where my father comes into the story. I'd told you that my mother had six of us, all different fathers. Well, I'm the only one who knows who my father is. This man used to come out to the orphanage to visit, and at the time I thought he was an uncle.

One day he said to me, 'I have something to tell you. It's a secret. You could ask your mother yourself, if you want to, but I'm your father'. He left me an address, and told me if I ever needed anything, to write and ask him.

So a little while later, I wrote to him, saying please could I have a case and a swim suit. Well, he came out and he brought a lovely case, huge, and it was packed with sweets and chocolate and lemonade. My eyes lit up when I saw that case. And when I opened it up and I saw all the sweets, it was like finding a treasure chest.

But being polite, you wouldn't take anything out while he was there, you know. So he said goodbye and went off. I was just walking into the dormitory, carrying the case, when one of the nuns came up and grabbed it off me.

'Give me that here,' she shouted. 'Who does he think you are? Does he think we don't feed you here?" I didn't dare answer back. I got the case back a few days later, but all the sweets were gone. It was completely empty. Nothing was said, no explanation. I suppose the nuns ate them all.

The other thing we never got were the dresses that our aunt left in for me and my sisters. Lovely dresses, apparently, but we never saw them. Didn't even know about them. I only found out about that recently.

But in all that time, there was one good thing that happened. Every year, we used to have a day out at the seaside in Rush in Co Dublin. Taxi-men from the local area organised it, and they'd drive us out in their taxis.

When we got to Rush, there were sandwiches laid out and lemonade and games and races, and you would get a little gift. It was so exciting, it really was wonderful. As soon as it was over, we'd be counting the days until next year and Rush again.

Otherwise, the only time we really got out was for our walk on Sundays. We'd walk maybe as far as Blackrock, two by two, in a long line, holding hands. We never had parties or anything — I never even knew when my birthday was.

But there was one time when a nun came in and said to me 'Forty-seven, today you're nine'. All the girls were laughing at me saying, 'you can't be nine, you're too small to be nine. You must be only seven.' That was the only one I remember. And it was just like an ordinary day. You did all your charges as usual — there was never anything special.

The charges were our duties. We did laundry every day. Monday there was washing, that was a very heavy day. Tuesday there was more washing. Wednesday was ironing. Thursday you'd finish the ironing. You'd have cleaning jobs as well, washing floors and that. At weekends you'd work harder — all the floors and all the wood had to be polished, for instance.

And we'd have to mind the babies as well. There was one incident where I remember one of the nuns slapping a little baby girl on the bare bottom with her open palm. And she slapped and slapped that child, on and on. I was wondering why is she doing this. The baby was only about nine months old.

It was my job to look after this baby, and I was standing in the yard holding her one time when her mammy came to visit. I remember feeling, 'I'd love to tell her about the beatings', but I couldn't say it. And that woman was playing with her little baby as if there was nothing wrong, as if the child was having a great time here. And I couldn't tell. Too much fear.

I remember the yard was always very quiet. I mean, my two kids would make more noise than that whole school. The windows on the back of the convent could see out into the yard, and you'd always have the fear they could see you. We all mainly sat in groups, talking. I'm not saying that we were perfect either. I remember some of the girls, the daring ones, would go off and rob orchards. They'd get badly punished for that.

Fruit, apples and that, would be a big treat. We'd never get them normally. The problem wasn't that we got bad food, it was just there just wasn't enough of it.

The teachers — that's what we used call the lay staff, they never actually taught us — they had their own dining room, and they had different food. They had lovely things. The scraps from their table were thrown in the pigs' bin. After the meal, we used to make a dive on that bin to see what we could get. There was muck and potato skins and slop and everything thrown there, but we used to eat it anyway, we'd be that hungry.

You'd be thirsty as well. We'd get a drink of half milk, half water with our dinner. But I clearly remember drinking water out of the toilet, I'd be so thirsty. What I used to do was flush the toilet and put my hand in, and when the water flowed out, I'd drink that.

And school, as far as education was concerned, I think we all learned through fear. I mean they were vicious — anything you didn't know, you got hit. So I never really learned much. I never had the chance to go to secondary school, for instance. I've only educated myself since. I've always had this terrible fear that if anybody ever asked me to do anything, I was going to do it wrong.

For a while, I had it fixed in my mind growing up that I was going to be a nun. They told me that I could go to Perth in Australia to be a novice. I was so holy as a child I used to cry at the Stations of the Cross. I used to be in agony, I really thought I was there with Our Lord in his suffering. It seems daft now, but it was the same with the Bible. I used to be in those stories, it was like watching a film. So being a nun was all I thought I was fit for.

I'm not at all religious now. Since this all began coming out, about what the nuns did in the orphanages, I don't really want to practice religion anymore. I still have my faith, I'm not a non-believer or anything. I just don't want to have anything to do with them anymore.

I met one of the Booterstown nuns again years later, when I was in hospital, in Jervis St, which was run by the

Mercy order. She heard I was in, and came to see me. She said she had something important to tell me.

'I came up here,' she said, 'because I want to apologise to you, but not only to you, to the many girls that were in school with you, for all the hurt you were caused and the way you were brought up.' She said that she had complained at the time, but that it wasn't liked and that she was sent away to another orphanage.

She was an old nun at this stage, and she's died since. She hadn't been the worst of them, but I was so taken aback, I couldn't believe it. I mean, a nun, who all my life I would have had to apologise to — even if I was right, and she was wrong — and here she was apologising to me. It didn't really mean anything to me. I was just so surprised, I thought I was hearing things.

You see, the whole thing hasn't just affected me. There's my own children, and it's going down to the next generation. My own child went out of control, I couldn't talk to her. I had to put her into care, and it broke my heart.

She's in a lovely place — nothing like the way I was reared. But still, I mean, people say to me, how could you do it? They don't understand the reason I put her there was because she'd have someone who would be able to control her and look after her. Because I can't. I mean, the way I was brought up has affected me so badly, I just fall to pieces on everything. I blame myself for everything. The way we're chatting here, I might come across to you as somebody normal, but I know myself how I feel inside.

I'm sure there are lots of women like myself who have just suppressed it. I used to cry in bed every time I thought about my childhood. I managed to tell my own children, but I know that there are lots who haven't been able to tell their own families. They still feel that they'll be looked down upon. Because we were all made to feel so ashamed. We were put into orphanages for being poor, it was like discrimination. You feel ashamed of your upbringing, and you feel ashamed that you don't have a good education.

And there's a particular look. I notice it especially whenever a group of us gather together. It's a kind of daunted look, of something wanting. It's hard to describe, and I think only someone who's been in an orphanage could pick it out. Sometimes I'm walking through town, and I see it and wonder were they in school with me. But the thing is, I probably have that same look too, and I just never realised it until now."

With her children now almost grown, Claire decided recently to try to find a job. She felt that all she would get was a cleaning job. But her local FAS office organised a position for her as a receptionist. Claire was amazed to discover that she had no problems doing the work. It has been her first step in rebuilding a self-confidence that she was never given the chance to develop.

Suffer the Little Children

Angela's Story, St Joseph's Industrial School, Cavan (Poor Clares), 1949–1963

"It's a terrible thing to have as your first memory, being dragged away screaming from your mother."

Born in 1947, Angela was the daughter of a single mother. They lived together just outside Cavan Town until Angela was almost two-and-a-half.

"My mother wanted to keep me, but the courts wouldn't let her. Apparently there had been a number of complaints about her in the town — I suppose they said that she shouldn't be allowed to keep a baby since she wasn't married.

I can remember so clearly this nun dragging me away from her. I was trying to hold on, but this terrifying person in long black clothing was pulling me away from her. When she was gone, it seemed to me like I sobbed for a year.

Everyone told my mother that it would be for my own good to be in the convent, that the nuns would look after me well and give me an education. But I never got an education. I was barely even noticed in the classroom — I was a very timid child, and I was always getting whacked on the back of my hands. When I wasn't in school, I was put scrubbing floors and stairs all day. I still have the scars on my knees from kneeling and scrubbing so much.

My mother came to visit me every third Sunday, which was visiting day. She never stopped caring about me. But the nuns treated her so badly, they just left her out in the cold courtyard. That's where we'd have to meet, even in bad weather.

All the better-off people, coming to adopt children for example, they'd be brought into the parlour. But not my mother. And the worst of it was that she was such a gentle person, she wouldn't complain or anything.

On the day of your sixteenth birthday [the day the State grant ran out], you were out the door so fast, with only your little battered case. I was sent off to skivvy for some relations

354

of the nuns. I never got the chance to do anything else except cleaning all my life.

That's my big gripe, that they never gave me the chance for any education. I've tried to better myself. When my own son was going through school, I went and did a course in maths so that I might be able to help him.

But the most difficult thing is that when you've been put down so much as a child, you just don't have any confidence. It really does hold you back. I've raised my son, and he's doing very well, has a good job, and now I've decided, it's my turn. I'm determined to get out there now, and make something of myself. Those nuns have kept me down for too long. I'm not going to let them do it any more."

Fourteen

The First Cracks

It was not until the 1960s in Ireland that there was any significant debate on the nature of care provided to children in need. This was almost half a century after Britain had engaged in such an examination and concluded that institutional care was harmful to children.

It is all the more remarkable that this debate did not occur in Ireland, particularly in the context of the enormous emphasis that this country had placed on the primary role of the family within society. During the late 1950s and into the 1960s, several organisations began to realise the considerable divergence between official thinking on the primacy of the family on the one hand, and on the other, the widespread use of industrial schools to deprive thousands of children of their families.

There had been a handful of voices pointing to this significant contradiction. The Joint Committee of Women's Societies and Social Workers kept up a barrage of correspondence on the matter with the Ministers for Health and Education throughout the 1950s and 1960s. This was an umbrella group representing seventeen different organisations, including the Irish Countrywomen's Association and the Mothers' Union. They argued that "Family life is the basis of our society and therefore no normal healthy child should be brought up in an institution if a suitable foster home can be found. Financial and other assistance should be made available to prevent the unnecessary removal of children from the care of their parents or guardians."[1]

The Department of Education, whose defence of the schools if anything intensified during this period, was contemptuously dismissive of this view. Department officials described the Joint

Committee as being prejudiced against industrial schools, saying that they obviously had no sympathy for "the excellent work being done in Irish orphanages and industrial schools for the homeless or deprived child". They concluded by saying that "it is difficult to see what contribution they [the Joint Committee] can make to the problem beyond airing the prejudices against the existing system."[2]

The Commission on Youth Unemployment, whose chairman was the Archbishop of Dublin John Charles McQuaid, also criticised the placement of large numbers of children in institutions. During the 1950s, this body advocated fostering as an alternative, combined with the breaking up of larger institutions into smaller, family-type units.[3] This view was publicly supported at the time by CK Murphy, a prominent member of the Society of St Vincent de Paul.[4]

However, during the 1950s, any criticism was invariably tempered with an enthusiastic defence of the religious orders running industrial schools. A representative flavour of this can be seen in the comments of the Rev Cecil Barrett, a leading advocate of adoption based on Catholic principles. In 1955, he argued that:

> … if I appear to feel very strongly against perm-anent institutional care for children whose parents are alive, it is because I consider the removal of children from parental custody to be a very serious matter and something that must be accepted only as a last resort. To remove any danger of being misunderstood may I emphasise that my criticism is aimed solely at the system and the method of dealing with industrial school cases. I can pay a tribute to the concern and consideration of the officials who have to administer the system, and I readily admit that no words of mine would be adequate to extol the meritorious work of the Sisters and Brothers who manage the schools.[5]

The first official criticism of the industrial schools system came in 1962 with the publication of the OECD (Organisation for Economic Co-operation and Development) report *Investment in Education.* This was critical of the operation of the schools, particularly in regard to the educational state of the children and the training provided within the institutions.[6]

In the same year, a most revealing questionnaire was completed by the Department of Education on the subject of the treatment of children in detention. It was only filled in after repeated requests, lasting over a period of two years, from the Department of Justice. The information was to be compiled into a European report, comparing the treatment of detained children in a number of countries. The questions were clearly based on assumptions of a system very far removed from the reality that existed in Ireland. For example, one question asked "what personnel is available to detained juveniles, e.g. physicians, psychiatrist, psychologists, teachers, monitors, social workers, probation officers, etc?" The response by the Department was "Religious Orders, nothing more". The answer to the question "Under what condition are punishments applied to minors, nature of these institutions and their rehabilitation?", the response was simply that "Discipline is maintained mainly by withdrawal of privileges but secondly by light corporal punishment." Armed with these somewhat terse answers, the Inspector of Industrial and Reformatory Schools in Ireland jetted off to Rome in 1962 to attend an international conference on juvenile detention. While the files contain much about the expense associated with this trip, there is little reference to what, if anything, was learnt from it.[7]

During 1962, the Department of Education had been involved in a more general Inter-Departmental Committee on Crime Prevention and Treatment of Offenders. This had been established in September under the chairmanship of Peter Berry, Secretary of the Department of Justice. As part of its remit, it examined the treatment of young offenders, and consequently it turned its attention to the industrial and reformatory schools.[8]

Despite meeting on several occasions, this Committee never published a report, and most of its recommendations on the schools were never acted on. Some of these were identical to those of the Kennedy Report, seven years later. However, the deliberations of the Inter-Departmental Committee were strangely never referred to by the Kennedy Report.

Among the Inter-Departmental Committee recommendations in 1962 were the following:

- The term industrial school should be abolished;
- Larger State grants should be made to industrial schools;
- A visiting committee should be appointed for every industrial school, and in appropriate cases after-care committees should be set up as well;
- The industrial schools should be inspected more frequently than is at present (the inspector had admitted that there were some schools that he had never even visited, due to pressure of work);
- To ensure that adequate, proper bedding, clothing, footwear etc. is issued to the inmates of industrial schools, the scale of issue — showing minimum standards — should be prescribed by regulations;
- Adequate financial provision should be made for carrying out of essential maintenance and repair work and for the supply of proper recreational, ablutionary etc. facilities at industrial schools;
- A matron or nurse should be appointed to the staffs of all industrial schools for boys and similar institutions;
- Generally speaking, boys from urban centres should not be sent to serve lengthy sentences in an industrial school in a rural environment.

The Inter-Departmental Committee also interviewed the Chaplain of Artane Industrial School, Fr Moore. He was scathing in his comments on the operation of the school. He told the Committee that he had been assigned to Artane by Dr McQuaid, Archbishop of Dublin, who he said was dissatisfied with the management of the school. The Archbishop had asked Fr Moore to submit a report to him on the matter, which he had duly done.

Fr Moore made a number of criticisms of Artane:

> The boys are badly clothed. They have no overcoats (unless they can pay for them out of their pocket

money), only raincapes. They have no vests and no change of footwear or socks; sometimes a boy's shoes are too small and give him sore feet. They have no handkerchiefs. There is no such thing as a boy having his own shirt or pyjamas — after washing, articles of clothing are distributed at random; Bed clothes are inadequate. The boys are undernourished. The medical facilities are appalling. There is no resident nurse or matron. The Brother who is in charge of the infirmary has no experience of nursing — he used to be employed on the farm. The surgical room is unsuitable for the purpose and the room smells.[9]

Fr Moore's comments were not only a condemnation of the Artane school, but they also reflected directly on the Department of Education, whose responsibility it was to ensure the welfare of the children placed there. The Department's officials emphatically rejected his criticisms of Artane. Three of them carried out a special inspection of the school in December 1962, and concluded that the boys were "well-fed, warmly clothed, comfortably bedded and treated with kindness by the Christian Brothers in an atmosphere conducive to their spiritual and physical development". They mentioned that complaints about the industrial schools in general, while not infrequent, were generally untrue. They concluded that "No serious faults could be found in Artane and the impression of the big happy family atmosphere which pervaded the entire institution was inescapable."[10]

Meanwhile, in the real world, the pressure on the industrial schools was intensifying. The numbers of children being committed by the courts was continuing to decline, placing increasing financial strain on the institutions. Public criticism was also becoming more vocal, and more pointed. Solicitor James O'Connor, writing in the Jesuit journal *Studies* in 1963, argued that "The system of institutional treatment in Ireland has serious defects and the courts, left with no alternative, impose it with reluctance". The strict segregation between boys and girls was noted, leading in his view to a "degree of sexual maladjustment in the inmates". Discipline in the schools, he said, was "rigid and severe, approaching at times pure regimentation, with the result that the inmates are denied the opportunity of developing friendly and spontaneous characters; their impulses become suffocated, and when they are suddenly liberated their reactions are often violent and irresponsible."[11]

In 1965, the fledgling RTE television became interested in the schools. Current affairs reporter Brian Cleeve wrote to a number of industrial schools asking permission to be allowed film in them. The correspondence files of John Charles McQuaid show that the Archbishop did not think that this was a good idea. Most of the schools refused permission to film inside their walls, and Dr McQuaid wrote that he was particularly glad that the Christian Brothers in Artane had forbidden such access. It should be remembered that Dr McQuaid, of course, was in possession of Fr Moore's report on the poor conditions for the boys in that particular institution.[12]

Another addition to the call for reform was a report entitled *Some of Our Children*, produced in 1966 by the London Branch of a group called Tuairim (meaning 'opinion' in Irish). It described itself as an association of people interested in ideas and not afraid to discuss them. They published eighteen pamphlets between the 1950s and early 1970s on a host of diverse topics. It is interesting that it was their London branch who took on the hot potato of the industrial schools, although at the time they had several branches all over Ireland.

Their report on the residential care of children argued for the need to replace the 1908 Children Act with modern legislation, and for all child care services to be co-ordinated by the Department of Health. Tuairim also examined private voluntary homes for children, noting that there were twenty-three homes that they were aware of, thirteen of them managed by religious orders catering for nearly 1,000 children. Tuairim remarked that the informal system by which children were admitted to these homes had the advantage of bypassing the courts system, but that the danger existed that "illegitimate children may be dumped and conveniently forgotten" in these homes.[13]

The Tuairim report contained a section dealing with punishment in industrial schools. It said that its committee had received "accounts from a number of ex-pupils of boys' schools alleging excessive corporal punishment in the past". They added that they had heard stories of recent punishments. These punishments they considered "either unsuitable or excessive". They went on to talk about the undesirability of administering corporal punishment to boys for what they called "sex offences". However, they reached no overall conclusion on the matter of punishment, remarking that in the absence of verification, the accounts of any excessive corporal punishment "must be treated as hypothetical".[14]

This level of caution is particularly interesting as a former inmate of the industrial school in Letterfrack was a member of the committee involved in drawing up the Tuairim report. This was Peter Tyrrell, who had attempted to write a book about his own childhood during the 1930s. He had stated that boys in Letterfrack were stripped and beaten naked for long periods. He also said that he himself had been raped by one of the Brothers. He had told a priest about this in confession, but the priest had said how dare he speak in this way about the Brothers, without whom he wouldn't have a roof over his head. Tyrrell had subsequently joined the British army and been taken prisoner during the Second World War. He had said that compared to Letterfrack, the German prisoner of war camp was like a tea party.

However, none of this was reflected in the final Tuairim report. Tyrrell felt that it had not properly exposed the horrors of the schools in the past, and he did not believe that the treatment of the children had improved in the 1960s. In despair, he committed suicide a year after the report's publication by setting himself alight on London's Hampstead Heath. It took the British police almost a year to identify his body. They traced the unburned corner of a postcard in his pocket to his friend Dr Owen Sheehy-Skeffington, himself a noted campaigner for reform in this area. Sheehy-Skeffington was able to confirm that he had indeed sent the postcard, and that the body was that of Peter Tyrrell.[15]

1966 also saw the publication of the Report of the Commission of Inquiry on Mental Illness. It recommended that "that the whole problem of industrial schools should be examined", and it regarded the "term industrial as applied to these schools as obsolete and objectionable".[16] In the same year a series of articles appeared in *The Irish Times*, written by Michael Viney, describing the often appalling conditions of some industrial schools. Viney, however, also commented on the poor funding for the schools, the difficult circumstances under which the religious orders had to conduct their work and the indifference of the State to their needs.[17] By this stage the drop in numbers of children in the schools had resulted in a most serious decrease in their income.

The theme of State indifference to the reformatory and industrial schools was repeated in an editorial in the *Carlow Nationalist* in 1965, following a meeting between George Colley, Minister for Education and his opposite number in Northern Ireland, William Fitzsimons. The editorial claimed that "the attitude of the Department of Education and the Department of Justice is stuck firmly in the nineteenth century and the extent of their neglect, indifference and inefficiency demand public exposure — which incidentally is near at hand. When it comes the current holders of these posts as well as those who occupied these Ministries in the past should be hounded out of public life."[18]

Paralleling these external commentaries on the operation of the schools, substantial changes were also occurring within the religious orders who managed them. The impact of Vatican II was to exert an enormous change on the role that the Catholic Church saw for itself in contemporary Ireland. Between 1964 and 1969, the religious orders had closed fourteen of their industrial schools, and some were attempting to break up their institutions into smaller, more child-centred units. It is clear that some at least had begun to take on board a portion of the criticisms being made of their approach to child care.

However, from the files in the Department of Education, it is evident that the primary concern of the religious orders at this time related to falling numbers of committals and their own declining income as a result. Their emphasis was on attempting to find ways in which more children could be detained in the schools, rather than proposing an alternative method of funding.[19]

It is at this stage that the Department's files indicate some slight shift in its own view of the long-term future of the schools. In 1964, the first doubts about the system begin to be voiced. An internal report stated that "thinking both here and abroad is against long-term detention in institutions which are situated in rural areas and are not equipped for psychiatric treatment, or the training of children from urban areas, and in general, with the exception of Artane, lack any kind of after-care organisation."[20]

Only a year previously, the Department had dismissed a proposal from the Irish Association of Civil Liberty, which had strongly advocated financially supporting the parents of children in order to maintain them at home rather than in an industrial school. The Association had written: "To remove a child from the care of its own parents solely for reasons of poverty appears to conflict with the spirit of the Constitution." The Department of Education had disdainfully described this as "a pipe dream, idealistic yet impractical".[21]

Even the Bishop of Cork and Ross, Dr Cornelius Lucey, joined in the general debate about the future of child care. In 1963, he pronounced "no matter how home-like an institution is, it is never really home for the child in it. I would prefer to see children left with careless parents even if they have to fend a little for themselves — though not, of course with really bad parents — to having them in even the best of institutions".[22]

The Kennedy Report

In 1966, Donough O'Malley was appointed as Minister for Education. He was to have probably the most important impact on education in Ireland since the foundation of the State. His implementation of free secondary education for all children had a fundamental and lasting effect on Irish society. It was also he who established the Kennedy Committee to investigate industrial and reformatory schools, a move which resulted in the effective dismantling of the system.

O'Malley had been concerned for some time about the schools. Possibly as a result of the considerable amount of adverse publicity surrounding the institutions at this time, he and Brian Lenihan, then Minister for Justice, had clearly discussed the issue during 1966. In a letter to O'Malley on the 24th August that year, Lenihan talked about the desirability of setting up visiting committees for the industrial schools, and recommended taking "a vigorous approach" to the religious managers of the schools.[23]

In early January 1967, O'Malley had a busy week dealing with the industrial schools. On the 5th of January, he sent a hand-written note to the Secretary of the Department saying that he wished to set up a three-person committee to report to him on the issue of the schools, and could the Secretary advise him. Also that same day, he received a letter from John Hurley (subsequently to be appointed to the Kennedy Committee) enclosing a report from a Fr Kenneth McCabe. This concerned the industrial and reformatory schools in general with a particular focus on St Conleth's in Daingean. It was a remarkably frank document about conditions pertaining in the schools. Later that evening, Brother MC Normoyle, Vicar General of the Christian Brothers, appeared on RTE television criticising the Government for inadequate funding of the industrial schools and saying that this was a factor in a number of recent closures.[24]

Taoiseach Jack Lynch sent around a note to O'Malley the following day wondering about Brother Normoyle's remarks on television. O'Malley wrote back saying that the managers of the schools had indeed repeatedly complained to the Department of Education about the low level of funding, adding that "there is of course something in this". He mentioned that one of the difficulties was that Daingean reformatory, which was "really suffering from very poor accommodation, understaffing and under-everything practically, is confused with the forty industrial schools of which the vast majority cater very well indeed for their children".[25]

Brother Normoyle's remarks on television were dismissed out of hand. O'Malley said that he didn't know exactly "what Br Normoyle was getting at and I have a shrewd idea that he wouldn't know either. It was probably his first appearance on television and his instinct was to fob off from the Order any blame that might be going on. On the whole, I would be inclined to let the matter go at that. He is not a man who normally opens his mouth much."[26]

This letter was also the first time that Donough O'Malley had formally communicated his intention to set up a committee to examine the schools. He was still, however, describing it as only an *ad hoc* group. He told the Taoiseach that "if it were to do nothing else, it might at least have the effect of allaying public unease".[27]

However, the report from Fr Ken McCabe that O'Malley had received on the same day as the Normoyle interview must have made for quite shocking reading at the time. Fr McCabe had joined the Jesuit order, and during his training he had spent a number of weeks observing conditions in Daingean during 1964. He resigned from the Jesuits in 1967, but remained a priest. He went to work with the homeless in the diocese of Westminster in England, where he still runs a number of residential centres for deprived children.

In his report, he described the system as "at best, punitive". Referring to the poor level of funding, he said "the result is as one would expect. The food is bad. Boys are disgracefully dressed." In Daingean, he said that "too much time, far too much, is spent in the school square; a large yard where the boys just hang around for hours at a time."

His report continued: "The system in all our reformatory and industrial schools is repressive. Given the facilities at the disposal of the schools, it seems unlikely that it could be otherwise. Boys are taken out of the natural (if defective) atmosphere of their homes and placed in an institution .... Perhaps the most obvious problem to begin with here is that of sex."

McCabe's report had a long section dealing with what can happen when adolescent boys are placed in the repressive atmosphere of these institutions, with no "positive sex instruction". He said that:

> ... there is no need to go into the detail of how sex can 'go wrong' at this stage and how habits can be acquired that will cause endless unhappiness in later life ... I also have definite evidence of serious incidents of homosexual practices in some schools. A

circumstance that doesn't help matters here is the very unsuitable situation of most industrial schools. Daingean is situated in a place where almost all outside contact is impossible. Letterfrack and Upton are even worse. It seems completely wrong to send a Dublin boy to an environment so different from his home environment.

On the matter of punishment of boys, Fr McCabe had some interesting points to make. Saying that the rules were being "widely and seriously abused", he added that severe punishment in Daingean was used frequently, "and in my opinion cannot in any circumstances be justified … [this] can do untold damage." He also mentioned that he had himself witnessed the shaving of boys' heads in Daingean as punishment, adding that "I also understand that it is done in other schools. The psychological effects need no comment."

In a very clear-sighted appraisal from a Catholic Church perspective of the effects of all this, he said that a boy "will associate all that is inhuman and harsh with the Church …. He may even come to 'hate' all they stand for."[28]

Armed with this information, Donough O'Malley rapidly pushed ahead with his plans to establish a committee of inquiry into the schools. He wrote to the Association of Resident Managers outlining his plans in broad terms, assuring them that the purpose of the committee was "not to find any fault with the conducting or management of the schools". Privately, O'Malley is quoted as having said that he wanted "the skin pulled off this pudding".[29]

In the middle of all this, T R Ó Raifeartaigh, the Secretary of the Department, paid a visit to the Daingean Reformatory. He returned with a glowing report which he submitted on the 27th February to Minister O'Malley. He extolled the virtues of the manager, Fr McGonagle. "Such is the spirit of dedication on the part of the staff, religious and lay, that one's principle feeling on leaving is that it is good to know that such people exist." He enthused about one particular recent reform, namely the introduction of regular visits to the reformatory by local members of the Irish Countrywomen's Association. "The ICA visitors have not only organised concerts for the boys, but have also held dances with them. The Reverend Manager and his staff consider that these dances, even though the woman partners in them are no longer in the teenager age group, have a very refining influence on the boys." There is unfortunately no record as to whether or not the boys had an opinion on this.

It is interesting to note in this regard that Donough O'Malley's original plan for the committee of inquiry into the schools did not include any officials from his own Department, or indeed any civil servants at all. He wanted John Hurley as the chair, who was described as "a cinema manager, has wide social interests". Fr Ken McCabe was also to be a member of the committee — he had been specifically recommended by Declan Costello TD, who had for many years taken a great interest in the issue of children with disabilities. The other members consisted of two representatives from Dublin Junior Chamber of Commerce, the Manager of Artane Industrial School, the Medical Director of John of God's Services for the Mentally Handicapped, and a nun who worked with the Limerick Social Service Centre.[30]

However, when discussed at Cabinet on the 5th September 1967, several changes were made. Most notable was the removal from the list of Fr Ken McCabe. No reasons were given. District Justice Eileen Kennedy of the Dublin Metropolitan Children's Court was to be asked to chair the committee, which was to include a nominee each from the Ministers for Education, Justice and Health. In this way, three civil servants were added to the Committee.[31]

Its terms of reference were very broadly defined: "To survey the Reformatory and Industrial Schools systems and to make a report and recommendations to the Minister for Education". This was subsequently extended to include all children in care.

The Kennedy Committee, as it was to become known, held its inaugural meeting on the 20th October 1967 at 3 p.m. It was preceded by a luncheon at the Gresham Hotel. There was a choice of two menus, but it being a Friday, both consisted of fish. Over the following three years, the members of the Kennedy Committee were to find out enough about the system of industrial and reformatory schools in Ireland to make them recommend its urgent abolition.

Geraldine's Story, Pembroke Alms House Industrial School, Tralee (Sisters of Mercy), 1961–1978

"At the school, we were known as the Nazareth children. The other girls from outside who lived with their families were warned not to have anything to do with us. We were like the plague, and we stood out a mile with our green Donegal tweed dresses. If one of the outside girls did something bold in class, the nun teaching us would pull one of the Nazareth children out and cane her across the back of the legs. She said this was what the outside girls would get if any of them misbehaved."

Geraldine was the youngest of eight children. Their parents were married, and lived in Co Cork. All the children were committed through the courts to industrial schools. The family was split apart, and spread across an amazing total of seven different schools. Most of them never even saw each other. The stated reason for their committal was that they were "found without any visible means of subsistence or guardianship". But Geraldine is still trying to find out exactly why so many of them were detained in this way when still babies. She was five months old when committed to the Tralee Industrial School (known as Nazareth House), run by the Sisters of Mercy.

"My first memory goes back to when I was about three or four years old. I was a very nervous child, and if there was any shouting or anyone being walloped I used to wet my knickers. When it happened this particular time, the nun put me in a cupboard under the stairs, where they kept the cleaning things.

It was dark in the cupboard, and I cried and cried, but I was left there all day. Eventually I fell asleep on the floor. I remember when they let me out I was dazzled by the light. I was stripped down to my vest and knickers and put across a cold table. Two big girls held me down, and this nun walloped me across my body with a black leather strap. She beat me black and blue, and I was put to bed hungry.

Suffer the Little Children

I was asleep in bed that night, when I woke up and saw a lady standing beside my bed. At first I was a bit afraid. She said she had a surprise for me under the blanket she was holding in her hand. She had brought me two marshmallow sweets. She gathered me up in her arms and carried me downstairs to where she had a lovely warm fire.

She was the night nurse and her name was Debbie. She was a wonderful woman. She would always take me down after that and give me a cuddle. Her love and hugs made me feel like a human being, she was like a mother to me. Without her, I'd never have survived the years ahead.

We used to say the rosary at six o'clock each evening, and it might often go on for over an hour. Sometimes I'd fall asleep, and be woken up with a slap on the face, and discover that I'd wet the floor with fright. Then I'd get walloped with the leather strap again.

There's a photograph of me as a little one, [see page 7 of photo section], and I think I have a black eye. It was taken in the play room, and it looks lovely. But we were only allowed into that room on special occasions. Normally, it was kept locked. But when visitors or the inspector came, we'd be dressed up and could play in there. They always seemed to know whenever anyone was coming.

In school, some of the nuns were nice. But in Senior Infants, the nun was so cross that I used to wet the floor again. She'd slap me across the face, and I'd fall to the ground. Another girl used to cry over this and hold my hand, and we became friends. She used to give me some of her lunch. But the nun who was our teacher saw us and grabbed me away by the arm. I was sent home to the nun in charge of the orphanage.

This nun punched me in the face, and my nose started to bleed. Then she told me to stand in the corner with my finger up to my lips, and not move from that spot.

A few day later, my little friend in school offered me some of her lunch again, but I said no. I was terrified of what they'd do to me. But then she brought in a special lunch just for me. When the head nun heard about this, she called me a beggar and beat me again.

That nun came into the classroom and in front of everybody she said that none of her girls were poor and that we did not need handouts. We had apples to throw on the floor, she said. But from then on, we Nazareth children were all sent to school with brown bread, milk and an apple for our lunch.

When I was about seven, my feet got very wet one day coming into school. It was a short walk from the orphanage, and I had holes in my shoes. I was leaving puddles all over the floor and the teacher asked me could she get in touch with my mum to get me nice and dry. I was speechless, and another girl hopped up and said, 'She's a Nazareth child, Miss.' The teacher, a lovely, kind woman called Miss Nolan, didn't understand the system at all, and she sent me back over to the nun again.

The nun called me a notice box and gave me a beating. I was told to get a bucket of water and scrub floor of the corridors — they were all tiles and they went on for ever.

Miss Nolan heard what had happened to me and she was so sorry. She gave me lots of hugs, and brought me in lovely drawing books and markers. I could see the sadness for me in her eyes. Two days after I made my Communion, she was killed by a drunk driver. I cried for days, and it was the start of a deep depression for me.

Christmas was the happiest time for me. The nun in charge was like a different person, helping us with the decorations and the preparations. Santa would come, and one of the nuns would call each child's name, and we'd have to go up and give him a big hug. Some of the little children were terrified of him, though, and I remember the nuns dragging them, screaming and kicking, up to Santa.

The head nun in the orphanage really did do her best to get us all presents, and make it a happy time. The other nuns would come down from the convent and admire what we'd got, and you could see that our nun would be so delighted with their praise.

She was such a strange person, this nun. She had her favourites, and she was so nice to them. I was desperate to try and please her. It sounds funny, but I really loved her. I picked daisies for her once and left them on the desk beside her. But she gave me a wallop on the face and told me to take that rubbish away. I cried and cried over this. I couldn't understand why she hated me so much.

She always told us we were dirt, that we came from dirt, and that none of us would ever amount to anything. She used to say we'd end up as fishmongers selling fish by the side of the street. I think looking back that maybe she was not a very stable person, but the problem was that we were at her mercy. And by God she showed me no mercy.

The most horrific experience I had was having to watch what happened to other girls. I used to feel physically sick watching them get punished. It disturbed me so much that I stopped eating and couldn't sleep. They tried to force feed me. I remember cutting my wrists at that time as well. The doctor came and gave me sedatives. They were careful not to leave us alone with the doctor in case we might tell him about the beatings.

All through this I used to beg Debbie, my friend who was the night nurse, to take me away. I called her 'Mammy' and we'd both cry when I'd show her the marks on my body from the beatings. I couldn't understand why she wouldn't take me home with her if she loved me. I didn't know that I had been put in there by the court and wasn't allowed to leave. Debbie would tell me that I'd be alright soon, I'd be a big girl and would have a lovely home of my own.

I ran away a couple of times from when I was about thirteen. The Guards always caught me and brought me back. But things were beginning to change in the orphanage at this stage. It was the mid-1970s, and the nun was trying to make things a bit better by organising outings and so forth. But it was too late for me. The abuse I had already suffered marked me for my whole life."

Geraldine is now married with three children and lives in Co Cork. She has suffered all her life with severe bouts of depression, and has become almost suicidal at times. But her husband always stood by her, and she has now found someone she describes as a wonderful counsellor, and is at last, she feels, well on the road to recovery.

"I never got an apology from that nun. I feel that if I had, I might have been saved all those years of depression. Because not all the nuns were like her — we did have some nice ones. And I met a beautiful nun in the Mercy order in later years, and she restored my faith in God. She was able to take away some of the pain of my childhood, but it's not until now, when all of this has finally come out, that I'm finally beginning to feel totally healed."

Marie's Story, St Joseph's Industrial School, Clifden (Sisters of Mercy), 1958–1973

"I remember hearing about this man who used to go round collecting kids and bringing them to Clifden. I never heard his name. I think maybe he had brought me there. When word came to us that he had died, we were all cheering and dancing. I think he was responsible for putting a lot of children into the place."

Marie went into St Joseph's Clifden when still only a baby. She is still not clear as to why she was separated from her family. She knows that her father died, but she has had no contact with her mother. What little information she has managed to discover comes from her half-brothers, who had themselves grown up in industrial schools.

"It's hard when you don't know much about yourself. My kids ask me about where I came from and about their grandparents, and I don't really know what to tell them. I know that my mother never wanted me, won't even talk to me. But how do I tell that to my own children?

What sticks out in my mind about Clifden is how the nuns always told us we were no good. From when I was about four or five, all I heard every day was 'You'll never be any good, your mother never wanted you, you'll end up in the gutter like her, no one will ever want you'. It's hard to forget that — it stays with you, and I suppose I do really have a low opinion of myself.

I ended up at about thirteen years old working for the nuns in the convent kitchen. I'd love to have gone on to secondary school, but they never gave me the chance. They told me they didn't have the money. I never learnt to read and write properly. I can read now, but I'm still not great at writing.

One of our jobs from the age of about nine or ten was to look after the babies. Each of us was given a toddler to mind. If they did anything wrong, we'd get punished for it. When I was small, the girl who looked after me was very nice. But I remember a gang of older girls throwing me on the floor once and urinating on me.

Another job I had to do was go over every Saturday and clean the Reverend Mother's room. I can still see her to this day, standing over me while I was on my knees scrubbing and polishing. It all had to be so clean that she could see herself in it.

You'd get beaten a fair bit for all sorts of things. Bed wetters had a very bad time. The nuns used to pull my hair a lot as punishment. There was one class in school where I always got the blame, no matter whose fault it was. It's a wonder I had any hair left by the end of it.

They had long canes and they'd whack you with them, and they usually left a mark. I remember doing Irish dancing, and if any of us got a step wrong, we'd get a lash of the cane across our legs.

The food was pretty bad — you could have stuck wallpaper on with the porridge. Even to this day, I can't eat porridge. The soup we'd get was covered in grease. I remember telling one of the nuns that I couldn't eat it, and she said, 'You'd better eat it because you're not getting anything else'. And then she tasted it herself, and she said, 'No, they can't eat that'. So she was good in that respect. The food got a bit better closer to when I was due to leave.

There was a lovely nun in the convent kitchen, Sr Elizabeth. She used to leave food out for me when she wasn't supposed to. There's not many of them that were nice, but she was brilliant.

Around 1969 a new nun took over, and things did improve. She gave us all our proper dates of birth. Up till then many of us didn't know our birthdays. We never had parties or presents or anything anyway, not even at Christmas or Easter. This nun also used to give us a bit of pocket money — that was when I had my first ice-cream. I was about twelve.

Most of us used to be fostered out to families for the summer months. When I was about ten or eleven, I was sent out to this family that had a farm, and they expected me to work the farm. But I hadn't a clue what to do, so they sent me back the next day. I was punished for that by the nuns. They said that I must have done something wrong.

Sometimes when you'd be sent out in the summer, it would be a great holiday. I met a wonderful family this way, and they wanted to adopt me for good. But it wasn't allowed. Whenever you got too attached to one foster family, the nuns would shift you and send to somewhere else. I never understood why that was.

There was one time I was sent to a family, and the parish priest was supposed to keep an eye on me. Myself and a girl from the family used to call in to visit him.

He used to sit me on his knee, and he'd be kissing and hugging me, and touching me down in my underpants. The other girl was much younger than me, and he never touched her, maybe because she had her parents nearby.

I didn't really know what was happening — at first I thought it was great because no one had ever hugged me before. But then I just decided I didn't want to go there any more. After that, if I said hello to that priest on the street he used to ignore me.

There was no one I could tell or ask about it — if you told the nuns something like that, they'd have locked you up in a mental home or a laundry. Because they'd never have taken my word over a priest's.

The nuns wouldn't have done anything anyway. There was a girl in St Joseph's with me, and her father came down to visit her one Sunday. He was obviously drunk, and he wanted to take her out for the day. Usually children couldn't go out like that, but this man was allowed to take his daughter out.

I'll never forget when she came back later that day. She was cut all over, particularly her legs. Her father had taken her up a big hill and tried to have sex with her and she ran for her life. But she couldn't tell the nuns about it, because they wouldn't have believed her.

But another time, one of the men who worked on the convent farm was actually caught in a shed with one of the girls. She was only about twelve. The nuns gave the man the sack, but they blamed the girl. They said that she had encouraged him.

But sure none of us had a clue about sex — there was no sex education of any kind in the place. Quite a few of the girls ended up pregnant shortly after they left, and were back working for the nuns, with their babies taken away and put into schools. It was sad to see history repeating itself like that."

When Marie left Clifden at sixteen, she worked in various cleaning and domestic service jobs. She is now married and living in the West of Ireland with her husband and four children. She feels that if she had the courage, she would dearly love to confront the priest who sexually abused her as a child.

"I put the whole thing about the abuse to the back of my mind for years. It was only when I had my own daughter that it really came back at me. I became very upset, I was even suicidal. I rang the Rape Crisis Centre, and that was the first time I had ever told anyone about the abuse.

It's something that I say now to my own children all the time, never to have secrets. That's how it starts, people saying 'This is our little secret, don't tell anyone else'. At least today people are more inclined to believe children. With us, they looked down on us so much that no one really cared what happened to you. So there really was no point in telling anyone."

Fifteen

A Terrible Legacy: 1970 to the Present

When the Kennedy Report was published in 1970, it was without doubt one of the most damning indictments of the operation of any State system ever produced in this country.

The report was an impressive piece of work. At 136 pages long, the committee visited all of the industrial and reformatory schools in the State, some of them on a number of occasions. It dealt with a total of fifty-six oral and written submissions, wrote seeking information from forty-five organisations, and consulted 113 publications during the three years of its deliberations. It met a total of sixty-nine times, on average once every two weeks during its existence.

Its report described the industrial school system as being "far from satisfactory ... haphazard and amateurish". It stated damningly that "there is, in general, a lack of awareness of the needs of the child in care". It lamented the lack of emphasis on the training of staff, saying that "we have come across one case at least where the Manager of a school took no active part in the running of the school except to veto the proposals made by the trained member of the staff."[1]

The report was severe about the perception among religious orders of the status accorded to those working in the industrial schools, saying that some of the congregations involved were engaged in "other work which is of more direct concern to them and which comes more into the public eye. There appears to be a tendency to staff the schools, in part at least, with those who are no longer required in other work rather than with those specially chosen for Child Care work."[2]

It was equally critical of the approach taken to the children, describing it as "institutional" and "depersonalised". The committee reported meeting with children within the system "who had so little contact with the outside world that they were unaware that food had to be paid for or that letters had to be stamped." It was considered "highly undesirable" to maintain rigid segregation between boys and girls.[3]

The report also condemned the system of inspection of industrial schools by the Department of Education as having been "totally ineffective", saying that not even its statutory obligations had been fulfilled. It also criticised the financial provisions made by the State as "totally inadequate", although it did point out that the increase to £8 and 5 shillings per week per child would undoubtedly serve to "ease the financial difficulties of those running the schools".[4]

Daingean Reformatory and Marlborough House were singled out for specific criticism. The committee recommended that both be immediately shut down. The children in Daingean were described as "ill-dressed and dirty", and the place itself was "depressing and decayed ... dirty and insanitary". The members of the committee said that they were "so perturbed" by Daingean, that they asked for immediate improvements to be made. The situation in Marlborough House was described as "deplorable and must be altered without delay". The committee wanted it to be urgently shut down, regardless of the fact that its replacement was not yet ready to be opened.[5]

Most fundamentally, the Kennedy Report sounded the death knell for the institutional model of child care which had remained remarkably resilient in this country for almost exactly 100 years. Its first major recommendation was that: "The committal or admission of children to residential care should be considered only when there is no satisfactory alternative." The report went on to say that "The present institutional system of residential care should be abolished and be replaced by group homes which would approximate as closely as possible the normal family unit."[6]

In total, the Kennedy Committee made thirteen major recommendations, all of them designed to structure a modern child care system, complete with fully trained staff, special educational supports, adequate after-care provisions, and a proper system of inspection. They also stated that the

Department of Health should in future have responsibility for the area, and that funding should no longer be based on the capitation system per child, but rather on an overall budget for the institution.

It appears that the Kennedy Committee was viewed with some hostility by the Department of Education right from the beginning. Although the vast majority of its files are mysteriously missing from the Department's archive, enough survives to illustrate a rather frosty relationship. The current Minister for Education, Micheal Martin, said in Dail Eireann that the "behaviour of many managers and officials has been described to me as at best silently obstructive".[7]

Tragically, the Minister responsible for setting up the Kennedy Committee, Donough O'Malley did not live to see its report published. He died in 1968, at the age of forty-seven. At that stage, the Kennedy Committee had not even been provided with administrative backup from the Department of Education. It was only as a result of the direct intervention of O'Malley's successor, Brian Lenihan, that they were given a proper secretariat.

Lenihan held the Education portfolio for only a year. However, some of the boys in Artane vividly remember a visit which he paid to the institution in 1968. When he was leaving, a fifteen-year-old went up to him and told him that the boys were being beaten by the Christian Brothers in charge of them every day of the week. "Stop them beating us," he begged the Minister. Lenihan is reported as having turned to his driver and said "Get me out of this fucking place". It became a catch-phrase among the boys — "Get me out of this fucking place" they used to say to each other, and then fall around laughing.[8] A year later, Artane had closed down, and their wish had come true.

While the publication of the Kennedy Report was greeted with considerable publicity and wide approval, it was clear that neither the State nor the Catholic Church shared that enthusiasm for change. Significantly, the report was never debated in the Dail; the only parliamentary debate on the issues it raised was in the Seanad, and even then had to wait until November 1973, three years after its publication. It was only through the determination of independent Senators Mary Robinson and Trevor West that it received any parliamentary recognition.

Some of the Senators criticised the lack of action by the Government in implementing the Report's recommendations. The Parliamentary Secretary to the Minister for Education, John Bruton, responded by saying that "to date there has been a certain amount of secretiveness in the approach of my Department and also of other Departments to this particular issue".[9]

A year after the report had been published, one of the civil servants on the Kennedy Committee was to receive the full brunt of criticism from the Catholic Church. At the Church's major seminar on child care in Killarney in 1971, he was called into a room and held to account by the Bishop of Kerry, Eamon Casey, and by Sr Stanislaus Kennedy, even at that stage a major force in the area of child care. They wanted to know how it was that the Department of Education could have presided over a report which gave the religious orders so little credit for their great work on behalf of children for so many decades.[10]

However, it was clear that the system of institutional industrial schools was at an end. Gradually they began to close, or to change into smaller units, termed 'family oriented centres'. When the Department of Health took over the area in 1984, fostering became the first option for children in need of care. A training course for child care workers was established in Kilkenny by Sr Stanislaus Kennedy in 1971.

However, the legacy of the old system was ever present. One of the first graduates of the new child care course, David Murray, secured immediate employment in St Joseph's Industrial School in Kilkenny, run by the Sisters of Charity. In 1997, Murray was sentenced to ten years imprisonment for the gross sexual abuse of several young boys in his care at St Joseph's. Judge Mathews at his trial stated that "Never in the history of child care in this State has one child care worker caused so much damage. If these sad facts teach us anything, it is that we must listen to those who cannot and have not in the past been heard."[11]

The case of David Murray was revealing in several different ways. His rape of so many boys had happened in an environment of considerable social enlightenment — St Joseph's was part of the complex of buildings housing Kilkenny Social Services, the most progressive such venture in the country. The industrial school itself had been one of the first to break itself up into smaller, more child-centred units, having implemented this policy even before the publication of the Kennedy Report. However, it is clear from the statements made by some of the Sisters of Charity to the Gardai during their investigation of child sexual abuse at the school, that there was an awareness of problems with a number of staff members. As it has now transpired, David Murray was only one of a staggering total of four staff members against whom allegations of sexual abuse have been made. Three have been convicted in the courts for this abuse, and, at the time of writing, the Gardai are still seeking the fourth, who is believed to be in England.

Despite this awareness, three of the abusers were allowed to continue working with the children in the school for long periods. Right throughout the 1970s, while the abuse continued, both the children and the nuns describe an institution which had not significantly changed in attitude, despite the supposedly new era heralded by the Kennedy Report. When the children complained, they were beaten and not believed. When outsiders complained, it was made clear to them that it was none of their business. When other staff members complained, no action was taken, and in one case, the staff member felt he had no option but to resign. What they all describe in graphic detail was a picture which was to repeat itself over and over again throughout the 1980s and 1990s.

The stark reality is that while the rhetoric associated with child care had changed, the closed and secretive practices which had allowed so much past abuse to occur were still very much in place. Despite the convictions of three separate child care workers for the abuse of the same group of boys, there was no official inquiry into the events at the Kilkenny school. Even more alarming was the fact that David Murray had worked in child care facilities all over the State for a period of twenty-five years, and yet it was not thought necessary to produce any report of the possible extent of the damage he had caused. It seemed that no one much cared how this extraordinary litany of abuse had occurred, who was at fault, and what lessons could be learnt from it in order to protect children in the future.

The contrast with the attitude taken to child abuse within the general community could not be more sharp. Just one month after the conviction of David Murray, the swimming abuse controversy arose with the conviction of coach Derry O'Rourke for the sexual abuse of young swimmers. Almost immediately an official inquiry was initiated by the State, headed by Dr Roderick Murphy SC. His report was published in full in June 1998.[12] It minutely analysed the practices within the swimming organisations where abuse had occurred, and made a series of recommendations to safeguard the welfare of children.

All of this, of course, was right and proper, as indeed were the investigations and full publication of reports into a number of cases of abuse of children within their families.[13] However, in relation to the abuse of children who were in the direct care of the State, no similar inquiry report has ever been published in full. This is in spite of a large number of such cases of abuse, parts of which have trickled into the public arena.

During the 1980s, many children from the travelling community were to suffer the most horrific aggravated sexual and physical abuse at Trudder House in Co Wicklow. This was a voluntary institution funded by the State, where it was considered that traveller children would be better off than with their families. It was reported in court that allegations of physical and sexual abuse were made against a number of members of staff, and in 1996 there was one conviction. An Eastern Health Board worker stated in 1996 that he had expressed concern to his superiors about the mistreatment of children at Trudder House in the early 1980s. Allegations of "homosexual activities" and beatings had also been made by a number of the children at this time. One child had made complaints as early as 1975.[14] However, as in the Kilkenny case, no official report as to how the abuse had been allowed to occur was produced. Once again, no one was interested in learning from the disastrous wreckage of Trudder House. The facility was shut down in April 1996, and that was the end of the matter.

In 1989, the Gardai began an investigation into the gross sexual abuse of children at Cualann in south Dublin, a small, child-centred and modern facility run by the Sisters of Our Lady of Charity of Refuge. It was this order who had run an industrial school and enormous Magdalen Laundry at High Park in Drumcondra, and who had disinterred and cremated the remains of the Magdalen women in order to sell some of their land. Some of the allegations in the Cualann case are literally stomach-turning, involving horrific allegations of abuse against boys as young as seven. However, no arrest was made — the alleged abuser is believed to have fled the country and is now thought to be in England.

Shortly after the first allegations of child sexual abuse were made at Cualann, the nuns simply shut down the facility, and removed the children elsewhere. Some of the children have since received compensation through the courts for the abuse they suffered, but their lives remain in ruins. Furthermore, in what had now become an established pattern, no official report on how such abuse could have occurred was produced, and once again no lessons were learnt. It is important to remember that all of these facilities were totally funded by the State.

A handful of courageous individuals had reported their suspicions of the abuse of children in residential centres during the 1980s. As the various agencies involved were primarily concerned with maintaining secrecy when such allegations arose, some of these whistle-blowers paid a heavy price for speaking out. One case concerned a senior civil servant, Loreto Byrne. While working in the Department of Education in the late 1980s, she had become aware of allegations concerning the sexual abuse of children in St Laurence's residential school in Finglas. This was run by the De La Salle Brothers. Allegations of abuse had been made against two of the Brothers.

However, as soon as she raised the issue within the Department, she was transferred out of Education and into the Department of Finance. An investigation was held, which concluded that no further action was warranted. Loreto Byrne resigned from the civil service in 1992, and continued to press for a full investigation in the abuse allegations at St Laurence's.[15]

In 1995, the Oireachtas Public Accounts Committee discussed the issue. Referring to Loreto Byrne, Des O'Malley TD stated that "the Department of Finance sent her to the gulags". She had written to Bertie Ahern TD (then leader of Fianna Fail in opposition) on the matter, and he in turn conveyed his concerns in writing to the Eastern Health Board. Finally, eight years after Loreto Byrne's original complaint, a full Garda investigation began. Over seventy former residents of St Laurence's have been interviewed.[16]

It should have surprised no one when once again allegations of child sexual abuse were made, this time relating to Madonna House, run by the Sisters of Charity (the same order which was in charge of the Kilkenny school). In 1993, the institution's maintenance man Frank Griffin was sentenced to four years' imprisonment for sexually abusing several children resident there during the 1980s and early 1990s. Madonna House was the largest child care facility in the Dublin region, catering for up to fifty children at any one time, and receiving funding of about £1 million a year from the State.

This time, both the State and the Sisters of Charity did take action. They jointly appointed a Committee of Inquiry in 1994, and it produced its report two years later. However, in an extraordinary move, the Government decided to delete all of the most critical sections from the published version of the report. The censored parts constituted a damning indictment of the management of the facility. In essence, they described an industrial school, run by the Sisters of Charity along the old and draconian institutional lines. The Government stated at the time that the reasons for the censorship were legal. The effect of its decision to accept this legal advice was to protect both the State and the Sisters of Charity from further opprobrium and, perhaps more importantly, from civil litigation by the victims.

What the entire Madonna House episode showed was that absolutely no one had learnt any lessons from the highly abusive climates of the past. The State had not learnt that complete openness is the only way to even begin to tackle child sexual abuse within the residential child care system. The Sisters of Charity had clearly learnt nothing from either their appalling experience in Kilkenny Industrial School during the 1970s, or from the general legacy of these schools in which they themselves had played a significant part.

Interestingly, this was not the first time that Madonna House had been embroiled in controversy. In 1978, a child care worker had kidnapped a boy who had been resident at the home and drowned him in the bath of an Edinburgh hotel. In response to calls for a public inquiry at the time into the practices employed in children's homes, Minister for Health Charles Haughey said that such an inquiry would serve no useful purpose.[17]

The censored sections of the 1996 Madonna House Report were revealed as part of the *States of Fear* documentary in May 1999. Two chapters had been completely removed: Chapter Six, dealing with the full extent of child abuse within Madonna House; and Chapter Seven, which detailed the incompetence of the management.

These chapters contained devastating evidence that child after child who had been sexually abused had told staff members of that abuse, in one case a full eight years before paedophile Frank Griffin was finally removed from Madonna House. According to the report, no fewer than nine members of staff knew of the abuse. Most of them had in turn reported it to the management. The report made it clear that the management team, including the nun in charge, Sr Anne Purcell, had taken no effective action either to stop the abuse or to protect the children in their care. "Incompetence and pervasive dysfunction", "unsafe", "dangerous", "secretive" and "closed" were just some of the words used in the report to describe the management culture of Madonna House.

The censored sections of the report also showed that the physical, sexual and emotional abuse of children at the home was far more extensive than had been indicated in the sanitised published version. The inquiry team described "harsh, punitive and humiliating practices affecting thirteen children". They established through extensive interviews that no fewer than seven staff members had knowledge of some or all of these practices. They also explained through precise examples how inappropriate and exploitative relationships had developed, particularly between one staff member and a girl resident at the home.

There were also further allegations of serious sexual abuse against another staff member. The alleged abuse occurred in 1980, when two boys were sexually assaulted by a trainee priest working at Madonna House. One of the victims has now taken a civil case for damages, which was heard in March 1999. Both the Sisters of Charity and the Eastern Health Board are contesting the case — part of their defence is that there was no clear awareness of child sexual abuse in the early 1980s.

It emerged in court that the alleged abuser had made a statement to Gardai in 1993, admitting the abuse. It was also stated that the Sisters of Charity do not deny that this abuse occurred. Bizarrely, no criminal prosecution ever took place. The civil case for damages taken by one of the victims was heard before Judge Cyril Kelly, who resigned from his position before he was able to deliver his judgement. It will now have to be re-heard before a new judge.

The hidden parts of the report also contained descriptions of children locked outside at night, in one case wearing only a bath towel. The child was seen "screaming in distress and seeking to be allowed indoors". Another child was so afraid of a particular member of staff that she soiled herself. One former resident graphically described waking one morning and seeing her younger sister, who lived in a different unit, outside in her bare feet and in tears. She also recalled one incident of a staff member putting soap in the mouth of another of her sisters.

These chapters also revealed that while many staff members were unaware of guidelines which existed on child abuse, there was one rule which was repeatedly pointed out to them and strictly enforced. This concerned what type of clothing should be worn particularly by the female child care workers. It was frequently and exhaustively discussed at internal meetings. The inquiry team discovered that "it appears that there was an inflexible rule that no members of female staff while on duty could wear trousers ... It would also appear that considerable significance was placed upon the type of skirt to be worn by female members of staff." In fact, one staff member told the inquiry team that the rules about the dress code were the only regulations of which she was made clearly aware by management.

The report concluded that "management failure was central to the organisation and culture of Madonna House". The inquiry team also revealed that they experienced considerable difficulty in "obtaining reliable information and disclosure in relation to the issues under review", and that these difficulties were compounded by the paucity and inadequacy of records. Ominously, they anticipated that "further concerns may emerge over time and this commentary is based on the information currently available".

It is clear that in the Madonna House case the public interest should have hugely outweighed any legal advice given with regard to full publication. The great strength of the complete, uncensored report lies in the extraordinary level of detail it gives on exactly how the management of such a child care facility can (and did) go wrong — with such tragic consequences for the children involved. This was a uniquely valuable piece of work, which should have become a Bible for all children's homes. Instead, petty concerns relating to the State's desire to protect itself from civil litigation were tragically allowed to prevail. To date, the missing sections of the Madonna House report have still not been published.

The Sisters of Charity closed Madonna House in 1995. This contributed to a crisis in child care from which the State has still not recovered. The resulting desperate shortage of places for children in need of short-term care has been the subject of almost weekly press reports, with some judges publicly condemning the Government for its lack of action in the area. Hundreds of children ended up in hospitals, bed and breakfasts or Garda stations simply because there was nowhere else to put them. The State's supine dependence on religious orders for the provision of its child care facilities had left it acutely vulnerable to such crises — it simply has no experience and little knowledge of how to establish an alternative system.

Two key recommendations of the Kennedy Report back in 1970 have still not been properly implemented. The first of these relates to the raising of the age of criminal responsibility from seven to twelve. It was only in September 1999 that this issue was finally addressed, with the proposal contained in the 1999 Children Bill, which has not yet been enacted.

The second crucial recommendation in 1970 related to the inspection of residential homes for children. The Kennedy Committee advocated the establishment of "an independent advisory body with statutory powers ... to ensure that the highest standards of Child Care are attained and maintained".[18] This recommendation has still not been implemented. The absence of such a body has undoubtedly contributed to the scale of child abuse in residential homes in the past thirty years.

In 1999, a new body was eventually appointed with some powers to inspect children's homes. This is the Social Services Inspectorate, which is based in the Department of Health. However, as yet it has no statutory basis, and bizarrely, has no jurisdiction over children's homes managed by voluntary agencies, including the Catholic Church. Homes managed by voluntary bodies are to be inspected by the Health Boards in which they are based.

The continuing fragmentation of the approach to protecting the welfare of children has resulted in the fact that no single body is even aware of the extent of abuse in residential children's homes, let alone in a position to do anything about it. The Department of Health has no knowledge of such abuse. Each Health Board deals with cases as they arise in their own local areas, usually in secrecy and in total ignorance as to how any other Health Board may be tackling the issue. So far, the remit of the Social Services Inspectorate remains narrowly defined. In essence, little has changed since the era of the industrial schools in the 1940s and 1950s.

Most shocking of all, however, is the absence of any specified independent inspection or complaints procedure in the new 1999 Children Bill. Part 3 of this Bill allows Health Boards to establish what are euphemistically termed special care units. These are intended for children who are deemed to require secure care or protection. Given the vulnerability of these children, and from what we know about past abuses in quasi-secure institutions, it would have been reasonable to assume that a range of clearly specified safeguards would have been a priority. Amazingly, no system of inspection is proposed for these special care units, no visiting committees, no annual reports on their operation, and no complaints procedures. Rather, the Bill simply says that regulations *may* be drawn up by the Minister, at some unspecified date in the future, to introduce provisions for the protection of the children in these units. In contrast, the protection provided in the Child Detention Centres is thorough and clearly specified in the Bill. It is somewhat ironic that the 1999 Bill affords considerably less protection to vulnerable children in need of care than to those who have committed offences.

This scandalous omission was also a feature of the earlier 1996 Children Bill, which was withdrawn to be re-drafted following the tabling of a large number of amendments. It is extraordinary that the re-draft of the Bill in 1999 did not include clear and specific child protection mechanisms. Its publication, of course, was in the middle of a deluge of publicity on the disastrous consequences in the past for children in institutions with little or no system of public accountability. It is clear that the country's legislators have created the potential for the future abuse of children in the care of the State.

The Challenges Facing the Commission

The Commission to Inquire into Childhood Abuse, established by the Government in May 1999, is entering into virgin territory for this country. Described by Government members as approximating to the South African Truth Commission, one of its functions will be to hear the testimony of survivors of child abuse from the industrial and reformatory schools. In terms of testimony to be given by the religious orders and by the alleged abusers, the Commission has yet to report on whether it will require powers to compel such witnesses to attend. This obviously raises the issue of immunity from prosecution for such alleged abusers, and equally the Commission has so far not indicated its views on these difficult issues.

However, there are some precedents for what this country is now trying to achieve in terms of dealing with its past. The Commission in Ireland will be able to draw on the wide experience of the abuse of children by members of religious congregations in other countries. Such experience is by no means unique to Ireland, with Australia and Canada having been shocked by revelations of similar abuse of children to that being examined by the Commission in Ireland. In a number of cases, the religious orders involved in both Canada and Australia have their origins in Ireland.

Christian Brothers have been found responsible for widespread and systematic sexual and physical abuse of children at their institutions in Canada and Australia.[19] Repeated allegations of severe physical abuse have also been made against the Sisters of Mercy with regard to their institutions in Australia and Canada.

Many of these allegations, particularly in Australia, centred initially on the treatment of child migrants[20] or indigenous children[21], but have now embraced all children placed in such institutions. In many cases, the descriptions of the regimes that operated in these institutions have an uncanny resemblance to what occurred in Ireland. Severe beatings; rigid discipline; window dressing of the institutions prior to inspection by State authorities; inspectors not talking to the children to ascertain their experience; a tacit policy of not upsetting the Catholic Church — these were all features of both the Australian and Canadian experience.[22]

In a cruel irony, one of the children abused at the Mount Cashel orphanage in Newfoundland, managed by the Christian Brothers, was Leo Gerard Rice. Born in 1958, he is a direct descendent of the family of Edmund Ignatius Rice, founder of the Christian Brothers. He and his four brothers were placed in the orphanage after the death of both their parents.[23] The abuse at Mount Cashel had started in the early 1970s. It was the subject of a police investigation in 1975, which had been hushed up, and two of the self-confessed abusing Brothers sent away for treatment. When survivors came forward in 1989, the case was re-opened.

The gross sexual abuse of so many boys, combined with the cover-up during the 1970s, shocked Canada to its core. The cover-up had involved the police, the Justice Department, the Catholic Church and the Christian Brothers. In Canada, the order is referred to as the Irish Christian Brothers, and so far twelve of their members have been convicted for the sexual abuse of children in their care. The story of the horror experienced by the children in Mount Cashel was powerfully told in the Canadian television drama *The Boys of St Vincent*, shown during 1999 on RTE.

As in Ireland, apologies have been offered by the religious orders responsible for the abuse of children in both Australia and Canada. The issue as to how the victims should be adequately compensated has been debated in detail.

The Forde Report, an examination of abuse in child care institutions in Queensland, Australia, concluded that "reparation will require the Government and responsible religious organisations to enter into a restorative process with survivors to redress the harm done." Significantly, the Australian inquiry team were of the view that "accountability for the harm done cannot be characterised as a legal issue only; the Government and religious organisations must also accept moral and political accountability."[24]

These issues of accountability were also raised by a discussion paper on institutional child abuse in Canada. As in other countries, this noted that a primary need identified by most survivors is an acknowledgement that what was done to them was wrong. The paper makes an interesting distinction between an acknowledgement and an apology. An apology, it is suggested, should be absolute, unqualified and offered voluntarily. The paper goes on to say that how that apology is expressed is also crucial. If it only states that the agency responsible is simply sorry that harm was caused, this is not sufficient. It must also explicitly acknowledge the abuse that caused the harm, their role in committing the abuse or in allowing others to commit it.[25]

The Canadian discussion paper also argues that descriptions of the needs of survivors often play down the issue of financial compensation, as "if there were something faintly distasteful about survivors seeking money for the harms they suffered … We see no need to gloss over both the desire and the need of survivors for financial compensation. In this, they are no different from any other victims of criminal injury, or anyone who has suffered a civil wrong. They have been harmed, both emotionally and physically, by the intentional wrongful acts of others and by the failure of those in authority to fulfil their duty to protect them. In many cases, the harms suffered limited their ability to earn a living."[26]

In light of this very thoughtful discussion paper, it is instructive to examine the apologies offered by the various Irish agencies who were responsibility for the incarceration and abuse of so many Irish children.

The Irish Sisters of Mercy were the first agency to publicly apologise. However, their statement was neither fully voluntary nor unconditional. It came largely in response to the adverse publicity experienced by the congregation following the showing of the television documentary *Dear Daughter* on RTE. While they claimed to apologise unreservedly to those who were harshly treated, they added a significant paragraph:

> Life in the Ireland of the '40s and '50s was generally harsh for many people. This was reflected in orphanages which were under-funded, under-staffed and under-resourced. In these circumstances many sisters gave years of dedicated service. Notwith-standing these facts, clearly mistakes were made.[27]

The Irish Sisters of Charity issued a press statement expressing their regret in the aftermath of the Madonna House scandal. This could not be described as a voluntary apology, insofar as it was issued in response to considerable public outrage. Also, their statement (issued in May 1996) did not acknowledge the responsibility of the order in allowing the abuse to occur. While the Sisters expressed their "deep regret" that children in their care had been abused, they went on to say that "it is important, however, not to lose sight of the many hundreds of children in our care, who experienced only love, care and safety from very committed staff".[28]

The Sisters of Charity also apologised for the horrific catalogue of sexual abuse suffered by the boys of St Joseph's in Kilkenny. While this was less conditional than their Madonna House apology, it still did not acknowledge the responsibility of the order for the fate of the small boys in their care. It, too, was only issued directly in the wake of the publicity surrounding the various convictions of the paedophiles who had been employed by the order to care for the children at St Joseph's. The Sisters stated that: "The abuse of the children at St Joseph's has caused untold misery for the men involved. Nothing can make up for what happened to them and we deeply regret their suffering."[29]

The Christian Brothers issued a statement in March 1998 stating: "We the Christian Brothers in Ireland, wish to express our deep regret to anyone who suffered ill-treatment while in our care". This order went a step further than any others by acknowledging their lack of response to previous complaints: "And we say to you who have experienced physical and sexual abuse by a Christian Brother, and to you who complained of abuse and were not listened to, we are deeply sorry." This was also a voluntary apology — while a number of members of their order had been arrested and were awaiting trial, the apology offered was not directly the result of any public outcry. However, they still did not acknowledge the overall responsibility of their order in allowing such widespread abuse of children in their care to have occurred.

In a statement issued to the *States of Fear* documentaries, the Oblates of Mary Immaculate (who ran the Daingean Reformatory) merely said that "we in the Order are distressed to learn of allegations of abuse made against any of our members". There was no acknowledgement of either the damage caused or the responsibility of the order in this. Further, the statement was not voluntary — it was made in response to a query from *States of Fear*.

The Rosminians (who ran industrial schools at Upton and Clonmel, in addition to the School for Blind Boys in Dublin) also issued a statement to *States of Fear*. It said: "The members of the Rosminian Institute are saddened and shamed that young people in our care were abused by members of our Order. We deeply regret, not only the abuse, but also the shadow cast on the lives of those abused. We abhor all mistreatment of children and we wish to express our profound sorrow."

As with all the other apologies, this order did not accept responsibility for its own role in the abuse suffered by children in its care. Indeed, it is a general feature of all the above statements that they tend to distance the order involved from the abuse, implying that while individual members were involved, the organisation itself does not share the blame. Equally they do not address issues of accountability for why abuse took place and was not responded to; nor do they fully acknowledge the powerless status of their victims and the sense of guilt and shame they often carry with them. Further, they do not outline a mechanism to provide a real opportunity for healing and do not indicate measures to ensure future abuse will not happen.

Following the controversy resulting from *Dear Daughter*, the Conference of Religious of Ireland established a telephone helpline for people who had been abused while in care. In its first year of operation it received more than 1,000 calls. By 1999, the number had risen to almost 5,000. The Irish Catholic bishops also produced a framework for responding to child sexual abuse by priests and religious in 1996.[30]

However, the religious orders continue to contest the civil cases being taken against them by survivors of the industrial schools. This has clearly influenced their attitudes to any public statements about their responsibility for abuse. Many of them repeatedly quote legal reasons as the basis for either refusing interviews or access to their archival records. Both the Christian Brothers and the Sisters of Mercy have engaged public relations firms, who have indicated that they will make available names to journalists of individuals who have positive stories to tell of their experiences of growing up in industrial schools. However, when this offer was taken up by *States of Fear*, no names were forthcoming from the Christian Brothers.

The apology of the Irish Government, issued on the 11th of May 1999, is at least more specific on how it aims to engage with the survivors of child abuse. Their starting point was "a sincere and long overdue apology to the victims of childhood abuse for our collective failure to intervene, to detect their pain, to come to their rescue". The Government went on to outline a series of measures to deal with the survivors of childhood abuse, the most significant being the Commission on Childhood Abuse. The outline terms of reference for the Commission include providing a sympathetic forum where victims can describe their abuse; to ascertain the nature and extent of the abuse suffered; and to produce a report which would include recommendations to ensure that such abuse will not occur in the future.

While the State also continues to contest the civil cases being taken against it by survivors of industrial schools, it has agreed to remove the Statute of Limitations from cases involving sexual abuse. The fact that it has not yet done so for those involving physical abuse has caused great anger among survivors.

As with the apologies of many of the religious orders, the State's intervention was hardly voluntary. It was issued as a direct response to the broadcast of the *States of Fear* programmes, which for the first time clearly identified the State's enormous role in the industrial schools system. Equally, there was no acknowledgement that the State was specifically to blame and should be held directly accountable for the miserable conditions and abuse suffered by the many tens of thousands of children it consigned to the industrial schools.

At the time of writing, the Commission has yet to publish its first report, which will deal with how it approaches its task. It is clearly an exercise of enormous potential value. But for the survivors there may be many pitfalls. The experience in other countries has shown that while such inquiries may provide a catalyst for redress, they also have a potential to do actual harm, unless handled sensitively and with direct material benefits to survivors.

Most importantly perhaps for the future of children in this country, the deliberations of the Commission may finally allow society to learn fully the lessons of the abusive past, a past that had generally been conveniently forgotten. Through that process, there may at last be a full acknowledgement in every aspect of the child care system, both in legislation and on the ground, that the potential for abuse is a constant reality. The children of this country have experienced so much of it in the past, that we should now be in a position to deal with it thoroughly and ruthlessly whenever it raises its most ugly head.

Appendix 1
Reformatory and Industrial Schools in Ireland (post 1922)

Schools marked with an * remained open after 1970. The majority of these schools remained certified as industrial schools until their transfer to the Department of Health on the 1st of January 1984.

Cavan
St Joseph's Industrial School for Girls, Cavan town. Poor Clare Sisters. Certified for eighty-seven children (closed 1966).

Clare
Our Lady's Industrial School for Girls, Ennis. Sisters of Mercy. Certified for eighty children (closed 1963).

Cork
St Coleman's Industrial School for Girls, Cobh. Sisters of Mercy. Certified for forty-six children (moved to Rushbrooke in early 1960s).*

Our Lady of Mercy Industrial School for Girls, Kinsale. Sisters of Mercy. Certified for 120 children (closed 1963).

Mallow Industrial School for Girls. Sisters of Mercy. Certified for sixty children.*

Mount St Joseph's Industrial School for Junior Boys, Passage West. Sisters of Mercy. Certified for fifty children.*

St Finbarr's Industrial School for Girls, Sunday's Well, Cork City. Sisters of the Good Shepherd. Certified for 172 children.*

St Joseph's Industrial School for Senior Boys, Greenmount, Cork City. Presentation Brothers. Certified for 220 children (closed 1959).

St Aloysuis' Industrial School for Girls, Clonakilty. Sisters of Mercy. Certified for 130 children (closed in 1965).

St Patrick's (or Danesfort) Industrial School for Senior Boys, Upton. Rosminians (Institute of Charity). Certified for 200 children (closed 1966).

Baltimore Fishing School for Senior Boys. Managed by Parish Priest. Certified for 150 children (closed 1950).

Dublin
Artane Industrial School for Senior Boys. Christian Brothers. Certified for 800 children (closed 1969).

St Anne's Industrial School for Girls, Booterstown. Sisters of Mercy. Certified for eighty children.*

St Vincent's Industrial School for Girls and Junior Boys, Goldenbridge, Inchicore. Sisters of Mercy. Certified for 130 children.*

St Mary's Industrial School for Girls, Lakelands, Sandymount. Irish Sisters of Charity. Certified for 100 children.*

Carriglea Park Industrial School for Senior Boys, Dun Laoghaire. Christian Brothers. Certified for 250 children. (Closed 1953)

St Joseph's Industrial School for Girls, High Park convent, Drumcondra. Sisters of Our Lady of Charity of Refuge. Certified for fifty children.*

Donegal

St Columba's Industrial School for Senior Boys, Killybegs. Managed by Parish Priest. Certified for 144 children (closed 1941).

Galway

St Brigid's Industrial School for Girls, Loughrea. Sisters of Mercy. Certified for 112 children (closed 1966).

St Josephs' Industrial School for Girls and Junior Boys. Clifden. Sisters of Mercy. Certified for 100 children.*

St Joseph's Industrial School for Senior Boys, Letterfrack. Christian Brothers. Certified for 165 children (closed 1973).

St Ann's Industrial School for Girls and Junior Boys, Lenaboy, Galway city. Sisters of Mercy. Certified for seventy-seven children.*

St Joseph's Industrial School for Senior Boys, Salthill. Christian Brothers. Certified for 200 children.*

St Joseph's Industrial School for Girls and Junior Boys, Ballinasloe. Sisters of Mercy. Certified for sixty children (closed 1968).

Kerry

St Joseph's Industrial School for Girls and Junior Boys, Killarney. Sisters of Mercy. Certified for 103 children.*

St Joseph's Industrial School for Senior Boys, Tralee. Christian Brothers. Certified for 145 children (closed 1970).

Pembroke Alms House (Nazareth House) Industrial School for Girls, Tralee. Sisters of Mercy. Certified for seventy children.*

Kilkenny

St Patrick's Industrial School for Junior Boys, Kilkenny town. Irish Sisters of Charity. Certified for 162 children (closed 1966).

St Joseph's Industrial School for Girls, Kilkenny town. Irish Sisters of Charity. Certified for 100 children.*

Limerick

St George's Industrial School for Girls, Limerick. Sisters of the Good Shepherd. Certified for 100 children.*

Mount St Vincent's Industrial School for Girls, Limerick. Sisters of Mercy. Certified for 130 children.*

St Joseph's Industrial School for Senior Boys, Glin. Christian Brothers. Certified for 190 children (closed 1966).

Longford
Our Lady of Succour Industrial School for Girls, Newtownforbes.
Sisters of Mercy. Certified for 145 children (closed 1970).

Louth
House of Charity Industrial School for Junior Boys, Drogheda.
Daughters of Charity. Certified for ninety-two children.*
St Joseph's Industrial School for Girls, Dundalk. Sisters of Mercy.
Certified for eighty children.*

Mayo
St Columba's Industrial School for Girls, Westport. Sisters of Mercy.
Certified for 105 children.*

Monaghan
St Martha's Industrial School for Girls, Monaghan Town. Sisters of St
Louis. Certified for 120 children (moved to Bundoran in 1957,
closed in 1965).

Offaly
St John's Industrial School for Girls, Birr. Sisters of Mercy. Certified for
eighty children (closed 1962).

Roscommon
St Francis Xavier's Industrial School for Girls (and later Junior Boys),
Ballaghaderreen. Irish Sisters of Charity. Certified for seventy-five
children (closed 1969).

Sligo
Benada Abbey Industrial School for Girls, Ballymote. Irish Sisters of
Charity. Certified for sixty children.*
St Lawrence's Industrial School for Girls, Sligo Town. Sisters of Mercy.
Certified for 155 children (closed 1957).

Tipperary
St Joseph's Industrial School for Senior Boys, Ferryhouse, Clonmel.
Rosminians (Institute of Charity). Certified for 190 children.*
St Augustine's Industrial School for Girls, Templemore. Sisters of
Mercy. Certified for sixty children (closed 1964).
St Francis's Industrial School for Girls, Cashel. Presentation Sisters.
Certified for 110 children (closed 1967).
Industrial School for Girls, Dundrum. Presentation Sisters. Certified
for sixty-five children.*

Waterford
St Michael's Industrial School for Junior Boys, Cappoquin. Sisters of
Mercy. Certified for fifty-one children.*

St Dominick's Industrial School for Girls, Waterford. Sisters of the
Good Shepherd. Certified for 160 children.*

Westmeath

St Joseph's Industrial School for Girls, Summerhill, Athlone. Sisters of
Mercy. Certified for 120 children (closed 1963).

Mount Carmel Industrial School for Girls, Moate. Sisters of Mercy.
Certified for fifty-three children.*

Wexford

St Aidan's Industrial School for Girls, New Ross. Sisters of the Good
Shepherd. Certified for seventy children (closed 1968).

St Michael's Industrial School for Girls, Wexford. Sisters of Mercy.
Certified for 106 children.*

Wicklow

St Kyran's Industrial School for Junior Boys, Rathdum. Sisters of
Mercy. Certified for fifty children.*

REFORMATORY SCHOOLS

St Kevin's Reformatory School for Boys, Glencree, Co Wicklow.
Oblates of Mary Immaculate (closed 1940).

St Conleth's Reformatory School for Boys, Daingean, Co Offaly.
Oblates of Mary Immaculate (closed 1974).

St Joseph's Reformatory School for Girls, Limerick. Sisters of the Good
Shepherd (closed 1975).

St Anne's Reformatory School for Girls, Kilmacud, Dublin. Sisters of
Our Lady of Charity of Refuge (closed 1984).

Appendix 2
The Department of Education, 1922 — 1973

Ministers for Education (who had ultimate responsibility for industrial and reformatory schools during their time in office):

Michael Hayes, January–August 1922
Eoin MacNeill, September 1922–November 1925
J.M.O'Sullivan, January 1926–March 1932
Thomas Derrig, 1932–1939
S.T. O'Kelly, 8th–27th September, 1939
Eamon de Valera, September 1939–June 1940
Thomas Derrig, 1940–1948
Richard Mulcahy, 1948–1951
Sean Moylan, 1951–1954
Richard Mulcahy, 1954–1957
Jack Lynch, 1957–1959
Patrick Hillary, 1959–1965
George Colley, 1965–1966
Donough O'Malley, 1966–1968
Brian Lenihan, 1968–1969
Padraig Faulkner, 1969–1973

Of these, only three appear from the Department's files to have taken any serious interest in the industrial schools — Thomas Derrig, Richard Mulcahy and Donough O'Malley. The others are barely even mentioned in the files.

Secretaries of the Department of Education (1923-1968)

Joseph O'Neill, 1923–1944
Michael Breathnach, 1944–1953
Labhras Ó Muirí, 1953–1956
Tarlach Ó Raifeartaigh, 1956–1968.

Notes

Abbreviations

D/Ed SpEd: Department of Education, Special Education Files on Industrial and Reformatory Schools, Athlone.

NA: National Archives.

NA D/T: National Archives Department of an Taoiseach.

NA D/J: National Archives Department of Justice.

NA D/H: National Archives Department of Health.

D/H: Department of Health Files, Hawkins House, Dublin.

IS: Industrial School

Two – The System

[1] D/Ed SpEd file G001a Boarding-out Arrangements.

[2] Saorstat Eireann (1933) *Committee of Inquiry into Widows' and Orphans' Pensions.* Dublin: Stationery Office, p.65.

[3] D/H. Miss Clandillon files, 1966.

[4] *Reformatory and Industrial Schools Systems Report, 1970* (The Kennedy Report). Dublin: The Stationary Office.

[5] Williams, G. (1902) *Dublin Charities.* Dublin: The Educational Depository, pp.127-128.

[6] Carroll, Sr MTA (1881)Leaves from the Annals of the Sisters of Mercy, Vol. 1, Ireland. New York: Catholic Publication Society. p.250.

[7] Hutch, W. (1875) *Nano Nagle: Her Life, Her Labours, and Their Fruits.* Dublin: McGlashan and Gill, pp.119-120.

[8] *12th Annual Report of St Brigid's Orphanage for Five Hundred Children* (1869) Dublin: W. Powell, p.1.

[9] Catholic Social Workers' Handbook, 1947. Dublin: The Society of St Vincent de Paul.

[10] Ibid.

[11] D/Ed SpEd G0021a Establishment of new Reformatory, Kilmacud. This reformatory school was specifically legislated for by the Children (Amendment) Act of 1949.

Three – Saving Little Souls: The Battle for Power

[1] *Artane – An Illustrated Souvenir,* by P.O. Ryan, Manager, Artane, 1905 (National Library of Ireland).

[2] Robins, J. (1980) *The Lost Children.* Dublin: Institute of Public Administration, p. 11.

[3] Ibid, p. 31.

[4] Young, Rev. H. (1821) *The Catholic Directory dedicated to St Patrick, Bishop, Apostle, and Patron of Ireland, which gives a useful and interesting information of the Dioceses of Ireland, also of the Parishes, Rev. Clergymen, Orphan Asylums, Catholic Schools, Pious Confraternities and all Charitable Institutions.* Dublin: John Coyle.

[5] Osler, T. (1834) *Account of Catholic Orphanages in Dublin, including Statistics of numbers therein, 1789-1832.* Ms. 640. National Library.

[6] Franciscan Library Killiney. Mss.c87. Rules of the Orphan Society of St Francis of Assisium.

402

[7] Atkinson, S. (1879) *Mary Aikenhead: Her Life, Her Work, and Her Friends, Giving a History of the Foundation of the Congregation of the Irish Sisters of Charity*. Dublin: Gill and Son, p.447.

[8] St Vincent's Glasnevin. *Centenary Annual, 1856-1956.* Dublin: Society of St Vincent de Paul.

[9] Bolster, Sister M. A. (1987) *Mercy in Cork 1837-1987: A Sesquicentennial Commemoration*. Cork: Tower Books, p. 13.

[10] Oates, M.J. (1995) *The Catholic Philanthropic Tradition in America.* Indiana University Press.

[11] Corish, P. (1985) *The Irish Catholic Experience: A Historical Survey.* Dublin: Gill and Macmillan.

[12] Barkley, J.M. (1966) *The Presbyterian Orphan Society, 1866-1966.* Belfast: BNL Printing Co pp.116-117.

[13] Barrett, R.M. (1884) *Guide to Dublin Charities.* Dublin.

[14] Barrett, R.M. (1902) Introduction to section v, Orphanages and Homes for the Young IN Williams, G. *Dublin Charities.* Dublin: The Educational Depository. p.123.

[15] Robins, J, (1980). *The Lost Children: A Study of Charity in Ireland, 1700-1900,* Dublin: Institute of Public Administration. p 292.

[16] Government of Ireland (1950) *White Paper on the Reconstruction and Improvement of County Homes.* Dublin: Government Publications Office, p.9; Department of Health (1968) *The Care of the Aged.* Dublin: Stationery Office.

[17] Report of Miss Kenny-Fitzgerald, Lady Inspector of Boarded-Out Children, Local Government Board Annual Report, 1907, p.159.

[18] Curry, J. (1884) Industrial Schools in Ireland. *The Irish Ecclesiastical Record*, Vol. 5, p.438.

[19] Foley, L. (1923) *The Reformatory System.* Dublin:Browne and Nolan, p.31.

[20] Ibid, p.6.

[21] The Londonderry Sentinel, May 2nd, 1861.

[22] Ibid.

[23] Report of the First meeting in aid of St Kevin's Reformatory School for Catholic Boys, Glencree, held at the Music Hall, Dublin, Wednesday, May 25th, 1859. *Freemans Journal*, May 26th, 1959.

[24] Foley, L. (1923) *The Reformatory System.* Dublin: Browne and Nolan, p.63.

[25] *Train Up a Child in the Way He Should Go.* A Paper on the Industrial Schools of Scotland and Dunlops Act, communicated to the Bristol Meeting of the National Reformatory Union in 1856.

[26] Quoted in May, M. (1973) *Innocence and Experience*: The Evolution of the Concept of Juvenile Delinquency in the Mid-Nineteenth Century. *Victorian Studies.* Vol. XVII, No. 1, p.7.

[27] 3rd Report of the Inspector appointed to visit the Reformatory Schools of Ireland (1865). Dublin: Thom and Co.

[28] Commission of Enquiry into the Reformatory and Industrial System of Ireland in 1884, p.567.

[29] Burke-Savage, R. (1955) *Catherine McAuley: The First Sister of Mercy.* Dublin: Gill and Son.

30 Letter from T.J. Butler, Manager Artane Industrial School, Co. Dublin 3/2/1900 to John Sweetman, Esq. Hon. Sec. County Council's General Council in Irish County Councils' General Council Publications. No.1. *Industrial Schools.* Dublin: ICCGC.

31 Thirty Sixth Annual Report of the Inspector appointed to Visit the Reformatory and Industrial Schools in Ireland (1898). Dublin: Thom and Co.

32 Thirty Seventh Annual Report of the Inspector appointed to Visit the Reformatory and Industrial Schools in Ireland (1899). Dublin: Thom and Co.

Four – Independence for Whom? (1921-1939)

1 Report of the Department of Education for the School Years 1925-26-27 and the Financial and Administrative Year 1926-27. Dublin: Stationery Office, p.91.

2 Carlebach, J. (1970) *Caring for Children in Trouble.* London: Routledge and Kegan Paul, p.89.

3 Home Office (1923) *First Report of the Children's Department.* London: HMSO, p.17.

4 Parker, R.A. (1990) *Away from Home: A Short History of Provision for Separated Children.* London: Barnardos.

5 Home Office (1938) *Fifth Report on the Work of the Children's Branch.* London: HMSO.

6 Glynn, J.A. (1921) The Unmarried Mother. *Irish Ecclesiastical Record*, Vol. xviii, p.466.

7 MacInerny, M.H. (1922) A Postscript on the Souper Problem. *Irish Ecclesiastical Record*, Vol. xix, p.254.

8 'Sagart' (1922) How to Deal with the Unmarried Mother. *Irish Ecclesiastical Record*, Vol. XX, p.150.

9 *Annual Report of the Department of Local Government and Public Health* (1928). Dublin: Stationery Office, p.113.

10 NA D/H A124/23 Repatriation of Pregnant Unmarried Irish Mothers.

11 Department of Local Government and Public Health, Annual Report, 1930-31, p.130.

12 D/H.. Children - General File - Unmarried Mothers in Great Britain and at Home.

13 NA D/T s2623a Reformatory and Industrial Schools Commission of Enquiry 1934.

14 *Commission of Inquiry into the Reformatory and Industrial School System Report, 1936* (The Cussen Report). Dublin: Stationery Office p. 49.

15 Ibid, p.36.

Five – An Act of Charity? How the Schools Were Funded

1 Luddy, M.(1995) *Women and Philanthropy in Nineteenth-Century Ireland.* Cambridge University Press.p.85.

[2] Sr Winifred (1972) Current Trends in Residential Child Care. From *Child Care - Papers of a Seminar held by the Council for Social Welfare.* Dublin: Council for Social Welfare.

[3] Mercy Sisters Express Regret. *Sunday Tribune,* 25/2/96.

[4] Coldrey, B. (1991) *The Scheme - The Christian Brothers and Child Care in Western Australia.* Argyle Pacific Publishing. p. 407.

[5] NA D/T s2623a Reformatory and Industrial Schools Commission of Enquiry 1934.

[6] NA D/H file A124/8 Children Acts, 1908-41 Amendment.

[7] Ibid.

[8] D/Ed SpEd G008/a/i Proposed Course in Institutional Management for Nuns in Industrial Schools.

[9] D/Ed SpEd G7b Scoileanna Ceartúcháin agus Saothair — Cruinniú de Chumann na mBrunscéirí.

[10] Ibid.

[11] Ibid.

[12] Ibid.

[13] Ibid.

[14] Ibid.

[15] Ibid.

[16] Ibid.

[17] Ibid.

[18] Ibid.

[19] Ibid.

[20] Ibid.

[21] D/Ed SpEd G001/e Daingean Reformatory.

[22] Ibid.

[23] Ibid.

[24] Ibid.

[25] Ibid.

[26] Ibid.

[27] D/Ed SpEd GA/ii, Establishment of a new Industrial School for boys at Celbridge.

Six – "Children in a Pitiable Condition"

[1] Barnes, J. (1989). *Irish Industrial Schools 1868 - 1908,* Dublin: Irish Academic Press.

[2] 27th Report of the Inspector Appointed to Visit the Reformatory and Industrial Schools of Ireland. (1889) Dublin: Alexander Thom and Co.

[3] Barnes, J (1989). *Irish Industrial Schools 1868-1908,* Dublin: Irish Academic Press. p. 113.

[4] D/Ed SpEd file G21/a, Report on Industrial and Reformatory Schools.

[5] D/Ed SpEd, Cappoquin IS Medical Inspection File, memo 11 September 1944.

[6] D/Ed SpEd, Rathdrum IS Medical Inspection File.

[7] D/Ed SpEd, Lenaboy IS Medical Inspection File.

[8] D/Ed SpEd, Rathdrum IS Medical Inspection File.

⁹ Ibid.
¹⁰ Ibid.
¹¹ D/Ed SpEd, Passage West IS General Inspection File.
¹² D/Ed SpEd, General Inspection File for Baltimore IS.
¹³ D/Ed SpEd, Baltimore IS Medical Inspection File.
¹⁴ D/Ed SpEd, Rathdrum IS Medical Inspection File.
¹⁵ D/Ed SpEd, Greemount IS General Inspection File.
¹⁶ D/Ed SpEd, Upton IS Medical Inspection File.
¹⁷ Ibid.
¹⁸ D/Ed SpEd, File G21/a.
¹⁹ Ibid.
²⁰ D/Ed SpEd, File: Circulars to Resident Managers.
²¹ D/Ed SpEd, General Inspection File, Letterfrack IS.
²² D/Ed SpEd, General Inspection Baltimore IS.

Seven – The Child Labourers
¹ Barnes, J, *Irish Industrial Schools, 1868-1908*, p. 91, 93/94.
² D/Ed SpEd G21/a. Inter-Departmental Committee on the Prevention of Crime and Treatment of Offenders.
³ Ibid.
⁴ *Commission of Inquiry into the Reformatory and Industrial School System Report, 1936* (The Cussen Report) Dublin: Stationery Office.
⁵ D/Ed SpEd, File G7/b, File G21/a.
⁶ D/Ed SpEd, File G21/a.
⁷ *Reformatory and Industrial Schools Systems Report, 1970* (The Kennedy Report), p. 39.
⁸ D/Ed SpEd Letter 8ᵗʰ March 1947.
⁹ D/H Unmarried Mothers in Great Britain and Home.

Eight – "A Disgrace to the Nation": An Outsider's View
¹ All of the Fr Flanagan material originates from the Boys Town Hall of History, Omaha, Nebraska, USA.
² 'The Supervision of Delinquents in Society' by Justice H. A. McCarthy, a chapter in *Some Problems of Child Welfare* edited by B.G.McCarthy M.A., PhD.; University and Labour Series No. 6, published by Cork University Press, 1945.
³ D/Ed SpEd file G003/e, Transfer of Borstal to Department of Education to be run by a Religious Order.

Nine – "Beating the Devil Out of Them"
¹ D/Ed SpEd, Circular on Discipline and Punishment in Certified Schools, 1/12/46.
² File G003/e, Department of Education Archive.
³ *Reformatory and Industrial Schools Systems Report* 1970 (The Kennedy Report) p.15; Report by Dr Anna McCabe, Medical Inspector of Reformatory and Industrial Schools, 1964 (Dept. Education Archive, File No. G21/a).

4 D/EdSpEd, General Inspection File, Greenmount IS.

5 D/Ed SpEd, Upton Medical Inspection File.

6 D/Ed SpEd, File G21/a.

7 D/Ed SpEd, Letterfrack Medical Inspection File.

8 D/Ed SpEd, Glin Medical Inspection File.

9 Ibid.

10 D/Ed SpEd, Bundoran IS General Inspection File.

11 D/Ed SpEd, file G18, Complaints from Past Pupils of Industrial Schools.

12 D/Ed SpEd, file G18/a, Complaints on behalf of Children in Industrial and Reformatory Schools.

13 D/Ed SpEd, file G21/a, Inter-Departmental Committee on Crime Prevention.

14 D/Ed SpEd, file G41A, Complaints Re. Corporal Punishment.

15 Ibid.

16 D/H Tipperary South Riding Boarding-out Files.

17 D/Ed SpEd, file G56, Marlborough House Complaints of Maltreatment of Detainees.

18 Ibid.

19 Ibid.

20 Ibid.

Ten – The Evil Within: Child Sexual Abuse

1 *Irish Times*, 4th July 1997.

2 North Western Health Board (1998) *'West of Ireland Farmer Case': Report of Review Group*.

3 Ferguson, H. (1998) McColgan Case - A Different Era. *Irish Times*, January 26th.

4 Shatter, A. (1998) Health Board must take the Blame. *Irish Times*, February 5th.

5 *Irish Times*, 19th May, 1999.

6 *States of Fear*, RTE Television, 11/5/99.

7 NA D/J H247/41a.

8 Ibid.

9 Ibid.

10 Ibid.

11 Ibid.

12 Cowen, P. (1960) *Dungeons Deep: A monograph on prisons, borstals, reformatories and industrial schools in the Republic of Ireland, and some reflections on crime and punishment and matters relating thereto*. Dublin: Marion Printing, p.31.

13 Letter to *The Irish Times*, May, 11th, 1999.

14 Coldrey, B. (1993) *The Scheme: The Christian Brothers and Child Care in Western Australia*. Argyle-Pacific Publishing.

15 Ibid.

16 Gill, A. (1998) *Orphans of the Empire: The Shocking Story of Child Migration to Australia*. Random House.p.350.

17 Ibid.

[18] Bean, P. and Melville, J. (1990) *Lost Children of the Empire Sydney*: Unwin Hyman, p. 20.

[19] Humphreys, M. (1994) *Empty Cradles*. Transworld Publishers. p.242.

[20] Gill, A. (1998) *Orphans of the Empire: The Shocking Story of Child Migration to Australia*. Vintage.pp.546-547.

[21] House of Commons — Select Committee on Health (1998) *Third Report - The Welfare of Former British Child Migrants*. London: HMSO.

[22] See *The Report of the Archdiocesan Commission of Enquiry into the Sexual Abuse of Children by members of the Clergy*. (1990) St John's Newfoundland: Archdiocese of St John's, and Steed, J. (1994) *Our Little Secret: Confronting Child Sexual Abuse in Canada*. Toronto: Random House.

[23] Coldrey, B. (1992) 'A Most Unenviable Reputation': The Christian Brothers and School Discipline over Two Centuries. *History of Education*, Vol. 21, No. 3, pp. 284-85.

[24] Coldrey. B (1999) *A Strange Mixture of Caring and Corruption. Residential care in Christian Brothers Orphanages and Industrial Schools During Their Last Phase, 1940s to the 1960s*. Unpublished manuscript.

[25] Congregation of Christian Brothers (1982) *Inheritance: Collection Two*. Private Circulation. p.295.

[26] *Sex in a Cold Climate*, Channel 4, 1998.

[27] Doyle, P. (1988) *The God Squad*. Dublin: Raven Arts Press. p.49.

Eleven – Sisters and Brothers

[1] *The Rules and Constitutions of the Religious Called Sisters of Mercy*. (1863). Dublin: James Duffy. p.4.

[2] Larkin, E. (1976) The Devotional Revolution in Ireland, 1850-75. IN Larkin, E. *The Historical Dimensions of Irish Catholicism*. The Catholic University of America Press.p.77.

[3] Carroll, Sr M.T.A. (1881) *Leaves from the Annals of the Sisters of Mercy. Vol. 1. Ireland*. New York: Catholic Publication Society.

[4] Clear, C. (1988) *Nuns in Nineteenth Century Ireland*. Dublin: Gill and Macmillan.

[5] O'Brien, S. (1988) *Terra Incognita*: the Nun in Nineteenth Century England, *Past and Present*, No. 145, pp.110-140.

[6] *The Rules and Constitutions of the Religious Called Sisters of Mercy*. (1863). Dublin: James Duffy. p. 39.

[7] Clear, C. (1987) *Walls within Walls: Nuns in Nineteenth-Century Ireland* IN Curtin, C., Jackson, P. And O'Connor, B. (Eds) *Gender in Irish Society. Studies in Irish Society 3*. Galway: Galway University Press.

[8] Murphy, J.N. (1873*) Terra Incognita or the Convents of the United Kingdom*. London: Longmans, Green and Co.p.194.

[9] NA D/HA122/34 St Martha's Industrial School — Monaghan and Donegal.

[10] O'Toole, F (1993) *Irish Times*, Sept 8th.

[11] Ibid.

[12] Kennedy, S. (1971) The Role of Religious in Child Care. In *Child Care: Papers from a Seminar held by the Council for Social Welfare*, March, 1971.

[13] Coldrey, B. (1988) *Faith and Fatherland. The Christian Brothers and the Development of Irish Nationalism, 1838-1921*. Dublin: Gill and Macmillan. p.22.

[14] Coldrey, B (1992) 'A Most Unenviable Reputation'. The Christian Brothers and School Discipline over Two Centuries. *History of Education*, Vol 21, No 3, PP 277-289.

[15] Flynn, S and Yeates, P (1985) *Smack*. Dublin: Gill and Macmillan, p. 276.

Twelve – Pity the Poor Orphans: How the Children Were Perceived
[1] D/Ed SpEd Memo 20/6/52.
[2] D/Ed SpEd, file G43.
[3] Ibid.
[4] D/Ed Annual Reports.

Thirteen – The State: "None So Blind..."
[1] D/Ed SpEd. Rathdrum IS Medical Inspection File.
[2] NA D/H a122/41. Section 47, Ennis Industrial School.
[3] NA D/Ha122/61 Section 47, St Dominick's Industrial School.
[4] Ibid.
[5] NA D/H 24/129. Offaly - Inspector's Report on Returns for September, 1965.
[6] D/H. Review of child care services.
[7] D/H. Miss Clandillon Files.
[8] Report of Mrs. Dickie, lady Inspector of Boarded-Out Children, Local Government Board Annual Report, 1905, p.480.
[9] D/Ed SpEd file G001/1 Boarding-out Arrangements.
[10] Breen, R. Hannon, D.F., Rottman, D. And Whelan, C.T. (1990) *Understanding Contemporary Ireland. State, Class and Development in the Republic of Ireland*. Dublin: Gill and Macmillan.
[11] D/Ed SpEd file G003/e Transfer of Borstal to Department of Education to be run by a Religious Order.
[12] D/Ed SpEd file G004/e/ii Capitation Grants: Memo, 16th Aug 63 from Secr. Educ. To Secr. Finance.
[13] D/Ed SpEd 6A2: Establishment of a new Industrial School for Boys at Celbridge.
[14] NA D/H a122/0 Section 47: Carriglea Park, Dun Laoghaire.
[15] D/Ed SpEd file G21/a Inter-departmental Committee on the Prevention of Crime and Treatment of Offenders.
[16] Ibid.
[17] Ibid.
[18] Ibid.
[19] Section 46(3) of the *Children Act, 1908*.
[20] D/Ed SpEd file G21/a, Inter-Departmental Committee on the Prevention of Crime and Treatment of Offenders.
[21] NA D/H file a122/96 St Brigid's Industrial School, Loughrea.

22 D/Ed SpEd file G56 Place of Detention, Marlborough House, Complaints of Mistreatment of Detainees; also D/Ed SpEd file G41/a Complaints of Corporal Punishment.

23 Ibid.

24 Ibid.

25 NA D/T s 1329oa.

26 NA D/T 98/6/156 Children – General.

27 D/Ed SpEd file G41/ii.

Fourteen – The First Cracks

1 D/Ed SpEd file G11/a, Correspondence with Joint Committee of Women's Societies and Social Workers.

2 Ibid.

3 *Commission on Youth Unemployment Report, 1951*. Dublin: Stationery Office.

4 Murphy, C.K. (1959) *The Lay Apostolate of Charity and Other Essays*. Cork: Cork University Press.

5 Barrett, C.J. (1955) The Dependent Child. *Studies*, Vol.XLIV, p.422.

6 Department of Education (1966) *Investment in Education*. Annexes and Appendices. Dublin: Stationery Office, pp.26-34.

7 D/Ed SpEd G37/b, Seminar on the evaluation of methods of prevention of juvenile delinquency held in Rome in October 1962.

8 D/Ed SpEd G21/a, Recommendations of the Inter-Departmental Committee on Crime Prevention and Treatment of Offenders.

9 D/Ed SpEd G21/a, Recommendations of the Inter-Departmental Committee on Crime Prevention and Treatment of Offenders. Note of interview given to Fr Moore, Chaplain to Artane Industrial School, 26 November, 1962.

10 D/Ed SpEd G21/a, Recommendations of the Inter-Departmental Committee on Crime Prevention and Treatment of Offenders. Report of the special inspection of Artane Industrial School with particular attention to food, clothing and general management.

11 O'Connor, J. (1963) The Juvenile Offender, *Studies*, Vol. ii, No.1, p.80-81.

12 From *John Charles McQuaid: What the Papers Say*, Esras Films 1998, written by John Bowman.

13 London Branch Study Group (1966) *Some of Our Children: A Report on the Residential Care of the Deprived Child in Ireland*. Tuairim Pamphlet No.13, p.33.

14 Ibid, p.39.

15 Arnold, M. and Laskey, H. (1985) *Children of the Poor Clares — The Story of an Irish Orphanage*. Belfast, Appletree Press.

16 *Commission of Inquiry on Mental Illness Report, 1966*. Dublin: Stationery Office, p.74.

17 Viney, M. (1967) *Irish Times*, November 16th.

18 *The Carlow Nationalist*. 6th August, 1965.

19 D/Ed SpEd G7 Farrarais ar Meadú sna rátaí capaitíochta. Note for Minister, June 1964.

[20] Ibid.

[21] D/Ed SpEd G011/b Correspondence with the Irish Association of Civil Liberty.

[22] *Cork Examiner*, May 8, 1963 Careless Parents Preferable to Even Best Institution.

[23] D/Ed SpEd G21/a, Inter-Departmental Committee on the Prevention of Crime and Treatment of Offenders.

[24] NA D/T 98/6/156. Children General.

[25] Ibid.

[26] Ibid.

[27] Ibid.

[28] D/Ed SpEd G41/ii Residential Homes and Special Schools. Visiting Committees. Juvenile Delinquency: Causes, Prevention and Treatment.

[29] Dail debates, Micheal Martin, Minister for Education and Science 13/5/99.

[30] NA D/T 98/6/156 Children — General.

[31] Ibid.

Fifteen – A Terrible Legacy: 1970 to the Present

[1] *Reformatory and Industrial School Systems Report, 1970* (The Kennedy Report). Dublin: The Stationery Office. pp. 13/14.

[2] Ibid. p. 15.

[3] Ibid. pp. 15/17.

[4] Ibid. pp. 28/29.

[5] Ibid. pp. 42/43/44.

[6] Ibid. p.6.

[7] Dail debates, Micheal Martin, Minister for Education and Science 13/5/99.

[8] *Irish Times*, 25th September 1999 — 'Artane Boys Faced Music and Straps', by Patsy McGarry.

[9] *Dail Debates*, Vol. 76, 15 November, 1973, Col. 139.

[10] O'Toole, F. (1999) Not Asking Questions Could Again Fail Children. *Irish Times*, 21/5/99.

[11] *Irish Times*, December 18th, 1997.

[12] First Interim Report of the Joint Committee on Tourism, Sport and Recreation (1998) *Protection of Children in Sport*. Dublin: Stationery Office.

[13] McGuinness, C. (1993) *Report of The Kilkenny Incest Investigation*. Dublin: Stationery Office; Keenan, O. (1996) *Kelly: A Child is Dead*. Interim Report of the Joint Committee on the Family. Dublin: Government Publications Office.

[14] *Irish Times*, 5th July 1996 (Mairead Carey).

[15] *Irish Times*, 20th January 1997 (Padraig O'Morain).

[16] *Irish Times*, 17th November 1997 (Padraig O'Morain).

[17] Dail Debates, Vol 303, No 2, Cols 283-4.

[18] *Reformatory and Industrial School Systems Report, 1970* (The Kennedy Report). Dublin: The Stationery Office, p.7.

[19] *The Report of the Archdiocesan Commission of Enquiry into the Sexual Abuse of Children by Members of the Clergy.* (1990) St John's Newfoundland: Archdiocese of St John's.

[20] Gill, A. (1998) *Orphans of the Empire: The Shocking Story of Child Migration to Australia.* Vintage.

[21] *Stolen Children*: Report of the National Inquiry into the Separation of Aboriginal and Torres Strait islander Children from their Families.

[22] Commission of Inquiry into Abuse of Children in Queensland Institutions. p.104.

[23] Harris, M. (1990) *Unholy Orders: Tragedy at Mount Cashel.* Viking.

[24] Commission of Inquiry into Abuse of Children in Queensland Institutions. p.288.

[25] Law Reform Commission of Canada (1998) *Discussion paper on Institutional Child Abuse.* p.22.

[26] Ibid. p.23.

[27] Various newspapers, 25/2/96.

[28] *Irish Times*, 10th May 1996.

[29] *Kilkenny People*, June 12 1998.

[30] Report of the Irish Catholic Bishops' Advisory Committee on Child Sexual Abuse by Priests and Religious (1996) *Child Sexual Abuse: Framework for a Church Response.* Dublin: Veritas.

Index

The Commission to Inquire into Childhood Abuse

If you suffered abuse as a child, you might like to contact the above Commission. It has been established by the Irish Government to hear testimony from victims of child abuse, and to inquire into the entire area of industrial and reformatory schools. It is a three-member body, chaired by Ms Justice Mary Laffoy of the High Court.

The Commission to Inquire into Childhood Abuse
Floor 2,
St Stephen's Green House,
Earlsfort Terrace,
Dublin 2,
Ireland.

Tel: *(from Ireland)*
  1850 20 11 20 (low cost)
  or 01 662 44 44
  (from UK)
  0845 309 81 39 (low cost)
Fax: 01 662 49 35

Freedom of Information

Under the Freedom of Information Act 1997, you are entitled to apply to the State for access to any records held on you personally. If you were in an industrial or reformatory school in Ireland as a child, you can phone, call in or write to the Department of Education, Freedom of Information Section, and they will inform you of the procedure.

Freedom of Information Section,
Department of Education,
Marlborough St,
Dublin 1.

Tel: 01 873 47 00